THE BATTLE OF CARHAM

THE BATTLE OF CARHAM
A THOUSAND YEARS ON

Edited by
Neil McGuigan
and
Alex Woolf

First published in Great Britain in 2018 by
John Donald, an imprint of Birlinn Ltd

West Newington House
10 Newington Road
Edinburgh
EH9 1QS

www.birlinn.co.uk

ISBN: 978 1 910900 24 6

Copyright © The contributors severally 2018

The right of contributors to be identified as the authors of this work has been asserted by them in accordance with the Copyright, Designs and Patents Act, 1988

All rights reserved. No part of this publication may be reproduced, stored, or transmitted in any form, or by any means, electronic, mechanical or photocopying, recording or otherwise, without the express written permission of the publisher.

British Library Cataloguing-in-Publication Data
A catalogue record for this book is available on request from the British Library

Typeset by Biblichor Ltd, Edinburgh
Printed and bound in Britain by
TJ International Ltd, Padstow, Cornwall

Contents

	List of Contributors	vii
	Preface	ix
	List of Abbreviations	xi
	Map of Bamburgh and Surrounding Region, c. 1000	xvii
	Map of Britain, c. 1000	xviii
1	The Battle of Carham: An Introduction Neil McGuigan	1
2	Southern Scotland as Part of the Scottish Kingdom: The Evidence of the Earliest Charters Dauvit Broun	33
3	Edinburgh's Renown in the Early Middle Ages Philip Dunshea	50
4	Carham: The Western Perspective Fiona Edmonds	79
5	Bamburgh and the Northern English Realm: Understanding the Dominion of Uhtred Neil McGuigan	95
6	Early Medieval Carham in its Landscape Context David Petts	151
7	A New Reading of Late Anglo-Saxon Sculpture in and around the Tweed Valley: Carham, Lindisfarne, Norham and Jedburgh Victoria Thompson	174
8	Annals 848 to 1118 in the *Historia Regum* David A. Woodman	202
9	The Diocese of Lindisfarne: Organisation and Pastoral Care Alex Woolf	231
	Index	241

Contributors

Dauvit Broun is Professor of Scottish History at the University of Glasgow.

Philip Dunshea previously lectured in Celtic History at the Department of Anglo-Saxon, Norse and Celtic, University of Cambridge.

Fiona Edmonds is Director of the Regional Heritage Centre and Lecturer in Regional History at Lancaster University, as well as Director of the Victoria County History of Cumbria.

Neil McGuigan completed his doctorate in 2015 at the University of St Andrews, where he regularly teaches.

David Petts is an Associate Professor in the Department of Archaeology, Durham University.

Victoria Thompson is an independent scholar specialising in early medieval sculpture and mortuary behaviour.

David A. Woodman is Fellow in History and Senior Tutor at Robinson College, Cambridge.

Alex Woolf is a Senior Lecturer in History at the University of St Andrews.

Preface

This volume was conceived in April 2014, in the aftermath of a conference commemorating the millennium of the battle of Clontarf. The scale of academic and popular participation in this event at Trinity College, Dublin was, to say the least, impressive. With the millennium of an analogous Scottish battle four years away (or so it was believed), it struck us that we as historians of Viking-Age Scotland and Northumbria had a duty to come up with some sort of commemoration. The battle of Carham, of course, has never quite captured the popular imagination in Scotland or northern England like Clontarf in Ireland. Nevertheless, turn to any general history of Scotland (or Northumbria indeed), and the chances are good that you will find the battle of Carham occupying a similar 'coming-of-age' role in Scotland's past. Carham has featured centrally in how the history of Scotland has been told by modern historians because it is one of the few things we can plausibly relate to the mysterious process of Scottish expansion beyond the Forth and into Anglo-Saxon territory of Northumbria in the period between the tenth and twelfth centuries. The outcome of this process, in turn, facilitated an expansion of what it meant to be 'Scottish', led to the ethnogenesis of the familiar Late Medieval and Early Modern Scottish 'Lowlander', and gave Scotland its familiar complexion as a territorial unit.

As some of the contributions in this volume suggest, when subjected to scrutiny the significance of the battle of Carham itself becomes less apparent. Much like a low-resolution photograph, the picture blurs when one 'zooms in' on the fine detail. Yet, the importance of the developments that Carham has come to represent remains undeniable. Lack of reliable evidence provides one of the reasons the process is still quite poorly understood, but the problem has been compounded by the fact that the 'Northern English' realm ruled from Bamburgh, the northern Northumbrian polity that stretched from the Forth to the Tyne, the region in which the battle took place, has tended not to attract as much interest from modern scholarship as its neighbours; i.e., Strathclyde, the Scottish kingdom and the 'Vikings' of southern Northumbria. Whereas modern scholarship has lifted these topics out of the illusory certainty provided by John of Fordun and the Icelandic sagas, by contrast, uncritical readings of extremely problematic twelfth-century material tend still to be relied upon whenever northern Northumbria emerges in passing. Things are changing, and all of the contributions in this text play a part in improving understanding of the region.

The volume provides an introduction to the problems associated with the battle itself, identifying its participants and dating the event. The precise location of the battle itself is not known, and no archaeology has ever been connected to the conflict with any authority. This volume does not, and probably could not, offer any study of the weapons or tactics used in the battle itself. However, as David Petts's offering demonstrates, a great deal of insight can be achieved through comparative scholarship as well as understanding of the archaeology and the landscape. Likewise, Victoria Thompson's new look at the sculpture of the Tweed basin in the era of the battle opens up another way of understanding the region, and recognising its importance and vitality. The contributions of the editors seek to understand the Bamburgh realm itself, and its political structures, secular and ecclesiastical, in more detail. The process by which a large part of the former Bamburgh realm was absorbed into Scotland, in the three centuries after Carham, is examined in Dauvit Broun's contribution. So important was this process that one power centre in the region south of the Forth eventually emerged as Scotland's capital. Philip Dunshea looks at early Edinburgh and how the fortress was perceived in the critical centuries around the battle, particularly among the Britons. Sticking with the Britons, Fiona Edmonds offers an understanding of the battle from the point of view of Bamburgh's main British neighbour, Strathclyde. Finally, one of the key sources for the battle, the twelfth-century chronicle compilation known as *Historia Regum*, provides the object of David Woodman's study.

The chapters of this volume reflect the interests of the scholars who were generous enough to lend their efforts to this commemoration. The editors would like to express their gratitude to all the contributors. Thanks are also due to Professor Thomas Owen Clancy, and to the publishers and to the work, patience and effort of Nicola Wood and Mairi Sutherland.

Neil McGuigan

List of Abbreviations

AClon	*The Annals of Clonmacnoise, being Annals of Ireland from the Earlies Period to AD 1408 / Translated into English AD 1627 by Conell Mageoghagan*, ed. D. Murphy (London, 1896)
AFM	*Annala Rioghachta Eireann: Annals of the Kingdom of Ireland / By the Four Masters, from the Earliest Period to the Year 1616; Edited from MS. in the Library of the Royal Irish Academy and of Trinity College, Dublin*, ed. and trans. M. O'Clery, 6 vols (Dublin, 1851)
ALC	*The Annals of Loch Cé: A Chronicle of Irish Affairs from AD 1014 to AD 1590*, ed. and trans. W. M. Hennessy, 2 vols, Rolls Series 54 (London, 1871)
ALD	*Annales Lindisfarnenses et Dunelmenses*, ed. W. Levison, 'Die "Annales Lindisfarnenses et Dunelmenses" kritisch untersucht und neu herausgegeben', *Deutsches Archiv für Erforschung des Mittelalters* 17 (1961), 447–506, at 478–89
Arch. Ael.	*Archaeologia Aeliana: Miscellaneous Tracts Relating to Antiquity* (1822–)
ASC	*The Anglo-Saxon Chronicle*. Cited by year, by manuscript; for MS A, see J. Bately (ed.), *The Anglo-Saxon Chronicle: A Collaborative Edition. Volume 3, MS A* (Woodbridge, 1986); for MS B, S. Taylor (ed.), *The Anglo-Saxon Chronicle: A Collaborative Edition. Volume 4, MS B* (Cambridge, 1983); for MS C, K. O'Brien O'Keefe (ed.), *The Anglo-Saxon Chronicle: A Collaborative Edition. Volume 5, MS C* (Cambridge, 2001);

	for MS D, G. P. Cubbin (ed.), *The Anglo-Saxon Chronicle: A Collaborative Edition. Vol. 6, MS D* (Woodbridge, 1996); for MS E, S. Irvine (ed.), *The Anglo-Saxon Chronicle: A Collaborative Edition. Volume 7*, MS E (Cambridge, 2004). For collated translation of the various MSS, see D. Whitelock with D. C. Douglas and S. I. Tucker (eds), *The Anglo-Saxon Chronicle: A Revised Translation* (London, 1961).
ASE	*Anglo-Saxon England* (1972–)
AT	*The Annals of Tigernach*, ed. W. Stokes, *Revue Celtique* 16–18 (1895–1897)
AU	*The Annals of Ulster (to AD 1131)*, ed. S. Mac Airt and G. Mac Niocaill (Dublin, 1983)
CASSS	Corpus of Anglo-Saxon Stone Sculpture
Chron. Fordun, i	John of Fordun, *Chronica Gentis Scotorum*, ed. W. F. Skene, The Historians of Scotland 1 (Edinburgh, 1871)
Chron. Fordun, ii	John of Fordun, *Chronicle of the Scottish Nation*, ed. W. F. Skene, trans. F. Skene, The Historians of Scotland 4 (Edinburgh, 1872)
Chronicon ex Chronicis	John of Worcester, *Chronicon ex Chronicis*, in *The Chronicle of John of Worcester*, 2 of 3 vols (Oxford, 1995–8); volume ii, ed. R. R. Darlington and P. McGurk, trans. J. Bray and P. McGurk (Oxford, 1995); volume iii, ed. and trans. P. McGurk (Oxford, 1998)
Chron. Wallingford	*The Chronicle Attributed to John of Wallingford*, ed. R. Vaughan, Camden Miscellany XXI (London, 1958), 1–67
CKA	*Chronicle of the Kings of Alba,* ed. and trans. B. T. Hudson, 'The Scottish Chronicle', *SHR* 77 (October, 1998), 129–61 (text at 148–61)
CMD	*Cronica Monasterii Dunelmensis*, ed. H. H. E. Craster, 'The Red Book of Durham', *EHR* 40 (1925), 504–32
Cogadh	*Cogadh Gaedhel re Gallaibh*, ed. and trans. J. H. Todd, Rolls Series 48 (London, 1867)

LIST OF ABBREVIATIONS

CPNS	W. J. Watson, *The History of the Celtic Place-Names of Scotland* (Edinburgh, 1926)
CS	*Chronicum Scotorum: A Chronicle of Irish Affairs, from the Earliest Times to AD 1135, with a Supplement Containing the Events from 1141 to 1150*, ed. and trans. W. M. Hennessy, Rolls Series 46 (London, 1866)
David I Chrs	*The Charters of King David I: King of Scots, 1124–53 and of his Son Henry Earl of Northumberland*, ed. G. W. S. Barrow (Woodbridge, 1999)
DNPB	*De Northumbria post Britannos*, ed. and trans. N. McGuigan, 'Ælla and the Descendants of Ivar', *NH* 52 (2015), 20–34, at 32–4
DOD	*De Obsessione Dunelmi*, ed. T. Arnold, *Sym. Op.*, i, 215–20
DPSA	*De Primo Saxonum Adventu*, ed. T. Arnold, *Sym. Op.*, ii, 365–84
EHD, i	*English Historical Documents: Volume I, c.500–1042*, ed. D. Whitelock, 2nd edn (London, 1979)
EHD, ii	*English Historical Documents: Volume II, 1042–1189*, ed. D. Douglas and G. W. Greenway, 2nd edn (London, 1981)
EHR	*The English Historical Review* (1886–)
ESC	*Early Scottish Charters prior to AD 1153*, ed. A. C. Lawrie, (Glasgow, 1905)
ES	*Early Sources of Scottish History 500 to 1286*, ed. A. O. Anderson, 2 vols (Edinburgh, 1922)
FAI	*Fragmentary Annals of Ireland*, ed. and trans. J. N. Radner (Dublin, 1978)
Gesetze	*Die Gesetze der Angelsachsen*, ed. F. Liebermann, 3 vols (Halle, 1903–16)
Glas. Reg.	*Registrum Episcopatus Glasguensis*, ed. C. Innes, 2 vols, Bannatyne and Maitland Clubs (Edinburgh and Glasgow, 1843)
GRA	William of Malmesbury, *Gesta Regum Anglorum*, ed. and trans. R. A. B. Mynors, with R. M. Thomson and M. Winterbottom (Oxford, 1998)

HR	*Historia Regum*, ed. T. Arnold, *Sym. Op.*, ii, 3–283
HSC	*Historia de Sancto Cuthberto*, ed. and trans. T. J. South, Anglo-Saxon Texts 3 (Cambridge, 2002); cited (where appropriate) by chapter, followed by editorial page range
IR	*The Innes Review* (1950–)
JSNS	*Journal of Scottish Name Studies* (2007–)
LDE	Symeon of Durham, *Libellus de Exordio atque procursu istius, hoc est Dunhelmensis, ecclesie*, ed. and trans. D. Rollason (Oxford, 2000); cited (where appropriate) by book section, followed by editorial page range
Lives of Ninian and Kentigern	*Lives of S. Ninian and S. Kentigern: Compiled in the Twelfth Century, Edited from the Best MSS*, ed. and trans. A. P. Forbes, Historians of Scotland 5 (Edinburgh, 1874)
NH	*Northern History: A Review of the History of the North of England* (1966–)
North Durham	*The History and Antiquities of North Durham*, ed. J. Raine (London, 1852)
Northern Chrs	*Charters of Northern Houses*, ed. D. A. Woodman, Anglo-Saxon Charters 16 (Oxford, 2012)
PSAS	*Proceedings of the Society of Antiquaries of Scotland* (1851–)
RCAHMS	Royal Commission on the Ancient and Historical Monuments of Scotland
RHC	Roger of Howden, *Chronica*, ed. W. Stubbs, 4 vols, Rolls Series 51 (1868–71)
RRAN, i	*Regesta Regum Anglo-Normannorum, 1066–1154*, volume i, ed. H. W. C. Davis, *Regesta Willelmi Conquestoris et Willelmi Rufi, 1066–1100* (Oxford, 1913)
RRAN, ii	*Regesta Regum Anglo-Normannorum, 1066–1154*, volume ii, ed. C. Johnson, *Regesta Henrici Prima, 1100–1135* (Oxford, 1956)
RRS, i	*Regesta Regum Scottorum*, vol. i, ed. G. W. S. Barrow, *The Acts of Malcolm IV, King of Scots, 1153–1165* (Edinburgh, 1960)

RRS, ii	*Regesta Regum Scottorum*, vol. ii, ed. G. W. S. Barrow in collaboration with W. W. Scott, *The Acts of William I, King of Scots 1165–1214* (Edinburgh, 1971)
RW	Roger of Wendover, *Chronica, sive, Flores Historiarum*, ed. H. O. Coxe, 5 vols (London, 1841–4)
SAEC	*Scottish Annals from English Chroniclers 500 to 1286*, ed. A. O. Anderson (London, 1908)
Sawyer	*Anglo-Saxon Charters: An Annotated List and Bibliography*, ed. P. H. Sawyer (London, 1968), online and expanded at 'The Electronic Sawyer' (<http://www.esawyer.org.uk/about/index.html>), cited by number
Scotia Pontificia	*Scotia Pontificia: Papal Letters to Scotland before the Pontificate of Innocent III*, ed. R. Somerville (Oxford, 1982)
SHR	*The Scottish Historical Review* (1903–28, 1947–)
Sym. Op.	*Symeonis Monachi Opera Omnia*, ed. T. Arnold, 2 vols, Rolls Series 75 (London, 1882–5)
TCWAAS	*Transactions of the Cumberland and Westmorland Antiquarian and Archaeological Society* (1874–)
TDGAS	*Transactions of the Dumfriesshire and Galloway Natural History and Antiquarian Society* (1862–)
TRHS	*Transactions of the Royal Historical Society* (1872–)
Triumph Tree	*The Triumph Tree: Scotland's Earliest Poetry, AD 550–1350*, ed. T. O. Clancy (Edinburgh, 1998)

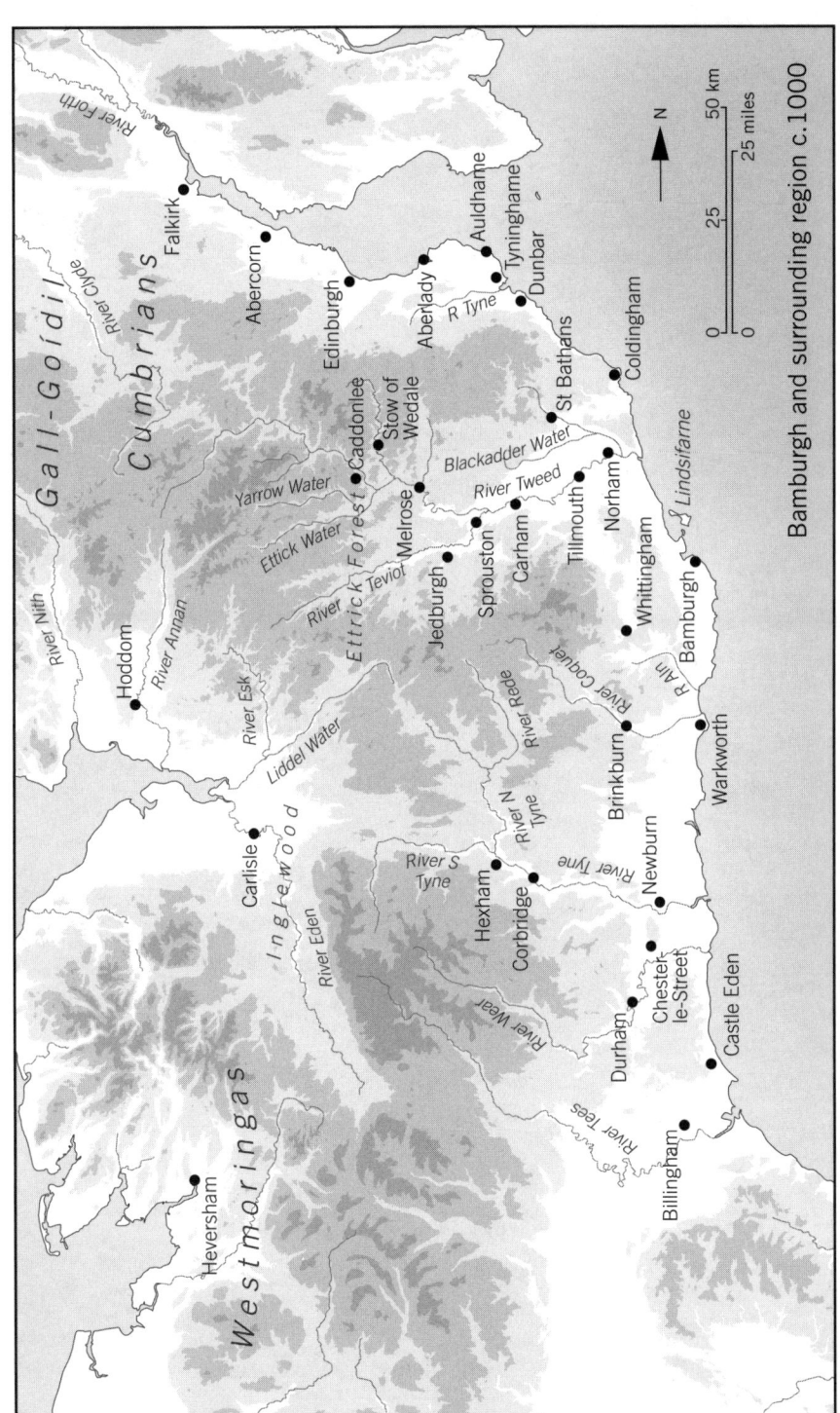

CHAPTER ONE

The Battle of Carham: An Introduction

NEIL MCGUIGAN

Rightly or wrongly, the encounter between the Northumbrians and their northern and western neighbours has long been regarded as one of Scotland's 'coming of age' battles.[1] Our most detailed notice of the battle of Carham contains the last clear reference to a king of Strathclyde, but the battle has also long been linked with the Scottish annexation of Lothian. The Victorian historian Thomas Hodgkin opined that the battle was 'more important than Brunanburh' adding that 'we might perhaps say only a little less important than Hastings'.[2] His contemporary Peter Hume Brown agreed with the comparison: 'it is with Hastings rather than Bannockburn that Carham must be reckoned in the list of British battles'.[3] More recently, the *Handbook of British Chronology* told its readers that Máel Coluim II (r. 1005–34) 'secured Lothian by the battle of Carham' and 'obtained Strathclyde . . . thus forming the kingdom of Scotland'.[4] The following chapter aims to provide an overview of the battle from the point of view of the modern historian, examining issues relating to the sources and dating of the battle, as well as the encounter itself, its participants and its consequences.

Sources

Northern Anglo-Latin annals
We have at least three distinct sources about the battle of Carham. The names of the battle's leaders are given most fully by a tradition of

---

1 For more on the battle's historiographic reputation, see D. Broun, 'Southern Scotland as Part of the Scottish Kingdom: The Evidence of the Earliest Charters', this volume, 33–49.
2 T. Hodgkin, *The History of England from the Earliest Times to the Norman Conquest* (London, 1906), 409.
3 P. Hume Brown, *History of Scotland to the Accession of Mary Stewart*, 3 vols (Edinburgh, 1899–1909), i, 43.
4 E. B. Fyrde *et al.* (eds), *Handbook of British Chronology*, 3rd edn (Cambridge, 1996), 56.

Latin-language 'annals' from northern England that, in surviving form, began to be woven together around 1120. When historians talk about 'annals', we are referring to records of events listed according to the year they took place and chronicled on a year-by-year basis over a longer period, usually centuries but sometimes only a few decades. We tend to use the term 'annals' when the events or 'notices' (of the events) occur in a list-like form, where there is no consistent attempt to create logical links between each year or integrate the events of multiple years into a unified narrative. Annals often survive in later single compilations and copies, but usually it is assumed (sometimes wrongly of course) that the original annals themselves were composed soon after the events that they document. Modern scholars often cite particular annals from a collection by writing 'under year x' or *sub anno* (abbreviated s.a.): for instance, a notice of the battle of Clontarf occurs in the *Annals of Ulster*, s.a. 1014.[5]

The Anglo-Latin annals that concern us here come from a northern English adaptation of (an early version of) *Chronicon ex Chronicis,* a collection nowadays attributed to John of Worcester (previously attributed to Florence of Worcester).[6] Occasionally, 'new' or unique material relating to northern England appears, added by an author with a distinct interest in more northerly affairs. The most famous of the northern adaptations include the later part of *Historia Regum* (occasionally attributed to Symeon of Durham), the early part of Roger of Howden's *Chronica*, and the early part of *Chronicle of Melrose* – but there are also lesser known recensions.[7] In *Chronicon ex Chronicis,* many of the annals

---

5 *AU* 1014.2.
6 The text is John of Worcester, *Chronicon ex Chronicis*, in *The Chronicle of John of Worcester*, 2 of 3 vols (Oxford, 1995–8); volume ii, ed. R. R. Darlington and P. McGurk, trans. J. Bray and P. McGurk (Oxford, 1995); volume iii, ed. and trans. P. McGurk (Oxford, 1998). It is cited in this volume simply as *Chronicon ex Chronicis.*
7 *Historia Regum*, ed. T. Arnold, *Symeonis Monachi Opera Omnia*, 2 vols, Rolls Series 75 (London, 1882–5), ii, 3–283 [hereafter *HR*]. The section influenced by *Chronicon ex Chronicis* might be called 'Part 2', which is ibid., ii, 95–283. 'Part 1' has been more recently edited by Cyril Hart, as *Byrhtferth's Northumbrian Chronicle: An Edition and Translation of the Old English and Latin Annals*, Early Chronicles of England 1 (Lewiston, 2006), 2–233. For a more detailed look at *Historia Regum* 'Part 2' and John of Worcester's work, see D. Woodman, 'Annals 848 to 1118 in the *Historia Regum*', this volume, 202–30. A major new edition of the whole *HR* text has been promised for many years. D. Rollason, 'Symeon of Durham's *Historia de Regibus Anglorum et Dacorum*', in M. Brett and D. A. Woodman (eds), *The Long Twelfth-Century View of the Anglo-Saxon Past* (Farnham, 2015), 95–111, at 95, has stated in print that it will

related to England appear to be based on a translation of a lost recension of the *Anglo-Saxon Chronicle*, annals originally written in Old English. The battle of Carham, unfortunately, is not mentioned in *Chronicon ex Chronicis*, nor indeed in any surviving recension of the *Anglo-Saxon Chronicle*. It is the unique northern material that gives us a notice, entered s.a. 1018, commemorating the battle.

There are two versions of the 1018 Carham annal, a short version and a long version. The short version is common to several variant recensions, including Roger of Howden's *Chronica* and the *Chronicle of Melrose*. For convenience, Roger of Howden's entry, *sub anno* 1018, will be used as the representative version:

Ingens bellum inter Anglos et Scottos apud Carrum geritur.

A massive battle between the English and the Scots is waged at Carham.[8]

---

become available in Oxford Medieval Texts under the title *Historia de Regibus Anglorum et Dacorum*. For Roger's work, see Roger of Howden, *Chronica* [hereafter *RHC*], ed. W. Stubbs, 4 vols, Rolls Series 51 (1868–71), with the annals up to 1148, sometimes known as *Historia post Bedam*, found at *RHC*, i, 3–211. A new edition of the *Chronicle of Melrose* is under preparation for the Scottish History Society. The first volume has been published in D. Broun and J. Harrison (eds), *The Chronicle of Melrose Abbey: A Stratigraphic Edition. Volume I: Introduction and Facsimile Edition*, Scottish History Society 6th Ser. (Edinburgh, 2007). A facsimile version was previously published, i.e. A. O. Anderson and M. O. Anderson (eds), *The Chronicle of Melrose: From the Cottonian Manuscript, Faustina B.IX in the British Museum* (London, 1936), but otherwise the latest printed edition in Joseph Stevenson's *Chronica de Mailros: e codice unico in Bibliotheca Cottoniana servato*, Bannatyne Club 52 (Edinburgh, 1835). Shorter annal sets with common source material include the unprinted Paris, Bibliothèque Nationale, Nouv. Acq. Lat. 692; Liège, Bibliothèque Universitaire, MS 369C; and London, British Library, Cotton Caligula A.viii. Other annals related to the tradition include Alfred of Beverley, *Annales*, ed. T. Hearne (Oxford, 1716), and some appear in later collections such as Ranulf Higden's *Polychronicon*. A good overview of the relationship between *Historia Regum* 'Part 2' and John of Worcester is M. Brett, 'John of Worcester and his Contemporaries', in R. H. C. Davis and J. M. Wallace-Hadrill (eds), *The Writing of History in the Middle Ages: Essays Presented to Richard William Southern* (Oxford, 1981), 101–26, especially 119–21. The most detailed discussion of these sources can be found in B. Meehan, 'A Reconsideration of the Historical Works Associated with Symeon of Durham: Manuscripts, Texts, and Influences', PhD thesis (University of Edinburgh, 1979). David Rollason, 'Symeon of Durham's *Historia de Regibus Anglorum et Dacorum*', 107, figure 6.1, provides a helpful illustration of how he understood some of these relationships in 2015.

8 *RHC*, s.a. 1018, ed. Stubbs, i, 87.

The longer version of this matter-of-fact annal appears in a collection of historical material found in Corpus Christi College MS 139, known today as *Historia Regum*. The following is its variant entry, similarly entered *sub anno* 1018:

> *Ingens bellum apud Carrum gestum est inter Scottos et Anglos, inter Huctredum filium Waldef comitem Northymbrorum et Malcolmum filium Cyneth regem Scottorum. Cum quo fuit in bello Eugenius Calvus rex Clutinensium.*

A massive battle was fought at Carham between the Scots and English, between Uhtred son of Waltheof earl of the Northumbrians and Máel Coluim son of Cinaed king of the Scots, with whom in battle was Owain the Bald king of the Clyde-folk.[9]

As Offler pointed out in 1971, neither the abbreviated Paris version of the annal nor Roger of Howden's *Chronica* nor the *Chronicle of Melrose* names any of the commanders.[10] That information is unique to the longer version, unique to *Historia Regum*. For some unknown reason, a contributor to *Historia Regum*, and he alone, working in or after 1129, was able (and willing) to produce this important extra detail.

Durham church histories

A lengthier account of the battle is found in a history of the church of Durham written 1104×1115, Symeon of Durham's *Libellus de Exordio*. The battle is dated to 1018:

> *Anno Incarnationis Dominice mille duodeuicesimo, Cnut regnum Anglorum disponente, Northanhymbrorum populus per triginta noctes cometa apparuit, que terribili presagio futuram prouincie cladem premonstrauit. Siquidem paulo post (id est post triginta dies) uniuersus a flumine Tesa usque Twedam populus, dum contra infinitam Scottorum multitudinem apud Carrum dimicaret, pene totus cum natu*

---

9 *HR*, s.a. 1018, ed. Arnold, ii, 155–6.
10 H. S. Offler, 'Hexham and the *Historia Regum*', *Transactions of the Architectural and Archaeological Society of Durham and Northumberland*, New Ser. 2 (1971), 52–62, at 57. B. Meehan, 'The Siege of Durham, the Battle of Carham and the Cession of Lothian', *SHR* 55 (1976), 1–19, at 12.

maioribus suis interiit. Episcopus audita populi sancti Cuthberti miseranda nece, alto cordis dolore attactus grauiter ingemuit, et 'O me', inquit, 'miserum! ut quid in hec tempora seruatus sum?'

In the year of our Lord 1018, while Cnut was ruling the kingdom of the English, there appeared to the Northumbrian peoples a comet, which persisted for thirty nights, presaging in a terrible way the future devastation of the province. For soon afterwards (that is after thirty days) the whole people between the river Tees and the river Tweed fought a battle at Carham against a countless multitude of Scots and almost all perished, including even their old folk. When the bishop heard of the miserable death of the people of St Cuthbert, he was stricken with deep sorrow of heart and sighed, saying 'O why – wretched as I am – was I spared to see these times?'[11]

The account continues to describe the bishop's longing for his own death, a prayer soon answered by God. The so-called *Annales Lindisfarnenses et Dunelmenses* or 'Annals of Lindisfarne and Durham', which appears to represent an earlier stage in Symeon's research, contain the following detail, added after notice of Bishop Ealdhun's death:

Cometa late spargens flammas visa est per Northymbriam per XXX noctes. Transactis post hoc XXX diebus fuit Carrum illud famosum bellum inter Northanhymbros et Scottos, ubi pene totus sancti Cuthberti populus interiit, inter quos etiam XVIII sacerdotes, qui inconsulte se intermiscuerant bello; quo audito prescriptus episcopus dolorem et vitam morte finivit.

A comet spewing flames was seen across Northumbria for thirty nights. When it passed after thirty days, the infamous battle of Carham was fought between the Northumbrians and Scots, where the entire *populus* of St Cuthbert met with the penalty of destruction, among them eighteen priests who had rashly got themselves involved in the fray; when he heard the news, the bishop, having ordered his affairs, ended his sadness and his life with death.[12]

---

11 *LDE*, iii.5, 154–7.
12 *ALD*, s.a. 1018, ed. Levison, 487.

Both versions show that Symeon is primarily interested in Ealdhun's end rather than Carham itself. This could mean that the information about the battle had passed to him as part of hagiographic traditions relating to the bishop, or that he himself was synchronising the death of the bishop and the battle for hagiographic purposes. The details about Bishop Ealdhun are more useful for reconstructing the twelfth-century historical imagination than the events of the 1010s, but the synchronisation of the event with the comet is of significant interest. Since the northern annals were probably produced after *Libellus de Exordio*, it is possible that the latter shaped their *sub anno* 1018 notice about Carham, a likelihood that increases if we believe that Symeon of Durham played a role in the provision of extra historical material to the annal tradition in the 1120s.[13]

Scottish king-list

A third source for the battle comes from a Scottish king-list. The list in question is one of Marjory Anderson's 'Y lists'.[14] It is a member of a variant set that commences with Fergus son of Erc rather than Cinaed son of Ailpín.[15] This Dál Riata–Scotland list is number five among the Scottish items in Paris, Bibliothèque Nationale, MS Latin 4126, the famous 'Poppleton manuscript'.[16] Among the events of the reign of Máel Coluim mac Cinaeda, *Malcolín, filius Kinet*, the king-list notes that:

> Hic magnum bellum fecit apud Carrun.

> He fought a great battle at *Carrun*.[17]

It has been argued by Dauvit Broun that surviving Scottish king-list material covering the Viking Age is based on tenth-century material updated in the reign of Donnchad son of Crínán, i.e. 1034–1040.[18] There is a possibility, then, that *magnum bellum fecit apud Carrun* had

---

13   See also Woodman, this volume.
14   E.g. M. O. Anderson, *Kings and Kingship in Early Scotland*, rev. edn (Edinburgh, 1980), 234.
15   For discussion of this set, see D. Broun, *The Irish Identity of the Kingdom of the Scots* (Woodbridge, 1999), 144–5.
16   These are described and printed in Anderson (ed.), *Kings and Kingship*, 235–60.
17   For an edition, see Anderson (ed.), *Kings and Kingship*, 253–4, at 254.
18   Broun, *Irish Identity*, 165–9.

been included in the material in the first half of the eleventh century. Against this, the Carham notice is absent from other king-lists. This particular king-list dates to the reign of King William and thus, alone, the notice cannot with certainty be dated earlier than William's reign, 1165–1214.[19]

The chances that the Scottish king-list is independent of *Historia Regum* and the Durham material would normally be very good. In this case, however, there is some reason for pause. For one thing, *ingens bellum* (used in the northern Anglo-Latin annals) and *magnum bellum* are similar enough to raise suspicions. More significantly, the manuscript in question originates in northern England where Roger of Howden's work enjoyed wide circulation and was regarded, even at Durham, as the standard work for the centuries after Bede.[20] One of the odd features of the Poppleton Dál Riata–Scotland king-list is that Donnchad mac Crínáin, Máel Coluim II's historical successor, is omitted: *Macbeth filius Findleg* follows Máel Coluim II's thirty-year reign.[21] The northern Anglo-Latin chronicles tell us that Macbeth succeeded Máel Coluim in 1034, also omitting Donnchad.[22] This 'error' seems to be rooted in how the common source of the northern annals used *Chronicon ex Chronicis*, attributed to John of Worcester. For documenting non-English affairs, *Chronicon ex Chronicis* often used the work of an eleventh-century predecessor, Marianus Scotus. Although based in Germany, Marianus was a Gael, probably from the north of Ireland. He took an interest in Scottish affairs, and among his annals there occurs an obit for Máel Coluim mac Cinaeda, entered s.a. 1034. Marianus's work also includes a notice, s.a. 1040, of Donnchad I's death and of Macbeth's accession; and, s.a. 1050, a notice about the activity of Macbeth on pilgrimage at Rome.[23] The 1034 and 1050 notices were reproduced by *Chronicon ex Chronicis* (and subsequently the northern Anglo-Latin annals), but the notice of Donnchad's accession was not used by *Chronicon ex Chronicis* and, thus, the s.a. 1040 notice of Donnchad's

---

19 Ibid., 144.
20 Offler, 'Hexham and the *Historia Regum*', 57.
21 Anderson (ed.), *Kings and Kingship*, 254.
22 *RHC*, s.a. 1034, ed. Stubbs, i, 89; *HR*, s.a. 1034, ed. Arnold, ii, 158.
23 Marianus Scotus, *Chronicon*, s.aa. 1034/1056, 1040/1062, 1050/1072, ed. G. Waitz, *Monumenta Germaniae Historica, Scriptores* 5 (Hannover, 1844), 481–562, at 556, 557, 558.

demise was unavailable to the northern revisers.[24] The latter, therefore, without any knowledge of Donnchad's reign seems to have added Macbeth's accession to its notice, s.a. 1034, in order to join up the dots of Scottish affairs. At any rate, for whatever reason it came about, an idiosyncratic error shared by the king-list and the annals is enough to raise a little doubt about the king-list's credentials as a source of independent information about Carham.

A fourth source?
A conflict between Máel Coluim II and Uhtred is mentioned in the Scoto-Latin chronicle tradition associated with the names of John of Fordun and Walter Bower. Although Fordun and Bower lived in the fourteenth and the fifteenth centuries respectively, their eleventh-century material was based on a chronicle put together at St Andrews in the thirteenth century.[25] They tell us that Máel Coluim II's career was marked by several victories over the Danes and by a struggle with Cnut, Danish conqueror of England. The source tells us that:

> *Ochtredum itaque comitem Anglicum sed Danis subditum, cuius inter eos simultatis exorte causam nescio, Cumbriam predari conantem, repceptis predis, iuxta Burgum bello difficili superauit.*

> As Uhtred, an English *comes* but subject to the Danes, was attempting to pillage *Cumbria* (the reason for the hostility that had arisen between them I know not) Máel Coluim took back the plunder and defeated him in a hard-fought battle near Brough.[26]

On the face of it, this battle has nothing to do with Carham. The chronicle appears to intend either Burgh-by-Sands near Carlisle (Cumberland) or Brough under Stainmore (Westmorland) as the location of this battle. We know of only one other battle that plausibly

---

24 *Chronicon ex Chronicis*, s.aa. 1034, 1050, ed. Darlington and McGurk, ii, 520–1, 552–3
25 D. Broun, *Scottish Independence and the Idea of Britain: From the Picts to Alexander III* (Edinburgh, 2007), chapter 9.
26 Walter Bower, *Scotichronicon*, iv.43, ed. and trans. J. MacQueen and W. MacQueen, *Scotichronicon by Walter Bower in Latin and English: Volume 2, Books III and IV* (Aberdeen, 1989), 400–3.

involved both Uhtred and Máel Coluim, but that was a Scottish defeat in 1006 (see below). One of the distinct, tendentious features of the thirteenth-century Scoto-Latin chronicle is the way it systematically attempts to portray *Cumbria* as a historical appanage of the Scottish kingship.[27] Máel Coluim [II], prior to his accession to the Scottish kingship, had served as ruler of *Cumbria* under King 'Grim'; subsequently, Máel Coluim provided *Cumbria* for his own successor, his grandson Donnchad. It is possible that the chronicle is a unique source for a third battle, not otherwise recorded; but it is also conceivable that this piece of narration was based on an account, perhaps very brief, that documented the battle of Carham; which the thirteenth-century Scoto-Latin chronicler relocated to Cumberland in order to accommodate his vision of eleventh-century Scoto-Cumbrian relations.[28]

Date

No extant source places the battle of Carham in any year except 1018, the year given by the Anglo-Latin annals and by *Libellus de Exordio*. As we have seen, in their final form all extant sources for the battle of Carham are post-1100. The independence of these sources is, as we have also seen, uncertain. Theoretically, it is conceivable that all of our dates originate in a speculative attempt by Symeon of Durham to synchronise an otherwise undated battle with the death of Bishop Ealdhun. No contemporary or near-contemporary source mentions the battle of Carham, but we do have one near-contemporary source with implications for its date. A group of entries included in the *Anglo-Saxon Chronicle* covering the period 983–1022 were written retrospectively at some point in the 1020s. The important notice, however, relates specifically to 1016. In

---

27 D. Broun, 'The Welsh Identity of the Kingdom of Strathclyde c.900–c.1200', *IR* 55 (2004), 111–80, at 130–5.
28 Opposite Carham, on the 'Scottish' side of the Tweed, lay Birgham. Very tenuously, perhaps the source the thirteenth-century chronicle encountered had referred to a battle of Birgham that was 'corrected' as part of the narrator's Cumbrian agenda. If so, the change was not the result of a simple scribal error; the spellings of the two places in twelfth- or thirteenth-century documents are not any more similar than the modern spellings and the separate etymologies would have been transparent to any medieval Anglophone. E.g. for Birgham, *Bricgham* in *RHC*, s.a. 883, ed. Stubbs, i, 45; but for Burgh-by-Sands, *Burgo* c. 1160, *Burch* c. 1180, etc., for which see A. M. Armstrong *et al.*, *The Place-Names of Cumberland*, English Place-Name Society 20-2 (Cambridge, 1950–2), i, 126–7.

that year, we are told about the activities of Edmund (d. 1016), son of King Æthelred 'the Unready' (d. 1016), who was at London preparing to fight Cnut and his ally, the Mercian ealdorman Eadric Streona (d. 1017):

> Then the atheling Edmund rode to Northumbria to Earl Uhtred, and everyone thought that they would collect an army against King Cnut. Then they led an army into Staffordshire and into Shropshire and to Chester, and they ravaged on their side and Cnut on his side. [Cnut] then went out through Buckinghamshire into Bedfordshire, from there to Huntingdonshire, and so into Northamptonshire, along the fen to Stamford, and then into Lincolnshire; then from there to Nottinghamshire and so into Northumbria towards York. When Uhtred learned this, he left his ravaging and hastened northwards, and submitted then out of necessity, and with him all the Northumbrians, and he gave hostages. And nevertheless he was killed by the advice of Ealdorman Eadric, and with him Thurcetel, Nafena's son. And then after that the king appointed Eric for the Northumbrians, as their earl, just as Uhtred had been . . .[29]

The essential problem is that if Uhtred died in 1016, which seems to be implied by the text above, he could not have appeared at Carham in 1018.

The problem invites several potential solutions. The most obvious, perhaps, is that Symeon of Durham's *Libellus de Exordio* and all northern Anglo-Latin annals simply got the year of the battle wrong. Since it is not possible to prove that these sources are independent authorities

---

[29] The text is *Ða rad se æþeling Eadmund to Norðhymbron to Uhtrede eorle, 7 wende ælc mon þæt hi woldon fyrde somnian ongean Cnut cyng. Þa fyrdedon hi into Stæffordscire 7 into Scrobsæton 7 to Legceastre, 7 hi heregodon on heora healfe, 7 Cnut on his healfe wende him ut þuruh Buccingahamscire into Bedanfordscire 7 ðanon to Huntadunscire swa into Hamtunscire andlang fennes to Stanforda 7 þa into Lindcolnescire þanon, ða to Snotingahamscire 7 swa to Norðhymbran to Eoferwicweard. Ða Uhtred geahsode þis, ða forlet he his hergunge 7 efste norðweard 7 beah ða for nyde 7 ealle Norðhymbro mid him, 7 he gislode, 7 hine mon ðeah hwæþere ofsloh ðuruh Eadrices ræd ealdormannes, 7 Þurcytel Nafenan sunu mid him. 7 þa æfter ðam gesette se cyng Yric into Norðhymbron him to eorle eal swa Uhtred wæs . . .*; see *ASC* MS C 1016, ed. K. O'Brien O'Keeffe (ed.), *The Anglo-Saxon Chronicle: A Collaborative Edition. Volume 5, MS C* (Cambridge, 2001), 100–1; trans. D. Whitelock, *The Anglo-Saxon Chronicle: A Revised Translation* (London, 1961), 94–5.

for either the date or the event, only a single misstep made either by Symeon or his source material need be responsible for an error. Elsewhere, *Historia Regum* and the other northern annals share common source material with *Libellus de Exordio*, and the latter was certainly used to supplement the former.[30] One error by *Libellus* or one of its sources could, then, account for all appearances of 1018 as the year of the battle. The historian most associated with the rejection of 1018 is the great Anglo-Saxonist and place-name scholar, Frank Stenton. Stenton accepted that Uhtred had participated in the battle of Carham, and pointed out, quite reasonably, that 'names are better remembered than dates'.[31] His reasoning put the battle back to 1016 or to some earlier year.

Another response to the problem is to accept that the battle happened in 1018, but that Uhtred had indeed died in 1016. By default, this is to reject the claim that Uhtred was the leader at the battle of Carham, a claim which, in fairness, is made only by *Historia Regum*. This solution appears to have been around long before Stenton's. It was implicitly favoured by John Hodgson in 1858, Eben William Robertson in 1862, and argued explicitly later in the century by William Forbes Skene and Edward Freeman, who were followed by other notable commentators in succeeding generations. With Uhtred dead two years before Carham, his brother Eadwulf emerged as the best candidate for leadership of the English, a corollary theory beginning at least as early as Hodgson.[32] Eadwulf is named as Uhtred's successor in the Anglo-Norman-era Northumbrian earl lists, but Eadwulf was also attractive because of another text, *De Obsessione Dunelmi* ('Regarding the Siege of Durham'). In *De Obsessione Dunelmi* we are told that during his time in Bamburgh Eadwulf was forced to cede Lothian to the Scots.[33] Although

---

30   For a fairly recent discussion of its sources, see Rollason, *LDE*, introduction, lxvi–lxxvi.
31   F. M. Stenton, *Anglo-Saxon England*, 3rd edn (Oxford, 1971), 418, n. 2.
32   J. Hodgson, *History of Northumberland, in Three Parts*, 3 vols (Newcastle-upon-Tyne, 1820–58), i, 162–3; E. W. Robertson, *Scotland under Her Early Kings: A History of the Kingdom to the Close of the Thirteenth Century*, 2 vols (Edinburgh, 1862), i, 95–7; W. F. Skene, *Celtic Scotland: A History of Ancient Alban*, 3 vols (1876–80), i, 393, and n. 15; E. Freeman, *The History of the Norman Conquest of England*, 6 vols (1867–79), i, 738; H. Maxwell, *The Early Chronicles Relating to Scotland* (Glasgow, 1912), 120. Notably John Pinkerton, *An Inquiry into the History of Scotland Preceding the Reign of Malcolm III*, 2 vols (London, 1789), ii, 189, does not seem to have noticed the issue.
33   *RHC*, s.a. 952, ed. Stubbs, i, 57; *HR*, s.a. 1072, ed. Arnold, ii, 197; *DPSA*, 383; *DOD*,

the author of *De Obsessione Dunelmi* shows no awareness of any battle at Carham, Eadwulf's predicament could be explained if we were to suppose he had been defeated in a large military encounter.

In the 1970s, A. A. M. Duncan offered a third solution, this one involving reinterpretation of the *Anglo-Saxon Chronicle*'s 1016 entry. Duncan focused on one key line:

> And nevertheless he was killed by the advice of Ealdorman Eadric, and with him Thurcetel, Nafena's son.

Duncan argued that this was a parenthetical comment prompted by the account of how Uhtred 'submitted ... and with him all the Northumbrians, and ... gave hostages'. Cnut had presumably come to be blamed for Uhtred's death by the 1020s, and the chronicler is reflecting on the injustice of it. The reflection is included in the text entered *sub anno* 1016, the year of Uhtred's peace with Cnut; but, according to Duncan, he is not necessarily saying that Uhtred's killing itself happened in 1016; Uhtred's 'reconciliation' in 1016 is just the opportunity for the parenthetical comment because Cnut's subsequent malevolence, in light of Uhtred's submissive behaviour, was unwarranted.[34] Avoiding his inevitable fate in 1016 Uhtred would theoretically be free to lead the Northumbrians at Carham in 1018 (or afterwards). In general, Duncan's explanation has impressed the scholarly community, and has gained acceptance among a significant portion of historians working on this era, enough that, at the time of this volume, it can probably be regarded as the closest thing we have to a 'consensus date'.[35]

218, trans. C. J. Morris, *Marriage and Murder in Eleventh-Century Northumbria: A Study of 'De Obsessione Dunelmi'*, Borthwick Papers 82 (York, 1992), 3. It is worth noting that Offler, 'Hexham and the *Historia Regum*', 57, was sceptical about Eadwulf's leadership.

34 A. A. M. Duncan, 'The Battle of Carham, 1018', *SHR* 55 (1976), 20–8. An additional complication is that Eadric died in 1017; i.e. he died at least a year before his advice could have killed Uhtred. Duncan argued that Eadric's role as arch-villain in these episodes explained this.

35 Not all historians have accepted Duncan's explanation. Christopher Morris, for instance, thought it 'more likely that the *Historia Regum* is mistaken' (*Marriage and Murder*, 11); it should be pointed out, however, that Duncan did not rest his case for this analysis on the dating of Carham, the case for 'parenthetical commentary' is possible without the evidence relating to Carham. See also T. Clarkson, *Strathclyde and the Anglo-Saxons in the Viking Age* (Edinburgh, 2014), 136–7.

As things stand, this 'consensus' is not unreasonable. One of our northern sources, *Libellus de Exordio*, places the battle in the same year, 1018, as the appearance of a comet. If Symeon of Durham was using a muddled source or a source with dating errors, we might expect the comet to be misdated too. Yet, the Saxon chronicler Thietmar of Merseburg, writing in the 1010s, documented the appearance of a comet in August 1018, one that 'was visible for more than fourteen days'.[36] The comet is also noted in Irish annals,[37] and in East Asian sources.[38] The comet presents some difficulties for anyone seeking to reject 1018. One possibility is that knowledge of the comet and its year existed in some astronomical record circulating in Symeon's time. Another is that a story of the comet was linked to the death of Bishop Ealdhun in oral or written tradition. That is to say, *Libellus de Exordio* was able to perform the synchronisation of 1018 and comet successfully because of reliable traditions about Ealdhun. The battle is only linked to the comet because Symeon speculatively added the battle of Carham to a body of older traditions about the death of Ealdhun, the bishop Symeon regarded as the founder of Durham. This type of solution can work, but the overall resulting argument is a little more convoluted than would be ideal. The truth is that if we are going to explain how Symeon in the twelfth century came, as seems to be the case, to have reliable information about a comet in 1018, the most economic explanation is probably that he did have access to reliable dating information that came along with a reliable account of the battle.

As a result of Stenton's argument, the year 1016 seems to have emerged as an alternative date, and often more cautious historians can be seen using 1016×1018 as the battle's date, i.e. no earlier than 1016 but no later than 1018. However, Stenton did not, at least not in his third edition, commit himself to 1016. Indeed, even accepting Stenton's argument, 1016 would not be particularly appealing as a correction to 1018. The northern Anglo-Latin annals do not say any leader died at the battle. While the *Anglo-Saxon Chronicle* does include a comment about Uhtred's death under commentary relating to 1016, it does not mention Carham; Uhtred is killed by the Danes, not the Scots. Carham may not

---

36 Thietmar of Merseburg, *Chronicon*, viii.29, trans. D. A. Warner, *Ottonian Germany* (Manchester, 2001), 281.
37 *AU* 1018.7; *ALC* 1018.5.
38 Clarkson, *Strathclyde*, 136; Rollason, *LDE*, 156, n. 17.

be mentioned s.a. 1018, but Carham would be a much stranger omission for the *Anglo-Saxon Chronicle* s.a. 1016, where the annal takes interest in Uhtred. Uhtred's activities in 1016 would have been affected by a major encounter with the Scots, but the annal has no suggestion of any such encounter. Uhtred met Cnut in southern Northumbria by moving northwards from the southern Danelaw, not heading southwards from Carham or the Tweed basin. Are we to believe that Uhtred would have been able and willing to raise an army and leave Northumbria if the Scots had just defeated him in a 'massive battle'? If we want to place the battle in 1016, we are left with what must have been a very small interval between submission to Cnut and death at Cnut's orders. That is not impossible, and Uhtred would have been more vulnerable to 'betrayal' had he just lost a battle to the Scots; but there is no particular evidence that requires us to squeeze his death into such a tight gap rather than, say, 1015 or 1014 or 1013 (and so forth). The range 1016×1018, therefore, is hardly much more rigorous than a specific year like 1016 or 1018.

Even for those who accept Stenton's argument, 1016 is only the latest possible year of the battle. It is worth noting, however, the other leaders mentioned by *Historia Regum*: Máel Coluim mac Cinaeda, king of the Scots; and *Eugenius Calvus*, 'Owain the Bald', king of the 'Clyde-folk'. Only Máel Coluim, reigning between 1005 and 1034, comes with a secure set of dates. If we knew that Uhtred did die in 1016 and that he did fight at Carham, the obvious date range for Carham would be 1005×1016. Unfortunately, Owain the Bald would not allow us to narrow that range further; nor does he provide much assistance with the date of the battle generally; he is not attested anywhere else, not with certainty at least. The closest we get is the B version of *Annales Cambriae*, which reports the death of a certain Owain son of Dyfnwal (*Owinus filius Dunawal*).[39] The B version of *Annales Cambriae* does not supply a year directly, but relative chronological order suggests that the original annalist had 1015 in mind – though 1014 and 1016 would also be possibilities. If we could be sure *Owinus* was *Eugenius Calvus*, and if we were sure of 1015 as the date of *Owinus*'s death, we could be sure that *Historia Regum* got the year wrong. Unfortunately, there does not seem to be much reason to be certain about either of these suppositions.

---

39   *Annales Cambriae*, ed. J. Williams ab Ithel, Rolls Series 20 (London, 1860), 22.

Although it is true that the name *Dunawal* tended to be used in northern Britain more than Wales (Dyfnwal in modern Welsh or Domnall in early Gaelic; i.e. 'Donald' in Scottish English, 'Donal' in Hiberno-English), use of such a name can be explained adequately if *Owinus* were a kinsman of *Eugenius Calvus*.[40] In any case, since the *Annales Cambriae* have no reference to Carham, we could only date Carham to 1005×1016, the same range we would get from accepting Stenton's position.[41]

Historia Regum is the only source to offer the names of the leaders at the battle of Carham, but not everyone has accepted the historical integrity of its 1018 annal. Hilary Seton Offler proposed that the original annal relating to the battle of Carham, s.a. 1018 in the surviving annals, had lacked the names of the leaders; he thought that someone in the mid twelfth century may have added names to the Corpus Christi College version of *Historia Regum* using a 'muddled addition from an unknown source'.[42] It should be noted that Offler's motivation for seeking this explanation rested on a 1016 date for the death of Uhtred and, writing in 1971, he had not been able to benefit from or reach a judgement about Duncan's argument. Nonetheless, Offler's position is still a reasonable one. Offler did not put *Historia Regum*'s names down to invention, however, but proposed an 'unknown source'. The reason for this proposal, surely, was the difficulties of explaining the inclusion of *Eugenius Calvus rex Clutinensium* otherwise. *Eugenius* is unrecorded (at least in this form) in any other extant source. To modern historians Eugenius is a plausible figure, while it is unlikely he was casually invented in the middle of the twelfth century, by which time the kings of Strathclyde had become a fading memory.

Uhtred and Máel Coluim mac Cinaeda both appear in *De Obsessione Dunelmi* and the northern Anglo-Latin annals, and so it is

---

40   Broun, 'Welsh Identity', 128, n. 66, provides perhaps the fullest recent discussion of this issue. See also Woolf, *From Pictland to Alba, 789–1070* (Edinburgh, 2007), 236; and, in this volume, Fiona Edmonds, 'Carham: The Western Perspective', 79–94. The survival of a nickname might indicate there was more than one prominent Owain in the family of the time, as it suggests that disambiguation was thought useful.

41   One advantage of a pre-1015 date is that we might be able to link Carham to the battle of Clontarf. We seem to know that the Scots and the 'Northern English' fought against each other at Clontarf in 1014. See *Cogadh*, c.87, 150–2, for the 'Northern English' in the 'Dublin army'; and for the participation of the Scottish mormaer of Marr, see *AU* 1014.2.

42   Offler, 'Hexham and the *Historia Regum*', 57.

possible that a scribe in the mid twelfth century, using those sources, could have synchronised the two rulers accurately. Even so, we would still be left trying to explain how the reviser obtained *Eugenius Calvus*. It is also unlikely that a 'king of the Clyde-folk' would be invented for a text of the 1100s. Doubtlessly, multiple speculative explanations for *Eugenius*'s appearance are possible; but the most economical explanation is that the scribe responsible for the names in *Historia Regum* obtained the synchronism of the three rulers from a single, older source, now lost. It is also worth noting that the appearance of all three rulers at the battle in an older source would not affect the security, either way, of 1018 as the year of the battle. The person responsible for the extra text in the Corpus Christi College version of the annal, as Offler suggests, may have been adding information about an event that a predecessor had already (perhaps incorrectly) dated. The appearance of *Eugenius Calvus* and a 1018 dating are, theoretically, independent.

Neither the obit of *Owinus* in *Annales Cambriae* nor the reference to Uhtred's death in the *Anglo-Saxon Chronicle* allow us to date the battle of Carham to a particular year. Of all the years in which it is possible to date the battle, 1018 is by far the best candidate. If we can rely on the works of Symeon of Durham, whose texts are the most specific about the date; and if we use what we know about the comet of that year, then we can surmise that the battle took place in either August or September 1018. That remains the only year supplied to us by any source. Nevertheless, the year is not certain and reasonable doubts are possible. All the sources that date the battle to 1018 may be the result of a speculative attempt by Symeon of Durham, in the early twelfth century, to add the battle of Carham to existing traditions about the death of Bishop Ealdhun, for instance. For historians seeking a more cautious dating, the range 1005×1018 could be recommended, perhaps alongside an extra cautious 1005×1034. The wider date range cannot really be questioned without robbing the battle of all identity and, thus, effectively disputing its existence.

Participants

Coalition: the Scots

Máel Coluim, almost certainly the commander of the Scots at Carham, was a member of the Alpinid dynasty, whom contemporaries called *Clann Cinaeda meic Alpín,* 'the children of Cinaed mac Ailpín' (i.e. Kenneth Mac Alpin; d. 858).[43] Máel Coluim was descended from Cinaed mac Ailpín's son Causantín mac Cinaeda (d. 877). Throughout the tenth century the line of Causantín mac Cinaeda shared power with the line descended from Causantín's brother, Áed mac Cinaeda (d. 878). However, the last royal descendant of Áed mac Cinaeda, Causantín mac Cuilén, was deposed in 997 by Cinaed mac Duib ('Kenneth Mac Duff'; d. 1005), a member of the rival branch. Máel Coluim II succeeded his kinsman Cinaed mac Duib in 1005, and soon afterwards appears to have launched an invasion of northern England. According to the *Annals of Ulster*, a large number of Scottish nobles were killed in battle with the English in 1006.[44] It is generally thought that the account of Uhtred's victory over the Scots presented in the Anglo-Norman-era text *De Obsessione Dunelmi* reflects some sort of memory of the 1006 victory, despite the fact that *De Obsessione Dunelmi* dated the event to 969 and confused the victory with a siege of Durham launched three and a half decades after 1006 by Máel Coluim's successor Donnchad mac Crínáin (d. 1040).[45]

Scotland, or *Alba* as it was known by its inhabitants, did not quite have the same territorial form in the early eleventh century that it has today. Until the thirteenth century the terminology was used only in reference to the territory north of the Forth, river and firth. In ideal terms, the men of Máel Coluim's polity may have conceived their kingdom encompassing all the lands north of the Forth. In reality, Máel Coluim's own power was probably very limited beyond the southeastern quarter of *Alba*. Although the Alpinids claimed to have Dál

---

[43] In notes added to genealogy, printed and translated by D. Broun, 'The Genealogy of the King of Scots as Charter and Panegyric', in J. R. Davies and S. Bhattacharya (eds), *Copper, Parchment, and Stone: Studies in the Sources for Landholding and Lordship in Early Medieval Bengal and Medieval Scotland* (Glasgow, 2016), c.7, appendix, 21–4, at 21, 23 (online at < http://eprints.gla.ac.uk/128834/1/128834.pdf >).

[44] *AU* 1006.5.

[45] Woolf, *From Pictland to Alba*, 233.

Riatan and Argyll ancestry, their power in that 'Scottish homeland' may have been confined to limited or irregular 'taxation'.[46] Many of the islands of western Scotland, in particular the Outer Hebrides, had been heavily settled in the early Viking Age by migrants from Scandinavia, foreign to the Scots both in allegiance as well as culture and language. A similar situation prevailed north of the Dornoch Firth, the land that the Scots called *Cait*. The area that later came to be Sutherland and Caithness was closer to Orkney and the Outer Hebrides in these terms than the southern side of the Moray Firth.[47]

It is also unlikely that, by 1018, Máel Coluim would have been able to exercise much direct authority over the southern Moray Firth region. In 1020, Irish annals note the death of a 'king of Scotland' named Findláech son of Ruaidrí ('Findlay son of Rory'); again, in 1029, they note the death of Findláech's nephew, another 'king of Scotland' named Máel Coluim son of Máel Brigte son of Ruaidrí.[48] This rising dynasty, Clann Ruaidrí, were probably based somewhere on the southern shore of the Moray Firth (or perhaps in Easter Ross) – the area occupied by their descendants in the twelfth century. The region had probably been part of the Alpinid realm, which seems to have included Forres among its major royal centres. It was at Forres where Dub mac Maíl Choluim was killed in 967, according to the *Annals of Ulster* by 'the Scots themselves' (*do marbad la h-Albanchu fein*).[49] There is no evidence that there was a separate Moravian kingship before the eleventh century, and the first 'king of Moray' is not recorded until the reign of Máel Coluim III.[50] The style 'king of Scotland' indicates affiliation with the Scottish political system, and so the sudden appearance of two 'kings of Scotland'

---

46 The Inner Hebrides appear to be styled *Innsi Alban* in the 900s: *AFM* 961.2. For Argyll and Scotland *c*. 1000, see recently P. Wadden, 'Dál Riata c. 1000: Genealogies and Irish Sea Politics', *SHR* 95 (2016), 164–81, and 178, for suggestions of taxation.

47 For recent overviews, see Woolf, *From Pictland to Alba*, 275–311; B. Crawford, *The Northern Earldoms: Orkney and Caithness from AD 870 to 1470* (Edinburgh, 2013), 80–144; A. MacNiven, T*he Vikings in Islay* (Edinburgh, 2015), 105–20.

48 *AU* 1020.6, for Findláech mac Ruaidrí (only *mormaer Moreb* at AT 1020.8); *AT* 1029.5 for Máel Coluim mac Maíl Brigte (without title at *AU* 1029.7); see also N. Evans, 'Alasdair Ross, *The Kings of Alba c.1000–c.1130*', *IR* 63 (2012), 101–10, at 105–6, responding to A. Ross, *The Kings of Alba: c.1000–c.1130* (Edinburgh, 2011), 90.

49 Anderson, *Kings and Kingship*, 267, 275, 283, 288; *AU* 967.1. Forres was the death place of Domnall mac Causantín (d. 900) according to one king-list (i.e. Anderson, *Kings and Kingship*, 274).

50 *AU* 1085.1.

suggests that a certain section of Scotland, perhaps all the Scots north of the Mearns (what later became Kincardineshire), replaced Máel Coluim but were not able to force other Scots to follow suit. One explanation for their discontent with Máel Coluim II might have been the defeat in 1006; another, perhaps, is political alienation resulting from the displacement of the line of Áed mac Cinaeda.[51]

Whatever the reason for the appearance of 'Moravian separatism' in the early decades of the eleventh century, Máel Coluim's power may not have extended north of 'the Mounth' (i.e. the 'Grampian' massif that protrudes into the Mearns). The territory that Máel Coluim governed directly around 1018, the lands that he habitually toured and resided, probably consisted of Perthshire, Fife, Angus and the Mearns – an area that in 1755, when we have our first detailed knowledge of Scotland's demographics, encompassed between a quarter and a fifth of the country's population.[52] It is still possible, however, that the Scottish army at Carham contained contingents from elsewhere. We have no way of knowing how exactly Máel Coluim and Clann Ruaidrí formalised their relationship, what rights and responsibilities were shared between the two. Custom may have allowed Máel Coluim the right to recruit westerners and northerners to join hostings directed at England; avarice and lust for glory may have supplied men on a voluntary basis – the opportunity to plunder the riches of Northumbria would have been hard for Moravians or Argyllmen to turn down.[53]

Coalition: the Clyde-folk

As we have seen, according to *Historia Regum*, Máel Coluim's Scottish forces at Carham had been joined by the 'Clyde-folk' and their king, Owain.[54] The kings of Strathclyde had been part of the political

---

51 A. Woolf, 'The "Moray Question" and the Kingship of Alba in the Tenth and Eleventh Centuries', *SHR* 79 (2000), 145–64; Woolf, *From Pictland to Alba*, 223–4, 240–2.
52 J. G. Kyd, *Scottish Population Statistics*, Scottish History Society, 3rd Ser. Vol. 44 (Edinburgh, 1952), 82.
53 We know from Aelred of Rievalaux's famous *Relatio de Standardo* that Orcadians fought for David I at the battle of the Standard in 1138, despite a very loose political connection (the perhaps recently appointed infant earl, Harald Maddadsson, was a member of David I's dynasty). For this text, see R. Howlett (ed.), *Chronicles of the Reigns of Stephen, Henry II, and Richard I*, Rolls Series 82, 4 vols (London, 1884–9), iii, 181–99, at 181.
54 See below, Edmonds, 'Carham: The Western Perspective', 79–94.

landscape of northern Britain just as long as the Alpinid Scots. Strathclyde, or 'Clydesdale' as it came to be known in the Scoto-English vernacular of the later Middle Ages, was probably very similar to what later became Lanarkshire. Owain's kingdom is generally called *Cumerland* (or some variation) in English,[55] 'Britain' (*Bretain*) or Northern Britain (*Bretain Tuaiscirt*) in Gaelic.[56] Their 'Cumbrian' and 'British' identity tells us that the dominant language of this polity was a British Celtic language, something very similar to Welsh and Cornish in the south-west of Britain. The men of Strathclyde probably called themselves *Cludwys* in their native British,[57] a term seemingly mirrored by the Latin of the *Historia Regum* entry for 1018 as well as the term *Bretain Chluada* known, elsewhere, in Irish.[58] At the height of their power, the kings of the Clyde-folk may have held sway over a greater area, perhaps much of what later became southern Scotland and north-western England. It is generally thought today that the Strathclyde kings, earlier in the Viking Age, had been able to expand into surrounding regions, including Tweeddale, Annandale and (the later English county of) Cumberland as well, perhaps, as Lothian.[59]

From the thirteenth to the twentieth century, historians portrayed Strathclyde as a subordinate appanage of the Viking-Age Scottish kingdom. Such a view would make sense of Owain's participation at the battle of Carham. Today, historians recognise that the evidence for such a view is very weak, and now proceed on the basis that the Cumbrian realm was no more or less independent than any of its neighbours, including the Scots.[60] Fiona Edmonds, in this volume, suggests that political pressures from its eastern and western neighbours had the effect of pushing the Cumbrians into a closer relationship with the Scots.

---

[55] *ASC* MS A 945, ed. Bately, 74; *ASC* MS D 945, 1000, ed. O'Brien O'Keeffe, 80, 88; *ASC* MS D 945, 1000, ed. Cubbin, 44, 50.

[56] *AU* 975.2; *AU* 997.5; *CKA*, 149, 150; *Corpus genealogiarum sanctorum Hiberniae*, ed. P. Ó Riain (Dublin, 1985), c.722.100, at p. 180. Use of *Bretain Tuaiscirt* may have been based on analogy with the Gaelic term for Northumbria, *Saxain Tuaiscirt*.

[57] A. Woolf, 'Reporting Scotland in the Anglo-Saxon Chronicle', in A. Jorgensen (ed.) *Reading the Anglo-Saxon Chronicle: Language, Literature, History* (Turnhout, 2010), 221–39, at 235.

[58] *Corpus genealogiarum sanctorum Hiberniae*, ed. Ó Riain, c.662, at p. 80.

[59] See F. Edmonds, 'The Expansion of the Kingdom of Strathclyde', *Early Medieval Europe* 23 (2015), 43–66, and, further, her contribution to this volume, at 88–90.

[60] See, in particular, Broun, 'Welsh Identity', 111–80, and Edmonds, 'Expansion of the Kingdom of Strathclyde', 43–66.

Doubtlessly, also, political opportunities presented to the Scots were just as appealing to the Cumbrians. Co-operation would have lowered the ceiling of booty for each side, but would also have brought increased safety.

The English
The English at Carham were not the people of the kingdom of England, *per se*. They were Northumbrians or 'Northern English'. As we have seen, there are some doubts about whether or not Uhtred fought at Carham. There is no doubt, however, that the 'English' at Carham were the followers and subjects of the rulers of Bamburgh, in whose territory Carham itself lay. After the Danish settlement of southern Northumbria in the 870s, the ancient citadel of Bamburgh on the North Sea, within sight of the Holy Island of Lindisfarne, emerged as the stronghold of the English rulers who had escaped subjection to the Danes. Bamburgh came to be ruled by the Eadwulfing clan, descendants of Eadwulf 'king of the Northern English' who died in 913. Uhtred was a member of this family, the son of Waltheof (fl. 994), son of Ealdred (fl. 958–9?), son of Oswulf (fl. 934–54), son of Eadwulf (d. 913). The Eadwulfing polity had frequently enjoyed a close relationship with the West Saxon kings of England prior to the 960s, but it was not directly part of the kingdom of England itself, no more than Strathclyde or Gwynedd were.[61] This is quite important to recognise because, contrary to expectations generated by later centuries, prior to the mid eleventh century the English kings south of the Humber would not *necessarily* have taken any particular side in a conflict between the Northern English and Scots.

The Eadwulfings, rather like the rulers of Strathclyde, enjoyed mixed relations with the Scots. The Alpinids and Eadwulfings had been allies at the battle of Corbridge in 918 and again in 952, united against the Hiberno-Norse rulers of the English Danelaw. However, Eadwulfing territory was invaded several times by Máel Coluim II's father, Cinaed mac Maíl Choluim. During one of these invasions, the Scots captured a 'son of the king of the English'.[62] In 1006, probably led by Máel Coluim II himself, in his inaugural invasion or *crech-ríge*, the Scots were defeated

---

61 See N. McGuigan, 'Ælla and the Descendants of Ivar', *NH* 52 (2015), 20–34; and 'Bamburgh and the Northern English Realm', this volume, 95–150.
62 *CKA*, 151, 161.

in a significant battle (location unknown).[63] The encounter of 1006, as we saw above, seems to have formed the basis for memory about a victory enjoyed by Uhtred, mixed with other traditions and confusingly reproduced by *De Obsessione Dunelmi*. It is the text's attribution of the victory to Uhtred that allows us to link it to the battle of 1006.[64]

For most of the tenth century the Eadwulfings presided over a territory stretching, roughly speaking, from the Forth to the Tyne, perhaps with a core collection of residences in the lower Tweed basin. However, from about 1006, the year of Uhtred's victory over the Scots, Eadwulfing power expanded significantly. Uhtred of Bamburgh was granted control of the ealdordom of York by Æthelred 'the Unready', king of England. The office was created in the 960s by Æthelred's father and predecessor Edgar (d. 975) as a means of managing West Saxon-controlled territories in southern Northumbria. The ealdorman was responsible for peace and justice in the region, and for defence against invaders. Uhtred became Æthelred's son-in-law too, marrying one of the monarch's daughters. Æthelred was probably seeking to utilise the resources of the Eadwulfings to maintain control of the north in the face of the increasing political instability and the growing threat of Danish conquest. It did not work, and Uhtred's alliance with the southern monarch led to his undoing. The Danes finally conquered the English kingdom in 1016; by 1017, at the latest, the new king Cnut had stripped Uhtred of the ealdordom. If Uhtred was still alive in 1018, he probably still controlled the areas subject to Bamburgh. However, he would have been a man on a sharp downward trajectory. If the Scots and Clyde-folk fought Uhtred or any Eadwulfing in 1018, they did so just as the family's fortunes were collapsing.[65]

Purpose of the battle

Rulers of polities like Scotland and Strathclyde had a perennial need to provide plunder for their leading inhabitants. Scottish armies invaded northern England at least once every generation from Cinaed mac Ailpín onwards. Successful invasions allowed kings to boost their prestige and provide their followers with proud memories and glorious

---

63 B. Hudson, *Kings of Celtic Scotland* (Westport, 1994), 112, was inclined to dispute its status as an inaugural *crech-ríge* based on his belief that the 1006 invasion was aimed at Durham.
64 *DOD*, 215–16, trans. Morris, *Marriage and Murder*, 1–2.
65 See McGuigan, 'Bamburgh and the Northern English Realm', this volume, 130–2.

deeds, but more importantly with precious metal, cattle, slave girls and other valued moveable goods.[66] The ability of kings to supervise such large-scale theft safely was usually doubtful – otherwise the neighbour in question would have little option but to pay tribute on a permanent basis. It is probable, particularly with the Scottish realm divided between two kingships, that the Scots, the Cumbrians and the Northern English of Bamburgh were, in relative terms, quite evenly matched in the 1010s. Windows of weakness, however, opened all of them up to predation by neighbours. Such a window was open on the Northern English from 1016. Therefore, the declining fortunes of the Eadwulfings in the face of Cnut is probably the best general explanation for the Scoto-Cumbrian invasion and why, in general terms, the battle took place.

At the same time, it is possible that the Scots or Cumbrians invaded with some more specific political goal. Unfortunately, we can only speculate what that could have been. It is not impossible that they had been invited to invade by Cnut. It is also possible that they sought to change the leadership in Bamburgh. Perhaps the 'son of the king of the English' captured by Máel Coluim's father Cinaed had grown up with Máel Coluim in the Scottish royal household. Now that Uhtred was on the way out, the Scots may have felt this was their time to establish a grateful dependent in the south, perhaps Eadwulf *Cudel*. After the disasters of the era, the Northern English people may also have preferred a leader with Scottish support, and it is possible that some leaders had invited the coalition to intervene. Even if no territorial question had been at stake, victory might have tempted the Scots or the Clyde-folk to demand concessions on a territorial basis, perhaps transfers of tribute or even of palace sites.

Modern historians are not able to say with any authority what sort of numbers might have participated in the battle of Carham. Any attempt to calculate the size of either side's contingent is wrought with intractable difficulties.[67] Documentary evidence from the Viking Age tends not to reveal much about the size of armies or number of participants in battles, and historians almost never believe numbers supplied by primary source

---

66 Particularly good discussion relevant to Scottish armies in this regard can be found in D. R. Wyatt, *Slaves and Warriors in Medieval Britain and Ireland: 800–1200* (Leiden, 2009).

67 Good introductions to war and musters relevant to this place and period can be found in N. Aitchison, *The Picts and Scots at War* (Stroud, 2003) and S. Davies, *Welsh Military Institutions, 633–1283* (Cardiff, 2004).

anyway. One source for the battle of Brunanburh, an encounter of 937 that was almost certainly larger in scale than Carham, tells us that the losing Scots and Hiberno-Norse had more than 35,000 men.[68] Since it is usually assumed that authors exaggerate the size of armies for rhetorical effect, there is a general tendency among modern historians to revise figures downwards. Figures provided by the twelfth-century writer Jordan Fantosme are a good example of where scepticism might also be employed. Describing the Scottish invasion force of 1173/4, he claimed that the mormaer of Angus alone commanded 3,000 Scots.[69] If other provincial commanders had similar numbers the Scottish invading army of 1174 would be in the 30,000 to 40,000 range! Few historians would believe such figures, and it is doubtful that many historians would be prepared to suggest anything over 10,000 even for a twelfth-century army.

However, if the Carham expedition was raised primarily for plunder, it is possible that the armies of Scotland and Strathclyde were very large; consisting, perhaps, of a sizeable proportion of middle- and upper-class males of fighting age. Armies above the 10,000 range cannot be entirely dismissed, therefore. Within each contingent, however, the quality of arms and armour would likely have varied with social rank and wealth. The Scottish and Strathclyde armies probably had many seasoned professional warriors, drawn from the households of the kings, mormaers and other local rulers; but the bulk of both armies likely consisted of 'amateurs', prosperous farmers who were not well disciplined. Lack of discipline in such armies was ruthlessly exposed by the Normans in the coming centuries. In 1174, in the vicinity of Alnwick (about 30 miles from Carham), the Scottish king William (d. 1214) was captured despite the presence of his very large army of Scots – distracted at the time by plundering. A tiny force of fully professional, highly mobile Norman knights took advantage of the situation and ended Scottish participation in the wider conflict (i.e. the revolt of Henry the 'Young King' against his father King Henry II of England).[70] Máel Coluim III, William's great-grandfather, may have been killed in similar circumstances

---

68 *AClon* 931 [937], ed. Murphy, 151.
69 Jordan Fantosme, *Chronique de la guerre entre les Anglois et les Écossois*, c.47, lines 473–4, ed. and trans. R. C. Johnston (Oxford, 1981), 36–7.
70 There is an excellent description of this in William of Newburgh, *Historia rerum Anglicarum*, ii.33, ed. and trans. P. G. Walsh and M. J. Kennedy, *History of English Affairs Book II* (Oxford, c. 2004), 134–9.

in 1093. Depending on how the encounter was initiated, the battle of Carham may also have involved only the smallest, most professional elements of the army. Without any detailed source on the battle it is impossible to say whether or not the battle was a full-scale engagement rather than just a large-scale encounter.

Scotland in the eleventh century was organised into a number of provinces such as Angus, Fife, Atholl, Gowrie, Mearns, Mar and so forth. The *Fír Alban*, the army of the 'men of Scotland', would have been raised by local officials and have marched province by province, perhaps under the banner of their local mormaer or 'clan chief' (the *toísech clainne* of the Book of Deer *notitiae*).[71] The Scots would have crossed the Fords of Frew on the Forth, and headed south towards their prearranged meeting point with the Clyde-folk. It is possible that the Scots took a route passing through Edinburgh and Stow of Wedale, and met the Clyde-folk at Caddonlee, Selkirkshire; alternatively, both armies may have met further north, perhaps at the monastery of Falkirk, Stirlingshire.[72] Woolf argues that Uhtred's army may have been forced to rely on levies from regions close to the battle site, from Berwickshire, Roxburghshire and the area between the rivers Tweed and Aln.[73] The mustering of the Scottish and Clydesdale armies would have taken time and planning and could not have been done in secret. Therefore, it is possible that Uhtred and the Northern

---

71 For the latest edition of these notes, see *Deer Notitiae*, ed. R. Ó Maolalaigh, trans. K. Forsyth, T. Clancy and D. Broun, in K. Forsyth, D. Broun and T. Clancy, 'The Property Records: Text and Translation', in K. Forsyth (ed.), *Studies on the Book of Deer* (Dublin, 2008), 136–43; see also K. Jackson, *The Gaelic Notes in the Book of Deer* (Cambridge, 1972), 110–11.

72 Caddonlee was a mustering point for Scottish armies in the later Middle Ages and a natural place for an army for a group originating north of the Forth to meet another originating in Clydesdale or Tweeddale, or beyond – however, in 1018 it may have lain in Northern English territory and a meeting there would have allowed the natives more of an opportunity to tackle each army separately; see Woolf, *From Pictland to Alba*, 238. In later sources, the pre-Norman monastery of Falkirk is known to have been positioned on the royal road linking Lothian and Clydesdale. It would have offered the early arrivers better facilities, and made it more difficult for the Northern English to ambush either party in the coalition. The same location hosted a meeting between Robert Curthose and Máel Coluim III in 1080. See *The Knights of St John of Jerusalem in Scotland*, ed. I. B. Cowan, P. H. R. Mackay and A. Macquarrie, Scottish History Society, 4th Ser. Vol. 19 (Edinburgh, 1983), no. 3; and *HR*, s.a. 1080, ed. Arnold, ii, 211.

73 Woolf, *From Pictland to Alba*, 236–9.

English, perhaps informed by travellers, merchants or even spies, had time to make some preparations.

Our sources are clear that the battle was a large-scale encounter. It is unlikely that the English side would have fought the battle against the will of its leaders. Even accepting that psychological issues of confidence and political pressure may have interfered somewhat with the decision-making process, we are still entitled to assume that the English army was close enough in size that fighting the battle was a rationally-justifiable risk. Perhaps some advantageous position or some opportunity to kill one of the coalition's kings or defeat a major component of the army encouraged the engagement. We can only speculate.

Carham the place

Carham as a place-name is of some interest. Modern spellings could suggest that the generic element derives from the relatively common Old English *ham*, meaning 'homestead', 'enclosure', 'abode', from which the modern English 'home' and Scots 'hame' derive. This interpretation of the name was in existence by the thirteenth century, but the earliest forms are not particularly supportive of a *-ham* etymology.[74] For instance, the form is *Carrum* in the eleventh-century *Historia de Sancto Cuthberto* and in the related twelfth-century *Libellus de Exordio* and *Historia Regum*.[75] It is more likely that the place-name is an Old English dative incorporating the Old Northumbrian word *carr*, 'rock', itself a borrowing from Celtic.[76] The Carham area became very significant militarily in the twelfth century as it emerged as the frontier of lands directly subject to the Norman (and later Angevin) kings of England. Richard of Hexham listed Carham among the five Northumbrian *oppida* seized by King David of Scotland in 1135, the others being Carlisle, Alnwick, Norham and Newcastle. Richard tells us that Carham (*Carrum*) was called 'Wark' in English (*quod ab Anglis Werch*), very likely Old English

---

74 For a survey, see A. Mawer, *The Place-Names of Northumberland and Durham* (Cambridge, 1920), 39, s.v. 'Carham-on-Tweed'.
75 *HSC*, c.7, 48–9; *LDE*, iii.5, 156–7; *HR*, s.a. 1018, ed. Arnold, ii, 155.
76 The word *carr* is used in several glosses to the Book of Mark in the Lindisfarne Gospels; see *Oxford English Dictionary*, s.v. 'carr', online at < http://www.oed.com/view/Entry/28210 >

[*ge*]*weorc*, 'work', 'building', 'structure'.[77] The name 'Carham' may have been taken into Richard's native Norman French, the language of England's aristocracy at the time, when they first arrived in the region; after the beginning of the French castle, the native English locals appear to have coined a new name, subsequently the only name of Wark Castle. The castle probably, then, originates with the Normans, with the original 'Carham' focused on the other high status place in the area, the church.

Carham was the site of what was probably, in 'national' terms, a medium-sized church, most likely under some sort of control by the Cuthbertine community further east. The eleventh-century *Historia de Sancto Cuthberto* claimed that Carham had become part of the Cuthbertine dominion in the days of King Ecgfrith (d. 685), a claim that is plausible but which cannot be verified with contemporary evidence.[78] Lack of adequate documentation means that the political status of much of the Tweed basin is uncertain until the reign of Henry I (r.1100–35). Carham was held by Walter Espec by the 1120s, a man who exercised vice-regal authority in the north of England on behalf of the king. Like most of the surrounding region, Carham must have been subject to some sort of Norman lordship from at least the 1090s, when we can be sure Norman lords were operating both at Carlisle and Bamburgh.[79] Wark Castle was probably built at Walter's instigation or at the instigation of some obscure predecessor.

In Northumbria, important ecclesiastical sites tended to be within a few miles of important royal centres: for instance, Lindisfarne and

---

77 He also provides two names for Carlisle, and so it is worth quoting more fully for this context: *Similiter et David rex Scottiae, eiusdem dominae avunculus, in provincia Norþamymbrorum v. oppida, scilicet Lugabaliam, quod Anglice Carlel dicitur, et Carrum, quod ab Anglis Werch dicitur, et Alnawic et Norham et Novum Castellum, mox circa Natale Domini cum magno exercitu praeoccupavit ac tenuit*; this text is from the Rolls Series edition by Richard Howlett, for which see *Chronicles of the Reigns of Stephen, Henry II, and Richard I*, ed. Howlett, iii, 145.

78 *HSC*, c.7, 48–9.

79 The established account of Norman penetration in the north is W. E. Kapelle, *The Norman Conquest of the North: The Region and its Transformation, 1000–1135* (London, 1979). For the Norman conquest of the north-west, see now R. Sharpe, *Norman Rule in Cumbria, 1092–1136*, Cumberland and Westmorland Antiquarian and Archaeological Society Tract 21 (Kendal, 2006). The importance of the 1090s horizon for this region will be discussed more fully in N. McGuigan, *Máel Coluim III Canmore* (Edinburgh, forthcoming).

Bamburgh, Tyninghame and Dunbar, and so forth. The closest major pre-Norman secular site to Carham appears to be Sprouston, three and a half miles distant. Sprouston was one of the first major residences in Teviotdale used by twelfth-century Scottish monarchs.[80] There is the possibility of a 30-by-8 metre hall 'unparalleled in Bernicia' [Smith] comparable in size and construction to the ninth- or tenth-century 'hall G' of Thetford, capital of Viking East Anglia.[81] Sprouston, however, like most major royal sites, also developed its own church and after 1100 became the centre of a distinct parish. Sprouston, today, is in Scotland; Carham in England. It is likely that Sprouston was obtained by David mac Maíl Choluim around 1113, when he exercised the office of earl in the region of Teviotdale. He handed over rights and responsibilities for the church of Sprouston (and its glebe) to the Tironensians of Teviotdale, an act that would also make it difficult for the successors of Cuthbert, who by the Norman era were based at Durham, far to the south on the Wear, to 'recover' their jurisdiction.[82]

The monks of Durham tried to obtain Carham from Queen Matilda sometime before 1118.[83] It was gained instead, as we have seen, by the king's military commander in the region, Walter Espec, who managed to have Carham (with its township) included in the holdings of his new Augustinian foundation of Kirkham Priory. Carham became the centrepiece of Kirkham's Northumberland franchise, and eventually ended up as a 'cell'. The earliest notice of Kirkham's property comes from a confirmation of Henry I, *c.* 1126, indicating that the churches of Carham, Kirknewton and Ilderton, as well as the villa of Titlington, had been among the gifts bestowed on the new Yorkshire house. Walter granted Kirkham the tithes of all his property in Northumberland and Yorkshire. The properties and services of Ulfchill *clericus* of Carham were also

---

80   *David I Chrs*, no. 14.
81   I. M. Smith, 'Patterns of Settlement and Land Use of the Late Anglian Period in the Tweed Basin', in M. L. Faull (ed.), *Studies in Late Anglo-Saxon Settlement* (Oxford, 1984), 177–96, at 186; see also I. M. Smith, 'Sprouston, Roxburghshire', *PSAS* 121 (1991), 261–94.
82   *David I Chrs*, no. 150, but possibly prefigured by the grant of the glebe, *David I Chrs* no. 14.
83   *RRAN*, ii, no. 1143; *North Durham*, Appendix no. 785. See also K. H. Vickers, *A History of Northumberland, Volume XI: The Parishes of Carham, Branxton, Kirknewton, Wooler, and Ford* (Newcastle upon Tyne, 1922), 12.

among the gifts received by Kirkham.[84] Durham does not appear to have given up trying to regain Carham until the episcopate of Hugh le Puiset.[85]

The three contiguous parishes of Carham, Kirknewton and Ilderton have the Teviotdale parishes of Sprouston, Linton, Yetholm and Morebattle to their west. Carham falls on the English side of what became the Anglo-Scottish border – but only just. The Anglo-Scottish border as it is today (and as it has been, in practice, since the twelfth century) ceases to follow the Tweed about 700 metres up river from the position of Carham's ecclesiastical site. The border leaves the Tweed at the 'Carham burn', and proceeds south and then east, far enough to mean that the immediate vicinity of the church of Carham came to be surrounded on three sides by the kingdom of Scotland. The same boundary came to mark the boundary between the parish of Carham and the parish of Sprouston, as well as between the deanery of Bamburgh within the diocese of Durham and the Glasgow-run archdeaconry and deanery of Teviotdale.

The site of the modern village, based on the medieval church, is close to fords on the Tweed. This raises the possibility that the battle occurred as one side, probably the Scots, tried to ford the river. As Alex Woolf points out in his contribution,[86] Carham lies opposite a site with the Old English name *Bricgham* (i.e. modern Birgham), indicating the presence of a bridge, perhaps a major bridge, over the Tweed. However, custom and ritual may also have played a role both in the location of the battle and in how it was fought. As long-term neighbours, it is not impossible that both sides took part in the battle in a way that offered one group the possibility of decisive victory while limiting the destruction and suffering on both sides – although, as we have seen, this is not quite what Symeon of Durham's accounts suggest. As David Petts points out in his contribution to this volume, there is no way to locate the

---

84 *RRAN*, ii, no. 1459. See also J. E. Burton, *Kirkham Priory from Foundation to Dissolution*, Borthwick Papers 86 (York, 1995), 2–6. As late as the second half of the twelfth century, Walter Corbet, overlord of Makerston in Roxburghshire, and the Tironensians of Kelso, competed with the canons of Kirkham for Kirknewton. For the problems caused by Kirknewton, see *English Episcopal Acta, Volume 24: Durham, 1153–1195*, ed. M. G. Snape (Oxford, 2002), nos. 80–7.
85 *English Episcopal Acta, Volume 24*, ed. Snape, no. 82; cf. Vickers, *A History of Northumberland, Volume XI*, 13.
86 See this volume, 'The Diocese of Lindisfarne', 231–9, at 234, n. 14.

battle specifically within the 'shire' of Carham and, thus, it is pointless to speculate much about tactics.[87]

Aftermath and significance

Lack of documentation means that the immediate aftermath of the Scottish victory is obscure and open to a large amount of speculation. Doubtless, the Scots and Cumbrians returned home with lots of booty. Whoever was ruler in Bamburgh at the time of the battle, the defeat would not have boosted their status or credibility. If *De Obsessione Dunelmi* can be believed, Uhtred met his end in Yorkshire when he and his party were killed by one Thurbrand, a hold (a senior Anglo-Danish aristocratic status, junior to earl). Despite a royal safe conduct, Uhtred was, so the account has it, killed in the king's presence.[88] It is difficult to evaluate the reliability of this account positively, and it is possible that the text is back-projecting a later feud; on the other hand, if Uhtred had taken part at Carham it would not be unreasonable to suppose that enemies at home became emboldened; such a defeat would have significantly decreased his chances of surviving more than a year. Perhaps Uhtred felt forced to risk a direct meeting with Cnut because the disaster of Carham had robbed him of options; perhaps Uhtred had to flee Bamburgh after 1018 and mistakenly believed he could take refuge with the Danish king. Unfortunately, however, these suggestions are purely speculative. We cannot date even Uhtred's death with any certainty. It is thus impossible to establish a strong link between his death and the battle of Carham.

In *De Obsessione Dunelmi*, Uhtred's successor Eadwulf *Cudel* is said to have handed over Lothian to the Scots.[89] This evidence has long been linked in modern historiography to the battle. For this reason, Hume Brown declared that '[a]t Carham the Celts of Alba overthrew the Saxons of Northumbria, and by the annexation of Lothian made possible the growth of a Teutonic Scotland distinct from a Teutonic England'.[90] Hume Brown was right, doubtless, that the acquisition of

---

87 See David Petts, 'Early Medieval Carham in its Landscape Context', this volume, 151–73, at 151–2.
88 *DOD*, 217–18, trans. Morris, *Marriage and Murder*, 3
89 *DOD*, 218, trans. Morris, *Marriage and Murder*, 3.
90 Hume Brown, *History of Scotland to the Accession of Mary Stewart*, i, 206. For Hume Brown Carham stood alongside the battle of Harlaw in 1411 where 'the victory of

Anglophone territory by the Scottish kings, and the failure to Gaelicise these territories, came to be important developments in Scottish history – if nothing else, important to the identity of nineteenth- and twentieth-century Scottish intelligentsia![91] The integration of Lothian and Scotland had important consequences for the makeup and identity of Scotland in earlier centuries too, a process documented so well in recent years by Dauvit Broun.[92] However, the connection of these events with the battle of Carham is opaque and its nature, therefore, questionable. It is possible that some region called 'Lothian', perhaps just a small area around Edinburgh, was lost to the Northern English after Carham; but we have no reliable sources that document such a transfer.

It is very likely that the rulers of Bamburgh still controlled East Lothian, Teviotdale and the Merse until at least the episcopate of Bishop Edmund II of Durham, the successor of Ealdhun who died *c.* 1040. In contemporary terms, Scottish control south of the Forth cannot be reliably documented until the reign of Máel Coluim III, in relation to East Lothian and the Merse.[93] Even then, it was not until the 1110s that Teviotdale was transferred to a Scottish ruler from Anglo-Norman control.[94] *De Obsessione Dunelmi* is only one of several Norman-era sources that claim to explain why the Scottish kings controlled 'Lothian'. According to one twelfth-century tradition, the grant of Lothian had actually taken place under King Edgar.[95] According to another, Lothian remained detached from Scotland until the time of Máel Coluim III, when the latter received the land from Edward the Confessor (d. 1066)

Saxon over the Celt' preserved Carham's legacy, a legacy that was in the early 1400s, apparently, under threat.

[91] For ethnicity and Scottish historiography, see M. H. Hammond, 'Ethnicity and the Writing of Medieval Scottish History', *SHR* 85 (2006), 1–27; for the general struggle between Anglo-British 'Teutonic' identity and the Celtic 'other' among Scottish and Irish intellectuals of the modern era, see also M. Pittock, *Celtic Identity and the British Image* (Manchester, 1999).

[92] See contribution in this volume for further discussion, Broun, 'Southern Scotland', 33–49.

[93] See the wording in *ESC*, nos 12 and 18 (=*North Durham*, Appendix, nos 1 and 8).

[94] See *English Episcopal Acta V: York, 1070–1154*, ed. J. E. Burton (Oxford, 1998), no. 6; E. Craster, 'A Contemporary Record of the Pontificate of Ranulf Flambard', *Arch. Ael.* 4th Ser. 7 (1930), 33–56, no. 6. For discussion of this and other sources that make such a chronology likely, see N. McGuigan, 'Neither Scotland nor England: Middle Britain, c.850–1150', PhD thesis (University of St Andrews, 2015), 128–31, 198–200.

[95] *DPSA*, 382–83; *Chron. Wallingford*, 54; *RW*, s.a. 975, ed. Coxe, i, 416.

in exchange for marrying Margaret.[96] All three of these explanations are probably just speculative attempts to account for an arrangement that, in the twelfth century, was seen as anomalous in cultural, linguistic and legal terms.[97]

This is not to say that the significance of the battle can be dismissed. No historian is in a position to rule out territorial gains resulting from Carham. During the era of Carham the evidence does suggest that the ecclesiastical structures of the area governed by Bamburgh were reorganised, with power and relics being concentrated further south on the Wear – clear evidence of some sort of crisis in the Tweed basin and heartlands of the Bamburgh realm.[98] The battle would also, most likely, have ended any Eadwulfing hopes of reacquiring the territories south of the Tyne or Tees, governed briefly by Uhtred, probably the last chance of reuniting Northumbria under Northumbrian leadership. The Bamburgh polity appears to have retained its ability to devastate the Cumbrians in the 1030s, but otherwise never again appears as a power of great significance in the north.[99] It is not unreasonable, then, to link Carham to a 'process' of changing power relations where the Scots expanded in power at the expense of the Northern English. That process was central to the emergence of the familiar, later medieval Anglo-Scottish border.

---

96 Orderic Vitalis, *Historia Ecclesiastica*, ed. and trans. M. Chibnall, 6 vols (Oxford, 1969–80), iv, 268–71.
97 McGuigan, 'Neither Scotland nor England', 141–55, 263–8. A fully published version of this work is intended for the near future.
98 Woolf, *From Pictland to Alba*, 235–6; N. McGuigan, 'Cuthbert's Relics and the Origins of the Diocese of Durham', forthcoming (but see also McGuigan, 'Neither Scotland nor England', chs 3 and 6).
99 *HR*, s.a. 1072, ed. Arnold, ii, 198; *RHC*, s.a. 952, ed. Stubbs, i, 58.

CHAPTER TWO

Southern Scotland as Part of the Scottish Kingdom: The Evidence of the Earliest Charters

DAUVIT BROUN

In the twentieth century the Battle of Carham was typically accorded a special place in Scottish history as the moment when the kingdom assumed much of its modern territorial shape. A classic statement is by W. Croft Dickinson in his *Scotland from Earliest Times to 1603*, published in 1961. He described how the battle 'confirmed the Scottish hold on the land between the Forth and the Tweed', and how, 'About the same time ... Malcolm II was able to place his grandson on the throne of Strathclyde'; as a result, 'when Duncan succeeded Malcolm II in 1034, and reigned as Duncan I, his kingdom included ... roughly the land of modern Scotland ...'[1] For Archie Duncan, similarly, 'Early in the eleventh century the kingdom of Scotland attained its "historical" frontiers: that is frontiers beyond which the kings were unable to make further conquests ...'[2] For Geoffrey Barrow, 'By winning the battle of Carham on Tweed in 1018 Malcolm II made sure of permanent Scottish possession of Lothian and brought strong pressure to bear on Cumbria ... When the native Cumbrian dynasty became extinct, Malcolm II set up as ruler of this region his grandson Duncan II ...'[3]

Implicit in these accounts is a sense that the Scottish kingdom – if not Scotland itself – was essentially the territory ruled by the king of Scots. On the face of it this seems perfectly natural and unobjectionable. At the same time, there has for a long time been some awareness that the situation was more complicated (albeit that this was obviated by retaining the Latin term *Scotia* for contemporary conceptions of 'Scotland).[4]

---

1 W. Croft Dickinson, *Scotland from Earliest Times to 1603* (Edinburgh, 1961), 39.
2 A. A. M. Duncan, *The Nation of the Scots and the Declaration of Arbroath*, Historical Association pamphlet (London, 1970), 6.
3 G. W. S. Barrow, *Kingship and Unity: Scotland 1000–1306* (London, 1981), 25.
4 W. F. Skene described the fact that 'Scotia ... was limited to the districts between the Forth, the Spey and Drumalban' as one of three propositions that 'lie at the very

Some have chosen to place these much less tidy aspects nearer the foreground. For example, Bruce Webster observed that 'The history of Scottish kingship from the eleventh century to the thirteenth is a mixture of consolidation and internal challenges. The client states of Strathclyde and Lothian were to remain subject to the kings of *Scotia*, 'Scotland'... though the term *Scotia*, like Alba, did not yet cover the areas to the south of the Forth and Clyde isthmus.'[5] For Webster, the Battle of Carham was only notable as apparently the last time we hear of a king of Strathclyde.

Once this untidiness is placed centre stage, it becomes apparent that the coincidence between people, country and kingdom (or state) which would in modern times be regarded as natural did not become the norm in the case of the Scottish kingdom until the late thirteenth century. This was not unusual: France and Poland spring to mind as comparable examples.[6] I have laboured repeatedly to trace in more detail how the kingdom came to be seen by its own inhabitants as a single country, 'Scotland', and a single people, the 'Scots'. I have also sought to emphasise how the kingdom up to the early thirteenth century was regarded as, in effect, a realm comprising of a number of 'countries' of which 'Scotland' itself was only one, typically identified as the region in the east between the Rivers Forth and Spey.[7] If we wish to understand this fully, however, we need to examine not only contemporary notions of

---

threshold of Scottish history': William F. Skene, *Celtic Scotland: A History of Ancient Alban* (Edinburgh, 1876), i, 3.

5 Bruce Webster, *Medieval Scotland: The Making of an Identity* (Basingstoke, 1997), 22–3.

6 See Dauvit Broun, 'Rethinking Scottish Origins', in Steve Boardman and Susan Foran (eds), *Barbour's* Bruce *and its Cultural Contexts* (Cambridge, 2015), 163–90, at 175–6 and literature cited there for the comparison with France. For Poland, see e.g., Aleksander Gieysztor, 'Medieval Poland', in Stefan Kieniewicz (ed.), *History of Poland*, 2nd edn (Warsaw, 1979), 23–137, at 64, referring to how the name of the 'core small state of the Polanes (Polanie)' was applied by foreigners to the whole kingdom (and subsequently adopted within the kingdom itself). It goes without saying that this process was different in each case. For example, although it would appear on the surface that 'Scotland proper' was the 'historic core', this was more likely to have been the region referred to until the early tenth century as Fortriu: see Dauvit Broun, 'The Origins of the *Mormaer*' (forthcoming).

7 See most recently Broun, 'Rethinking', and Dauvit Broun, 'Kingdom and Identity: A Scottish Perspective', in Keith J. Stringer and Angus J. L. Winchester (eds), *Northern England and Southern Scotland in the Central Middle Ages* (Woodbridge, 2017), 31–85.

country and people – of 'Scotland' and 'Scots' – but in particular their idea of the *kingdom*.[8] This, indeed, holds the key. From a modern perspective Lothian, and later Strathclyde/Cumbria, became part of the Scottish kingdom by virtue of falling under the authority of the king of Scots. In this chapter I want to focus on the fact that for a long time after the Battle of Carham the areas ruled by the king of Scots south of the Forth were not regarded intuitively or naturally as integral parts of the Scottish kingdom. I have explored elsewhere how this changed by the end of the twelfth century, particularly in the minds of the scribes of charters.[9] In this chapter I will consider how the areas south of the Forth were imagined in relation to the Scottish kingdom before the kingdom proper came to be regarded as a single entity stretching south to the Tweed and Solway. Rather than regarding it as normal, or even inevitable, that the realm of the king of Scots came to be seen as one country and (eventually) a single people, I will argue that it was at least possible – and might even have been easier and more likely – that the king of Scots would have come to be seen, and regard himself, as ruling a composite entity, with Lothian, and maybe also Strathclyde (or 'Cumbria'), viewed as distinct from the kingdom itself.

I will argue that an important reason why this did *not* occur becomes apparent by considering the earliest extant charters of Edgar and David I as king. Although these are royal, they can be taken as representing the perspective of major lords whose interests were focused in what is now southern Scotland, rather than north of the Forth. There are specific reasons why these charters can be seen in this light. As a general point, though, it is useful to remember that virtually all the documents we have from the twelfth and thirteenth centuries are those that were kept and cherished by their beneficiaries, and that they were largely produced at their behest. They are best seen as much as a record of what royal authority could do for those exercising lordship than as an index of royal policy and direction.

Why might it seem odd for southern Scotland to be regarded as part of the kingdom itself? The answer lies in how the topography of the kingdom was imagined. Matthew Paris, in his map of Britain, portrays the landmass north of the Forth as an island linked to the rest of Britain

---

8   See Broun, 'Kingdom and Identity', 32–5.
9   *Ibid.*, 43–65.

by Stirling Bridge alone.[10] The same idea is found regularly in other maps.[11] It also appears, most strikingly of all, in the *Scotichronicon* of Walter Bower, who as abbot of Inchcolm actually lived in the Firth of Forth itself. Writing in the 1440s, he explained that someone at Glastonbury Abbey had described the Battle of Bannockburn taking place 'beside the royal burgh of Stirling in Scotland, lying on the boundary of Britain'.[12] Bower added that 'it is said that the bridge over the Forth at Stirling lies between Britain and Scotland, forming the border of both'.[13] Although this seems bizarre to us now, it can readily be understood as reflecting the experience of crossing this area before modern times. By land there were only a couple of established routes across the boggy terrain immediately north of the River Forth.[14] The easiest passage was by boat across the Firth: for those without boats of their own there was both the Queensferry and Earlsferry.[15] For anyone with a boat the only obstacles were occasional skerries – nothing to compare with the treacherous sandbanks of the Firth of Tay. It was, presumably, through these sea-crossings that the idea of the landmass north of the Forth as an island became established so firmly in the minds of those both near and far. Another reflection of this was that the Firth of Forth itself was generally referred to in the Middle Ages as the 'Scottish Sea'.

10   P. D. A. Harvey, 'Matthew Paris's Maps of Britain', in P. R. Coss and S. D. Lloyd. (eds), *Thirteenth Century England IV* (Woodbridge, 1992), 109–21, at 114–16.
11   G. R. Crone, *Early Maps of the British Isles AD 1000–AD 1579* (London, 1961), plates 2–8.
12   Norman H. Shead, Wendy B. Stevenson and D. E. R. Watt (eds), *Scotichronicon by Walter Bower in Latin and English*, vol. vi (Aberdeen, 1991), 356: *qui locus est juxta burgum regium de Strivelyne in Scocia ad fines Britannie constitutus*.
13   *Ibid.*, vi, 356: *Dicitur enim quod pons Striveline de Forth situatur inter Britanniam et Sciciam utriusque marginem apprehendens*. It is striking that, in William the Lion's assize relating to the calling of guarantors to vouch for disputed goods, no-one was expected to cross the Forth: cases involving people south of the Forth were meant to be resolved in meetings at Stirling Bridge (Broun, 'Rethinking', 172; for the assize see Alice Taylor, '*Leges Scocie* and the Lawcodes of David I, William the Lion and Alexander II', *SHR* 88 (2009) 207–88, at 218–19, 223–6, 234–5; 251–5 (§1) and 274 (§16) (text), 280–1 and 285 (translation)).
14   The causeway and Drip Ford near Stirling, and the Fords of Frew: see Dauvit Broun, *Scottish Independence and the Idea of Britain from the Picts to Alexander III* (Edinburgh, 2007), 54.
15   Free passage for pilgrims was established by Queen Margaret (d. 1093) and Earl Donnchad I of Fife (d. 1154). These routes are likely to be much older, however. For Earlsferry, see Simon Taylor with Gilbert Márkus, *The Place-Names of Fife*, vol. 3, *St Andrews and the East Neuk* (Donington, 2009), 272.

The significance of this for our purposes is that ultimate secular authority was imagined as islands, long before there was any idea of kingdoms as we might intuitively think of them today – namely, as independent jurisdictions defined by their borders with neighbouring jurisdictions. The idea of a pre-eminent king of Ireland can be traced throughout the early Middle Ages. By the eleventh century there was a clear sense that it had been a kingdom since prehistoric times.[16] Æthelstan (d. 939), regarded today as the first king of England, was in his own charters proclaimed as 'raised by the favour of the All-Accomplishing One on the throne of the whole kingdom of Britain'.[17] As far as *Alba* as 'Pictland' is concerned, in the 860s or 870s it is possible to imagine that the landmass north of the Forth was an ancient kingdom with a succession of over a hundred kings.[18] The core kingdom was not envisaged as 'Scotland' – the country between the Rivers Forth and Spey. It was the entire 'island' north of the Forth. This was less clearly imagined in the west, but it was maybe because of this sense of the kingdom as an island landmass that it was possible to think of Iona as a Pictish island and Loch Lomond as in the Pictish realm (*in regione Pictorum*).[19]

There were, of course, many regional kings in Britain and Ireland before the thirteenth century. Only those who claimed in some sense to be rulers of a major island, however, were considered to be pre-eminent: the king of England as ruler of Britain, rulers of Wales as rightful king of Britain, kings of Irish provinces as high-king of Ireland, and kings of Scots as ruler of the landmass north of the Forth. So profound was this idea that it was possible to understand the Welsh word for island, *ynys*, as referring to a kingdom – as in the phrase *tair ynys Prydain*, 'the three realms of Britain'. Geoffrey of Monmouth (writing in the mid-1130s) evidently took this to mean England, Wales and Scotland.[20] It is also

---

16   Broun, *Scottish Independence*, 44–5. For the kingship of Tara as a kingship of Ireland, see now T. M. Charles-Edwards, *Early Christian Ireland* (Oxford, 2000), 481–521.
17   *per omnipatrantis dexteram totius Britannię regni solio sublimatus*: the phrase is found in originals that have been identified as the work of the scribe 'Æthelstan A', a member of Æthelstan's household: see Simon Keynes (ed.), *Facsimiles of Anglo-Saxon Charters* (Oxford, 1991), 9, for comment on this scribe. On kings of England as rulers of Britain, see George Molyneaux, 'Why were some Tenth-Century English Kings Presented as Rulers of Britain?', *TRHS* 21 (2011) 59–91.
18   Broun, *Scottish Independence*, 75–9.
19   Thomas Owen Clancy, 'Iona in the Kingdom of the Picts: A Note', *IR* 55 (2004) 73–6.
20   Broun, *Scottish Independence*, 52–3.

striking that in the Hereford *Mappa Mundi*, made *c.* 1300, even though the kingdom of Scotland is recognised as extending to the Tweed and Solway, it is still portrayed (rather bizarrely) as an island.[21]

Seen in this light, it should not be surprising that Lothian and Strathclyde (or 'Cumbria') should have been seen as separate from the Scottish kingdom. This is maybe easier to appreciate in the case of Strathclyde/'Cumbria', whose memory as a distinct kingdom was cherished by bishops of Glasgow. In the *Life of Kentigern* commissioned by Bishop Jocelin from his namesake, Jocelin of Furness, soon after his consecration as bishop of Glasgow in 1175, the bishop of Glasgow was himself represented as invested with the authority of the kings of the old kingdom.[22] This was not meant for a moment to deny the bishop's allegiance to his patron, the king of Scots. It was, rather, an attempt to forestall the possibility that the bishop of St Andrews might become archbishop of a province that embraced the entire realm, including Glasgow.[23] If the bishop of St Andrews was to be archbishop, it was hoped (from Glasgow's point of view) that this would be of the kingdom proper, north of the Forth. For Lothian, by contrast, there was barely any sense that it had ever been a kingdom (except in the eyes of Glaswegian tradition).[24] At best it was regarded as an earldom.[25] It could also – apparently quite naturally – be seen as part of England.[26] This could still have political force as late as 1195. In that year, William the Lion came within a whisker of ratifying an agreement with Richard I that would have seen Richard acquire the castles of Lothian until his nephew, Otto of Brunswick, married William's elder daughter, Margaret.

---

21 Broun, 'Rethinking', 187.
22 Broun, *Scottish Independence*, 125; *Lives of Ninian and Kentigern*, 55, 182–3.
23 *Ibid.*, 135–44.
24 In the Life of Kentigern written for Bishop Herbert (d. 1164) Kentigern's maternal grandfather is said to have been King 'Leudonus' from whom a region in northern Britain was named (i.e., Lothian): *Lives of Ninian and Kentigern*, 125, 245.
25 The earls of Dunbar were sometimes referred to as earls of Lothian, although the evidence that they did so themselves is less clear; by the late twelfth century they clearly preferred 'earl of Dunbar': see Elsa Hamilton, *Mighty Subjects. The Dunbar Earls in Scotland, c.1072–1289* (Edinburgh, 2010), 34–5, esp. 35 n. 12.
26 Note also the much-quoted statement (*c.* 1180) by its prior that Dryburgh was 'in the land of the English and in the kingdom of the Scots' (*in terra Anglorum, et in regno Scotorum*): Adam of Dryburgh, *De tripartito tabernaculo*, in J.-P. Migne (ed.), *Patrologiæ cursus completes . . . series Latina*, 217 vols (Paris, 1844–57), cxcviii. cols 609–792, at col. 723.

The hoped-for outcome was that Otto would succeed William the Lion as king and be invested in Northumberland and Cumberland, thereby making good William's claim to the earldom of Northumberland which he had been deprived of in 1157.[27] Archie Duncan described this as 'the final occurrence of Lothian as an annexe to the kingdom of Scotland'.[28] It seems likely, moreover, that Lothian, as well as Northumberland and Cumberland, would have been formally acknowledged not only as part of England, but within the realm of the king of England. This, at least, would be consistent with allowing Richard to hold the castles of Lothian while William held the castles of Northumberland and Cumberland until the marriage was solemnised; if William held castles in connection with his right to these counties as earl, then Lothian's castles could have signalled a tacit recognition of the English king's overlordship over the region. That aspect of the agreement was, indeed, dangerously reminiscent of the humiliating terms of the Treaty of Falaise, when castles south of the Forth were offered, and some surrendered, to Henry II's keeping as a guarantee that William would abide strictly to the terms of his subjection.[29] It might therefore have harboured a more perilous ambiguity about the extent of the king of England's authority, which from the king of England's point of view would not unnaturally have held echoes of the idea of being king of Britain. In the Treaty of Falaise itself, of course, the entire Scottish realm north and south of the Forth was acknowledged as under Henry II's overlordship.[30]

This way of thinking about Lothian as separate from the kingdom proper, but within the realm of the king of England, is found exactly a century earlier, in the earliest of King Edgar's charters, dated 29 August 1095. A distinction between Lothian and the Scottish kingdom can also be detected in the sole charter of Edgar's half-brother, Donnchad II, in

---

27 See Broun, 'Kingdom and Identity', 36–7, for more detail and references.
28 A. A. M. Duncan, *The Kingship of the Scots 842–1292: Succession and Independence* (Edinburgh, 2002), 108.
29 E. L. G. Stones (ed.), *Anglo-Scottish Relations 1174–1328: Some Selected Documents* (Oxford, 1970), no. 1 (at pp. 6–7).
30 A distinction between Scotland proper, north of the Forth, and the rest of the king's territories south of the Forth is, nevertheless, apparent in the text: see Duncan, *The Kingship of the Scots*, 100–1, who discusses how *Scotia* and the king's 'other lands' relates to the distinction between 'Scotland' north of the Forth and the king's territories south of the Forth, and how the Scottish realm is referred to throughout as the 'land (*terra*) of the king of Scots'.

1094 (which I will return to).[31] In both cases the beneficiary – Durham Cathedral Priory – not only instigated the charters, but produced them, too.[32] As Geoffrey Barrow has observed, there is no indication that any predecessors of Donnchad II authorised the production of formal documents in their name.[33] Although Durham scribes cannot definitely be identified as responsible for all Edgar's surviving original charters, it is probable that they were.[34] It is likely, therefore, that it is not just an accident of survival that all Edgar's charters, as well as Donnchad's sole example, are for Durham. At that time Durham was alone in wanting formal documents from either of them.

Unfortunately Edgar's earliest charter only survives in fifteenth-century copies.[35] Its original existence is not, however, in dispute, nor is its date (29 August 1095), nor the terms of the transaction: all this is established beyond reasonable doubt by the grant of Edgar's gift by William II (Rufus), king of England, in a charter which survives as two almost identical originals. (One is in a Durham hand, the other by a royal scribe, datable on internal evidence to between 1094 and 2 January 1096.)[36] These were presumably produced when William was

---

31 See below, 41–2. These charters are discussed in detail in A. A. M. Duncan, 'Yes, the Earliest Scottish Charters', *SHR* 78 (1999) 1–38, at 8 (responding to J. Donnelly, 'The Earliest Scottish Charters?', *SHR* 68 (1989) 1–22); and see most recently Duncan, *The Kingship of the Scots*, 55–7. The gifts in Donnchad's and Edgar's charters were ineffective.

32 As far as Donnchad's only charter is concerned, Barrow has observed that 'it is Durham that is declaring the new king's legitimacy, Durham providing the trusted scribe, Durham doubtless fashioning the king's equestrian seal, and Durham making sure that it will receive a sizeable slice of Scottish territory': G. W. S. Barrow, 'The Kings of Scots and Durham', in David Rollason *et al.* (eds), *Anglo-Norman Durham, 1093–1193* (Woodbridge, 1994), 311–24, at 314.

33 G. W. S. Barrow, 'The *Capella Regis* of the Kings of Scotland, 1107–1222', in H. L. MacQueen (ed.), *The Stair Society Miscellany V* (Edinburgh, 2006), 1.

34 The earliest extant sealed document produced in Scotland is likely to be a brieve of Alexander I (1107–1124): Durham Cathedral Muniments, housed in Durham University Library, Archives and Special Collections [hereafter DCM], Miscellaneous Charter 563. Its final sentence reads as if it was dictated by the king himself. For text and translation, see now John Reuben Davies, 'The Standardisation of Diplomatic in Scottish Royal Acts down to 1249. Part 1: Brieves', Feature of the Month, December 2015, *Models of Authority* website: <http://www.modelsofauthority.ac.uk/blog/standardisation-brieves/>.

35 Edgar's charter, of which a copy is DCM, Miscellaneous Charter 559, is published in *ESC*, no. 15, and Duncan, 'Yes, the Earliest Scottish Charters', 16 and 22–3.

36 DCM, Miscellaneous Charters 558*, 973: see *RRAN*, i, no. 365; T. A. M. Bishop and Pierre Chaplais (eds), *Facsimiles of English Royal Writs* (Oxford, 1957), 9–10.

at Newcastle in July–August 1095. There can be no doubt, therefore, that Edgar's charter was created more than two years before he ousted his uncle Domnall Bán from the kingship. It is far from certain, by this stage, that Edgar controlled the region immediately north of the Tweed where the settlements given to Durham in the charter were located; the charter's place-date – Norham – makes it possible that it was produced when Edgar, travelling from Newcastle, arrived at the Tweed before entering the Merse. There is every reason to regard this charter as Edgar's first demonstration of his kingship on parchment – a demonstration made at Durham's prompting and dependent on Durham's experience in producing charters. It is a safe guess that Edgar's seal-matrix was also created by Durham; its most remarkable feature is that Edgar is represented with a crown, something that was not repeated in subsequent royal seal-matrices until the minority of Alexander III.[37]

It is striking that Edgar's kingship as stated in the charter's address is defined in a way that distinguishes Lothian – the region where Durham hoped to exercise lordship – from the 'kingdom of Scotland'. Edgar is described as 'possessing the entire land of Lothian and the kingdom of Scotland by the gift of my lord William, king of the English, and by paternal inheritance' (*totam terram de Lodeneio et regnum Scotie dono domini mei Willelmi Anglorum regis et paterna hereditate possidens*). Archie Duncan has argued that William's gift was Lothian and that the Scottish kingship was by paternal inheritance.[38] This is consistent with identifying the landmass north of the Forth as the kingdom proper. It is also possible that Durham sought to emphasise that the king of England was the ultimate authority that would guarantee their lordship. It will be recalled that they obtained a confirmation charter from William II. In Donnchad's charter no such distinction between Lothian and the kingdom proper is immediately apparent. Instead he was proclaimed as *constans heriditarie rex Scotie*, 'king of Scotland, established by heredity' as he made gifts to Durham in the eastern Borders.[39] In the light of

---

37   Broun, *Scottish Independence*, 208 (n. 37); Duncan, *The Kingship of the Scots*, 146.
38   Duncan, 'Yes, the Earliest Scottish Charters', 30; Broun, *Scottish Independence*, 104.
39   Donnchad's charter is DCM, Miscellaneous Charter 554, edited (for example) in *ESC*, no. 12, and A. A. M. Duncan, 'The Earliest Scottish Charters', *SHR* 37 (1958) 103–35, at 119. A photographic reproduction is in Duncan, 'Yes, the Earliest Scottish Charters', 8 (fig. 2).

regnum Scotie in Edgar's charter, it is likely that *Scotia* in Donnchad's charter also referred to the landmass north of the Forth. The ancestral kingdom was located north of the Forth, but (as far as Durham was concerned) it was as king of Scots and not earl of Lothian or some other title that authority was wielded by Edgar and Donnchad over the region between the Forth and the Tweed (although only in Edgar's case was this explicitly by gift of the king of England).

A different perspective is offered by the other famous charter I wish to discuss – David I's charter for Robert Bruce giving him Annandale. The succession of David I, 'ruler of the Cumbrian realm', brought to an end a period when a large part of what became southern Scotland lay outside the direct rule of the king of Scots (Alexander I).[40] From the outset of David's reign, however, David ruled the 'Cumbrian realm' as king of Scots, just as his father Máel Coluim III appears to have done.[41] His charter giving Robert Bruce Annandale is typically regarded as David's first extant charter as king.[42] Although this cannot be established with certainty, it is dated at Scone, where David was inaugurated in May 1124. The charter, with its Norman beneficiary and almost wholly Anglo-Norman cast of witnesses, has been taken as evidence of David I's identification with foreign personnel and customs, and his lack of a meaningful relationship with magnates north of the Forth.[43] Its real significance, however, is revealed by the strong likelihood that Bruce had already been lord of Annandale for a number of years.[44] The charter was

---

40 The title *Cumbrensis regionis princeps* is given to David in the inquest into the lands and churches of the bishop of Glasgow conducted before David became king of Scots: *David I Chrs*, no. 15.

41 For Máel Coluim's conquest as far south as Cumberland, see Dauvit Broun, 'The Welsh Identity of the Kingdom of Strathclyde, *c*.900–*c*.1200', *IR* 55 (2004) 111–80, at 138–40. The fact that David was already close to Henry I was presumably crucial in ensuring the English king's acceptance of the major change in the balance of power in northern Britain: see especially Judith A. Green, 'Henry I and David I', *SHR* 75 (1996) 1–19.

42 *David I Chrs*, no. 16.

43 Richard D. Oram, *Domination and Lordship: Scotland, 1070–1230* (Edinburgh, 2011), 65–6: 'Quite simply, the structure of the document reflects very strongly David's personal preferences, cultural inclinations and experience.' He goes on to say that 'Gaelic Scotland was alien to him', and that, based on the little that is known of David's itinerary, 'it is perhaps significant that there is little sign that he came north of Fife after 1124 until *c*.1139–40'. David I's itinerary in Scotland is based on his charters, and therefore is a direct reflection of the lack of extant charters for beneficiaries north of Fife before 1140.

44 R. M. Blakely, *The Brus Family in England and Scotland, 1100–1295* (Woodbridge,

intended to show that, now that David was king, Annandale was part of the realm of the king of Scots.

It is tempting to regard this charter as David I's initiative, particularly if it was, indeed, created immediately after his inauguration when he might have been keen to assert his new authority. Royal charters to laymen, however, were a rarity at this time: Matthew Hammond has argued that they only became a regular feature from the 1160s.[45] In general terms, therefore, it might seem more likely that they were prompted by the beneficiaries rather than produced at the king's behest, regardless of whether they were written by a royal scribe or not. Are there any clues in the charter itself that could indicate whether it was driven primarily by Bruce's or David's needs? It has frequently been observed that David I's charter is notably less detailed than William the Lion's charter 'restoring' Annandale to Bruce's son:[46] it merely refers to Bruce's existing (very extensive) powers as lord of Annandale, and makes no mention of what is due to David himself. In William's charter not only is the knight service specified, but the administration of crown pleas is carefully delineated. This difference between David's charter and William's has been cited as an example of how the drafting of documents became more specific with practice.[47] Alice Taylor, however, has highlighted how the two charters, when taken together, 'show a clear development in formal juridical language'.[48] She argued that this reflects actual differences in how the lordship of Annandale was conceived in both theory and practice, and that the later charter is not therefore merely a more detailed exposition of arrangements that had pertained in 1124. The use in King William's charter of the dispositive verb *reddere*, 'give back', reinforces this sense that it represented a fresh start.

2005), 20, 23–4; W. E. Kapelle, *The Norman Conquest of the North: The Region and its Transformation, 1000–1135* (London, 1979), 207.

45   Matthew H. Hammond, 'The Adoption and Routinization of Scottish Royal Charter Production for Lay Beneficiaries, 1124–1195', in David Bates (ed.), *Anglo-Norman Studies XXXVI* (Woodbridge, 2014), 91–115.

46   *RRS*, ii, no. 80. The primary dispositive verb is *reddere*, 'to restore / give back'.

47   Dauvit Broun, *The Charters of Gaelic Scotland and Ireland in the Early and Central Middle Ages* (Cambridge, 1995), 15–16; Dauvit Broun, 'The Writing of Charters in Scotland and Ireland in the Twelfth Century', in Karl Heidecker (ed.), *Charters and the Use of the Written Word in Medieval Society* (Turnout, 2000), 113–31, at 122.

48   Alice Taylor, *The Shape of the State in Medieval Scotland, 1124–1290* (Oxford, 2016), 51.

The likelihood that David I's charter was produced at Bruce's instigation would explain not only the charter's exclusive emphasis on the benefits to Bruce, but the way his rights in Annandale are viewed in the charter from Bruce's perspective.[49] His authority is defined by referring to a neighbour rather than in relation to the king of Scots (as in William's charter).[50] We are told that Bruce held Annandale 'with all those customary rights (*consuetudinibus*) which Ranulf Meschin ever had in Carlisle and in his land of Cumberland on that day in which he ever had them best and most freely'. Henry I had removed Ranulf Meschin from his Cumbrian powerbase sometime in 1121 or 1122.[51] Ruth Blakely has argued convincingly that Ranulf had been established there as part of the same policy for controlling the inner Solway, masterminded by Henry I, that had seen Bruce take Annandale.[52] There may therefore have been some ambiguity about Bruce's position in relation to Henry I. By defining Annandale on parchment as the *gift* of David I, Bruce not only legitimised his quasi-regal powers as derived from royal authority, but also put in writing an expectation that David I would maintain him in Annandale against any attempt to remove him – perhaps with Henry I particularly in mind.[53] Seen in this light, the selection of witnesses reflected the broader Anglo-Norman context of Bruce's lordship:[54] they, not the magnates of Scotland north of the Forth, were

---

49 I am very grateful to Joanna Tucker for this insight.
50 Blakely, *Brus Family*, 23–4, where the possibility is raised that there was an earlier charter, but without pushing this too far.
51 Richard Sharpe, *Norman Rule in Cumbria, 1092–1136*, TCWAAS, Tract Series (Kendal, 2006), 51–2.
52 Blakely, *Brus Family*, 19–20.
53 On the significance of *dare* as the dispositive word in a charter, guaranteeing that an equivalent replacement for the donation be provided to the beneficiary if the gift was successfully challenged, see John Reuben Davies, 'The Donor and the Duty of Warrandice: Giving and Granting in Scottish Charters', in Dauvit Broun (ed.), *The Reality behind Charter Diplomatic in Anglo-Norman Britain* (Glasgow, 2011), 120–65. It has been noted that 'the political temperature rose' in 1121–2 (Green, 'David I and Henry I', 9–10 [quotation at 9]), and suggested that both Bruce and David I had then fallen under Henry's suspicion: Blakely, *Brus Family*, 25–6.
54 The nature of Anglo-Norman networks is brought out vividly in David Bates, *The Normans and Empire* (Oxford, 2013), 130–41, taking a charter of 1144 by Adam I de Brix (a member of the Bruce family) for the abbey of Saint-Sauveur-le-Vicomte (in the Cotentin in Normandy) as a starting-point. For the late twelfth century, see especially Matthew H. Hammond, 'A Prosopographical Analysis of Society in East Central Scotland, circa 1100 to 1260, with Special Reference to Ethnicity', PhD thesis (Glasgow University, 2005); available at <http://theses.gla.ac.uk/1076>, 137–8.

the people that Bruce as well as David I would have looked to defend the charter's terms, particularly should Henry I intervene again in the region.[55]

There is one aspect of the charter, however, that was unchanging from one document to the next, and must reveal David's perspective: his seal. Unfortunately no good examples survive.[56] It is, like the English royal seal, double-sided, with an enthroned king on one side and the king on horseback on the other. There are key differences with seals of kings of England in this period, however. David was not apparently crowned, and the same legend appears on both sides: 'David by God the ruler king of Scots' (*Deo rectore rex Scottorum*). This is what is found on the seals of William II and the first two seal-matrices of Henry I (with a different legend: 'By God's grace king of the English', *Dei gratia rex Anglorum*). William the Conqueror, however, had used the opportunity afforded by the double-sided seal to identify himself on one side as king of the English and on the other as duke of the Normans. Henry I eventually followed suit, as did Stephen.[57] Now that David was king, there might, hypothetically, have been an opportunity for him to be 'king of Scots' on one side and 'ruler of the Cumbrians' on the other (albeit that he had not used the title on his seal before 1124).[58] In fact, he identified himself so closely with his predecessor's kingship that David's seal-matrix as king is simply a slightly adapted re-use of Alexander's. It has been pointed out, for example, that in both cases the final 'm' in *Scottorum* is missing from the obverse.[59] Perhaps there was no time to get a fresh

---

55   See D. Broun, 'The Presence of Witnesses and the Writing of Charters', in Broun (ed.), *Reality behind Charter Diplomatic*, 235–90, for witnessing charters, and especially 273, for the obligation undertaken by being a witness. See also more generally D. Postles, 'Choosing Witnesses in Twelfth Century England', *Irish Jurist*, new ser., 23 (1988) 330–46.

56   http://db.poms.ac.uk/record/matrix/6555/ (accessed 17 January 2018), including information taken from J. H. Stevenson and Marguerite Wood, *Scottish Heraldic Seals*, 3 vols (Glasgow, 1940), i, 2–3 (nos 6 and 7).

57   Pierre Chaplais, *English Royal Documents, King John–Henry VI, 1199–1461* (Oxford, 1971), 2–3.

58   On his seal before becoming king of Scots David identified himself as brother of Queen Matilda: http://db.poms.ac.uk/record/matrix/6178/ (accessed 17 January 2018), including information taken from Stevenson and Wood, *Scottish Heraldic Seals*, i, 40.

59   http://db.poms.ac.uk/record/matrix/6171/ (accessed 17 January 2018), including information taken from Stevenson and Wood, *Scottish Heraldic Seals*, i, 2 (nos 4 and 5).

matrix cut. It is difficult, though, to accept that such a fundamental symbol of the king's authority would have been rushed like this to the extent of repeating a flaw. The alternative would be to see it as a deliberate choice because it was assumed that he was continuing Alexander I's kingship without any modification.

In territorial terms, of course, David I's realm was strikingly different from Alexander I's. Alexander ruled Lothian north of the Lammermuirs directly, and had only limited authority further south.[60] The extension of the realm as far south as Annandale meant that David now ruled over regions that were distant from the kingdom proper north of the Forth and interacted with different networks. Now that David was king, the balance between the kingdom proper and the rest of his domain altered dramatically – all the more so from 1141 when David's realm reached as far south as the Ribble in the west and the Tyne or Tees in the east.[61] Presumably this would have heightened the perception that the king of Scots ruled a complex polity united only by the king himself.[62] The

---

60 *RRS*, i, no. 37. An example of Alexander's authority in relation to David's Cumbrian principality is that he saw it as his business to intervene with the Pope on behalf of Bishop John of Glasgow when John was under pressure to profess obedience to the archbishop of York: *Scotia Pontificia*, no. 10. For indications that the region north of the Lammermuirs continued in David's reign to form a unit along with the kingdom north of the Forth, see Kenji Nishioka, 'Scots and Galwegians in the "Peoples Address" of Scottish Royal Charters', *SHR* 87 (2008) 206–32, at 221–2.

61 See especially Keith J. Stringer, 'State-Building in Twelfth-Century Britain: David I, King of Scots, and Northern England', in J. C. Appleby and P. Dalton (eds), *Government, Religion and Society in Northern England, 1000–1700* (Stroud, 1997), 40–62, for the extent to which northern England was integrated into David's kingdom. There is nothing to suggest, however, that the realm was regarded as the 'kingdom of Scotland/the Scots' (and, as a result, I would resist the convenience of 'Scots' and 'Scottish' in this context, for example, 'Scottish rule' in the north of England, or 'Scots' tightening their grip: Stringer, *State-Building*, 48). Stringer's preferred term for David's realm is a 'Scoto-Northumbrian kingdom' (coined, as he notes, in G. W. S. Barrow, *David I of Scotland (1124–1153): The Balance of Old and New* (Reading, 1985), 18). Oram, *Domination and Lordship*, c.3, places David's southward expansion alongside the extension of his power in the north and west, which he refers to as 'imperialistic' (at 75).

62 From a contemporary Irish perspective, David died in 1153 as *rí Alban & Saxan* ('king of Scotland and the English'): *AT* 1153.4 (<http://www.ucc.ie/celt/published/G100002/>). For further references and discussion, see Broun, *Scottish Independence*, 13–14, 30, n. 71. Royal charters with address clauses listing peoples presumably reflected a royal viewpoint of the realm's diversity. This is particularly marked in the 1160s and 1170s when, as Kenji Nishioka has shown, 'French, English, Scots and Galwegians' became a regular form without regard for the location of the

claim to be not just a king, but the focus of ultimate secular authority, however, rested on the idea of the landmass north of the Forth as a kingdom-island.

The Battle of Carham may have played a part in consolidating the rule of the king of Scots as far as the Tweed, and ultimately to the Solway (and, for periods, beyond). The areas south of the Forth within the realm of the king of Scots, however, only came to be regarded as fully part of the Scottish kingdom when a new sense of the 'kingdom proper' emerged by around 1200. The image of the landmass north of the Forth as an island did not entirely lose its gravitational force on how the kingdom was imagined, as we have seen. Indeed, it played a central part in the way the first continuous narrative of Scottish history from its origins was constructed, probably in the 1260s.[63] In the late twelfth century, however, charter scribes increasingly began to refer to the entire realm as the kingdom of Scotland or kingdom of the Scots, and to define lordship in relation to this. In Edgar's charter the kingdom proper was a topographical entity; by the end of the twelfth century scribes saw it as an abstract concept that related intrinsically to the realm as a whole.[64]

I have argued elsewhere that this change has its roots in growing expectations that society should be defined in standard ways, initially in the context of the Church.[65] A key part of this process was that judicial powers were defined in relation to a superior authority. As a result, those wielding these powers acquired a new identity within a standard framework. Among the earliest examples is the Church as a whole. There was a tendency to regard kingdoms as the standard unit of ecclesiastical governance below the pope; as such, the 'kingdom of Scotland' first began to acquire a new identity as the entire realm of the king of Scots – but only in that context. Another context was when judicial functions in the secular sphere began to be defined in relation to royal authority, a process that Alice Taylor has first identified in the 1160s, and has shown was gathering pace in the 1180s.[66] In the process a

---

matter-in-hand or of the place where the charter was produced: Nishioka, 'Scots and Galwegians', 214–18, 224–5.
63 Broun, *Scottish Independence*, 252–8, 262–3.
64 Broun, 'Kingdom and Identity', 34–9.
65 For what follows, see Broun, 'Kingdom and Identity', 66–73.
66 Alice Taylor, *The Shape of the State*, 158–61.

variety of lords, great and small, gained a new identity within a standard framework that was, by definition, seen as applying across the entire realm of the king of Scots. As a result, the 'kingdom of Scotland' or 'kingdom of the Scots' gained force as primarily an abstract concept, overriding the older image of the kingdom as in its essence primarily defined by topography.

Alice Taylor has shown the value of seeing the relationship between royal authority and aristocratic power, not as a binary opposition, but a joint enterprise. Royal authority existed through aristocratic power; aristocratic power, in turn, was enhanced by royal authority.[67] Seen in this light, it should not be so much of a surprise that the earliest charters of Edgar and David I can be seen as attempts by major lords south of the Forth to harness Scottish royal authority to protect or enhance their regional power. In neither instance, however, was there reference to standard norms of lordship. Indeed, the reverse is true: all we see is a raw invocation of the king's authority. In the case of Durham this was articulated within the king of England's overlordship; in the case of Robert Bruce the charter was, in all likelihood, an appeal to an alternative to English royal authority. Be this as it may, lordship in Annandale and the Merse was identified with the king of Scots. Although it was not yet possible to imagine these regions as part of the kingdom proper, it is noteworthy that there was a limited appetite for seeing the king of Scots south of the Forth as exercising his power simply as an earl of Lothian or ruler of the Cumbrians. The earl of Dunbar is reported by Roger of Howden to have been one of the keenest opponents to William the Lion's plan in 1195 that could have risked establishing Lothian as part of a Northumbrian earldom under the overlordship of the king of England.[68] It was this willingness to identify local lordship with Scottish royal authority that was one of the key ingredients in the eventual emergence of a sense of the entire realm as a single country.

---

67   *Ibid.*, e.g., 445–6.
68   *RHC*, ed. Stubbs, iii. 299; Broun, 'Kingdom and Identity', 37.

Acknowledgements

I am very grateful to Joanna Tucker for discussing the charter evidence in this chapter with me, and for some crucial insights into this and also into ways of thinking about the kingdom; to Alice Taylor for reading the final draft and making many very helpful suggestions and clarifications; and to Keith Stringer for editing an earlier version of parts of this chapter. I am also very grateful to the editors for the invitation to contribute this piece, and for their feedback. I am, as ever, solely responsible for any errors and misconceptions that remain.

Finally, I am grateful to the Arts and Humanities Research Council for funding the project of which this is an outcome: AH/L008041/1 Models of Authority: Scottish Charters and the Emergence of Government 1100–1250.

CHAPTER THREE

Edinburgh's Renown in the Early Middle Ages

PHILIP DUNSHEA

Introduction

The Scots reportedly took possession of Edinburgh some six decades before the Battle of Carham, in the reign of Ildulb mac Causantín. Whether or not it seemed a momentous occasion at the time is unknown. Our sole notice of the event is an interpolation in the *Chronicle of the Kings of Alba*, and may postdate the mid-tenth century by 200 years or more. As we shall see, the passage is also worded so that the taking of Scotland's future capital sounds almost like an accident. With such flimsy evidence we can only really speculate about Edinburgh's significance in the transformations of the tenth century. If the kings of Alba harboured long-standing ambitions to wrestle Lothian from English control, it is tempting to see Edinburgh as the bridgehead that allowed them to extend their authority south of the Forth, to the point where southern rulers had little option but to recognise a *fait accompli*. Equally Scottish possession of Edinburgh may have been significant only in retrospect. In the twelfth century, when the grip of the Scottish crown on the lands south of the Forth gradually comes into sharper focus, Edinburgh has almost immediate prominence in the written sources. From then onwards, there was good reason to invest the site with a relevant political history.

In Welsh texts from the central Middle Ages, Edinburgh (or something like it) is consistently depicted as a British site whose political credentials were already ancient. The most concentrated set of references is in *Y Gododdin*, a series of poems on the North British kingdom of Gododdin. Surviving in a manuscript of the 1260s (*Llyfr Aneirin*, 'The Book of Aneirin'), *Y Gododdin* is a key component of the Welsh literary construct known as *yr hen ogled*, the 'Old North'. One important aspect of this tradition is that a fortress called *Eidyn* had been the seat of Gododdin's rulers during the later sixth or early seventh century.

The onomastic link between *Eidyn* and modern Edinburgh is usually treated as one of *Y Gododdin*'s 'safe zones'. The careful arguments of Ifor Williams and Kenneth Jackson established a consensus that references to *Eidyn* (and in particular phrases describing a 'fort of *Eidyn*') in the thirteenth-century manuscript refer to the locality of Edinburgh, and a stronghold on the summit of Castle Rock.[1] Long-running debate over *Y Gododdin*'s date and provenance has not disturbed this accord: a summary of the poetry might state that it is 'about' *Catraeth*, identified with Catterick on the northern edge of the Yorkshire Dales, but that it is also 'about' a fort at Edinburgh. This chapter does not undermine the '*Eidyn* = Edinburgh' equation, but probes the significance of this link, its date and provenance.

Y Gododdin and beyond: the view from medieval Wales

We begin with a brief survey of the name *Eidyn* as it appears in early Welsh manuscripts. This exercise illustrates the range of meanings *Eidyn* seems to have had, and shows the difficulty of tracing how this changed over time. The name had kaleidoscopic literary connotations which, in many of the texts, all but obscure its probable relationship with Edinburgh. Even where *Eidyn* does seem to signify an important place in the north, it is not always clear how precisely this was understood, in a geographical sense. The survey is not meant to be comprehensive, but sketches out a literary background against which to measure material discussed later in this chapter, where references to Edinburgh can be linked to more definite historical contexts. The table below brings together the more certain examples in *Y Gododdin*, following their order in the manuscript. The first four are in the hand of scribe A, the second four of scribe B.

With these examples it is unclear whether the sound /d/ or /ð/ is intended with any degree of uniformity; after wrestling with the issue at some length, Williams decided that the medial sound had originally been /d/, later shifting to /ð/ in Welsh usage.[2] One observation is that, in at least some of these instances, *Eidyn* might be read as a personal name as well as a place-name. Another is that, while *Din Eidyn* seems to have become the standard form of reference for modern scholars

---

[1] *Canu Aneirin*, ed. I. Williams (Cardiff, 1938), xxxvi–xl; K. Jackson, *The Gododdin: The Oldest Scottish Poem* (Edinburgh, 1969), 75–8.
[2] *Canu Aneirin*, ed. Williams, xxxviii–xl. Usage in *Llyfr Du Caerfyrddin* indicates medial /ð/, as Williams notes; 'ond nid yw ei orgraff yn brawf pendant a therfynol'.

Reference	*Llyfr Aneirin* (page, line)[3]	*Canu Aneirin* (*awdl*, line)[4]	Clancy's translation in *The Triumph Tree* (stanza, page)[5]
eidyn ysgor	4.5–6	XIII, 113	'Eidyn's fortress' (A13, 50)
kynted eidyn	5.9–10	XVII, 157	'Eidyn's great hall' (A17, 51)
eidyn eu ruchawc	5.18–19	XVIII, 183	'gold-smithed Eidyn' (A18, 51)
rac eidyn	19.15	LXVII, 951	'before Eidyn' (A73, 64)
dineidin	33.5	XCIV, 1158	'Din Eidyn' (B17, 71)
called a med eidin	33.17	XCIV, 1167	'Eidyn's forests and mead' (B19, 72)
ut eidin uruei	35.11	C, 1220	'Eidyn's lord, Urfai' (B26, 74)
eidin vre	36.18	CI, 1224	'Eidyn's hill' (B32, 75)

(arguably because it closely approximates a Welsh translation of Gaelic *Dùn Èideann*, 'Edinburgh'), it occurs just once in *Llyfr Aneirin*. And in fact the pairing is very rare in early Welsh manuscripts, as we will see.

There are two further instances in the same manuscript, one more certain than the other. The first and more problematic is cited as a reference to *Eidyn* in John Koch's 'reconstructed' *Gododdin of Aneirin*, as well as in Thomas Clancy's translation.[6] Obtaining the translation 'first out of Eidyn's bright fort' requires emendation from *echeching gaer* to Old Welsh **ec etin-cair*, 'from the fortress of Eidyn'.[7] More reliably, we also have an example in the *Gwarchanau*, a set of poems preserved in

---

3   Llyfr Aneirin: Cardiff, South Glamorgan Library, 2.81 (Wales, s. xiii); *Llyfr Aneirin: Ffacsimile*, ed. D. Huws and J. Gwenogvryn Evans (Aberystwyth, 1989).
4   *Canu Aneirin*, ed. Williams.
5   *Triumph Tree*, ed. T. O. Clancy.
6   *Llyfr Aneirin*, 5.1–3; *Canu Aneirin*, ed. Williams, 140–4; *Triumph Tree*, 50 (A-text, stanza 16).
7   J. T. Koch, *The Gododdin of Aneirin: Text and Context from Dark-Age North Britain* (Cardiff, 1997), 68, 190; J. Rowland, 'Notes on *The Gododdin*', in M. J. Ball, J. Fife, E. Poppe and J. Rowland (eds), *Celtic Linguistics/Ieithyddiaeth Geltaidd: Readings in the Brittonic Languages* (Amsterdam/Philadelphia, 1990), 333–42, at 334–5. On *echeching*, see *Canu Aneirin*, ed. Williams, 113–14.

Llyfr Aneirin which share certain themes with *Y Gododdin* but are not part of it.[8] Under the red-ink rubric *Ema weithyon e dechreu gorchan kynvelyn* ('Here now begins the *Gwarchan* of Kynvelyn'), but identified by Katherine Klar as part of a separate poem, *Gwarchan kynvelyn ar ododin* ('Kynvelyn's *gwarchan* on Gododdin'), we have *eidyn gaer gleissyon glaer*, 'Eidyn's fortress, splendid bright'.[9] The name *Kynvelyn* is given as a patronymic in several versions of Triad 31 ('Teir Gosgordd Adwyn Enys Prydein'): *Melyn mab Kynuelyn* is listed as leader of one of the 'three noble retinues of *Enys Prydein*', for instance.[10] The same triad also has *Gosgord Mynydawc Eidyn*, 'the retinue of Mynyddawg Eidyn'. *Kynvelyn* is part of what might be termed *Eidyn*'s literary collateral, more of which is discussed below.

Staying with the encyclopaedic triads, the various recensions of Triads 33 and 34 demonstrate further ambiguities in *Eidyn*'s currency. Triad 33, 'Teir Anvat Gyflauan Enys Prydein' ('Three Unfortunate Assassinations of the Island of Britain'), is straightforward enough as packaging for some North British names:

Heidyn mab Engyn a ladavd Aneiryn Gwavtryd Mech deyrn Beird,
a Llavgat Trwm Bargavt Eidyn a ladavt Auaon mab Talyessin,
a Llouvan Llav Diuo a ladavd Vryen mab Kynvarch.

Heidyn son of Enygan, who slew Aneirin of Flowing Verse, Prince of Poets,
and Llawgad Trwm Bargod Eiddyn ('Heavy Battle-Hand of the Border of Eiddyn') who slew Afaon son of Taliesin,
and Llofan Llaw Difo ('Llofan Severing Hand') who slew Urien son of Cynfarch.[11]

---

8 *Llyfr Aneirin*, 25.1–30.11. For commentary see *Canu Aneirin*, ed. Williams, lviii–lx, 348–89; K. Klar, 'What are the *Gwarchanau*?', in B. F. Roberts (ed.), *Early Welsh Poetry: Studies in the Book of Aneirin* (Aberystwyth, 1988), 97–138.
9 *Llyfr Aneirin*, 27.15; *Canu Aneirin*, ed. Williams, 1385.
10 *Trioedd Ynys Prydein*, ed. R. Bromwich, 2nd edn (Cardiff, 1978), 65–7, 323, 467–9. *Trioedd Ynys Prydein* ('Triads of the Island of Britain') is the name given to the medieval Welsh triads collated principally from four manuscripts: National Library of Wales, Peniarth 16 (Wales, s. xiii); *Llyfr Gwyn Rhydderch*, National Library of Wales, Peniarth 4 and 5 (Wales, s. xiv); *Llyfr Coch Hergest*, Jesus College, Oxford, 111 (Wales, s. xvi) and *Llyfr Du Caerfyrddin*, National Library of Wales, Peniarth 1 (Wales, s. xiii). On the manuscripts and the provenance of the triads, see *Trioedd Ynys Prydein*, xi–cxxi.
11 *Trioedd Ynys Prydein*, ed. Bromwich, 70–3, 405, 419, 424. As Bromwich points out

A related triad in *Llyfr Gwyn Rhydderch*, however, labelled 33W by Rachel Bromwich, shows how the elements of the assemblage might become corrupted:

> *Llofuan Llav Difuro a ladavd Vryen ap Kynuarch*
> *Llongad Grvm Uargot Eidin a ladavd Auaon ap Talyessin,*
> *a Heiden ap Euengat a ladavd Aneirin Gvavt ryd merch teyrn-beird – y gvr a rodei gan muv pob Sadarn yg kervyn eneient yn Talhaearn – a'e trevis a bvyall gynnut yn y fen.*

> Llofan Llaw Difro ('Llofan Exiled Hand') who slew Urien son of Cynfarch,
> Llongad Grwm Fargod Eiddyn ('Llongad the Bent of the Border of Eiddyn') who slew Afaon son of Taliesin,
> and Heiden son of Efengad who slew Aneirin of Flowing Verse, daughter of Teyrnbeirdd – the man who used to give a hundred kine every Saturday in a bath-tub to Talhaearn. And he struck her with a wood-hatchet on the head.[12]

Bromwich's response to this is worth quoting in full ('W' is her label for the redactor of the triads in *Llyfr Gwynn Rhydderch*):

> W's ill-conceived misinterpretations reach their height of absurdity in the rendering of this triad: *mechdeyrn* has become *merch teyrn-beird*, and Aneirin's identity has been so far forgotten that the Prince of Poets has become a girl, hit with a hatchet on *her* head – *yn y fen*. A misinterpretation seems to have arisen with respect to *Talhaearn*: it looks as though the redactor of W has mistaken for a place-name what is in fact the name of another of the renowned *Cynfeirdd* listed by Nennius – *Talhaern Tataguen*.[13]

Finally, there is also Triad 34, 'Teir Anvat Vwyallavt Enys Prydein', 'Three Unfortunate Hatchet-Blows of *Enys Prydein*', which opens with

---

(424), this triad is not necessarily inconsistent with the narrative on Urien's death in *Historia Brittonum* (c.63); Triad 33's overall interest in figures mentioned in chapters 62 and 63 of *Historia Brittonum* is also worth noting.
12 *Trioedd Ynys Prydein*, ed. Bromwich, 70–3.
13 *Ibid.*, 72.

Bvyallavt Eidyn ym pen Aneiryn, 'The Blow of Eidyn on the Head of Aneirin'.[14] The form *Eidyn* (given here for Triad 33's *Heidyn/Heiden*) may have been influenced by the place-name, as Bromwich notes, but equally it may have been intended, 'since each of the assassinators in triad 33 belongs to the northern British kingdoms'.[15] Despite the apparent breakdown in configuration, the triads taken together confirm that *Eidyn* was associated exclusively with the north. There is little sign of anything more precise, though, and *Eidyn*'s use as a geographical epithet or a personal name is noteworthy.

The well known figure of Clydno Eidyn, consistently associated with the *gwŷr y gogledd* ('men of the north'), reinforces this impression.[16] The form given in the thirteenth-century *Llyfr Du Caerfyrddin* is *Clytno Idin* ('Englynion y Beddau', lines 63.2–69.22).[17] A passage from the roughly contemporary *Llyfr Du o'r Waun* (Peniarth 29) and the related legal manuscript 'E' (British Library Additional 14931) links Clydno with a northern warband which invades Arfon (Gwynedd) to avenge the death of Elidir Mwynfawr.[18] The warband later retraces its steps to *auon Guerit*, 'the river Gweryd', which on the testimony of the twelfth-century tract *De situ Albanie* is understood to refer to the Forth.[19] Gwynedd's perceived links with that part of the north are stated in the ninth-century *Historia Brittonum* and have long been linked with the composition or preservation of *Y Gododdin* itself.[20] Clydno's halter is listed as one of *Tri Thlws ar Ddeg Ynys Brydain* ('The Thirteen Treasures of *Ynys Prydain*'), and his

---

14 Ibid., 74.
15 Ibid., 74.
16 P. Bartrum, *A Welsh Classical Dictionary: People in History and Legend up to About AD 1000* (Aberystwyth, 1993), 149.
17 National Library of Wales, Peniarth 1 (Wales, s. xiii). See *Llyfr Du Caerfyrddin*, ed. A. O. H. Jarman (Cardiff, 1982), 37.
18 M. E. Owen, 'Royal Propaganda: Stories from the Law-Texts', in T. M. Charles-Edwards, M. E. Owen and P. Russell (eds), *The Welsh King and His Court* (Cardiff, 2000), 224–54 (text and translation at 252–4). See also T. Lewis, 'Copy of the Black Book of Chirk Peniarth Ms. 29 National Library of Wales Aberwystwyth,' *Zeitschrift für celtische Philologie* XX (1936), 30–96, at 75; *Trioedd Ynys Prydein*, ed. Bromwich, 309–10, 501–3.
19 M. O. Anderson, *Kings and Kingship in Early Scotland,* revised edn (Edinburgh, 1980), 240–43; D. Howlett, 'The Structure of *De Situ Albanie*', in S. Taylor (ed.), *Kings, Clerics and Chronicles in Scotland, 500–1297* (Dublin, 2000), 124–45.
20 E.g. G. R. Isaac, '*Canu Aneirin* Awdl LI Revisited: Gildas and the *Gododdin*', *Zeitschrift für Celtische Philologie* 54 (2004), 144–53, at 152–3.

presence as a *cynghoriad varchoc* ('counsellor-knight') at Arthur's court is also noted.[21]

Clydno Eidyn also features in several genealogies of the *gwŷr y gogledd*, including Peniarth 45 (late 1200s), as well as in *Bonedd y Saint*.[22] In the older Harleian genealogies the same figure is perhaps represented by *Clinog Eitin*: Egerton Phillimore suggested *Clinog* is a misspelling of *Clitgno*, although this is not certain.[23] Clinog's pedigree – *Clinog eitin map Cinbelim map Dumngual hen* – is listed below those of other descendants of Dumngual, an apical figure for various dynasties linked with Alt Clut (Dumbarton Rock).[24] There are other strands that might be pursued. Clinog's geneaology in Harleian 3859 is also preceded and followed by those of kings listed at the siege of *Insula Medcaut* in *Historia Brittonum*: *Riderch Hen*, *Urbgen*, *Guallauc*, and *Morcant*. *Riderch* ('Rhydderch Hael' in later Welsh tradition), meanwhile, is listed alongside Clydno Eidyn in the northern invasion of Arfon recounted in *Llyfr Du o'r Waun*.[25] Lastly, one of *Y Gododdin*'s honorands, Cynon, is named as *mab klytno clot hir*, 'son of Clydno of far fame'.[26]

The final Welsh literary examples discussed here come from the Arthurian poem 'Pa Ŵr yw'r Porthor?', 'What man is the gate-keeper?', in *Llyfr Du Caerfyrddin* (lines 94.1–96.16). As Rachel Bromwich noted, the 'narrative background of the poem is obviously similar to that

21 *Trioedd Ynys Prydein*, ed. Bromwich, 240, 251.
22 *Early Welsh Genealogical Tracts*, ed. P. Bartrum (Cardiff, 1966), 57, 73. Bromwich argues that *Bonedd Gwŷr y Gogledd* postdates the Harleian genealogies and was probably compiled in the twelfth century, on the basis of the insertion of Maxen Wledic, a figure who became increasingly popular around this time, at the head of BGyG 11: see *Trioedd Ynys Prydein*, cxxx.
23 E. Phillimore, 'The *Annales Cambriae* and the Old-Welsh Genealogies from Harleian MS 3859', *Y Cymmrodor* IX (1888), 141–83, at 173, n. 3. An *erratum* here is corrected in the following volume, *Y Cymmrodor* X (1889), 248. See also H. M. Chadwick, *Early Scotland: The Picts, the Scots and the Welsh of Southern Scotland* (Cambridge, 1949), 145.
24 *Early Welsh Genealogical Texts*, ed. Bartrum, 10. On the composition vowels displayed by some of the names in this group, see P. Russell, 'Old Welsh *Dinacat*, *Cunedag*, *Tutagual*: Fossilised Phonology in Brittonic Personal Names', in J. H. W. Penney (ed.), *Indo-European Perspectives in Honour of Anna Morpurgo Davies* (Oxford, 2004), 447–60.
25 H. M. Chadwick and N. K. Chadwick, *The Growth of Literature*, 2 vols (1932–40), i, 150–1.
26 *Llyfr Aneirin*, 15.8; *Canu Aneirin*, ed. Williams, 416; *Triumph Tree*, 56 (A-text, stanza 37). On Cynon, see *Trioedd Ynys Prydein*, ed. Bromwich, 323–4.

of a part of *Culhwch ac Olwen*, another text famous for its north British interests.[27] 'Pa Ŵr?' mentions *Eidyn* in a similarly fabulous context:

Ac anguas edeinauc.
a lluch. llauynnauc.
Oetin doffreidauc
ar eidin cyminauc.

And Anwas the Winged, and Llwch of the Striking Hand,
They were defending Eidyn on the border.

Ew a guant penpalach.
in atodev. dissethach.
ym minit eidin.
amuc. a. chinbin.

He smote the 'Cudgel-head' in the settlements of Dissethach,
on the mountain of Eidyn he fought with the 'Dog-heads'.[28]

The *d* in *Eidin* here represents /d/, preceded in the second instance by *minit* where *t* is /ð/. It is tempting to link *Minit Eidin*, 'the mountain of Eidyn', with the personal name *Mynydavc Eidin* in Triad 31, which in

---

27 R. Bromwich, 'Celtic Elements in Arthurian Romance: A General Survey', in P. B. Grout *et al.* (eds), *The Legend of Arthur in the Middle Ages* (Cambridge, 1983), 41–55, at 46. *Culhwch ac Olwen* is preserved in *Llyfr Gwyn Rhydderch*, National Library of Wales, Peniarth 4 (Wales, s. xiv) and in *Llyfr Coch Hergest*, Jesus College, Oxford, 111 (Wales, s. xiv). See R. Bromwich and D. Simon Evans (eds), *Culhwch and Olwen. An Edition and Study of the Oldest Arthurian Tale* (Cardiff, 1992), 94 (line 282). The extant redaction may date to as early as the eleventh century, although Rodway's recent argument maintains that it cannot be proved to have been composed any earlier than the mid-twelfth century. See S. Rodway, 'The Date and Authorship of *Culhwch ac Olwen*: A Reassessment', *Cambrian Medieval Celtic Studies* 49 (2005), 21–44; T. M. Charles-Edwards, 'The Date of *Culhwch ac Olwen*', in W. McLeod *et al.* (eds), *Bile ós Chrannaib: A Festschrift for William Gillies* (Ceann Drochaid, 2010), 45–56; S. Rodway, *Dating Medieval Welsh Literature: Evidence from the Verbal System* (Aberystwyth, 2013), 169.

28 *Llyfr Du Caerfyrddin*, ed. Jarman, 66–8; translated in Bromwich, 'Celtic Elements in Arthurian Romance', 45–6. See also P. Sims-Williams, 'The Early Welsh Arthurian Poems', in R. Bromwich, A. O. H. Jarman and B. F. Roberts (eds), *The Arthur of the Welsh: The Arthurian Legend in Medieval Welsh Literature* (Cardiff, 1991), 33–72, at 39–46.

turn seems to be a variant of the *Mynydawc* who commands the British forces in *Y Gododdin*.[29] Phrases such as *Gosgord Mynydawc*, 'Mynyddawg's retinue', occur in Triad 31 as well as in the twelfth-century court poem *Hirlas Owain*.

To sum up this section, there are a few forms to deal with: principally *Eidyn/Eidin*, but also *Eidyn Ysgor, Dineidin, Eidin Vre, Minit Eidin, Eidyn Gaer* and *Kynted Eidyn*, respectively 'fort', 'hill-fort', 'hill', 'mountain', 'fortified city' and 'royal hall'. Alt Clut, Dumbarton Rock, was given a similarly wide range of names in medieval texts.[30] At this point it might be tempting to give precedence to the *Eidyn* celebrated in *Y Gododdin*, with other (perhaps later) texts using the name in various ways, often in a more overtly fabulous setting. But the distinction may be illusory: there is nothing especially consistent about *Eidyn*'s usage in *Y Gododdin*. And without firm dating for many of our texts, any insinuation that *Eidyn* lost definition in proportion to distance from its 'original' status in *Y Gododdin* would be misleading. There is no diachronic scale in which to situate these synchronic references, and therefore no discernible 'process'. One further point may be made: while the generic element varies, albeit more widely in a lexical than in a semantic sense, the specific *Eidyn* does so in orthographic terms only. So *Eidyn* had a standard form, but its associated fort does not seem to have done so. This flexible onomastic schema clearly lent itself to poetic usage, and may well have been shaped by that usage.

Edinburgh before 1100: Scottish and Irish annals

We now move on to search for a fort at Edinburgh in the wider textual record. If Welsh scribes understood *Eidyn* to signify Edinburgh, what might have inspired the latter's literary fame? The earliest attestation by some distance is a reference to a seventh-century siege of *Etin* in various versions of the Irish annals. The relevant item falls under 638:

1. *Kl. Ianair. Bellum Glinne Mureson 7 obsessio Etin.*
2. *Cronan moccu Loeghde, abbas Cluana Moccu Noise, obiit.*

---

29 For Bromwich's comments on these names, see *Trioedd Ynys Prydein*, 467–9.
30 K. Jackson, 'Edinburgh and the Anglian occupation of Lothian', in P. Clemoes (ed.), *The Anglo-Saxons: Some Aspects of their History and Culture*, 35–42, at 39.

1. The kalends of January. The battle of Glenn Mureson, and the siege of Etin.
2. Crónán moccu Lóegde, abbot of Clonmacnoise, died.[31]

This information was probably derived from the monastery on Iona, where some contemporary elements of the pre-740 'Chronicle of Ireland' were drawn up. *Etin* might well signify Edinburgh, as Kenneth Jackson demonstrated, and in support James Fraser notes that there is a 'sequence of annals relating to Northumbrian affairs in the Irish chronicles in these years'.[32] The Iona chroniclers' putative interest in sieges was also noted by John Bannerman, although the cluster of *obsesio* entries relating to northern Britain only commences properly in the 680s.[33]

Etin is found only in the *Annals of Ulster*. In the *Annals of Tigernach* and *Chronicum Scotorum* the forms given are respectively *Etaín* and *Etain*. The latter are presumably 'translations' into Irish from the original Latin. They may be compared with *Eadain*, which occurs in the *Leabhar Leacain* copy of the 'second recension' metrical *Dindsenchas* ('Carn Máil', line 15), and which is listed in Edmund Hogan's *Onomasticon Goidelicum*.[34]

> *Lughaidh Mál as mór do mhill,*
> *do h-indarbadh é a h-Erinn,*
> *lucht secht long do mhac an rígh*
> *a h-Erinn a n-Albain tír.*

---

31 *The Chronicle of Ireland*, ed. T. M. Charles-Edwards, 2 vols (Liverpool, 2006), i, 141; *AU* 638.1, ed. Mac Airt and Mac Niocaill, 121; *CS* 638, ed. Hennessy, 85; *AT* 640.1, ed. Stokes, 184. A reference to Edinburgh under 934 in the *Annals of Clonmacnoise* has been shown by Alex Woolf to be a misnomer. The seventeenth-century translator had a 'bad habit of modernising and anglicising personal names': '*Dunfoither* (Dunottar) becomes "Edenburrogh" doubtless because he did not recognise *Dunfoither* but knew Edinburgh (*Dún Etin*) to be the obvious target for any English invasion of Scotland in his own day.' See *AClon* 928 [*recte* 934], ed. Murphy, 149; A. Woolf, *From Pictland to Alba*, 163–4.
32 Jackson, 'Edinburgh and the Anglian Occupation of Lothian', 35–42; J. Fraser, *Caledonia to Pictland: Scotland to 795* (Edinburgh, 2009), 170.
33 J. Bannerman, *Studies in the History of Dalriada* (Edinburgh, 1974), 15–16.
34 Royal Irish Academy MS 23 P 2 (Ireland, s. xv); E. Gwynn, *The Metrical Dindsenchas Part IV* (Dublin, 1924), 134–5; E. Hogan, *Onomasticon Goidelicum: Locorum et Tribuum Hiberniae et Scotiae* (Dublin, 1910), s.v. *eadain*. On the 'Book of Lecan' *Dindsenchas* and its relationship with the other manuscripts, see E. Gwynn, *The Metrical Dindsenchas Part V* (Dublin, 1935), 5–6.

> *Ro chosain na tíri thair,*
> *a chathaibh, a comhlannaibh,*
> *ó Eadain co Lochlaind* láin,
> *ó indsibh Orc co h-Espáin.*

> Lughaidh Mal, who destroyed much,
> Was banished out of Eire,
> With a fleet of seven ships the king's son sailed
> From Eire to the land of Alba.
> He fought for the eastern country
> In battles, in conflicts,
> From Eadain to the wide-spreading Lochlann,
> From the Islands of Orc to Spain.[35]

Other manuscripts give *Letha*, 'Brittany', and Étar, 'Howth', in place of *Eadain*.[36] Given these variations it would be unwise to read too much into the fact that, as a description of Alba from the tenth century through to the twelfth and beyond, 'Edinburgh to wide-spreading Lochlann' works rather well. All of this significantly postdates the seventh century, of course, and our ability to substantiate *Y Gododdin*'s claim of an early medieval fortress at Edinburgh must rest on the identification with *Etin* in the *Annals of Uster*.

We are then faced with a 300-year hiatus in the sources, bringing us to the reign of Ildulb mac Causantín, king of Alba from 954 to 962. This is the period referred to in the introduction, when the Scots kings may have begun to assert meaningful political power in Lothian. Ildulb, whose name is likely to represent Germanic 'Hildulf' (perhaps Norse 'Hildulfr', via intermarriage between the Alpínids and a dynasty of Scandinavian descent), was a son of Causantín mac Áeda and thus a great-grandson of Cináed mac Ailpín. His death in 962 is noted in *Chronicum Scotorum* and the *Annals of Clonmacnoise*.[37]

The reference in question is a component of the *Chronicle of the Kings of Alba*, a text that demands another short excursus.[38] The only

---

35 Printed in full in J. O'Donovan, *Miscellany of Celtic Society* (Dublin, 1849), 66–7.
36 Gwynn, *The Metrical Dindshenchas Part IV*, 135.
37 *CS* 960 [*recte* 962], ed. Hennessy, 185; *AClon* 956 [*recte* 962], ed. Murphy, 157.
38 The most recent edition of the *Chronicle of the Kings of Alba* was published by B. T. Hudson in 'The Scottish Chronicle', *SHR* 77 (1998), 129-62, text and translation at

surviving exemplar is in the 'Poppleton' manuscript, Paris Bibliothèque nationale, Latin 4126, a product of the fourteenth century. The *Chronicle* therein is structured around a regnal list and is not strictly annalistic (as opposed to, for example, the Irish annals). This original framework was probably put together during the reign of Cináed mac Maíl Coluim (971–95); soon after the project seems to have been abandoned, as Cináed is not given a reign length, in contrast to the eleven other kings who come before him. The process by which other material was spliced onto this list of kings' names and reign lengths remains uncertain, but it was probably carried out in a number of stages up to *c.* 1200. According to Hudson, late Old Irish and early Middle Irish words and phrases in the text are consistent with a date of composition from the mid ninth to the late tenth century, suggesting that some of the 'chronicle' material may represent a 'contemporary or near contemporary record of the events described'.[39] It is not always clear how accurately this material was synchronised with the reign-lengths in the regnal list, however.

The reference to Edinburgh is embedded in the eighth reign of twelve recorded in the *Chronicle*:

Idulfus tenuit regnum viii annis. In huius tempore opidum Eden uacuatum est ac relictum est Scottis usque in hodiernum diem. Classi[s] Somarlidiorum occisi sunt in Bucham.

Idulb held the kingship for eight years. In this time the *oppidum* of Eden was vacated and left to the Scots, as it is right up to this day. A fleet of *sumarliðar* were slain in Buchan.

Firstly, use of the term *opidum* demands comment. Previously in the *Chronicle*, under the reign of Domnall mac Causantín, mention is made of the destruction of *Opidum Fother*, Dunnottar in Kincardineshire. As Hudson notes, 'the spelling *opidum* is not uncommon in Latin texts written by Gaelic-speakers, nor is the use of *oppidum* for *dún*, "royal

---

148–61 [hereafter *CKA*]. On the provenance of the text, see David Dumville, 'The Chronicle of the Kings of Alba', in S. Taylor (ed.), *Kings, Clerics and Chronicles in Scotland, 500–1297* (Dublin, 2000), 73-86; Woolf, *From Pictland to Alba*, 88–92; D. Broun, 'Dunkeld and the Origins of Scottish Identity', *IR* 48 (1997), 112–24.

39 Hudson, 'The Scottish Chronicle', 133.

fortress"'.[40] Secondly, and unusually for the *Chronicle*, no information is apparently given about Ildulb's death. But is this in fact the case? Alex Woolf has suggested that the information concerning *opidum Eden* is an interpolation, the work of a later copyist who then miscorrected the grammar of the final phrase and garbled the passage's meaning.[41] The original king-list behind the *Chronicle* probably read something like 'Idulb held the kingship seven years and was slain by a fleet of *sumarliðar* in Buchan.' We therefore need to separate the information concerning Edinburgh from its (probably) late-tenth-century packaging. *Eden* here also looks like a relatively late form.

Having established that this allusion to Alba's expansion south of the Firth of Forth is retrospective, not least because of *in hodiernum diem*, it is difficult to assess the synchronism with Ildulb's reign. In support of its essential accuracy, one might have expected a twelfth-century fabrication to have made more of the event's symbolic overtones. Hudson also points to one of the later stanzas in the equally problematic 'Prophecy of Berchán', a Middle Irish text recounting the exploits of Irish and Scottish kings from Máel Sechnaill of Mide (died 862) to Domnall Bán. 'Woe to the Britons and Saxons during his time,' the 'Prophecy' says of Ildulb, 'and joy to the Scots with him':

Ni gerradh gearradh agu
Albainn ethrach find-fhoda
is tuilled chuíge fogheibh
da thúaith aineoil ar éiccin.

A shortening will not be a shortening among them, Scotland of fair long ships; it is an addition to her territory she will receive, from a foreign land, by might.[42]

Hudson attributes these verses to the second of three authors responsible for composing the 'Prophecy of Berchán'. The parts of this writer's work devoted to the kings of medieval Scotland are generally among the more 'accurate' components of the work, and enlargement of Alba's

---

40 *Ibid.*, 149, n. 18.
41 Woolf, *From Pictland to Alba*, 193–5.
42 *The Prophecy of Berchán*, ed. B. Hudson (Westport, 1996), 48, 88 (lines 161–2).

territories at the expense of both Britons and Saxons during the central decades of the tenth century is, if vaguely recalled, at least plausible. That said, Hudson also makes the argument that the verses on Ildulb's career were composed during the reign of Máel Coluim III (r. 1058–93), during and after which renewed political and literary focus fell on this part of Scotland, as we shall see.[43]

The Kentigern dossier and Geoffrey of Monmouth: Lothian renewed

The next task is to compare the presentation of Edinburgh, and Lothian more generally, in two sets of twelfth-century material, both perhaps illustrative of intensified literary contact between Scotland and Wales at the time. These are, firstly, the dossier of hagiographical material relating to Saint Kentigern and, secondly, Geoffrey of Monmouth's block-buster *Historia Regum Britanniae*.[44] An entry in the early versions of *Bonedd y Saint* ('Lineage of the Saints', probably thirteenth century) gives the ancestry of Saint Kentigern:

> *Kyndeyrn garthwys m. Ewein m. Vryen, a Denw verch Lewdwn luydawc o Dinas Eidyn yn y gogledd y vam.*[45]

The descent of Kentigern from Owain ab Urien and *Denw*, daughter of *Lewdwn* 'of the hosts' from '*Dinas Eidyn* in the north', is well known from the fragmentary 'Herbertian' *Vita* of the saint. In this work, composed by an anonymous Glasgow clerk for Bishop Herbert between 1147 and 1164, the names are rendered *Ewen*, *Taneu* and

---

43 *Ibid.*, 16–19.
44 Links between the 'Kentigern dossier' and the works of Geoffrey of Monmouth have long been recognised but are notoriously difficult to delineate. There is insufficient space here to go into detail but see, for example, O. Padel, 'Geoffrey of Monmouth and the Development of the Merlin Legend', *Cambrian Medieval Celtic Studies* 51 (2006), 37–65, at 54–60; J. Reuben Davies, 'Bishop Kentigern among the Britons', in S. Boardman, J. Reuben Davies and E. Williamson (eds.), *Saints' Cults in the Celtic World* (Woodbridge, 2009), 66–90.
45 *Early Welsh Genealogical Texts*, ed. Bartrum, 56; see also *Canu Llywarch Hen*, ed. I. Williams (Cardiff, 1935), xxvi. On *Bonedd y Saint*, see T. M. Charles-Edwards, *Wales and the Britons* (Oxford, 2013), 616; D. Huws, *Medieval Welsh Manuscripts* (Cardiff, 2000), 58. The oldest manuscript is National Library of Wales, Peniarth 16, iv (Wales, s.xiii).

Leudonus. It has recently been proposed that the 'Herbertian' *Vita* (of which only the preface and the first eight chapters survive) is the work of Simeon, archdeacon of Teviotdale.[46] The latter jurisdiction was added to the Glasgow see probably by the young Earl David, future king of Scotland, prior to the death of his older brother Alexander in 1124.[47] In any event, the author famously claimed to have made use of an older *codicellus* (or *codicelli*), probably the same source referred to as the *codicilus ... stilo Scottico dictato* in Jocelin's slightly later *Vita*.[48] Kenneth Jackson proposed that this refers to a lost work written not in Gaelic but in 'the Gaelic style of Latin', and perhaps a product of the eleventh century.[49] The author of the 'Herbertian' *Vita* also included material *viva voce fidelium mihi relata*, 'told me orally by trustworthy people'.

One feature of the 'Herbertian' text that has attracted frequent comment is the detailed geographical setting, which seems to be confined to the shores of the Firth of Forth. This goes beyond mere toponymy to include familiarity with what Jackson referred to as 'Strathclyde oral saga', but which might more accurately be characterised as a stock of North British (or Cumbric) names and tales.[50] The most impressive demonstration of this is made in the first chapter, where Kentigern's father is described as *juvenis quidam elegantissimus, Ewen videlicet filius Erwegende, nobilissima Brittonum prosapia ortus ... in gestis historiarum vocatur Ewen filius regis Ulien*, 'a most graceful young man, namely, Ewen, the son of Erwegende, sprung from a most noble stock of the Britons ... in the Deeds of the Histories he is called Ewen, son of king Ulien' (that is Forbes'

---

46 D. Howlett, *Caledonian Craftsmanship: The Scottish Latin Tradition* (Dublin, 2000), 96–7. For details on Simeon, see A. Beam, J. Bradley, D. Broun, J. Reuben Davies, M. Hammond, M. Pasin (with others), *The People of Medieval Scotland, 1093–1314* (Glasgow and London, 2012), www.poms.ac.uk (accessed 1 February 2018).

47 G. Barrow, *The Kingdom of the Scots: Government, Church and Society from the Eleventh to the Fourteenth Century*, 2nd edn (Edinburgh, 2003), 203–7; N. Shead, 'The Origins of the Medieval Diocese of Glasgow', *SHR* 48 (1969), 220–5.

48 *Vita S. Kentigerni* (also known as *Vita Kentegerni Imperfecta*), BL, MS Cotton Titus A.xix, fols 76r–80v: ed. A. P. Forbes, *Lives of Ninian and Kentigern*, 123–33 (translation), 242–52 (text), at 243. For the *Life* by Jocelin of Furness, see 159–242 in the same volume.

49 K. Jackson, 'The Sources for the Life of St Kentigern', in N. K. Chadwick (ed.), *Studies in the Early British Church* (Cambridge, 1958), 273–357, at 275–7.

50 *Ibid.*, 286.

reading; the manuscript gives *in gestis histrionum*, 'in the deeds of the actors', with the *o* altered from an *a*).[51] Jackson argues that *Ewen filius Erwegende* represents the form the author found in his source; the parenthetical *in gestis* is a gloss which, Sims-Williams suspected, may postdate the twelfth-century composition of the 'Herbertian' *Vita*, perhaps considerably.[52]

While it is true that Urien and his son were well known in Wales at the time, and may also have been familiar in places like Strathclyde in the eleventh and twelfth centuries, it is the case that, when the 'Herbertian' *Vita* was being compiled, the pair had recently been reintroduced to the world by Geoffrey of Monmouth. Even if the text behind the 'Herbertian' *Life* was considerably older than Geoffrey's work, updating could have occurred over a number of stages, right up to the production of the manuscript in the 1400s. *Ewen filius Ulien* in the 'Herbertian' *Life* and *Hiwenus filius Vriani* in *Historia Regum Britanniae* are clearly different forms, but awareness of Urien and his son among the Glaswegian clergy and their contacts may not have been entirely unrelated to Geoffrey's rapidly felt influence.[53] We should be wary of necessarily attributing knowledge of such names to popular folklore. On the other hand, it is doubtless a coincidence that Geoffrey's *Historia Regum Britanniae*, completed in the second half of the 1130s, was apparently known in his own lifetime as *Gesta Britonum*.[54] There is room for further research on the subject.

Returning to the presentation of Lothian in the Kentigern material, the geographical setting is striking in its detail. Kentigern's maternal grandfather is named as *Leudonus* (*Lewdwn* in the earliest version of *Bonedd y Saint*):

---

51 *Vita S. Kentigerni*, ed. Forbes, 125, 245. On the names here, see Jackson, 'The Sources for the Life of St Kentigern', 283–6. On the various readings, see P. Sims-Williams, 'Breton *Conteurs* and the *Matière de la Bretagne*', *Romania* 116 (1998), 72–111, at 94–5, n. 83.
52 Jackson, 'The Sources for the Life of St Kentigern', 285. Sims-Williams, 'Breton *Conteurs* and the *Matière de la Bretagne*', 95. The manuscript (British Library, Cotton Titus A.xix) is fifteenth-century.
53 Geoffrey of Monmouth, *Historia Regum Britanniae*, ed. M. Reeve and N. Wright (Woodbridge, 2007), 250–1.
54 Geoffrey of Monmouth, *Life of Merlin*, ed. B. Clarke (Cardiff, 1973), 36. As Clarke points out (155), the words *libellum quem nunc ... uocant*, 'the book which they now call', may suggest that Geoffrey or his readers had previously used a different name.

66　　　　　PHILIP DUNSHEA

> *Rex igitur Leudonus, vir semipaganus, a quo provincia quam regebat Leudonia nomen sortita in Brittannia septentrionali, filiam habuit novercatum que Thaney vocobatur.*

So a certain king Leudonus, a man half pagan, from whom the province over which he ruled obtained the name of Leudonia in northern Britannia, had a daughter under a stepmother, and the daughter's name was Thaney.[55]

Leudonus, as Jackson notes, looks 'suspiciously like an artificial ethnonym for the province', and is sometimes also linked with the figure of *Lleu*, prominent in Welsh mythology.[56] John Koch draws attention to a possible reference to the latter in '*Awdl* LI' in *Y Gododdin*, a much studied section of the B-text, where he interprets *Leech leud ud tut leu ure* as 'the rock of Lleu's tribe, the folk of Lleu's mountain stronghold'.[57] This, he says, 'is probably Din Eidin'. Koch's enthusiasm for grounding the contents of this paricular *awdl* in Lothian is further demonstrated when he translates *tramerin* three lines later as 'from over the Firth'.[58]

The *Leudonus* of the Kentigern material, on the other hand, is linked with a handful of identifiable place-names: *mons Dumpelder*, identified by Watson as Traprain Law; *insula May*, the small basalt island five miles off the south-east coast of Fife; and finally *Collenros*, Culross, on the north side of the Firth of Forth some forty miles to the west.[59] There is also *Kepduf*, which Jackson argued may have been a Gaelic name for Traprain Law, and *Aberlessic*, now lost but presumably a

---

55　*Vita S. Kentigerni*, ed. Forbes, 125, 245.
56　Jackson, 'The Sources for the Life of St Kentigern', 282; *Trioedd Ynys Prydein*, ed. Bromwich, 420–2. *Lliw Lleudiniawn* features in work by the court poet Gwalchmai ap Meilyr, active in North Wales between roughly 1130 and 1180. See J. E. Caerwyn Williams and P. I. Lynch (eds), *Gwaith Meilyr Brydydd a'i Ddisgynyddion*, Cyfres Beirdd y Tywysogion 1 (Cardiff, 1994), 210, no. 9.155.
57　*Llyfr Aneirin*, 34.6; Koch, *Gododdin of Aneirin*, 2, 3, 131. See also J. T. Koch (ed.), *Celtic Culture: A Historical Encyclopedia*, 5 vols (Santa Barbara, 2006), 1191–2; 1165–6; 1202–3.
58　This is presumably on the basis that a figure from *tra merin Iodeo* ('beyond the sea of Iudeu') appears three stanzas later. On (*Urbs*) *Iudeu/Giudi*, see J. Fraser, 'Bede, the Firth of Forth and the Location of *Urbs Iudeu*', *SHR* 223 (2008), 1-25; D. Hicks, 'Language, History and Onomastics in Medieval Cumbria: An Analysis of the Generative Usage of the Cumbric Habitative Generics *Cair* and *Tref*, unpublished PhD thesis (University of Edinburgh, 2003), 272–3.
59　*Vita S. Kentigerni*, ed. Forbes, 131, 249–50; *CPNS*, 345.

river-mouth or confluence in the same area.[60] *Eidyn* does not occur, although at this point it may be worth reiterating that, in *Bonedd y Saint*, Kentigern's grandfather *Lewdwn* is stated to come from *Dinas Eidyn* 'in the north'. *Dunpeleder*, meanwhile, features alongside Edinburgh in the list of churches founded in Alba by Saint Monenna, in the *Vita* by the Irishman Conchubranus (see below).

A final point may be raised in relation to the Kentigern material. It is well known that David endowed the refounded Glasgow see with a cluster of estates in the area around Tweeddale and Teviotdale.[61] Recent research by Neil McGuigan discusses the possibility that, perhaps later, territories in Lothian may have been added to Glasgow's ecclesiastical jurisdiction, such that when Bishop John departed for Rome in 1125, he was referred to as *biscop of Loþene*, 'bishop of Lothian', in the 'E' recension of the *Anglo-Saxon Chronicle*.[62] Not long afterwards these lands along the southern shores of the Firth of Forth were subsumed into the dioceses of St Andrews and Dunkeld, but their short-lived status as possessions of Glasgow may have encouraged the latter's clergy to pursue Lothian-related themes.[63] Edinburgh, however, remains absent under any identifiable name in their surviving output. A tentative conclusion is that *Dinas Eidyn* represents a twelfth-century addition to the legend.

We now return to *Historia Regum Britanniae*. Geoffrey's typically idiosyncratic take on the history of early medieval Scotland has recently been reappraised by Alex Woolf. The following passage from Book Four is noteworthy:

Erant ibi tres fratres regali prosapia orti, Loth uidelicet atque Vrianus nec non et Auguselus, qui antequam Saxones praeualuissent principatum

---

60 Jackson, 'The Sources for the Life of St Kentigern', 289–92. *Kepduf*, the site of Thaney's attempted execution in the 'Herbertian' *Life*, is replaced with *Dunpelder* in Jocelin's text. Cf. N. McGuigan, 'Neither Scotland nor England', unpublished PhD thesis (University of St Andrews, 2015), 265–6, n. 288.
61 *David I Chrs*, no. 15.
62 *The Anglo-Saxon Chronicle: A Collaborative Edition. Vol. 7: MS E*, ed. S. Irvine (Cambridge, 2004), 126–7.
63 I am grateful to Neil McGuigan, of the University of St Andrews, for sharing a part of his doctoral thesis on this subject prior to its completion. On the growth of Kentigern's cult in northern Britain, see J. Reuben Davies, 'Bishop Kentigern among the Britons', 72–83.

illarum partium habuerant. Hos igitur ut ceteros paterno iure donare uolens, reddidit Auguselo regiam potestatem Scotorum fratremque suum Vrianum sceptre Murefensium insigniuit. Loth autem, qui tempore Aurelii Ambrosii sororem ipsius duxerat, ex qua Gualguainum et Modredum genuerat, ad consulatum Lodonesiae ceterarumque comprouinciarum quae ei pertinebant reduxit.

Attending the king [Arthur] were three brothers of regal descent, Loth, Urianus and Auguselus, who had been princes in the region before the Saxons took control. Wishing to return their ancestral rights to them too, [Arthur] restored to Auguselus royal power over the Scots and made his brother Urianus king of Moray. Loth, who in the reign of Aurelius Ambrosius had married the king's sister and fathered Gawain and Modred, recovered the earldom of Lothian and its associated provinces.[64]

'This tripartite division of the northern realm,' Woolf writes, 'would seem to reflect quite realistically the situation pertaining in the early twelfth century when Moray retained its own king and when Lothian and neighbouring provinces, such as Teviotdale and Clydesdale, were held by a cadet of the royal house.'[65] Woolf also draws attention to Geoffrey's use of the provincial form *Muref-*, which seems to reflect 'vernacular Scoto-Latin usage' of the time.[66]

Geoffrey refers to Edinburgh on just the one occasion, using labels that are somewhat obscure:

Condidit etiam Ebraucus urbem Aldclud uersus Albaniam et oppidum Montis Agned, quod nunc Castellum Puellarum dicitur, et Montem Dolorosum.

Ebraucus also built the city of Dumbarton towards Alba, the town of *Mons Agned*, now called *Castellum Puellarum*, and *Mons Dolorosus*.[67]

---

64 Geoffrey of Monmouth, *Historia Regum Britanniae*, ed. Reeve and Wright, 202–4.
65 A. Woolf, 'Geoffrey of Monmouth and the Picts', in McLeod *et al.* (eds), *Bile ós Chrannaibh: A Festschrift for William Gillies*, 269–80, at 271.
66 *Ibid.*, 278, n. 11.
67 Geoffrey of Monmouth, *Historia Regum Britanniae*, ed. Reeve and Wright, 34–5.

Here, as Richard Coates has argued, Geoffrey seems to be indulging his taste for 'toponymic kleptomania'.[68] Firstly, Geoffrey's *Mons Agned* must surely be connected with *mons qui dicitur Agned*, one of the twelve battles of Arthur recorded in the ninth-century *Historia Brittonum*.[69] The latter is known to be one of the texts on which Geoffrey based his work (another is Bede's *Historia Ecclesiastica*, where Geoffrey surely learned of *urbs Aldclud*).[70] *Mons Agned* has never been satisfactorily identified, despite numerous attempts, but 'Geoffrey was clearly prepared to believe it was Edinburgh.'[71] *Castellum Puellarum*, Geoffrey admits, is a recent coining, but is it his own?[72] In his *Celtic Place-Names of Scotland*, Watson sought to link *Castellum Puellarum* with an otherwise unattested community of nuns on the summit of Castle Rock, a foundation whose existence he postulated on the basis of a reference to the same site in a list of churches founded by the female Saint Monenna (see below).[73] More recently Coates has suggested Geoffrey came across stories about Qaṣr al-Banāt, 'castle/palace of the maidens', introduced into Western Europe in the aftermath of the First Crusade.[74] But Geoffrey was not the first to associate Edinburgh with maidens, as we shall see.

---

68 R. Coates, 'Maiden Castle, Geoffrey of Monmouth and Hārūn al-Rašīd', *Nomina* 29 (2006), 5–60, at 32.
69 *Historia Brittonum*, ed. T. Mommsen, in *Chronica Minora saec IV.V.VI.VII*, 3 vols (Berlin, 1892–93), iii, 111–222, at 200. For a translation, see J. Morris, *Nennius: British History and the Weslsh Annals* (Chichester, 1980), 25.
70 Bede has *Urbs Alcluith* (i.12). See his *Historia Ecclesiastica Gentis Anglorum*, ed. B. Colgrave and R. A. B. Mynors (Oxford, 1969), 40-1.
71 Coates, 'Maiden Castle', 31. See also K. Jackson, 'Arthur's Battle of Breguoin', *Antiquity* 23 (1949), 48–9; A. Breeze, '*Historia Brittonum* and Arthur's Battle of *Mons Agned*', *Northern History* 40 (2003), 167–70; N. Higham, *King Arthur: Myth-Making and History* (London, 2002), 146.
72 The name is discussed by Jonathan Oldbuck and Sir Arthur Wardour in Walter Scott's novel *The Antiquary*: '"The Pictish maidens of the blood-royal were kept in Edinburgh Castle, thence called Castrum Puellarum." / "A childish legend," said Oldbuck, "invented to give consequence to trumpery womankind. It was called the Maiden Castle, *quasi lucus a non lucendo*, because it resisted every attack, and women never do."' *The Antiquary*, 3 vols (Edinburgh, 1816), i, 68.
73 *CPNS*, 342.
74 Coates, 'Maiden Castle', 23–8. The idea may not be all that far-fetched: Baldock (Herts), after all, is the Old French name for Baghdad. See *The Concise Oxford Dictionary of English Place-Names*, ed. Ekwall, 4th edn (Oxford, 1960), 24.

The cult of Monenna: a missing link?

The *Vita* of Monenna attributed to Conchubranus, usually dated in its extant form to the eleventh century, has the saint founding no fewer than seven churches *in Albania, id est in Scotiam*:

> *Peruenerat etiam in Albania id est in Scotiam in qua edificauerat ecclesias in Christi nomine quarum hec sunt nomina. Una est Chilnecase in Galuueie. Altera uero in cacumine montis qui appellatur Dundeuenel . . . Tercia autem in alio montis Dunbreten. Quarta in castello qui dicitur Striuelin. Quinta uero Dunedene qui anglica lingua dicitur Edeneburg. Sexta enim mons Dunpeleder et illic transfretauit mare in Albaniam ad sancte Andream. Post hec uero exiit ad Aleethe ubi modo est optima ecclesia quam Lonfortin edificauit cum quodam fonte sanctissimo . . .*

> She had also been to Albainn, that is Scotland, where she had built churches in the name of Christ. These are their names. One is Chilnecase in Galloway. Another is on the summit of the hill which is called Dundevenal . . . A third is on another hilltop, Dumbarton. A fourth is in a fortress called Stirling. Yet a fifth is Duneden, which in the language of the English is called Edeneburg. A sixth is the hill of Dunpeleder, and there she crossed the sea into Albainn, to St Andrews. Then after this she went to Alyth, where there is now a fine church which she built with a very holy spring at Luncarty . . .'[75]

This text is known only from a twelfth-century English manuscript (British Library, Cotton Cleopatra A. ii), probably copied at Burton

---

[75] Conchubranus, *Life of St Monenna* iii.8, *Seanchas Ardmhacha: Journal of the Armagh Diocesan Historical Society* 10.2 (1982), 440–1. On the place-names, see Geoffrey of Burton, *Life and Miracles of St Modwenna*, ed. R. Bartlett (Oxford, 2003), xvi–xvii. The list of Scottish churches is not found in the material relating to Monenna preserved in the fourteenth-century *Codex Salmanticensis*, some of which may be considerably older than the text redacted by Conchubranus. 'Vita S. Darercae seu Moninnae Abbatissae' in *Vitae Sanctorum Hiberniae ex codice olim Salmanticensi nunc Bruxellensi*, ed. W. W. Heist (Brussels, 1965), 83–95. See M. Esposito, 'Sources of Conchubranus' Life of St Monenna', *EHR* 35 (1920), 71–8. For further discussion of the list of church foundations, see J. MacQueen, *Ninian and the Picts* (Whithorn, 2007), 10–12.

from an Irish exemplar. The translation of *Dunedene* into *Edeneburg* perhaps represents a gloss or interpolation, though need not have been the work of an English scribe. Geoffrey of Burton's *Vita Sancte Moduenne Uirginis*, a reworking of the Irish *Vita* of Monenna attributed to Conchubranus, has *in cacumine celsi montis qui uoactur Dunedene, qui et Edeneburg*, 'on the summit of the high hill called Dunedin, also known as Edinburgh'.[76] The Conchubranus *Life*, in an earlier chapter, describes the same foundation in more detail:

> *Post hec uero cepto itenere Christo comite sancte uirgines trans mare in Scotiam ad sanctum Andream et iterum transfretauerunt in Brittanniam et edificauerunt ecclesiam in honore sancti Michaelis archangeli in cacumine montis, qui modo uocatur Edeneburd.*

> After this, beginning their journey with Christ as companion, the holy virgins crossed over the sea to Scotland, to Saint Andrews, and again to Britain, and built a church in honour of Saint Michael the archangel on the summit of a mountain which is now called Edinburgh.[77]

The five virgins, who are all given names, then reside at Edinburgh for five years before embarking on a pilgrimage to Rome. Geoffrey of Burton also said of the church at *Dunedin* that it was dedicated *in honorem sancti archangeli Michaelis*, 'to the archangel Michael', *pro altitudine rupis*, 'because of the height of the rock'.[78] The alleged dedication here is intriguing. David I founded a church dedicated to St Michael at Linlithgow, around fifteen miles to the west, and the cult was strongly associated with the Stewarts and their royal palaces during the later Middle Ages, but there seems to be no further evidence for the assertion that there was a chapel dedicated to the archangel at Edinburgh.[79] That said, Mont Saint-Michel in Normandy, St Michael's Mount in Cornwall and Skellig Michael off the south-west coast of Kerry demonstrate the type of site Michael was associated with in his

---

76 Geoffrey of Burton, *Life and Miracles of St Modwenna*, c.30, ed. Bartlett, 122–3.
77 Conchubranus, *Life of St Monenna* iii.3, 432–3.
78 Geoffrey of Burton, *Life and Miracles of St Modwenna*, c.30, ed. Bartlett, 122–3.
79 D. McRoberts, 'The Cult of St Michael in Scotland', in Marcel Baudot (ed.), *Millénaire monastique de Mont Saint-Michel* (Paris, 1971), 471–9.

role as a heavenly messenger.[80] Edinburgh Castle Rock could plausibly have been among them.[81]

The core of the list of Monenna's churches, as W. F. Skene long ago pointed out, looks like a roll-call of the 'principal fortified posts in the country' (or in the country to the south of the Forth, at any rate).[82] If *Chilnecase in Galuueie* has been correctly identified as Whithorn in Galloway (*Candida Casa*), however, the list would seem to be book-ended by two famous churches, with St Andrews as the eastern counterpart.[83] Mapped out from the Machars to Fife, via the Ayrshire plain, the 'Eye of Scotland' and the Lothians, the list is broadly representative of a route from the Irish Sea to St Andrews. Whatever its provenance (a document relating to the missionary activities of Ninian, *Moninn*, has been proposed), the majority of the place-names given begin with the element *dun*, 'fort'.[84] Only Stirling, *Striuelin*, lacking the *dun* element, is described as a *castellum*: whoever compiled the original list probably understood the significance of the Gaelic term. We have already encountered *Dunpelder*, probably Traprain Law, a key setting in the 'Herbertian' *Vita* of Saint Kentigern. Aside from (possibly) *Chilnecase*, these are all labels that could have been current in southern Scotland during the eleventh and twelfth centuries.

The tale of Monenna and her nuns does not have to be the final explanation for the name *Castellum Puellarum*, but it must imply that the association with maidens is older than Geoffrey of Monmouth. Trying to account for Monenna's association with Edinburgh looks

---

80 J. Wilkie, *St Michael and Inveresk* (Edinburgh, 1894), 29–30.

81 *Chronicle of the Kings of Alba* refers to an *ecclesia sancti Michaelis* during its account of the reign of Ildulb's son Cuilén (967–71). This is identified by the editor with the chapel of St Michael the Archangel in St Andrews, but this seems to represent an educated guess. See *CKA*, 160, n. 67.

82 W. F. Skene, *Celtic Scotland: A History of Ancient Alban*, 3 vols (Edinburgh, 1876–80), ii, 37.

83 P. A. Wilson, 'St Ninian: Irish Evidence Further Examined', *Transactions of the Dumfriesshire and Galloway Natural History and Antiquarians Society* 46 (1969), 140–59, at 154; MacQueen, *Ninian and the Picts*, 12. It has been noted that the earliest hagiographical material on St Monenna, in the *Codex Salamanticensis*, restricts the saint's activities almost entirely to Ireland. The sole exception to this is when Monenna sends one of her nuns to *Rosnat*, an Irish place-name meaning something like 'little headland' which would seem to be yet another name for Whithorn. See F. Edmonds, *Whithorn's Renown in the Early Medieval Period: Whithorn, Futerna and Magnum Monasterium* (Whithorn, 2009), 25–6.

84 MacQueen, *Ninian and the Picts*, 10.

daunting, particularly in the era of 'magpie historiography', but a possible lead is to be found in the saints' calendars.[85] Monenna's feast day is variously listed as 5 or 6 July; under 5 July a saint *Etain* ('Edana' or 'Edaoin') is also listed.[86] The *Martyrology of Tallaght*, for instance, compiled during the first half of the ninth century, has *Etain virginis Tuama Noadh* under 5 July and then *Moninni Sleibi Culinn quae et Darerca prius dicta est* for 6 July.[87] Ó Riain comments:

> On visiting Tumna in 1837, John O'Donovan was shown the grave of St Héidin (Eidin), or 'Edaoin in Irish'. The saint's pedigree... is also preserved, as is the record of her feast on 5 July. In the seventeenth century, her name began to be confused with the form 'Moduena' which was probably borrowed from a gloss on Moninne in the list of the following day. In Scotland, where her name was given the Latin form Medana, the saint was remembered variously on 5 July and 19 November.[88]

Ó Riain's seventeenth-century 'confusion' is attested in the genealogies compiled by Míchél O Cléirigh and his colleagues, where *Edaoin* is glossed with *Moduena* (presumably by his contemporary John Colgan).[89] But arguably the gloss speaks not of confusion but of an association long understood, if obscure. Another interpolation made in O Cléirigh's 'Martyrology of Donegal' draws the same link.[90] The association might predate the seventeenth century considerably, not least because it would account, via a 'folk-etymology', for Edinburgh's status in the *Vita* by the Irishman Conchubranus. Esposito maintained that it

---

85 T. Clancy, 'Magpie Historiography in Twelfth-Century Scotland: The Case of *Libellus de Nativitate Sancti Cutherberti*', in J. Cartwright (ed.), *Celtic Hagiography and Saints' Cults* (Cardiff, 2003), 216–31.
86 Noted by Skene (*Celtic Scotland: A History of Ancient Alban*, ii, 38). See *Corpus Genealogiarum Sanctorum Hiberniae*, ed. P. Ó Riain (Dublin, 1985), 62, 69 (nos 401 and 510).
87 *Martyrology of Tallaght*, ed. R. Best and H. Lawler (London, 1931), 53. For the date of the text, see P. Ó Riain, 'The Tallaght Martyrologies, redated', *Cambridge Medieval Celtic Studies* 20 (1990), 21–38.
88 *A Dictionary of Irish Saints*, ed. P. Ó Riain (Dublin, 2011), 279. On Moninne, see 495–7.
89 *Genealogiae Regum et Sanctorum Hiberniae*, ed. P. Walsh (Dublin, 1918), 59.
90 *The Martyrology of Donegal: A Calendar of the Saints of Ireland*, ed. J. Todd and W. Reeves (Dublin, 1864), 186–7.

was Conchubranus who confused 'first, a Darerca or Moninne of Killeevy... whose activities were confined to Ireland, and secondly, a Monenna or Moduenna (or Modwenna)... who founded the monastery near Burton-on-Trent and various churches in Scotland'.[91] But there are further intricacies in the relationships between these identities that still need unpicking, and there may also be a third saint involved.

Did a name for Edinburgh, *Eden* or something similar, come to be associated with Moduenna and Etain by virtue of similarities in pronunciation? Moduenna seems to have retained a following in Lothian, at any rate, according to the Scot David Camerarius, who was active around the same time as Míchél O Cléirigh. The calendar embedded in his 1631 work *De Scotorum Fortitudine* has *Sancta Moduenna Virgo in Laudonia and Galouida Scotiae prouincijs celebris* under 5 July.[92] There are two Galloway dedications that may further illustrate the point: Kirkmaiden parish in the Rhinns, and Kirkmaiden in the parish of Glasserton in the Machars, both dedicated to *Medana* (which Watson took as 'a latinized form of *M'Etáin*').[93] One speculative reconstruction is that the place-name *Eden* underwent a form of lexeme substitution, a process catalysed by knowledge of a saint and her cult (*Moduenna* or *Etain*, or more likely a conflation of both) among Gaelic or English speakers in southern Scotland.

Royal connections: Edinburgh in the reign of David I

By the 1150s at the very latest, Scottish royal charters were using *Castellum Puellarum* and *Castrum Puellarum* to refer to Edinburgh Castle. It is a label that seems to bear witness not to Geoffrey's influence, rapidly felt though it undoubtedly was, but to the site's perceived hagiographical status.[94] It is around this time, in the first half of the twelfth century, that archaeologists can detect the earliest structural remains of defences on the summit of Castle Rock.[95] Tucked inside them of course is little St Margaret's

---

91 M. Esposito, 'Sources of Conchubranus' Life of St. Monenna', 78.
92 A. Forbes, *Kalendars of Scottish Saints* (Edinburgh, 1872), 238.
93 *CPNS*, 163.
94 Charter references from the twelfth century are drawn together in G. Chalmers, *Caledonia*, 3 vols (London, 1807–24), ii, 557.
95 S. Driscoll and P. Yeoman, *Excavations within Edinburgh Castle in 1988–91* (Edinburgh, 1997), 226–9, 232.

Chapel, dating perhaps to the second quarter of the twelfth century, and popularly associated with the wife of Máel Coluim mac Donnchada (Malcolm III).[96] Though this amounts to little more than a legend ('the closing scenes of her life are strikingly associated with the Castle', wrote Daniel Wilson in the late nineteenth century), it has skewed interpretation of the site's archaeology.[97] Anderson was more circumspect:

> Fordun says (V, 21; cf. i, 422: Bower, V, 26, i, 274), professing to quote from Turgot, that queen Margaret died in Edinburgh Castle; and that the castle was besieged by Donald Bán with a large force before her body had been removed. She was carried out by a postern on the western side, under cover of a miraculous mist, and brought safely to Dunfermline. If this had been true, Turgot's Life would surely have mentioned it.[98]

Anderson was right, in fact: Turgot refers only to Margaret's 'oratory' (*oratorium*), and it is impossible to prove whether this was at Edinburgh.[99] Yet in their publication of the excavations at Edinburgh Castle, Steven Driscoll and Peter Yeoman take it for granted that the site was occupied by a royal castle during the reign of Máel Coluim, and that the kerbed path which leads from the west towards the summit of the rock was 'the route by which the body of the saintly Queen Margaret was secreted out of the Castle to be buried in her church at Dunfermline'.[100] Yet can we even be certain Edinburgh was a royal castle before the reign of David I?

The *Chronicle of Melrose* gives no further information on the location of Margaret's final days, although it does record the foundation of the

---

96 E. Fernie, 'Early Church Architecture in Scotland', *Proceedings of the Society of Antiquaries of Scotland* 116 (1986), 393–411, at 400–3. The type of chevron decoration on the chancel arch of St Margaret's was apparently first seen in Britain on the later parts of Durham Cathedral, built between 1093 and 1133. It is also featured on one of the doorways at nearby Holyrood Abbey, founded by David I in 1128.
97 D. Wilson, 'Notice of St Margaret's Chapel, Edinburgh Castle', *Proceedings of the Society of Antiquaries of Scotland* 21 (1887), 291–316, at 292–3.
98 *ES*, ii, 86, n. 1. See *Chron. Fordun*, i, 219.
99 *ES*, ii, 58–88, at 83; Turgot, *Vita S. Margaretae Scotorum Reginae*, ed. J. Hodgson-Hinde (Durham, 1868), 234–54, at 252 (xiii).
100 Driscoll and Yeoman, *Excavations within Edinburgh Castle in 1988–91*, 229. The authors admit, however, that the dating evidence for the kerbed path, which sealed an earlier midden, is 'scant'.

church at Holyrood in 1128, noting the latter's proximity to *Edeneburc*.[101] But then the *Chronicle of Melrose* was not redacted until the 1170s, by which time Edinburgh had become one of the most important Scottish burghs, and was indisputably a royal fortification. While Margaret's association with Castle Rock and the chapel there may have a basis in truth, one might argue that the story was not widely promulgated until the reign of David I, when there was concerted political focus on the lands to the south of the Forth, in Lothian and Teviotdale.

The greatly increased number of references to Edinburgh in the twelfth century is of course to some extent a reflection of the much greater volume of our surviving sources, but they may also supply some measure of this new focus to David's kingdom, and that of his successors. The kings of the Scots had every reason to make their hold on Lothian look as old, and preferably also as sanctified, as possible. Linking Margaret with Castle Rock, a place perhaps already famous for attracting saintly women, may have served an important political purpose for David and his family. Though this is more speculative, it may also have been around this time that the capture of *opidum Eden* was added to the *Chronicle of the Kings of Alba*. It is of course very possible that the latter addition was made during the eleventh century, but the point is that Edinburgh will have been very much more famous after the 1120s.

Conclusion

In conclusion, it must be admitted that there is very little historical or archaeological evidence for the importance of Edinburgh before the twelfth century (although we must allow for the very limited chances of survival for early medieval remains, given subsequent activity within the site's narrow confines). Where does this leave *Y Gododdin*? I would hesitate to suggest that *Eidyn* and its variants were actually drafted into the poetry at this late a date. But certainly the name might have acquired more contemporary significance in the twelfth century, particularly in the guise of *Din Eidyn* and so on. Perhaps that is why Clydno Eidyn is linked with the Forth in the Black Book of Chirk, and why, in *Bonedd y*

---

101 *ES*, ii, 171; *The Chronicle of Melrose from the Cottonian Manuscript, Faustina B. IX, in the British Museum*, ed. A. O. Anderson and M. O. Anderson (London, 1936), 32.

Saint, Kentigern's maternal lineage was linked with *Dinas Eidyn yn y gogledd*. While the twelfth-century 'northern' Kentigern documents, drawn up under the supervision of the Glasgow diocese, had associated the saint with Traprain Law and the Firth of Forth, this was replaced by *Dinas Eidyn* in the Welsh text perhaps because the latter had more contemporary connotations of high status. Edinburgh's new currency in Wales may have been reinforced by events such as those described in *Brut y Tywysogion* for the year 1114:

> *Yghyfrwg y petheu hyny y brenhin a anfodes trillu. Vn o gernyw a deheubarth a freig a saesson o dyued agilbert ap richard yn dywyssawc ar nadunt. A llu arall or gogled a phrydein a deu dywyssawc ar nadunt nyd amgen alexander ap moel kwlwm a mab hu yarll kaerllion. Ar trydyd llu gyd ac ef ehunan.*

> In the meantime the king [Henry I] got together three hosts: one from Cornwall and Deheubarth and French and Saxons from Dyfed, with Gilbert fitz Richard as their leader, and another host from the North and Scotland with two leaders over them, namely, Alexander son of Malcolm, and the son of Hugh, earl of Chester, and the third host along with him.[102]

Alexander I, David's older brother, had accompanied Henry I of England in an attack on Gruffudd ap Cynan of Gwynedd; like Clydno's retinue, the Scottish army had descended from *y gogledd*, 'the North', and must afterwards have returned to the Forth and Scotia beyond. But we are still no closer to seeing what *Eidyn* might have meant in Wales in previous centuries, or whether it was widely known that *Eidyn* meant Edinburgh, and that Edinburgh had been the Gododdin's royal stronghold. We might expect more to have been made of the latter, were it indeed the case. In the triads, as we have seen, and possibly even in *Y Gododdin* itself, *Eidyn* can function as a personal name and a geographical epithet just as frequently as it does a place-name. I will finish with some more speculative thoughts.

---

102 *Brut y Tywysogion MS. 20*, ed. T. Jones (Cardiff, 1941), 59; see also *Brut y Tywysogion, or the Chronicle of the Princes, Peniarth MS. 20 Version*, ed. T. Jones (Cardiff, 1952), 37.

The possibility remains, and no more, that *Eidyn* represents a North British place-name which is genuinely early, in the sense that it attests to a sixth- or seventh-century fortification on Castle Rock, all trace of which has otherwise been lost. Such was the site's obscurity in the intervening centuries that it is perhaps unlikely to have been placed so much in *Y Gododdin*'s foreground through antiquarian sensibility. That holds true perhaps until the twelfth century, when there may have been a certain obviousness to seeing the dramatic new seat of the Scottish kings as the most illustrious stronghold of the 'Old North'. But *Eidyn* was almost certainly present in Welsh literature before that point, as *Clinog Eitin*'s place in the Harleian genealogies shows. What it might have meant to an educated Welshman in the ninth or tenth centuries is difficult to establish, but perhaps we should allow for the possibility that *Eidyn*'s significance underwent a long spell of literary vagueness before being revived, along with its eponymous fortress, in the 1100s. Might this have been the period when *Y Gododdin* achieved new fame and relevance, as Owain Cyfeiliog's court poem *Hirlas Owain* seems to suggest?[103] Places in the 'Old North' were once again making the headlines, after all.

---

103 T. Gwynn Jones, 'Catraeth, and Hirlas Owain', *Y Cymmrodor* 32 (1922), 1–57; Isaac, '*Canu Aneirin* Awdl LI revisited', 144–53. The full text of *Hirlas Owain* is given in K. A. Bramley *et al.* (eds), *Gwaith Llywelyn Fardd I ac Eraill o Feirdd y Ddeuddegfed Ganrif*, Cyfres Beirdd y Tywysogion 2 (Cardiff, 1994), 226–37. The most recent editor, Gruffydd Aled Williams, also argues that Cynddelw had a significant role in the poem's composition (119–206). On links between *Hirlas Owain* and *Y Gododdin*, see also 206–9.

The only source to name the Cumbrian and English leaders at the battle of Carham is *Historia Regum*, a twelfth-century text within Corpus Christi College, Cambridge, MS 139. The notice of the battle is placed *sub anno* 1018. The entry for 1018 occurs on folio 94v, beginning from first rubricated 'A' on the left column. (Image reproduced by permission of The Parker Library, Corpus Christi College, Cambridge)

This is the *Historia Regum, sub anno* 1018, as it appears in folio 94v of Cambridge, Corpus Christi College, MS 139. The original entry in the *Chronicon ex Chronicis* attributed to John of Worcester contained information about a payment of Danegeld and about observance of the laws of King Edgar of England (r. 959–75). In *Historia Regum, sub anno* 1018, notices of the death of Bishop Ealdhun and the battle of Carham have been interpolated, interfering with the link between the Danegeld payment and the agreement of the Danish army to obey English law. (Image reproduced by permission of The Parker Library, Corpus Christi College, Cambridge)

St Cuthbert's church, Carham, looking north. The current structure is largely nineteenth century but maintains the site of an earlier building. (Photograph by David Petts)

Lidar image (1 m resolution) of Carham church (shown in black). The wedge-shaped current churchyard running south from the church clearly sits within a larger circular embanked enclosure, which is overlain by medieval ridge and furrow.

A view of Carham looking eastwards from the churchyard. This includes the area defined by the earthworks of the larger enclosure. (Photograph by David Petts)

A view from Carham church westwards towards Kelso. (Photograph by David Petts)

A view looking north-east from Hadden over Carham with Hirsel Law in the distance. (Photograph by David Petts)

Ambitious and well-modelled interlace on one of the Carham cross-fragments. (Carham 1B Picture Copyright G. Finch for the Corpus of Anglo-Saxon Stone Sculpture; Vol. I, County Durham and Northumberland, ill. 857)

Fragments of numerous crosses at Norham church were remodelled into a pillar in the nineteenth century. (Norham Pillar (East Face) Picture Copyright T. Middlemass for the Corpus of Anglo-Saxon Stone Sculpture; Vol. I, County Durham and Northumberland, ill. 1164)

The panel from Jedburgh has some of the most confident and charming inhabited vine scroll in the whole of Anglo-Saxon sculpture, though there is no early shrine recorded at the site. (Jedburgh Shrine Panel Picture Copyright T. Middlemass for the Corpus of Anglo-Saxon Stone Sculpture; Vol. I, County Durham and Northumberland, ill. 1429)

Lindisfarne 3 depicts Christ enthroned, surrounded by the four evangelists, two seated and two standing. (Lindisfarne 3A Picture Copyright T. Middlemass for the Corpus of Anglo-Saxon Stone Sculpture; Vol. I, County Durham and Northumberland, ill. 1051)

Lindisfarne 8 shows two men facing each other and grasping a post or cross. A parallel from Clonmacnoise suggests the scene may depict the foundation or refoundation of the church. (Lindisfarne 8A Picture Copyright T. Middlemass for the Corpus of Anglo-Saxon Stone Sculpture; Vol. I, County Durham and Northumberland, ill. 1061)

CHAPTER FOUR

Carham: The Western Perspective

FIONA EDMONDS

The battle of Carham is renowned as one of the defining events in the emergence of the Anglo-Scottish border. Yet the identities of the leaders involved in the battle reveal that Carham was no simple encounter between English and Scottish forces. Three leaders were present: Máel Coluim II, king of Scots, Uhtred, earl of Bamburgh and Owain, king of the Cumbrians. In this article, I focus attention on Owain's kingdom, the one remaining polity of the North Britons, which stretched from the Clyde Valley to the Lake District during its heyday. Shortly to be lost to history, the Cumbrian kingdom was still a going concern at the start of the eleventh century. Historians have traditionally viewed Cumbria as a sub-unit of the kingdom of the Scots, but its relative independence is stressed in recent scholarship. This raises questions about why a Cumbrian king fought at the battle at all, and why he made common cause with the king of Scots. I argue that the early eleventh century saw pressure on Cumbria from both the west and the east, with the result that the Cumbrians looked north for support.

The Cumbrian king and the battle

First it is necessary to tackle some difficulties surrounding the dating of the battle and the individuals who were present, including the identity of the Cumbrian king. These matters are discussed elsewhere in the volume,[1] but it is necessary to establish my position in order to contextualise the involvement of the Cumbrians in the conflict. Historians have differed on the date of the battle, placing it in either 1016 or 1018. Latin annals from northern England, preserved in later texts, place the battle in 1018; the texts include the extensive historical compendium *Historia Regum*. It

---

[1] See Neil McGuigan, 'The Battle of Carham: An Introduction', this volume, 1–32.

appears to have been drawing on earlier northern English material here, rather than the other main source, John of Worcester's chronicle.[2] In *Libellus de Exordio*, Symeon of Durham provided additional information about a comet that preceded the battle.[3] This detail correlates with astronomical events in August 1018, and indeed, the comet was reported in the contemporary 'Annals of Ulster' (then kept in Armagh).[4] I am therefore persuaded that the battle of Carham took place in September 1018.

A more difficult question is how this date may be reconciled with the purported involvement of Uhtred, the renowned warlord and earl of Bamburgh, given that he apparently died in 1016. This much has been gleaned from a strand of material that appears in three manuscripts of the 'Anglo-Saxon Chronicle' (C, D and E).[5] The relevant entries reveal that Uhtred supported the English king Æthelred and his son Edmund Ironside, prompting Cnut to take an army into Northumbria in 1016. Uhtred submitted but was slain nevertheless; some medieval writers identified the Yorkshire magnate Thurbrand as the culprit, linking this event to a famous northern English blood feud.[6] One way to reconcile this death date with Uhtred's alleged involvement in the battle is to

---

2   *HR*, 155–6. The northern English material also features in the *Chronicle of Melrose* and *Historia post Bedam*, which provide brief information about the battle; see below, 82. The textual history is discussed by David Woodman, 'Annals 848 to 1118 in the *Historia Regum*', this volume, 202–30, at 202, n.4.

3   *LDE*, iii.5, 154–7.

4   *AU* 1018.7, ed. Mac Airt and Mac Niocaill 454–5; Marjorie Ogilvie Anderson, 'Lothian and the Early Scottish Kings', *SHR* 39 (1960), 98–112, at 111 n. 2; Gary W. Kronk, *Cometography: Volume 1, Ancient–1799: A Catalog of Comets* (Cambridge, 1999), 168–9; Alex Woolf, *From Pictland to Alba, 789–1070* (Edinburgh, 2007), 236; Tim Clarkson, *Strathclyde and the Anglo-Saxons in the Viking Age* (Edinburgh, 2014), 135–6.

5   *The Anglo-Saxon Chronicle: A Collaborative Edition. Vol. 5: MS C*, ed. Katherine O'Brien O'Keeffe (Woodbridge, 2001), 101; *The Anglo-Saxon Chronicle: A Collaborative Edition. Vol. 6: MS D*, ed. G. P. Cubbin (Woodbridge, 1996), 61; *The Anglo-Saxon Chronicle: A Collaborative Edition. Vol. 7: MS E*, ed. Susan Irvine (Cambridge, 2004), 74. For the textual history of this strand, see Cecily Clark, 'The Narrative Mode of the *Anglo-Saxon Chronicle* before the Conquest', in Peter Clemoes and Kathleen Hughes (eds), *England before the Conquest: Studies in Primary Sources presented to Dorothy Whitelock* (Cambridge, 1971), 224–30, esp. 228; *ASC D*, ed. Cubbin, xxxix–xlx; Simon Keynes, 'Manuscripts of the *Anglo-Saxon Chronicle*', in Richard Gameson (ed.), *The Cambridge History of the Book in Britain* (Cambridge, 2011), 537–52, at 545.

6   *Chronicon ex Chronicis*, ii, 482–3. A more extensive account of the killing, and the story of the feud, appears in *De Obsessione Dunelmi*, for which see below n. 8. Cnut may have exploited local tensions to dispose of Uhtred, as suggested by Timothy Bolton, *The Empire of Cnut the Great: Conquest and the Consolidation of Power in Northern Europe in the Early Eleventh Century* (Leiden, 2009), 119–20.

assume that Uhtred was erroneously placed at the battle in the entry in *Historia regum*; indeed, Symeon did not include the earl in his account in *Libellus de Exordio*.[7] Another Durham text, *De obsessione Dunelmi*, blames Uhtred's successor, Eadwulf *Cudel*, for the loss of Lothian to the Scots.[8] The Northumbrian defeat at the battle of Carham might be explained as a consequence of Eadwulf's military weakness and the absence of the experienced Uhtred.[9] Eadwulf has even been seen as an active mover in events, contriving to hold the northern portion of Northumbria under the Scots and failing to oppose them at the battle.[10] An alternative interpretation is that Uhtred was killed in 1018, following his defeat at the battle of Carham.[11] Indeed, the line *and hine mon þeahhwæþere ofsloh* 'and nevertheless he was killed' in the various versions of the *Anglo-Saxon Chronicle* is rather vague about the timing of Uhtred's death. One scenario is that Thurbrand killed Uhtred during a moment of weakness following the defeat at the battle of Carham. On balance, then, I favour the view that Uhtred was present at the battle. The Scots and Cumbrians may have seized an opportunity to strike a blow against Uhtred, a formerly powerful foe weakened by his tussle with Cnut.

An even more significant problem for current purposes is the identity of the Cumbrian king who fought at the battle. The only account to divulge the name of the king is the entry that was incorporated in

---

7   *HR*, 155–6; *LDE*, iii.5, 154–7.
8   *DOD*, 218. Aspects of the content may date from the late eleventh century, as suggested by Bernard Meehan, 'The Siege of Durham, the Battle of Carham and the Cession of Lothian', *SHR* 55 (1976), 1–19, at 18. However, the tract relates to a land dispute that continued to be relevant in the early twelfth century, when the text is likely to have been completed: Christopher J. Morris, *Marriage and Murder in Eleventh-Century Northumbria: A Study of 'De obsessione Dunelmi'*, Borthwick Papers 82 (York, 1992), 9–10; David Rollason, 'Symeon of Durham's *Historia de regibus Anglorum et Dacorum* as a Product of Twelfth-Century Historical Workshops', in Martin Brett and David A. Woodman (eds), *The Long Twelfth-Century View of the Anglo-Saxon Past* (Farnham, 2015), 95–112, at 100.
9   As suggested, for example, by William E. Kapelle, *The Norman Conquest of the North: The Region and its Transformation, 1000–1135* (London, 1979), 21; Richard Fletcher, *Bloodfeud: Murder and Revenge in Anglo-Saxon England* (Oxford, 2003), 111; Clarkson, *Strathclyde*, 136–40.
10 Anderson, 'Lothian', 111.
11 A. A. M. Duncan, 'The Battle of Carham, 1018', *SHR* 55 (1979), 20–8; A. A. M. Duncan, *The Kingship of the Scots 842–1292: Succession and Independence* (Edinburgh, 2002), 28; Woolf, *From Pictland to Alba*, 236–8.

Historia regum. It states: *Ingens bellum apud Carrum gestum est inter Scottos et Anglos, inter Huctredum filium Waldef comitem Northanhymbrorum, et Malcolmum filium Cyneth regem Scottorum. Cum quo fuit in bello Eugenius Calvus rex Clutinensium*.[12] The information most likely derives from a northern English source, which also underpinned the entries on the battle in the *Chronicle of Melrose* and the Durham compilation *Historia post Bedam*. The latter was closely related to *Historia regum*.[13] All three describe the battle as *ingens bellum . . . inter Scottos et Anglos* but the latter two omit the information about the participants. Similarly, a mid-twelfth-century Scottish writer saw the battle as one of the highlights of the reign of Máel Coluim mac Cináeda but did not mention the other two leaders.[14] Yet it is hard to imagine why a twelfth-century writer would fabricate the information about the Cumbrian king, not least since it complicates the picture of the battle as an encounter between northern English forces and the Scots. The suggestion that the Cumbrian king played a supporting role seems consistent with the political circumstances of the time.[15]

Eugenius (Owain) is a plausible name for a Cumbrian king since it occurred repeatedly in the Cumbrian dynasty and amongst their forebears. An Owain appears in the pedigree of Rhun ab Arthgal of Dumbarton (d. 872), which is likely to have been incorporated into a genealogical collection in North Wales during the reign of Rhodri Mawr (d. 878). This collection was in turn included in the mid-tenth-century Harleian genealogies.[16] A King Owain took part in a great royal meeting

---

12 *HR*, 155–6: 'An enormous battle was fought between the Scots and the English at Carham, between Uhtred son of Waltheof, earl of the Northumbrians, and Máel Coluim son of Cináed, king of Scots. With him in the battle was Owain the Bald, king of the Clydefolk.'

13 *The Chronicle of Melrose from the Cottonian Manuscript, Faustina B.IX in the British Museum. A Complete and Full-size Facsimile in Collotype*, ed. A. O. Anderson and M. O. Anderson (London, 1936), 21. For the textual history of *Historia post Bedam*, see Rollason, 'Symeon of Durham's *Historia de regibus Anglorum et Dacorum*', 105–8. This *Historia* – including the notice of the battle of Carham – was incorporated into Roger of Howden's *Chronica* (see especially, *RHC*, i, 87).

14 As evidenced by a note in the king-list in the Poppleton manuscript, ed. M. O. Anderson, *Kings and Kingship in Early Scotland* (Edinburgh, 1973), 254; the date of the note is discussed in *Kings and Kingship*, 68–9.

15 See below, 90–4.

16 *Early Welsh Genealogical Tracts*, ed. P. C. Bartrum (Cardiff, 1966), 10, no. 5. This understanding of the textual history of the Harleian genealogies draws on Ben Guy,

on the River Eamont near Penrith in 927 in the company of Athelstan king of the English, Constantín king of Scots, Ealdred of Bamburgh and the leading Welsh king Hywel Dda. The 'northern recension' of the *Anglo-Saxon Chronicle* listed Owain's kingdom as Gwent, but historians tend to favour William of Malmesbury's description of Owain as *rex Cumbrorum* 'king of the Cumbrians'.[17] Twelfth-century authorship notwithstanding, William's identification makes much better sense in the geopolitical context.[18] Furthermore, there was a tendency at this point for Scottish and Cumbrian kings to work together in their dealings with the English king. In *Libellus de Exordio*, Symeon of Durham portrayed Athelstan as putting both Owain *rex Cumbrorum* and Constantín to flight in 934.[19] In 935, Athelstan's entourage included the *subreguli* Constantín and Owain, who witnessed a charter together at Cirencester, where they were accorded a higher position than the Welsh kings. Owain witnessed another charter later that year in a similarly prominent role.[20] There is, then, no doubt that there was an influential mid-tenth-century Cumbrian king named Owain, whose name echoed that of an antecedent in the kingdom of Dumbarton.[21]

The next member of the dynasty known to have been called Owain is the *Owinus filius Dunawal* whose killing is placed in 1015 in the 'Breviate chronicle', or B manuscript of *Annales Cambriae*.[22] The entry

'The Textual History of the Harleian Genealogies', *Welsh History Review* 28 (2016), 1–25.

[17] *ASC* D [926 = 927], ed. Cubbin, 41; *GRA*, i, 214–15. Thomas Charles-Edwards, *Wales and the Britons, 350–1064* (Oxford, 2012), 511–12, argues that both Owain of Gwent and Owain of Cumbria were present.

[18] Cf. Fiona Edmonds, 'The Emergence and Transformation of Medieval Cumbria', *SHR* 93 (2014), 195–216, at 202–4, where I suggest that the Cumbrians' support for the Hiberno-Scandinavian leader Guðrøðr antagonised Athelstan.

[19] *LDE*, ii.20, 136–41.

[20] Sawyer, nos 1792 and 435 (< http://www.esawyer.org.uk/>, accessed 11 Mar. 2018). For the status of the kings, see S. Keynes, 'Welsh Kings at Anglo-Saxon Royal Assemblies (928–55)', *Haskins Society Journal* 26 (2015), 69–122, at 92–3. Keynes argues that Owain is the *Eugenius* who witnessed a charter at Worthy (Hants) in 931 alongside several Welsh *subreguli*: 'Welsh Kings', 81.

[21] For further information about the mid-tenth-century Owain, see Alan Macquarrie, 'The Kings of Strathclyde, c. 400–1018', in Alexander Grant and K. J. Stringer (eds), *Medieval Scotland: Crown, Lordship and Community: Essays Presented to G. W. S. Barrow* (Edinburgh, 1993), 1–19, at 14–15; Clarkson, *Strathclyde*, 75–102.

[22] *Annales Cambriae*, ed. John Williams ab Ithel (London, 1860), 22; see now Henry Gough-Cooper, *Annales Cambriae*, http://croniclau.bangor.ac.uk [b1036.1] (Owain's death is placed in the year before Cnut's conquest of England, 1016).

also appears in Welsh chronicles that were based on a Latin chronicle similar to *Annales Cambriae*.[23] Thus it seems that Owain's death was recorded in the core material that underpins these texts, a Latin chronicle kept year by year at St Davids in south-west Wales.[24] Owain has been identified as a member of the Cumbrian dynasty on the basis that he was the son of Dyfnwal, who enjoyed a long reign over the kingdom until 975.[25] Yet the entry poses a problem because Owain's death is dated three years before the battle of Carham, and there is no hint in the surrounding entries that the Welsh chronicler's dating was three years off-target. Dauvit Broun's solution is that Owain the Bald was a nephew of the earlier Owain,[26] and I find this suggestion plausible given the popularity of the name Owain in the dynasty. Indeed, a northern English chronicler may have included the epithet *calvus* 'the bald' to distinguish the Owain who fought at Carham from a near-contemporary namesake. To sum up the discussion so far, I am persuaded that a Cumbrian king named Owain the Bald fought at the battle of Carham in 1018. He was supporting Máel Coluim, king of Scots, against Uhtred, earl of Bamburgh. The battle was a significant victory for the Scots and the Cumbrians.

The nature of the Cumbrian kingdom

The question remains why the Cumbrian king fought at the battle of Carham. From the late medieval period to the twentieth century, historians saw his participation as an inevitable consequence of Scottish

---

23 *Brut y Tywysogion or the Chronicle of the Princes. Peniarth MS 20 Version*, ed. and trans. Thomas Jones, 2 vols (Cardiff, 1952), i, 14; ii, 11; *Brut y Tywysogion or the Chronicle of the Princes. Red Book of Hergest Version*, ed. and trans. Thomas Jones (London, 1955), 20–1; *Brenhinedd y Saesson or the Kings of the Saxons*, ed. and trans. Thomas Jones (Cardiff, 1971), 52–3.

24 The textual relationships were first elucidated by J. E. Lloyd, 'The Welsh Chronicles', *Proceedings of the British Academy* 14 (1928), 369–91. For this strand of material, see Kathleen Hughes, 'The Welsh Latin Chronicles: *Annales Cambriae* and Related Texts', in *Celtic Britain in the Early Middle Ages*, ed. David Dumville (Woodbridge, 1980), 67–85, at 74–5.

25 For Dyfnwal's career, see Macquarrie, 'The Kings', 15–16; Clarkson, *Strathclyde*, 103–18.

26 Dauvit Broun, 'The Welsh Identity of the Kingdom of Strathclyde, *c.*900–*c.*1200', *IR* 55 (2004), 111–80, at 128, n. 66. Cf. Duncan, *Kingship of the Scots*, 29; Charles-Edwards, *Wales and the Britons*, 572.

domination. Yet recent scholarship has called into question the extent of Scottish influence in the Cumbrian kingdom, and refocused attention on Cumbria's operation as an independent unit. I would argue that the kingdom functioned autonomously until the early eleventh century, but that the circumstances of its expansion rendered its border zones especially vulnerable. This fragility was becoming increasingly apparent in the build-up to Carham.

First, I will briefly discuss the notion of the Scottish domination of Cumbria. The idea can be traced back to John of Fordun, who was writing in the later fourteenth century. Fordun stated that Constantín mac Áeda set Cumbria aside to be ruled by heirs to the Scottish kingship, a notion that has been accepted by historians down to the twentieth century.[27] Yet Dauvit Broun has undermined this portrayal by identifying Fordun's key source as a work of the mid-thirteenth-century writer Richard Vairement, who was influenced by the position of Gascony as an appanage.[28] Benjamin Hudson removed another plank in the argument for Cumbria's subordination by reinterpreting a supposed reference to the election of a member of the Scottish royal dynasty to the Cumbrian kingship. The reference appears in the complex text known as the *Chronicle of the Kings of Alba*, which incorporated a tenth-century king-list as well as later elements. Yet the reference is in fact to an Irish king and is irrelevant to Cumbrian rulership.[29] Even the longstanding impression of inextricable links between Strathclyde (Cumbria's forerunner) and the nascent Scottish kingdom in its early days has been reappraised.[30] It is true that the Scottish and Cumbrian kings might operate together, as already noted in relation to the years 934–5. Yet there was also strife, such as the killing of the Scottish king Cuilén and his brother, Eochaid, by Britons (presumably the Cumbrians)

---

27 *Chron. Fordun*, i, 163–4; ii, 155. Cf. D. P. Kirby, 'Strathclyde and Cumbria: A Survey of Historical Development to 1092', *TCWAAS*, 2nd ser. 62 (1962), 77–94, at 77, 85, 88–94.
28 Dauvit Broun, *Scottish Independence and the Idea of Britain: From the Picts to Alexander III* (Edinburgh, 2007), 215–68, esp. 259–60; cf. Broun, 'The Welsh Identity', 131 n. 84.
29 *CKA*, 150, 157.
30 For my views on this complex matter, see Fiona Edmonds, 'The Expansion of the Kingdom of Strathclyde', *Early Medieval Europe* 23 (2015), 43–66, at 60, where I am heavily influenced by T. O. Clancy, 'Scottish Saints and National Identities in the Early Middle Ages', in Alan Thacker and Richard Sharpe (eds), *Local Saints and Local Churches in the Early Medieval West* (Oxford, 2002), 397–421, at 416–20.

in 971.[31] In 945, the English king, Edmund, ravaged *Cumbra land* and granted it to Máel Coluim, king of Scots on condition that he would be an ally in military activities. Yet this grant only had a temporary effect, for a Cumbrian king appeared in his own right at Edgar's royal summit in Chester in 973.[32] Other parties may have briefly dominated the Cumbrians, such as the Scandinavian dynasty of Ívarr, but the effects were equally ephemeral.[33] Thus I see Cumbria as a unit that was still autonomous from, if closely linked with, the Scottish kingdom at the time of the battle of Carham.

This interpretation raises the question of how the Cumbrian kingdom emerged and operated. One long-held view, which I have recently defended, is that the kingdom of Strathclyde expanded southwards during the early tenth century. It was originally based on Dumbarton Rock, and shifted its focus to the Clyde Valley following the siege of the great citadel in 870. The implosion of the Northumbrian kingdom offered opportunities for gains of lands further south.[34] Charles Phythian-Adams has challenged this interpretation, arguing that there were two Brittonic kingdoms: Strathclyde to the north of the Solway Firth and Cumbria to its south.[35] Against this, however, the term Cumbria was applied to the area north of Solway in a diverse range of material including an eleventh-century Anglo-Saxon *mappa mundi*.[36] The term *Cymry* must

---

31   *CKA*, ed. Hudson, 151–2, 160.
32   The events of 945 appear in various version of the *Anglo-Saxon Chronicle*: *The Anglo-Saxon Chronicle: A Collaborative Edition. Vol. 3: MS A*, ed. Janet Bately (Cambridge, 1986), 74; *The Anglo-Saxon Chronicle: A Collaborative Edition. Vol. 4: MS B*, ed. Simon Taylor (Cambridge, 1983), 53; *ASC* C, ed. O'Keeffe, 80; *ASC* D, ed. Cubbin, 44; *ASC* E, ed. Irvine, 55. The late-tenth-century English writer Ælfric provided an early reference to the presence of the Cumbrians at the meeting in 973: 'Life of St Swithun', ed. Michael Lapidge, in Lapidge, *The Cult of St Swithun* (Oxford, 2003), 606–7. Other references are cited in Edmonds, 'The Expansion', 61 n. 94.
33   Edmonds, 'The Expansion', 61, discussing an idea put forward by D. N. Dumville, 'Old Dubliners and New Dubliners in Ireland and Britain: A Viking-Age Story', *Medieval Dublin* 6 (2004), 78–93, at 85–6. The relationship between Strathclyde and the dynasty of Ívarr is fully outlined in Clare Downham, *Viking Kings of Britain and Ireland: The Dynasty of Ívarr to AD 1014* (Edinburgh, 2007), 159–70.
34   See W. F. Skene, 'Notes on Cumbria', *apud Ninian and S. Kentigern*, 330–1, for an early depiction of the expanded kingdom. Cf. Edmonds, 'The Expansion', 44–6, 50–5.
35   Charles Phythian-Adams, *Land of the Cumbrians: A Study in British Provincial Origins, AD 400–1200* (Aldershot, 1996), 109–14; cf. Kirby, 'Strathclyde and Cumbria'.
36   P. A. Wilson also noted the use of Cumbrian terminology for the areas north and south of Solway: 'On the Use of the Terms "Strathclyde" and "Cumbria"', *TCWAAS*

have been in use amongst the inhabitants of Dumbarton/Strathclyde and their neighbours for centuries, for the term had been borrowed into English by the seventh century. Even so, poets and chroniclers in several languages developed a new enthusiasm for Cumbrian nomenclature (as opposed to the term 'Strathclyde') following the expansion of the kingdom beyond the Clyde Valley.[37] I have argued that the Cumbrian kings expanded their kingdom relatively rapidly by a piecemeal process of making deals with co-operative local nobility and expropriating land from less compliant parties. The units of regional governance remained in place during shifts in rule at the highest levels, hence the likely antiquity of some regional units within northern England and southern Scotland.[38] My proposed model for expansion helps to explain why the Brittonic speech of the Cumbrian kings thrived in some areas, whereas other inhabitants retained Northumbrian or Gaelic-Scandinavian culture.[39] The coastal areas around the Firth of Clyde and western Cumbria continued to be susceptible to influence from the Insular Scandinavian world, a connection that is evident in the sculpture at the political centre of Govan.[40] Alan James has argued that Cumbrian expansion was fuelled by economic as well as political factors, and indeed the foothills that

---

2nd ser. 66 (1966), 57–92. The term *Camri* appears to the north of Hadrian's Wall on the Cotton map; this has hitherto escaped attention in discussions of the Cumbrian kingdom. See British Library, Cotton Tiberius MS B.V, fol. 56v, viewed at http://www.bl.uk/onlinegallery/onlineex/unvbrit/a/001cottibb00005u00056v00.html (accessed 11 Mar. 2018). I am grateful to Bill Shannon for bringing this to my attention.

37 Edmonds, 'The Emergence', esp. 205–6. In his late-tenth-century Latin chronicle, Æthelweard selected the term *Cumbri* to replace the *Strecledwalas* of the Anglo-Saxon Chronicle: *Chronicon Æthelweardi: The Chronicle of Æthelweard*, ed. Alistair Campbell (London, 1962), 41. For the borrowing of the term into Northumbrian English, see Alex Woolf, 'Reporting Scotland in the Anglo-Saxon Chronicle', in Alice Jorgensen (ed.), *Reading the Anglo-Saxon Chronicle: Language, Literature, History* (Turnhout, 2010), 221–39, at 225, 230–2.

38 G. W. S. Barrow, 'The Pattern of Lordship and Feudal Settlement in Cumbria', *Journal of Medieval History* 1 (1975), 117–38.

39 Edmonds, 'The Expansion', 55–66.

40 S. T. Driscoll, *Govan from Cradle to Grave*, Govan Lecture (Glasgow, 2004), 8–13; B. E. Crawford, *The Govan Hogbacks and the Multi-Cultural Society of Tenth-Century Scotland*, Govan Lecture (Glasgow, 2005), 18–23; Courtney Helen Buchanan, 'Scandinavians in Strathclyde: Multiculturalism, Material Culture and Manufactured Identities in the Viking Age', in Anna Ritchie (ed.), *Historic Bute: Land and People* (Edinburgh, 2012), 17–32.

ringed the Solway Firth and the Clyde Valley were well suited to the development of intensive cattle agriculture.[41]

In developing this argument I focused on Cumbrian expansion southwards and around the coast. It is worth considering whether the same process had ramifications further east, in order to elucidate the geopolitical context of the battle of Carham. At the southern edge of the Clyde Valley, the watershed around Beattock Summit not only offers access to the Solway Firth, but also a route into Tweeddale. While there are no certain Roman roads going this way, the route offered connections between several major roads of Roman origin.[42] A Roman road certainly headed north-east from the Solway via Eskdale to the fort at Raeburnfoot, and probably into Teviotdale.[43] Cumbrian lords may have spotted opportunities in this area following the retraction of Northumbrian rule during the turbulence of the Viking Age. By the tenth century, the core of the Northumbrian polity lay far south in York, while the house of Bamburgh had significant assets around the Tyne and the lower reaches of the Tweed. Indeed, at the time of the Northumbrian expansion in the seventh century, the lower and upper areas of the Tweed Valley had developed different cultural characteristics; Brittonic speech and institutions apparently survived for longer in the more westerly areas.[44] It may be that this distinction persisted under the veneer of Northumbrian rule, predisposing the upper part of the valley to Cumbrian influence. It is worth noting the proximity of the kingdom of Dumbarton, which continued to exercise pressure on the area after Northumbrian expansion.[45]

A considerable number of Brittonic place-names have been traced in Tweeddale; the question is whether they are relics of pre-Northumbrian times or whether they reflect the arrival of new Cumbrian lords.[46] Some

---

41 'A Cumbric Diaspora?', in O. J. Padel and D. N. Parsons (eds), *A Commodity of Good Names: Essays in Honour of Margaret Gelling* (Donington, 2008), 188–203.
42 For Roman influence in Tweeddale, see Allan Wilson, 'Roman Penetration in Eastern Dumfriesshire and Beyond', *TDGAS* 73 (1999), 17–62, at 54–5.
43 Ivan D. Margary, *Roman Roads in Britain*, 3rd edn (London, 1973), 461–2.
44 Ian M. Smith, 'Brito-Roman and Anglo-Saxon: The Unification of the Borders', in Peter Clack and Jill Ivy (eds), *The Borders* (Durham, 1983), 9–48, at 31–5; W. Elliot, 'Prehistoric, Roman and Dark Age Selkirkshire', in J. M. Gilbert (ed.), *Flower of the Forest. Selkirk: A New History* (Selkirk, 1985), 9–18.
45 Clare Stancliffe, *Bede and the Britons*, Whithorn Lecture 14 (Stranraer, 2007), 28–30.
46 Bethany Fox, 'The P-Celtic Place-Names of North-East England and South-East Scotland', *The Heroic Age* 10 (2007), http://www.heroicage.org/issues/10/fox.html

Brittonic place-names in this area demonstrably pre-date the Viking Age, the name of the major church at Melrose being a renowned example.[47] The place-name *Penteiacob*, the future Eddleston (Peeblesshire), has been noted for the pristine survival of its Brittonic elements (**pentai Jacob* 'Jacob's outhouses').[48] This appearance may reflect long-term endurance of Brittonic speech in an area of little English influence. On the other hand, nearby Cardrona contains the element **cair* (with a debatable second element); **cair* names are thought to have proliferated from the tenth century onwards.[49] Traquair (*Treferquyrd* 1113x1124) features the element **trev*, which experienced a similar surge of popularity at this time, as well as the definite article and the name of the Quair Water.[50] Other aspects of Brittonic culture remained vibrant in Tweeddale. The northern British tale known as 'Lailoken B', which concerns the wildman Lailoken, features an episode set in Drumelzier (Peeblesshire). The tale is found in a fifteenth-century manuscript but was already extant in the twelfth century, when it influenced Geoffrey of

---

(consulted 11 Mar. 2018); and Stancliffe, *Bede and the Britons*, 26–7, 33–5 both explore the names from the perspective of the Northumbrian era. For the likelihood of later Brittonic influence in Tweeddale and West Lothian, see Davyth A. Hicks, 'Language, History and Onomastics in Medieval Cumbria: An Analysis of the Generative Usage of the Cumbric Habitative Generics *cair* and *tref*', unpublished PhD thesis (Edinburgh University, 2003), 24, 41–2, 60, 314.

47 This place-name appears in early eighth-century texts such as Bede's *Historia ecclesiastica gentis Anglorum*, III.26, ed. Bertram Colgrave and R. A. B. Mynors (Oxford, 1969), 308–11. The Brittonic etymology of *mel* 'bald hill' and *rōs* 'high ground' (with possible Gaelic influence) is discussed in Alan James, 'Brittonic Language in the Old North', 3 vols, ii, 273: http://spns.org.uk/resources/bliton (accessed 11 Mar. 2018).

48 *CPNS*, 135, 354; Alan James, 'Dating Brittonic Place-Names in Southern Scotland and Cumbria', *JSNS* 5 (2011), 57–114, at 76. The name could have been lost but it was preserved shortly before it changed in the late twelfth century: Fiona Edmonds and Simon Taylor, 'Languages and Names', in Keith J. Stringer and Angus J. L. Winchester, *Northern England and Southern Scotland in the Central Middle Ages* (Woodbridge, 2017), 137–72, at 150–1.

49 Different interpretations of the second element appear in *CPNS*, 369; Fox, 'The P-Celtic Place-Names'; Hicks, 'Language, History', 146, 150; James, 'Brittonic Language', ii, 66, 368. For the dating of *cair*- names, see Kenneth H. Jackson, 'Angles and Britons in Northumbria and Cumbria', in H. Lewis (ed.), *Angles and Britons: O'Donnell Lectures* (Cardiff, 1963), 60–84, at 80–1; Hicks, 'Language, History', 85–6, 105–12; James, 'Dating', 79–80.

50 For Traquair, see *CPNS*, 360; Hicks, 'Language, History', 290–1; James, 'Brittonic Language', 366. For the dating of *trev*- names, see Hicks, 'Language, History', 220–315; Alan G. James, 'Cumbric *trev* in Kyle, Carrick, Galloway and Dumfriesshire', *TDGAS*, 3rd ser., 88 (2014), 21–42.

Monmouth's *Vita Merlini*.[51] A further indication that this area fell under the Cumbrian sphere of influence is the inquest that the future David I (d. 1153) conducted into the estates of the church of Glasgow in his capacity as *Cumbrensis regionis princeps*. The estates included several in Tweeddale in addition to Clydesdale, Annandale and Teviotdale.[52]

So far I have argued that the Cumbrian kings extended their area of rule eastwards in the same way that they expanded southwards towards the Lake District. The eastward expansion of Cumbria has been relatively neglected by historians, but it may not have been insignificant. Indeed, as Neil McGuigan has pointed out, the kingdom may even have extended towards the Firth of Forth; certainly it was portrayed in that way in the twelfth century.[53] Just as Cumbrian southward expansion ceased in the wooded border zone around Inglewood Forest, so too the wilderness of Ettrick Forest may have become a frontier between Cumbrian and Northumbrian spheres of influence. It is in this border area that the Cumbrian king is likely to have mustered his forces and met the Scottish king for the approach to Carham.[54]

Western and eastern pressures

Finally, I ask why Owain the Bald decided to support the king of Scots in the battle of Carham. It is tempting to see the eleventh century as the era when the Cumbrian and Northumbrian kingdoms were definitively squeezed out of existence from the north and the south. Yet Carham was not an archetypal Anglo-Scottish border battle. Instead, I see the main pressures as being exerted from the east and the west, prompting an alliance between the Scots and the Cumbrians.

Turning first to the east, Earl Uhtred may well have seemed a significant threat to both of his neighbours. Uhtred's main powerbase lay north of the Tyne, but he had gained control of the Scandinavian-dominated earldom of York, partly on account of his loyalty to Æthelred.[55] According to *De*

---

51 Winifred and John MacQueen, 'Vita Merlini Silvestris', *Scottish Studies* 29 (1989), 77–93, at 77–82; Geoffrey of Monmouth, *Vita Merlini*, ed. and trans. Basil Clarke, *Life of Merlin* (Cardiff, 1973), 64–73.
52 *Glas. Reg.*, i, 4–5; *David I Chrs*, 60–1.
53 'Neither Scotland nor England: Middle Britain, *c*.850–1150', unpublished PhD thesis (University of St Andrews, 2015), 154, 232.
54 Woolf, *From Pictland to Alba*, 238–9.
55 Dorothy Whitelock, 'The Dealings of the Kings of England with Northumbria in the

obsessione Dunelmi, Uhtred attained this position after spectacularly beating off a Scottish raid on Durham *c*. 1006.[56] There has been debate about whether, or when, the raid took place; *De obsessione* is far from a contemporary witness.[57] Nevertheless, it is plausible that Uhtred and the Scottish king came to blows, not least if the Scots had established a foothold south of the Firth of Forth near to Dere Street. This is one possible reading of the tradition that Edinburgh had been vacated and left (*relictus*) to the Scots during the reign of Ildulb (d. 962).[58] On the other hand, there are indications that part of the area south of the Forth remained under the control of the Cuthbertine church as late as the 1020s.[59] Thus there was scope for frequent conflict over the area between Lammermuir and the Forth.

Uhtred's assumption of the earldom of York gave him access to westerly routes leading towards the Cumbrian kingdom. Raiding parties headed in this direction, as seen in the ravaging of Westmorland by Thored, son of Gunnar (an ealdorman) in 966.[60] Uhtred had more concrete ambitions in the west, to judge by the bestowal of the name Gospatric on one of his sons. Gospatric is a Brittonic name that honours St Patrick, whose cult flourished in the Cumbrian kingdom. The name may have come into the house of Bamburgh through familial links, or it may be an instance of 'predatory naming'; if so, Uhtred was envisaging a role for Gospatric in newly acquired western territory.[61] This scenario

Tenth and Eleventh Centuries', in Peter Clemoes (ed.), *The Anglo-Saxons: Studies in Some Aspects of their History and Culture Presented to Bruce Dickins* (London, 1959), 70–88, at 77–84; Kapelle, *The Norman Conquest*, 32; George Molyneaux, *The Formation of the English Kingdom in the Tenth Century* (Oxford, 2015), 3.

56 *DOD*, 217–18.
57 Most notably, Bernard Meehan argued that the raid had been confused with a later raid in the 1040s ('The siege of Durham').
58 *CKA*, 151, 159; for extensive discussion, see Anderson, 'Lothian'. As McGuigan points out, there is no concrete evidence that the tradition originated before the twelfth century: 'Neither Scotland nor England', 148–9, and 153 for Dere Street.
59 Woolf, *From Pictland to Alba*, 234–6.
60 *ASC* D, ed. Cubbin, 46; *ASC* E, ed. Irvine, 58; cf. Molyneaux, *The Formation*, 178.
61 Fiona Edmonds, 'Personal Names and the Cult of Patrick in Eleventh-Century Strathclyde and Northumbria', in Steve Boardman *et al.* (eds), *Saints' Cults in the Celtic World* (Woodbridge, 2009), 42–65. Cf. T. O. Clancy, 'The Cults of Saints Patrick and Palladius in Early Medieval Scotland', in Boardman *et al.* (eds), *Saints' Cults*, 18–41; Clancy, 'The Big Man, the Footsteps and the Fissile Saint: Paradigms and Problems in Studies of Insular Saints' Cults', in Steve Boardman and Eila Williamson (eds), *The Cult of Saints and the Virgin Mary in Medieval Scotland* (Woodbridge, 2010), 1–20, at 15. For the naming strategy, see David E. Thornton, 'Predatory Nomenclature and

may be borne out by 'Gospatric's writ', if Gospatric son of Uhtred was the man responsible for the text (the other candidate is his nephew, Gospatric son of Maldred). Gospatric's writ reveals the extent of Northumbrian influence *on eallun þam landann þeo weoron Combres*, 'in all the lands that were Cumbrian', by the mid-eleventh century, notably in Allerdale (Cumberland).[62] Further indications of a Northumbrian push to the west are found in *Norðleoda laga*, a text associated with the circle of Archbishop Wulfstan II (d. 1023). The text contains provisions for Britons; there is a resemblance to much earlier laws of Ine of Wessex, but the decision to include them indicates that Northumbrian dominance of Brittonic territory was a pressing contemporary matter.[63] The use of the term *Clutinenses*, 'Clydefolk', in the northern source for the battle of Carham may also indicate that the Cumbrian kingdom was contracting to its Strathclyde core.[64]

The push to the west may have been carried out relatively independently of Æthelred, albeit with his tacit approval given that he campaigned against the Cumbrian kingdom and the Isle of Man in 1000.[65] Yet Uhtred's fortunes took a turn for the worse when he fell foul of Cnut; the Yorkshire earldom fell out of the grasp of the house of Bamburgh and went to Earl Eric instead.[66] The Durham writers obfuscate this fact by focusing on Eadwulf *Cudel*, the successor north of the Tyne.[67] It is possible that Uhtred's power base was constrained during the period 1016–18, a situation exploited by the Cumbrians and the Scots at the battle of Carham.[68]

Dynastic Expansion in Early Medieval Wales', *Medieval Prosopography* 20 (1999), 1–22.

62 The most recent edition and translation is David Woodman, *Northern Chrs*, 370–1. For the debate about Gospatric's identity, see Phythian-Adams, *Cumbrians*, 174–81.

63 *Norðleoda Laga*, in *Gesetze*, i, 458–61, at 460–1. For Wulfstan's role, see Patrick Wormald, *The Making of English Law: King Alfred to the Twelfth Century* (Oxford, 1999), i, 391–4.

64 See above, n. 12.

65 For the English kings' relatively loose control of the Bamburgh earls, see David Rollason, *Northumbria, 500–1100: Creation and Destruction of a Kingdom* (Cambridge, 2003), 267–70; and N. McGuigan, 'Bamburgh and the Northerrn English Realm', this volume, 95–150, at 121–9. For the campaign of 1000, see n. 69, below.

66 The traditional view is that Eric gained the Yorkshire earldom in 1016, but the key piece of evidence need not necessarily be read this way; see McGuigan, 'The Battle of Carham: An Introduction', this volume, 10–16.

67 See references in ns 5 and 8 above; Dorothy Whitelock, 'The Dealings', 82–3; Molyneaux, *The Formation*, 3.

68 Duncan, 'The Battle'.

Finally, there was mounting pressure from the opposite direction, the seaboard of the Cumbrian kingdom. The Cumbrians enjoyed a cordial relationship with the Islesmen, to judge by the sculptural influences around the Solway Firth and the Firth of Clyde. An accord, perhaps even a marriage alliance, between these parties would explain Æthelred's two-pronged raid on *Cumberland* and the Isle of Man in 1000.[69] Yet there were new, unpredictable players in the Irish Sea region, notably the leading Irish king Brían Bórama and his descendants. Brían's involvement in Dublin led naturally to an interest in the Isles, for the Dubliners had long enjoyed intermittent influence in the Hebrides and Man.[70] Brían's ambitions are to some extent reflected in the extensive account of the battle of Clontarf in *Cogad Gáedel re Gallaib*, although its author viewed events through the lens of Brían's great-grandson, Muirchertach.[71] A notable episode features Brían levying a tribute from the Saxons and the Britons, Argyll and the Lennox. These areas lay on Britain's west coast, and they may have been prey for Brían once he began to show an interest in the Isles. The Lennox had once been a core part of the kingdom of Dumbarton, and it was vulnerable to incursions from the Firth of Clyde.[72] Meanwhile, another political grouping was emerging even closer to home, on the southern edge of the former Dál Riatan territory in Argyll. These people became known as *Gall-Goídil*, 'Foreigner Gaelic speakers', presumably to distinguish them from the *Gaill*, 'Foreigners' on *Innse Gall*, the Hebrides.[73] Their first known king was Suibne mac Cináeda, who died in 1034.[74] Thomas Clancy has

---

69   ASC C, ed. O'Keeffe, 88; ASC D, ed. Cubbin, 50; ASC E, ed. Irvine, 63. For the idea of a marriage alliance, see Downham, *Viking Kings*, 167–70.
70   Colmán Etchingham, 'North Wales, Ireland and the Isles: The Insular Viking Zone', *Peritia* 15 (2001), 145–87, at 180.
71   For the date of composition, see Máire Ní Mhaonaigh, 'The Date of *Cogad Gáedel re Gallaib*', *Peritia* 9 (1995), 354–77.
72   *Cogadh*, c.78, 136–7; Seán Duffy, *Brian Boru and the Battle of Clontarf* (Dublin, 2013), 148–9; Patrick Wadden, 'Dál Riata *c.* 1000: Genealogies and Irish Sea Politics', *SHR* 95 (2016), 164–81, at 175; Clare Downham, 'Scottish Affairs and the Political Context of *Cogadh Gaedhel re Gallaibh*', in Christian Cooijmans (ed.), *Traversing the Inner Seas: Contacts and Continuity in and around Scotland, the Hebrides and the North of Ireland* (Edinburgh, 2017), 86–106, at 93–4.
73   For cultural boundaries, see Clare Downham, 'The Break-Up of Dál Riata and the Rise of Gall-Goídil', in Howard B. Clarke and Ruth Johnson (eds), *The Vikings in Ireland and Beyond: Before and After the Battle of Clontarf* (Dublin, 2015), 189–205, at 192–3.
74   *AU* 1034.10, ed. and trans. Mac Airt and Mac Niocaill, 472–3; *AT* 1034.3, ed. and trans. Stokes, ii, 266.

argued that the Gall-Goídil were first based on the Firth of Clyde before expanding southwards into what is now Galloway in the eleventh century.[75] These expansionist aims threatened the Cumbrian kingdom, and indeed by 1030 the Britons (that is, most likely, the Cumbrians) were being ravaged both from across the sea and from the east.[76] Any respite provided by the battle of Carham did not last.

In conclusion, I have explored the presence of Owain the Bald, king of the Cumbrians, at the battle of Carham in 1018. I have set Owain's role in the context of current scholarly approaches to the Cumbrian kingdom. Owain and his antecedents were relatively autonomous, notwithstanding their tendency to work with the king of Scots. Their kingdom had expanded relatively rapidly, and its peripheral areas were settled by a combination of Brittonic-speaking lords and those who might develop allegiances to other groups. These circumstances rendered the edges of the kingdom vulnerable, and by the early eleventh century the Northumbrians were starting to encroach on eastern areas. Several new political groupings were emerging who were capable of threatening Cumbria's western seaboard. Owain's response was to support the king of Scots in his fight against Earl Uhtred at the battle of Carham.

---

[75] The crucial piece of evidence is a reference to St Bláán's feast day in a possibly tenth-century addition to *The Martyrology of Tallaght*. It locates Kingarth (Bute) in the territory of Gall-Goídil: *The Martyrology of Tallaght*, ed. R. I. Best and Hugh Jackson Lawlor (London, 1931), 10 August, 62; Thomas Owen Clancy, 'The Gall-Ghàidheil and Galloway', *JSNS* 2 (2008), 19–50. Downham, 'The Break-Up', 204, places the expansion of Gall-Goídil earlier than Clancy. I think there were two waves of Gaelic-Scandinavian influence in the Solway: a tenth-century, Norse-speaking wave, and eleventh-century Gaelic-speakers (here drawing on David Parsons, 'On the Origin of "Hiberno-Norse Inversion Compounds"', *JSNS* 5 (2011), 115–52).

[76] *AT* [1030], ed. and trans. Stokes, ii, 262. Broun, 'The Welsh Identity', 136–7 suggests that this entry refers to a carve-up of the kingdom between Northumbrians and Gall-Goídil, the latter operating under the aegis of the Dubliners.

CHAPTER FIVE

Bamburgh and the Northern English Realm: Understanding the Dominion of Uhtred

NEIL MCGUIGAN

In the early eleventh century speakers of English dominated Britain between the Firth of Forth, the Severn and the English Channel. Although the majority were governed by the 'West Saxon' kings of England, the land between the Tyne and the Forth was ruled by the Eadwulfings, the lords of Bamburgh. The *Angli* who fought Máel Coluim at Carham were followers of the latter. Contemporaries also called them the 'Northern English' or 'North English'. History, language and identity made this people both 'Northumbrian' and 'English' – though modern geography would make them half 'Scottish'. To the modern historian, they remain one of the most poorly understood major political groups in Viking-Age Britain. In the last few decades, an upsurge in interest regarding the Cumbrians of Strathclyde and the Scandinavians of southern and western Northumbria has significantly improved our understanding of 'Middle Britain', the large multi-cultural middle zone that in the Viking Age lay between the new kingdoms of Scotland and England; but the Northern English polity centred on Bamburgh has remained relatively neglected.[1] Today, the Bamburgh

---

1   For Strathclyde, see B. T. Hudson 'Elech and the Scots in Strathclyde', *Scottish Gaelic Studies* 15 (1988), 145–9; A. MacQuarrie, 'The Kings of Strathclyde, *c.* 400–1018', in A. Grant and K. J. Stringer. (eds), *Medieval Scotland: Crown, Lordship and Community: Essays Presented to G. W. S. Barrow* (Edinburgh, 1998), 1–19; D. Broun, 'The Welsh Identity of the Kingdom of Strathclyde *c.* 900–*c.* 1200', *IR* 55 (2004), 111–80; C. Phythian-Adams, *Land of the Cumbrians: A Study in British Provincial Origins, AD 400–1120* (Aldershot, 2006); and most recently T. Clarkson, *Strathclyde and the Anglo-Saxons in the Viking Age* (Edinburgh, 2014); F. Edmonds, 'The Emergence and Transformation of Medieval Cumbria', *SHR* 93 (2014), 195–216 and 'The Expansion of the Kingdom of Strathclyde', *Early Medieval Europe* 23 (2015), 43–66. For the Norse of the southern Northumbria/Danelaw, where the upsurge has been even more intense, it is impossible to summarise fairly in a note. For important general works, see A. P. Smyth, *Scandinavian York and Dublin: The History and Archaeology of Two Related Viking Kingdoms*, 2 vols (Dublin, 1979); P. Sawyer, *Anglo-Saxon Lincolnshire*

polity has found itself at the margins of Scottish, English and even Northumbrian history.[2] This contribution is aimed at redressing the balance somewhat and, hopefully as a result, better understanding of the politics surrounding the battle of Carham.

Political Status: From Kings to Earls

In the 860s and 870s the Scandinavian 'Great Army' brought disaster to three of the major Anglo-Saxon polities of Britain: Northumbria, Mercia and East Anglia. Their territories were subjected to large-scale settlement, which transformed most of central and northern England into the Scandinavian settlement-zone we have come to call 'the Danelaw'. The development, however, facilitated the expansion of the other great Anglo-Saxon kingdom, Wessex, which would lead in turn to the realisation of a unitary realm of England. Until it was subdued by these rising West Saxons in the course of the tenth century, the Danelaw hosted multiple independent or semi-independent potentates and political communities. Among them was a particularly powerful succession of kings who counted York and Lincoln, along with Dublin and much of the Irish Sea region, among their possessions (see below). Nonetheless, native English kingship outside Wessex survived the initial onslaught, at least for a short time. Even in the relatively small kingdom of East

---

(Lincoln, 1998); D. M Hadley, *The Northern Danelaw: Its Social Structure, c. 800–1100* (London, 2000); C. Etchingham, 'North Wales, Ireland and the Isles: The Insular Viking Zone', *Peritia: Journal of the Medieval Academy of Ireland* 15 (2001), 145–87; B. Hudson, *Viking Pirates and Christian Princes: Dynasty, Religion and Empire in the North Atlantic* (Oxford, 2005); D. M. Hadley, *The Vikings in England: Settlement and Culture* (Manchester, 2006); C. Downham, *Viking Kings of Britain and Ireland: The Dynasty of Ívarr to AD 1014* (Edinburgh, 2007); D. Griffiths, *Vikings of the Irish Sea* (Stroud, 2010); M. Townend, *Viking Age Yorkshire* (Pickering, 2014).

2 For instance, in D. Rollason's very good *Northumbria, 500–1100: Creation and Destruction of a Kingdom* (Cambridge, 2003), the book's forty-four-page chapter on the Viking Age gives them only a paragraph, at p. 249. The fullest treatments on our topic are D. Whitelock,'The Dealings of the Kings of England with Northumbria', in P. Clemoes (ed.), *The Anglo-Saxons: Studies in Some Aspects of their History and Culture Presented to Bruce Dickins* (London, 1959), 70–88; W. E. Kapelle, *The Norman Conquest of the North: The Region and its Transformation, 1000–1135* (London, 1979); R. Fletcher, *Bloodfeud: Murder and Revenge in Anglo-Saxon England* (London, 2002). However, there are many important observations in the works cited above, and in A. Woolf, *From Pictland to Alba, 789–1070*, The New Edinburgh History of Scotland 2 (Edinburgh, 2007). See also N. McGuigan, 'Ælla and the Descendants of Ivar', *NH* 52 (2015), 20–34.

Anglia, at least two native monarchs succeeded to the kingship after the martyring of St Edmund in 869. We are not able to date the end of their reigns, but kings named Oswald and Æthelred are known from numismatic evidence.[3] A rump of Mercia endured beyond the settlement of the 870s, surviving as a semi-independent monarchy based in western regions until 918.[4] In Northumbria, native kings persisted even longer.

Post-1100 chronicle material that seems to incorporate some reliable information from the Viking Age tells us about native Northumbrian kings right up to a certain Ecgberht II, a monarch who reigned for an indefinite period *after* the settlement of 876.[5] Another potential king, Osberht, is said to have been expelled from the *regnum* in 901. This notice occurs among a series of annals covering 888 to 957 reproduced in Corpus Christi College Cambridge, MS 139, a section of *Historia Regum* – what I have called the *Chronicle of 957*.[6] The eleventh-century *Historia de Sancto Cuthberto* refers to a certain *princeps* named Eardwulf, whose lifetime is said to have coincided with the reign of Edward the Elder (899–924).[7] The precise status and details of Osberht and Eardwulf remain obscure, but the names and death years of two kings are supplied by tenth-century Irish annals. The *Annals of Ulster*, s.a. 913, commemorate a certain 'Eadwulf King of the Northern English' (*Etulbb ri Saxan Tuaiscirt*).[8] The obit of one of his sons is

---

3 M. Blackburn, 'Expansion and Control: Aspects of Anglo-Scandinavian Minting South of the Humber', in J. Graham-Campbell, R. Hall, J. Jesch and D. Parsons (eds), *Vikings and the Danelaw: Select Papers from the Proceedings of the Thirteenth Viking Congress, Nottingham and York, 21–30 August 1997* (Oxford, 2001), 125–42, at 127.

4 On the last, see M. Bailey, 'Ælfwynn, Second Lady of the Mercians', in N. J. Higham and D. H. Hill (eds), *Edward the Elder, 899–924* (London, 2001), 112–27; and on the second last, see F. W. Wainwright, 'Æthelflæd, Lady of the Mercians', in Clemoes (ed.), *The Anglo-Saxons*, 53–69. For Mercia and Wessex in the time of Alfred 'the Great', see S. Keynes, 'King Alfred and the Mercians', in M. A. S. Blackburn and D. N. Dumville (eds), *Kings, Currency and Alliances: History and Coinage of Southern England in the Ninth Century* (Woodbridge, 1998), 1–46; for the time of Edward the Elder, see S. Keynes, 'Edward, King of the Anglo-Saxons', in Higham and Hill, *Edward the Elder*, 40–66. See also below, 99.

5 *DPSA*, 377; *Series Regum Northymbrensium*, in *Sym. Op.*, ii, 389–93, at 391; *RW*, 347–8.

6 Cambridge, Corpus Christi College, MS 139, fol. 75r; for the printed edition, see *Chronicle of 957*, s.a. 901, ed. Arnold, *Sym. Op.*, ii, 91–5, at 92.

7 *HSC*, c.24, 62–3.

8 *AU* 913.1; see also *FAI* no. 456 s.a. 912 [913], with *Etalbh, rí Saxan tuaisgirt*.

recorded in the *Annals of Clonmacnoise*, an early seventeenth-century English translation of a pre-existing set of Irish annals. Among events relating to 934, the death of one *Adulf mcEtulfe, King of the North Saxons* is noted.⁹ The descendants of Eadwulf who died in 913, the Eadwulfings, would dominate the Bamburgh polity until the mid-eleventh century (see Appendix). *Adulf mcEtulfe* is the last to be styled king and named directly in surviving sources, but it has to be stressed that coverage of Northumbrian rulers seems to be sporadic. Historians cannot treat the existing evidence base for this topic as exhaustive. The notices we have barely survive at all, and it is possible there were several more kings after *Adulf mcEtulfe*. Prior to Eadwulf of 913, the last Northumbrian ruler to be commemorated in the Irish annals was Ælla, the 'King of the Northern English' (*Alli, rex Saxan Aquilonalium*) who died at York in 867.¹⁰

The kings of the Northern English reigned in the shadow of the Scandinavian settlement-zone and its rulers. Men of royal status were ruling there from the 890s at the latest, although the Great Army may have contained multiple kings at various times. Around 918 southern Northumbria and other parts of the northern Danelaw came under control of a Hiberno-Norse leader named Rögnvald. Rögnvald's wider kingroup is known to modern historians by the Irish name *Uí Ímair* (pronounced, very roughly, wī īvar or ī īvar), the 'grandsons' or 'descendants of Ivar' (one of the leaders of the Great Army). The Uí Ímair exercised power over many of the islands to the west of Britain and over much of the Irish Sea, including Dublin, the region's emerging trading hub. Rögnvald defeated an army of Scots and Eadwulfing-aligned Northumbrian natives at the battle of Corbridge in 918. Rögnvald managed to gain control of York, but died three years after Corbridge. Rögnvald's brother Sigtrygg, known to the Irish as *Sitric Cáech*, 'Sigtrygg the One-Eyed', succeeded Rögnvald in 921.¹¹ The vastness of Northumbria doubtlessly contributed much of the manpower of the Uí

---

9   *AClon* 928 [934], ed. D. Murphy (London, 1896), 149. The *Annals of Clonmacnoise* exist only in an English translation prepared by Conell Mageoghagan around 1627. The text is related closely to the *Annals of Tigernach* (*AT*), which survive in the original language; *AT* may have provided this entry in the original Irish if its coverage of the era had not been lost.

10 *AU* 867.7.

11 For the dynasty and their deeds in this era, see again Downham, *Viking Kings of Britain and Ireland*.

Ímair; and it is possible some of the Uí Ímair claimed to be kings of Northumbria (their West Saxon successors certainly appear to have taken this position), but the Uí Ímair were used to urban power centres, of which Northumbria had only one. Sigtrygg had coins minted at Lincoln, which was probably as important to them as York; and it is known that his successors Olaf son of Guthfrith and Olaf son of Sigtrygg as well as Sigtrygg himself had coins struck in the southern Danelaw.[12]

Sigtrygg was courted by the West Saxon king, Æthelstan, and in 926 Sigtrygg married Æthelstan's sister. It is possible that Æthelstan was seeking to replicate the programme used to acquire 'English Mercia'. Mercia's last distinct king, Æthelred II, had been brought into a junior relationship with the West Saxons and had married King Alfred's daughter Æthelflæd. King Æthelred of Mercia died in 911, and was succeeded as ruler by his West Saxon royal wife; after her death in 918, their daughter Ælfwynn succeeded in turn, but soon afterwards Alfred's son King Edward the Elder brought the kingdom under direct West Saxon control.[13] It was in this way that Mercia and Wessex came to be united. However, the West Saxons did not have to wait as long to seize control of the Anglo-Danish kingdom, with Sigtrygg dying the year after the marriage.[14]

Despite the relative rapidity of Æthelstan's initial achievement, the area ruled by Sigtrygg raised more challenges than Æthelred's 'English Mercia'. Æthelstan had to survive very serious attempts to restore the position of the Uí Ímair in Scandinavian England, including the famous battle of Brunanburh in 937. The latter was a resounding victory over the king of Dublin, Olaf Guthfrithson, and his Scottish ally Causantín mac Áeda (Constantine II), but the incredibly risky confrontation appears to have brought the West Saxons little gain. The Uí Ímair renewed their efforts after Æthelstan's death in 939, achieving some success against his brothers Eadmund and Eadred; however, in the early

12 M. Blackburn, 'The Coinage of Scandinavian York', in R. A. Hall, *et al.* (eds), *Aspects of Anglo-Scandinavian York*, 325–49, at 327; and 'Expansion and Control', 133, 137–8; P. Grierson and M. Blackburn, *Medieval European Coinage 1* (Cambridge, 1986), 323–5; Downham, *Viking Kings of Britain and Ireland*, 98.
13 See fn. 4.
14 A surprisingly long account of this affair is produced by *GRA*, ii.134.2, ed. and trans. Mynors *et al.*, 206–9, 212–17.

950s Eadred, probably in alliance with the Northern English 'High Reeve' Oswulf (see below), managed to overcome the last two independent kings, Olaf Cuarán and Erik.[15] After 954, to all appearance, the West Saxon English kings enjoyed uncontested lordship over at least the south of Northumbria, as well as the rest of the northern Danelaw.[16]

Around 980, the West Saxon ealdorman Æthelweard presided over a translation into Latin of (a non-surviving recension of) the *Anglo-Saxon Chronicle*. Æthelweard's text contains an obit of the same Eadwulf who appears in the Irish annals. Eadwulf was 'he who then presided as *actor* over the fortress called Bamburgh' (*qui tum præerat actori oppidi Bebbanburgh condicti*), and died in the lands or coastlands (*orae*) of Northumbria, in 913.[17] Æthelweard's term *actor*, 'agent', is very unusual; it may reflect a reluctance, *c.* 980, to think of the native Northumbrian rulers as independent kings rather than the dependents of West Saxon sovereigns. It would not be unreasonable, on that basis, to deduce that Bamburgh's *actores* had given up the title of king by 980. It would also be reasonable to assume that the rulers of Wessex, both in 913 and in 980, may have had some apprehension about recognising the royal status of more junior Anglo-Saxon rulers. Then again, Æthelweard's text as a whole has a significant amount of unusual vocabulary and usage. It is worth noting that Æthelweard has more opportunities to use titles for an analogous ruler, Æthelred of Mercia: Æthelweard refers to Æthelred as ealdorman (*dux*) but also as 'king' (*rex*).[18] Perhaps Æthelweard would have given Eadwulf other titles, including *rex*, if Eadwulf had made more appearances in the text.

The next ruler we know about after *Adulf* is his brother Oswulf. No surviving source calls Oswulf 'king'. From 946 to 950, during the reign

---

15 For the complex chronological problems here, see P. H. Sawyer, 'The Last Scandinavian Kings of York', *NH* 31 (1995), 39–44; A. Woolf, 'Erik Bloodaxe Revisited', *NH* 34 (1998), 189–93; C. Downham, 'Chronology of the Last Scandinavian Kings of York', *NH* 40 (2003), 25–51, and 'Eric Bloodaxe – Axed? The Mystery of the Last Scandinavian King of York', *Mediaeval Scandinavia* 14 (2004), 51–77 (and further, *Viking Kings of Britain and Ireland*, 107–20).

16 The texts that say this directly are not particularly unproblematic or reliable; however, contemporary evidence is entirely consistent with 954 as the end of formal alternatives to the West Saxon kingship in Scandinavian England.

17 Æthelweard, *Chronicon*, iv.4, ed. and trans. A. Campbell (London, 1962), 52–3.

18 For *rex*, Æthelweard, *Chronicon*, ed. A. Campbell, 50; for *dux*, *Chronicon*, 46; see also *Chronicon*, 53, for *Mycriorum superstes* ('survivor of the Mercians'), translated by Campbell as 'lord of the Mercians'.

of King Eadred, Oswulf appears in West Saxon royal charters, and in a few of these he is described as 'high reeve' or 'high reeve at Bamburgh'.[19] Modern scholars have often sought to understand this usage of 'high reeve' as a peculiar feature of Northumbrian society. Part of the reason for this is that the title is mentioned in *Norðleoda laga*, a legal tract offering a synthesis of Anglo-Danish and Anglo-Saxon society in northern England. The status of 'high reeve' is listed with a wergild half the equivalent due to an ealdorman, equal to that of the Anglo-Danish 'hold'.[20] The tract doubtlessly contains information that would have been relevant to Northumbrian and Anglo-Scandinavian society in the previous century or two, but the final form is not earlier than the early eleventh century, the era of Archbishop Wulfstan II of York (d. 1023).[21]

In Roger of Wendover's annals Erik, the last king of the Northumbrian Danes, is killed by an act of treachery performed at Stainmore (Westmorland). Responsibility for the treachery is assigned to a certain *consul* Macon and to *comes* Oswulf.[22] The composition date of the annal is unknown, but there is a chance this represents a vernacular Northumbrian annal translated into Latin. With this possibility in mind, we might look with interest to some Cuthbertine glosses made in

---

19 In 946 *Osulf Hæhgerefa*, for which see *Sawyer*, no. 520; and as *Osulf ad Bebb' hehgr'* (*Sawyer*, no. 544) in 949.
20 Printed *Gesetze*, i, 458–60; trans. *EHD*, i, no. 51, at 469–70. See also the recent translation of Wulfstan's 'political' writings, A. Rabin, *The Political Writings of Archbishop Wulfstan of York* (Manchester, 2015), 65–75. The other reason is surely an early entry in the northern version of the *Anglo-Saxon Chronicle*, which names three Northumbrian high reeves: see *ASC* MS D 778, ed. G. P. Cubbin, *The Anglo-Saxon Chronicle: A Collaborative Edition. Volume 6, MS D* (Woodbridge, 1996), 15; D. Whitelock (trans.), *The Anglo-Saxon Chronicle: A Revised Translation* (London, 1961), 34.
21 It has been suggested that the inclusion of a 'king' must date the tract to the period before the mid-950s, but there are numerous grounds for questioning this logic. Firstly, the tract is normative and thus may be intentionally conservative to boost the authority of its prescriptions. Secondly, it is not certain, in fact, that the area covered by the law was without junior kings in 1000; besides the 'Northern English' of Bamburgh whose rulers, at home, may have maintained royal status, there are huge blank spots in the west potentially subject to various British or Hiberno-Norse local rulers – who is to say that the predecessors of the eleventh-century kings of *Na Renna* (around Whithorn) were not paralleled in regions like Allerdale, Annandale, or Westmorland? Thirdly, Northumbrians in 1000 did have at least one king, the West Saxon English monarch, who could theoretically be slain by his northern subjects. For this text at the 'Early English Laws' project, see 'Norðleoda Laga': < http://www.earlyenglishlaws.ac.uk/laws/texts/norleod/>.
22 *RW*, s.a. 950, ed. Coxe, i, 402–3; translation based on *EHD*, i, no. 4, at 284.

the 970s, to a tract on Roman titles (contained in Durham Cathedral Library, MS A.IV.19). Here the scribe glosses *comes* as both *heghgeroefa* 'high reeve' and *heretoga* 'war leader'; *consul/proconsul* is glossed *hereges larwu* (perhaps 'judge of the host', 'counsellor of the host').[23] George Molyneaux has pointed out that another tenth-century Cuthbertine gloss, to the Lindisfarne Gospels, used both *undercyningum* (*undercyning*, 'underking') and *hehgeroefum* (*hehgeroefa*, 'high reeve') for *praesides* (*praeses*, 'governor'); in the same text, ealdorman is equated with *princeps*.[24] The glosses suggest that the power or status of a 'high reeve' was more like that of an autonomous ruler than the familiar local 'reeve' (a 'reeve' is essentially what we today would call a 'manager'). Oswulf, indeed, does not appear to have had low status in Eadred's eyes. When he appears in Eadred's charters, Oswulf is listed very high among the witnesses; in two 949 charters Oswulf occurs between Welsh kings and the first *duces*. The title 'high reeve' appears to stress Oswulf's *relationship* with Eadred not his *status*; it is his relationship that is defined by the concept of 'reeve' – in pure status terms Oswulf is clearly more like an 'underking'. The presentation of the office in *Norðleoda laga*, with half the wergild of an ealdorman, may have more to do with events or processes that unfolded later in the century.

Oswulf's title of 'high reeve' is very unusual; on that basis, we may wonder whether or not 'high reeve' had an earlier, special Northumbrian meaning. However, the term is only important because it is a term used for Oswulf not in Northumbrian sources but in West Saxon royal charters. A 'high reeve' as a type of 'reeve' is a subordinate official, a manager who exercises power by delegation and on behalf of the legal owner of the land. Inclusion of 'high' can be read as status-signalling, but the whole title 'high reeve' was clearly and primarily designed not to

---

23   K. L. Jolly, *The Community of St Cuthbert in the Late Tenth Century: The Chester-le-Street Additions to Durham Cathedral Library A. IV. 19* (Columbus, 2012), 342–5. See *An Anglo-Saxon Dictionary Based on the Manuscript Collections of Joseph Bosworth. Supplement*, ed. T. Northcote Toller and A. Campbell (Oxford, 1972), s.v. 'láreów'. Aelred of Rievaulx in the twelfth century glosses the word *larwa* as *doctor* (*id est doctorem*), for which see *The Priory of Hexham*, ed. J. Raine, 2 vols, Surtees Society 44, 46 (Durham, 1864–5), ii, 190. Perhaps the judicial nature of the office of consul, as understood by Anglo-Saxons, could be the key to the expertise held by the 'láreów of the *here*'. Cf. where Causantín mormaer of Fife presides as judge with the 'army' of Fife; see *ESC*, no. 80.

24   G. Molyneaux, *The Formation of the English Kingdom in the Tenth Century* (Oxford, 2015), 61, n. 62.

communicate status but to stress a relationship. During the reign of Æthelred 'the Unready' the title of 'high reeve' is used for other royal subordinates with significantly less responsibility and autonomy and of much lower status.[25] Wessex in the ninth century had relied on figures called ealdormen (see below) to exercise regional government, but the expansion of West Saxon power saw the enlargement of the regions assigned to this official, creating a terminological hole below the ealdorman that was eventually filled by the 'shire reeve', or sheriff.[26] As the title of 'high reeve' is only used for the ruler of Bamburgh in King Eadred's reign (and only for Oswulf), it may be that it represents some sort of temporary accommodation between Oswulf and King Eadred. Oswulf had been present at Eadred's inauguration in 946, and with the 'treachery of Stainmore' proved himself a valuable ally against Eadred's Northumbria-based Norse enemies.[27] So it is possible that scholars have been distracted by a misguided search for the exotic unchanging norms of Northumbrian society, and that Oswulf's title was something new or even peculiar to Eadred's reign.[28]

Adulf mcEtulf happens to be the last ruler of Bamburgh both named directly and styled 'king' in our meagre collection of surviving sources; despite this, and despite the fact that *Adulf mcEtulf*'s successor Oswulf is consistently titled 'high reeve' in West Saxon charters, there is evidence that their successors continued to be thought of as kings later in the tenth century. The *Chronicle of the Kings of Alba*, written towards the end of the tenth century, tells us that the Scottish king Cináed mac Maíl Choluim (r. c. 977–95) captured 'a son of a king of English' during an invasion of England.[29] Since this cannot be a West Saxon English royal son, it must refer to the son of the ruler of the 'Northern English'.

---

25 *ASC* MS A 1001, ed. J. M. Bately, *The Anglo-Saxon Chronicle: A Collaborative Edition. Vol. 3, MS A* (Cambridge, 1986), 80, trans. Whitelock, 85; *ASC* MS C 1002, ed. K. O'Brien O'Keeffe (ed.), *The Anglo-Saxon Chronicle: A Collaborative Edition. Volume 5, MS. C* (Cambridge, 2001), 89.
26 L. Roach, *Æthelred the Unready* (New Haven, 2016), 97–8.
27 See below, 143.
28 For important discussions of the 'reeve' and 'high reeve', see H. M. Chadwick, *Studies on Anglo-Saxon Institutions* (New York, 1963) 228–39; and (emphasis on later era) J. Campbell, *The Anglo-Saxon State* (London, 2000), 201–25, originally printed as 'Some Agents and Agencies of the Late Anglo-Saxon State', in J. C. Holt (ed.), *Domesday Studies* (Woodbridge, 1987), 201–18; see also, recently, Molyneaux, *The Formation of the English Kingdom*, 181, and n. 309, for discussion of later 'high reeves'.
29 *CKA*, 151, 161.

Only two other certain Northern English rulers appear in the tenth century in contemporary documents, Eadwulf *Yvelcild* and Waltheof, and they are both styled *dux*. Waltheof's son Uhtred appears in contemporary sources from the early eleventh century, but only as the holder of a West Saxon ealdordom or 'earldom'. Uhtred's son Eadwulf is the next to be named in contemporary documents. The C and D versions of the *Anglo-Saxon Chronicle* note that in 1041 Harthacnut killed someone of that name; this Eadwulf is called *eorl* by the C version, but untitled in the D version.[30] Nonetheless, none of this compels the historian to believe that the rulers of Bamburgh were styled 'king' in the eleventh century; certainly it is very difficult to believe they used the title 'king of Northumbria', a style used occasionally by the monarchs of West Saxon England.[31] It is conceivable, too, that the title in the Scottish source is conservative.

Identity: Bamburgh and the Northern English

Æthelweard stressed the connection between Eadwulf and Bamburgh, and the significance of this fortress is confirmed by manuscript D of the *Anglo-Saxon Chronicle*. In its description of the events that followed the death of Sigtrygg, Æthelstan is said to have met with Ealdred son of Eadwulf of Bamburgh (*from Bebbanbyrig*) alongside the kings of Scotland and Wales, who together participated in a ceremony of pledge- and oath-giving for Æthelstan's benefit. The ceremony took place at a *stow* (usually signifying a church site) described *æt Eamotum*, very likely the minster of Dacre, in Leath ward, Cumberland.[32] The annalist

---

30   *ASC* MS C 1041, *swac Harðacnut Eadulf eorl under his griðe*, ed. O'Brien O'Keeffe, 107; cf. *ASC* MS D 1041, ed. Cubbin, 66, *Harðacnut Eadulfe under gryðe*. In *De Primo Saxonum Adventu* the event is place during Edward's reign, but that is corrected by the tract *De Omnibus Comitibus Northimbrensibus*, the tract inserted into *Historia Regum*, s.a. 1072, and Roger of Howden's *Chronica* (also known as *Historia post Bedam*), s.a. 952 (or 952×955). The man responsible for *De Omnibus Comitibus Northimbrensibus* appears to have had access to the contemporary annal used by *ASC* MSS C and D; see *DPSA*, 383; *HR*, 198; *RHC*, i, 57–9.

31   E.g. *Sawyer*, no. 677, which in the style *rex Merciorum et Norðanhymbrorum* appears to show that King Edgar used the title prior to becoming ruler of all England – though it should be noted that the title continues *atque Brettonum*, a position of overlordship that did not, so far as we know, have any existence as an independent kingship title.

32   *GRA*, ii.134.2, 214–15; and see also Woolf, *From Pictland to Alba*, 151–2. Dacre is also the only major pre-Conquest monastic church in the area, but another reason to be

identifies the other rulers with their territorial realms like 'Scotland' and 'Gwent', but *from Bebbanbyrig* is the closest the annalist is prepared to go for Ealdred.[33] Ealdred's brother Oswulf was also associated with Bamburgh in several later West Saxon English charters, in a way that suggests lordship of Bamburgh and the rulership of the far north were synonymous.[34] Bamburgh had been the chief fortress of Bernicia, the 'tribal' polity central to the formation of the larger Northumbrian kingdom in the mid 600s.[35] The fortified rock may have retained enough cultural and ritual significance that lordship there could be seen as a proxy for wider authority; but we should not forget, either, the practical utility of possessing one of the most formidable fortresses on the east coast of Britain.

The association of polities and powerful regional strongmen with important fortifications or urban sites was common in England and in western Europe at this period – the various 'county' names of England and France, like Yorkshire (based on York) and Anjou (from Angers), are a modern reminder of this. Identification of the Eadwulfings with such a site is not, therefore, unusual. However, for all such polities, the resources offered by the population and land in the adjacent country were ultimately more important than the central stronghold. Judging by their only surviving tenth-century chronicle, the Scots referred to the Bamburgh realm as *Saxain*, 'England' or 'the English', Latinised as *Saxonia*. A larger quantity of Irish sources, however, make it clear that in Gaelic usage the territory was *also* referred to as 'Northern England'. As well as being used to describe the territory of the only two tenth-century rulers named in Irish sources, *Etulbb ri Saxan* and

---

confident that Dacre was the location is that no known source material that might have been used by William gives any sign that the meeting took place in (what is today) the north-west of England. As a monk who spent most of his life in Wiltshire he is unlikely to have independently identified *et Eamotum* with this region much less taken a successful shot in the dark at a place-name so close to the river Eamont.

[33] For the meeting, see *ASC* MS D 926 [927], ed. Cubbin, 41, trans. Whitelock, 68–9. The other rulers were Hywel king of the West Welsh (*Huwal Westwala cyning*), Causantín king of Scotland (*Cosstantin Scotta cyning*), and Owain king of Gwent (*Uwen Wenta cyning*). But see F. Edmonds, 'Carham: The Western Perspective', this volume, 79–94, at 83.

[34] *Osulf bebbanbyrig* (*Sawyer*, no. 550) as *Osulf ad Bebb' hehgr'* (*Sawyer*, no. 544) in 949, and in 950 as *Osulf Bebbanburg* (*Sawyer*, no. 552a).

[35] For the importance of Bamburgh to early Northumbria, see J. Fraser, *From Caledonia to Pictland: Scotland to 795*, The New Edinburgh History of Scotland 1 (Edinburgh, 2009), 149–53.

Adulf mcEtulfe, King of the North Saxons, it was used for their ninth-century ancestor King Ælla (died 867). 'Northern England' was just what the Irish had come to use to refer to Northumbria. For instance, 'Northern England' (*Saxain Tuaiscirt*) is used for the early kingdom in the tenth-century Irish-language 'Life of Adomnán', *Betha Adamnáin*.[36] It is worth stressing that 'Northern England' is never used in reference to the Scandinavian settlers of Northumbria or their rulers. The Northumbrian Anglo-Danes, and the people of the Great Army more generally, were called *Gaill*, 'Norse', or *Dubgaill*, 'dark Norse'.[37] In Irish eyes, the Uí Ímair were never kings of Northumbria. This is a point worth making, because in West Saxon sources 'Northumbria' and 'Northumbrian' are often used to differentiate the northern segment of the Great Army from the East Anglian section, which split after Halfdan's settlement in 876. West Saxon kings appear to have regarded themselves as kings of Northumbria after 927, something that may have been connected more to the ideology of kingship generally than to reality. Responsibility for protecting the church was a critical element in tenth-century Christian kingship. York contained the former Roman province's (and indeed the island's) second archiepiscopal seat, so when the West Saxons came to occupy York and adjacent territory the triumphant kings naturally came to regard themselves as kings of Northumbria as well as protectors of all Britain.[38]

---

36   *Betha Adamnáin: The Irish Life of Adamnán*, ed. and trans. M. Herbert and P. Ó Riain, Irish Texts Society 54 (Dublin, 1988), 54–5. See also P. Wadden, '*Trácht Romra* and the Northumbrian Episode in *Betha Adamnáin*', *Ériu* 62 (2012), 101–11.

37   *AU* 867.7, 875.3, 877.5, 893.3, 914.3, 917.3, 918.4, 921.4, 927.2; cf. *CS* 941 (for Guthfrith son of Sigtrygg Cáech). The two groups (and their previous identification as 'Danes' and 'Norwegians') are discussed in a number of important articles: see A. Smyth, 'The Black Foreigners of York and the White Foreigners of Dublin', *Saga-Book of the Viking Society for Northern Research* 19 (1974–7), 101–17; D. N. Dumville, 'Old Dubliners and New Dubliners in Ireland and Britain', *Celtic Essays, 2001–2007*, 2 vols (Aberdeen, 2007), i, 103–22; and C. Downham, '"Hiberno-Norwegians" and "Anglo-Danes"', *Mediaeval Scandinavia* 19 (2009), 139–69.

38   For references to the settlers or their polity as 'the Northumbrians' or something similar, see *ASC* MS A 893, 896, 900, 905, 910, [919]; *ASC* MS C 944, 946; *ASC* MS D 927, 941, 947, 948, 954; *ASC* MS E 948, 952; Æthelweard, *Chronicon*, iv.3, iv.4, iv.7, ed. and trans. A. Campbell (London, 1962), 51, 52, 55; but cf. *ASC* MS A 920, where the northern English emerge separately. For Northumbria in the royal titles of Æthelstan, see *Sawyer*, no. 392, *rex Angulsexna and Norþhymbra imperator paganorum gubernator Brittanorumque propugnator*, and similarly at Eadred's coronation, *Sawyer*, no. 520.

Although we have no sources from the region itself, the distinctions visible in Irish sources are probably best explained as a reflection of usage in the lands subject to the ruler of Bamburgh and elsewhere in northern England; and, thus, more reliable than West Saxon descriptions.[39] The rulers of Bamburgh were both the leaders of the ethnic English in the north and the custodians of the old kingdom of Northumbria. Descended, so they appear to have claimed, from King Ælla via a daughter, their Northumbrian royal credentials were likely part of their authority as rulers within northern England. Danes elsewhere in Britain and Ireland told stories about the old rivalry between King Ivar and King Ælla, with Ivar taken to represent the Anglo-Danes and their ruling dynasty, the Uí Imair.[40] Nonetheless, the rulers of Bamburgh were not the only locally-based leaders of English Northumbria. The other major figures were the archbishops of York. They presided over what had once at least been among the most respected seats of learning in western Europe, the *alma mater* of the Carolingian scholar Alcuin. The archbishops were credible figures internationally and, as the kingdom's senior churchman, they had a strong incentive to keep the idea of Northumbria alive.[41] From 927 at least, the ethno-political and geographical mandate of the West Saxon rulers overlapped with that of the Bamburgh kings;[42] and from the 950s, with the translation and accession of Oscytel, the archbishops of York were intimately tied to the southerners.[43] In *Grið*, a judicial text on sanctuary connected to Archbishop Wulfstan II of York and composed *c.* 1000, 'Northenglish law' (*Norðengla lage*) is referred to as one of the

---

39 For what it is worth, a clear distinction between the 'English' and the 'Danes' is observed by *Historia de Sancto Cuthberto* in relation to Northumbrian politics of the Viking Age. *HSC*, c.13, 52–3.
40 McGuigan, 'Ælla and the Descendants of Ivar', 20–34.
41 There is scepticism, however, about how much of York's old school and library survived the Viking Age, for instance D. Rollason, 'Anglo-Scandinavian York: The Evidence of Historical Sources', in R. A. Hall, *et al.* (eds), *Aspects of Anglo-Scandinavian York*, The Archaeology of York 8, Anglo-Scandinavian York (York, 2004), 305–24, at 306–7.
42 *ASC* MS D 926 [927], ed. Cubbin, 41, trans. Whitelock, 68.
43 The ethnic and ideological mandate of the Southumbrian monarchs is a much discussed topic, but for recent discussions see S. Foot, *Æthelstan: The First King of England* (New Haven, 2011), 212–26, and Molyneaux, *Formation of the English Kingdom*, 195–230. For the kings of England and archbishops of York, see Whitelock, 'The Dealings of the Kings of England with Northumbria', 72–6.

different system of customs used in England.[44] A set of edicts, possibly also connected with Wulfstan, uses the practices of three Yorkshire minsters to model 'Northumbrian law' relating to sanctuary.[45] Nonetheless, if law is any guide, the divisions of the tenth century were deep enough to survive another century or so. Yorkshire is still included among the shires under 'Danish law' in a text that that dates to the Norman era.[46]

Northern English territory and politics

At its height in the eighth century Northumbria had extended from the Peak District and the Humber to Kyle (central Ayrshire) and the Firth of Forth. We know that Norse settlement reduced this to a rump, depriving it of York and other southerly and westerly regions. The exact

---

44 For *on Cantwara lage*, see *Grið*, c.6, in *Gesetze*, i, 470–3, at 470; for *on Suðengla lage*, see *Grið* c.9, in *Gesetze*, i, 470; and for *on Norðengla lage* and *be Norðengla lage*, see *Grið* c.13, *Gesetze*, i, 471.
45 *Norðhymbra Cyricgrið*, in *Gesetze*, i, 473; with discussion and translation in Rabin, *Political Writings of Archbishop Wulfstan*, 82–4.
46 The text may have been written prior to the conquest of the Bamburgh polity; it is *þe Syren and Hundredes of engelonde*, from Oxford, Jesus College, MS 29, folios 194r-195r, probably based on a text originally composed 1086×1130 (though written in 'updated' English of a later era); it lists York under Danish law, but has Northumberland unshired, as well as *loðen and westmara-lond and cumberland and Cornwale*, also noting *scotlaund and Brutlaund and wyht*, with Cornwall having seven 'small shires' (*lutle schire*); for text, see *An Old English Miscellany Containing a Bestiary, Kentish Sermons, Proverbs of Alfred, Religious Poems of the Thirteenth Century: From Manuscripts in the British Museum, Bodleian Library, Jesus College Library, etc*, ed. R. Morris, Early English Text Society 49 (London, 1872), 145–6; see also B. Hill, 'The History of Jesus College, Oxford MS. 29', *Medium Aevum* 32 (1963), 203–13, at 203; another vernacular list in the *Red Book of the Exchequer*, following *Leges Henrici Primi* and a 'County Hidage', omits York from the list of shires under Danish law; this is printed in *General Report on the Public Records* (London, 1837), 166; see also *The Red Book of the Exchequer*, ed. H. Hall, 3 vols, Rolls Series 99 (London, 1896), i, lxxxvi-lxxxvii. The tradition of this text is substantial, often found in conjunction with *notitia dignitatum* material in a tradition strongly reminiscent of *Historia Brittonum*, e.g. in *De Primo Saxonum Adventu*, 382; *Series Regum Northymbrensium*, 392–3 (here closely related to *þe Syren and Hundredes*); Henry of Huntingdon, *Historia Anglorum*, i.3, ed. and trans. D. Greenway (Oxford, 1996), 12–15, and *Historia Anglorum*, i.5, 16–19; Alfred of Beverley, *Annales*, ed. T. Hearne (Oxford, 1716), 99; *Chronicles of the Picts, Chronicles of the Scots*, ed. W. F. Skene (Edinburgh, 1867), 153–4; and *Munimenta Gildhallae Londoniensis*, ed. H. T. Riley, 3 vols, Rolls Series 12 (London, 1859–62), ii, 624–6 (from MS British Library Cotton Claudius D. ii.); for discussion of variations and date, see F. Liebermann, *Über die Leges Anglorum Saeculo XIII* (Halle, 1894), 6–9.

boundaries of this 'rump' are not immediately obvious; particularly in the tenth and early eleventh centuies. Even at its lowest point, its territory must have remained substantial enough to support rulers able to compete on relatively equal terms with the rulers of the Anglo-Danes, as well as Scotland and Strathclyde. For reasons established above, Bamburgh is the natural starting point for analysis. The Eadwulfing capital, like nearby Lindisfarne, lies on the southern edge of territory drained by the Tweed and its tributaries, the most important of which are the Teviot, Till, Leader, Yarrow, Bowmont–Glen and the two Adders. The basin encompasses what is now 'Scottish Borders' council area in addition to much of Northumberland; as well as Bamburgh, the area hosted major high status sites like Lindisfarne, Sprouston, Melrose and Jedburgh, as well as the ancient site of Yeavering Bell.

It is clear that language and place-names offer information about post-settlement politics in the north. Place-names coined in Old Norse survive throughout East Anglia, eastern Mercia and southern Northumbria, most particularly in Yorkshire, the region of the 'five boroughs', and in East Anglia – a zone that, for the most part at least, almost certainly marks the set of regions settled by the Great Army in the 870s.[47] By contrast, a relative absence of Norse toponyms is a feature of the area between the Forth and Tyne. Judging by this place-name evidence, the settlement of 876 did not extend significantly beyond the Tyne, leaving an 'English zone' in the north of the kingdom, analogous to the unsettled western part of Mercia and, perhaps, to the much less Scandinavianised southern part of East Anglia, Suffolk.[48] On the Forth itself, the evidence seems to suggest a boundary between Celtic and Old English somewhere around the East Lothian Esk – at least in the twelfth

---

[47] R. H. C. Davis, 'East Anglia and the Danelaw', *Transactions of the Royal Historical Society* 5th ser. 5 (1955), 23–39, at 30; G. Fellows-Jensen, 'Scandinavian Settlement in Yorkshire – Through the Rear-View Mirror', in B. E. Crawford (ed.), *Scandinavian Settlement in Northern Britain: Thirteen Studies of Place-Names in their Historical Context* (London, 1995), 170–86, at 176.

[48] For the 'regionality' of this pattern, see M. Townend, 'Viking Age England as a Bilingual Society', in D. M. Hadley and J. D. Richards (eds), *Cultures in Contact: Scandinavian Settlement in England in the Ninth and Tenth Centuries* (Turnhout, 2000), 89–105; see also L. Abrams and D. N. Parsons, 'Place-Names and the History of Scandinavian Settlement in England', in J. Hines et al. (eds), *Land, Sea and Home: Proceedings of a Conference on Viking-Period Settlement, Cardiff, July 2001* (Leeds, 2004), 379–431; W. F. H. Nicolaisen, *Scottish Place-Names* (Edinburgh, 1976), 109–55; and McGuigan, 'Ælla and the Descendants of Ivar', 30, n. 44.

century, when place-name forms begin to be attested in number.[49] The core of the Northern English polity, it is reasonable to deduce, consisted of the lands between the Tyne and Forth. Patterns of place-name evidence like those cited above can provide us a broad picture, but they cannot tell us much about the nuances of any particular point in the Viking Age. Northumbria may have remained, ideologically at least, a unity for some period in the late ninth and early tenth century, first under Norse hegemons and then under Eadwulf of Bamburgh.[50] Place-names cannot tell us, for example, whether or not or for how long the Northumbrian English rump acknowledged the political superiority of the 'Anglo-Danes' as a price of survival.

A twelfth-century text tells us that during the reign of Edgar the king of England left territory 'between the Tees and *Myreforth*' (*a Teisa usque Myreforth*) to Oswulf of Bamburgh's successor Eadwulf *Yvelcild*.[51] The vast majority of commentators have identified *Myreforth* with the Firth of Forth, though the possibility of an unidentified ford has left some uncertainty.[52] The surviving manuscripts of *De Primo Saxonum Adventu* give *Myreforth* and *Myreford*, and so it is much more likely that forms represent a vernacular ð rather than *d*, and thus not the English word *ford*. In the tenth century at the very least, *i* or *y* could be used by English scribes to render the first vowel in Gaelic *Muiredach*.[53] The B version of the St Andrews foundation legend uses the term 'mur' (*muir*) to mean 'estuary' or 'firth', as in *Slethemur* for 'Firth of Tay', *Ihwdenemur* for 'Firth of Forth'.[54] *Myreforth* seems to be a borrowing from Celtic terminology, meaning 'Forth Sea' or 'Firth of Forth', a term that later must have become defunct (though 'Forth' in modern English/Scots is a borrowing from Gaelic). Alternatively, it has

---

49 E.g. Nicolaisen, *Scottish Place-Names*, 96–7.
50 Discussed by Woolf, *From Pictland to Alba*, chs 2 and 4.
51 *DPSA*, 382, where the editor chooses *Myreford*.
52 For some uncertain (and alternative) suggestions, see M. O. Anderson, 'Lothian and the Early Scottish Kings', *SHR* 39 (1960), 98–112, at 105–6; G. W. S. Barrow, *The Kingdom of the Scots: Government, Church and Society from the Eleventh to the Fourteenth Century*, 2nd edn (Edinburgh, 2003), 123; A. A. M. Duncan, *The Kingship of the Scots, 842–1292: Succession and Independence* (Edinburgh, 2002), 24.
53 For Muiredach/Myrdah, see for instance N. Brooks, M. Gelling and D. Johnson, 'A New Charter of King Edgar', *ASE* 13 (1984), 137–55, at 141.
54 *St Andrews Foundation Account B*, ed. and trans. S. Taylor, *The Place-Names of Fife*, 5 vols (Donington, 2006–2013), iii, 567–79, at 573; for commentary, see *The Place-Names of Fife*, 593.

also been suggested that the *Myre* element stands for 'mire', hence 'Forth mire'.[55] *De Primo Saxonum Adventu*, however, is twelfth century, and even in the best case scenario, if the core of the account has been influenced by an earlier text (which is very possible – see below), the boundary specified would only relate to the time of Edgar. Thus, we could not use it to discuss the territory of Ealdred son of Eadwulf in the 920s, for instance. Nonetheless, as far as the broad picture is concerned, there is a reassuring harmony between this description and place-name evidence discussed above.

Another way to approach the subject is to utilise the evidence of ecclesiastical jurisdiction. Of the few things we know for certain about the Northern English polity in the Viking Age, one is that it contained the ancient episcopal church of Lindisfarne. The great spiritual capital of ancient Bernicia lies on an island close enough to Bamburgh as to be almost a sacred annex of the fortress. By the twelfth century, Lindisfarne itself had come to be part of the diocese of Durham. Durham was an episcopal seat by 1041, at the latest, when the first man named as bishop of Durham in a contemporary source appears.[56] By the 1100s, Durham was remembered as the foundation of the Eadwulfing Uhtred.[57] There is no reason to believe, however, that the Lindisfarne *familia* and the jurisdiction of Lindisfarne as a 'mother church' had ceased to exist by the eleventh century, nor that it had ceased to function as a serious principle of organisation prior to the conquest of the Tweed basin by the Scots and Normans. The latter process had begun in the eleventh century, and was complete by 1124. Norman control of the Lindisfarne region seems to have begun with the earldom of Robert de Mowbray. He may have taken power in the region as early as 1086, but perhaps as late as the 1090s. The first accounts of Lindisfarne's boundaries come only from the decades around 1100, and so at worst are a good guide to

---

55 A 'mire' reading is not an unreasonable one. Roman writers from Tacitus through Ptolemy to the *Ravenna Cosmography* called the Forth *Bodotria*, *Boderia* and *B[o]dora*, identified with Celtic terms meaning 'muddy water'; the Welsh called the Forth *Gweryd*, analysable as 'muddy', with which the Scottish term *Forth* is cognate; see Watson, *CPNS*, repr. with corrigenda, addenda and intro by S. Taylor (Edinburgh, 2004), 51–2; M. O. Anderson, *Kings and Kingship in Early Scotland*, rev. edn (Edinburgh, 1980), 242.

56 *ASC* MSS CD 1041, trans. Whitelock, 106; his see is revealed to be Durham on his resignation, for which see *ASC* MS D 1056, ed. Cubbin, 75, trans. Whitelock, 132.

57 *LDE*, iii.2, 148–9.

what the Normans found *c.* 1100 or what native Anglo-Saxons around 1100 believed had existed in the Viking Age.[58]

In *Historia de Sancto Cuthberto*, a text dating to the mid or late eleventh century (but with access to some earlier source material), there is a sketch of the 'Boundaries of the Land of Lindisfarne'. The text outlines the church's land in the lower Tweed basin, in addition to 'all the land that pertains to the monastery of St Balthere' at Tyninghame.[59] The 'Boundaries of the Land of Lindisfarne' claim that Lindisfarne's own *terrae* stretched from the headwaters of the Warren burn, the Breamish, and Till to the headwaters of the Leader and *Adre*.[60] Across the Lammermuir it encompassed the territory subject to the minster of St Balthere at Tyninghame, so extending Lindisfarne's properties as far west as *Esce muthe* (Inveresk, East Lothian). Use of the Esk as a western boundary, probably very similar to the western border of Old English in the 1100s, gives this description an extra air of credibility. The fact that Tyninghame's lands are claimed separately, however, should be cause for restraint – particularly as the area was in Scottish hands during the reign of Máel Coluim III (r. 1058–93) and during the episcopate of Fothad II of St Andrews (d. 1093); Máel Coluim's son Donnchad II (d. 1094) issued a charter authorising its 'return' to St Cuthbert.[61] Tyninghame was a hot property in the decades around 1100.

---

58 A charter of Bishop William de St Calais endows the Durham Benedictines with the churches of Lindisfarne and Norham (*Duas quoque ecclesias Lindisfarnensem scilicet que sedes primitus fuit episcopalis cum uilla sibi adiacente nomine Fennum, et Norham quam ipse ibi corpore quiescendo illustrauerat cum sua etiam uilla nomine Scoreswurthin*), for which see H. S. Offler (ed.), *Durham Episcopal Charters, 1071–1152*, Surtees Society 179 (Gateshead, 1968), no. 3 (relevant text at p. 8). Its editor regarded the final complete document as a forgery, but it may be based on something genuine. It is clear that Bishop Walcher, William's predecessor, did not control anything significantly north of the Tyne and it may not have been until the 1090s that the Normans of Durham actually gained control of Lindisfarne and Norham. For this potential late date of Robert's tenure, see Frank Barlow, *William Rufus* (London, 1983), 168–9. The consequences of a very late date of Norman arrival in the Tweed basin will be explored further in N. McGuigan, *Máel Coluim III Canmore* (forthcoming), but see also N. McGuigan, 'Neither Scotland nor England: Middle Britain, *c.* 850–1150', PhD thesis (University of St Andrews, 2015), 125–7.

59 *HSC*, c.4, 46–7; although the mouth of the Warren Beck (by Bamburgh) is listed, the point furthest south is effectively the Aln since 'the land . . . on both sides of the river Breamish up to the place where it rises' is included in the diocese.

60 Contrary to Barrow, *The Kingdom of the Scots*, 122, the text uses the Tweed as a reference point, not a boundary.

61 *ESC*, no. 12 (=*North Durham*, no. 1).

There is another description of the bishopric of Lindisfarne among Northumbria-related extracts inserted into a recension of John of Worcester's *Chronicon ex Chronicis*: in *Historia Regum* ('Part 2' or 'Section 8'), s.a. 854 (and in Roger of Howden's *Chronica*, s.a. 882). The description, 'Properties of the Diocese of Lindisfarne', contains information that is likely to have been taken from *Historia de Sancto Cuthberto* (or the related *Cronica Monasterii Dunelmensis*), but includes a list of dependent *mansiones* not included in earlier extant sources.[62] All of the *mansiones* appear to be significant regional minsters separated (when we can tell) by similar distances. Carlisle and Norham open the list, which proceeds to Carham, *Culterham* (unidentified), Melrose, *Tigbrethingham* (unidentified, perhaps Stow of Wedale), Abercorn, Edinburgh, Pefferham (probably Aberlady), Auldhame, Tynninghame, Coldingham, Tillmouth then back to *Northam supradictam*; that is, west from Norham up the Teviot, back down again and north over the moor, and east again through Lothian, circling the moor again to Coldingham, Tillmouth, and back to Norham.[63] Carlisle is entered into the text in a way that breaks up the text's logic. This suggests an earlier core, one altered to facilitate Cuthbertine ambitions on the church of Carlisle, whose status was unsettled until the 1120s (when Henry I consented to the creation of an independent bishopric there). The text makes much more sense if Carlisle is omitted, then it reads like a circuit of the Lammermuir beginning and terminating with Norham.[64] How much older than the 1120s, however, is not particularly obvious. It should be noted, however, that the description of the 'ancient' Cumbrian see in the 'Glasgow Inquest' of the same era fits into the 'Properties of the Diocese of

---

62 *CMD*, 523–9.
63 *HR*, s.a. 854, ed. Arnold, ii, 101; *RHC*, s.a 882, ed. Stubbs, i, 45. The first to draw attention to the significance of this extract in recent times was Woolf, *From Pictland to Alba*, 81–2. See also A. Woolf, 'The Diocese of Lindisfarne: Organisation and Pastoral Care', this volume, 231–9, and D. Woodman, 'Annals 848 to 1118 in the *Historia Regum*', this volume, 202–30, at 206–7.
64 Norham is named as the location of the body of Cuthbert in a list of saint relic resting places brought together between 1013 and 1031 (D. Rollason, 'Lists of Saints' Resting-Places in Anglo-Saxon England', *ASE* 7 (1978), 61–93, at 63–8). I have argued elsewhere that Norham, then called *Ubbanford*, was probably the *de facto* episcopal centre of the diocese of Lindisfarne prior to its merger into Durham; for which, see N. McGuigan, 'Cuthbert's Relics and the Origins of the Diocese of Durham', forthcoming, and 'Neither Scotland nor England', 64–79.

Lindisfarne' almost like a jig-saw. One wonders if David I, or some other potentate, had promoted a similar inquest for Lindisfarne in the early 1100s.[65]

The reliability of the above descriptions may be limited by the self-interest and knowledge of their architects. 'The past' for Anglo-Norman-era writers was worth remembering primarily when it reinforced self-serving beliefs or desires about 'the present', how it ought to be or how they would like it to be. Due to Scottish incursions prior to the 1100s, doubt and controversy probably surrounded the northern and western boundaries of Lindisfarne's sphere. The 'Properties of the Diocese of Lindisfarne' comprehended churches as far west as Edinburgh and Abercorn; but there are no claims west of the Esk in the 'Boundaries of the Land of Lindisfarne' nor elsewhere in *Historia de Sancto Cuthberto*. The southern sphere of the church's lands was probably not quite as topical *c.* 1100, which may potentially explain why the southern boundaries of the two descriptions are in concordance. Both accounts agree, however, on a central core running between the Aln and Forth. If we could put some potential sources of scepticism aside for the sake of argument, the boundaries outlined above might tell us about the lords of Bamburgh and the geography of their authority. Episcopal boundaries were, after all, closely tied to secular boundaries. Therefore, these descriptions might offer a guide to what the 'inner zone' of the 'Northern English' Bamburgh polity looked like, the region most intimately familiar to the Eadwulfings, where the lords of Bamburgh made 'circuit' throughout the period.

The inner zone is politically important in an era of extremely decentralised polities where relatively small areas provided a base for more 'extensive' royal authority encompassing a much larger region. The mighty kings of England rarely ventured outside a small zone in southern and south-western England, even though they also presided over a polity that reached, by the 950s, as far north as (what later became) County Durham. In the north, even in the Tweed basin it is unlikely that the rulers of Bamburgh extended their itinerary into Tweeddale (i.e. Peeblesshire). Although the region might have been subject to tribute, this was a British-speaking region that was separated from Anglo-Saxon Teviotdale by a large forested (but not thickly forested)

---

65   *David I Chrs*, no. 15; McGuigan, 'Neither Scotland nor England', 198.

march region later known as the 'Forest of Selkirk' or 'Ettrick Forest' (its boundaries are similar to the later sheriffdom of Selkirk, Selkirkshire).[66] Nonetheless, the core jurisdictions outlined in both the 'Boundaries of the Land of Lindisfarne' and the 'Properties of the Diocese of Lindisfarne' are accompanied by notes about further acquisitions. It is almost certain that, at one point or another, the dominion of the ruling family encompassed vassals, estates and halls at different locations further south as far as the Tees and perhaps beyond.[67]

The settlement of 876 clearly cut the geographic authority of Northumbria's native kings, since it is unlikely that Ecgberht II or any of his immediate successors took leadership of the Great Army.[68] With further Norse settlement 'English Northumbria', or at least the authority of native English rulers, probably continued to contract. In *Historia de Sancto Cuthberto*, an eleventh-century text but one that conveys accurate information about the reign of Edward the Elder, areas between the Tyne and Tees are said to have fallen under the domination of King Rögnvald, leader of the Uí Ímair. Prior to the latter's victory at the battle of Corbridge (in 918), the English aristocracy of the Tyne–Tees region had been protected by Ealdred son of Eadwulf.[69] However, rather than being permanent territorial loss, it is more likely that the Tyne–Tees zone evolved into an intermediate region where Norse and Northern English rulers competed for overlordship and

---

66 For an idea of the size of this forest, and of other march zones bounding the 'Northern English' realm in the west, see J. M. Gilbert, *Hunting and Hunting Reserves in Medieval Scotland* (Edinburgh, 1979), 360.

67 The same text goes on to add other churches and estates to the Lindisfarne–Norham collection, including Whittingham and Warkworth in Northumberland and several south of the Tees, *HR*, ed. Arnold, ii, 101–2, and *RHC*, ed. Stubbs, i, 45. The estates of Lindisfarne–Norham are clearly presented as a component of the larger diocese of Durham, which interests us here because it might be conservative and thus illustrative of our topic; but it is not to suggest that the Cuthbertine church and its properties were confined to such a small area. Cuthbert's was a pan-English cult in the tenth century (see M. Gretsch, *Ælfric and the Cult of Saints in Late Anglo-Saxon England* (Cambridge, 2005), 65–126). We have very good evidence that the Cuthbertine see was the recipient of grants from Danelaw magnates, for which see *Northern Chrs*, nos 18–19; D. Rollason and L. Rollason (eds), *Durham Liber Vitae: London, British Library, MS Cotton Domitian A.VII*, 3 vols (London, 2007), i, 140.

68 It is worth noting, however, that Alex Woolf has argued for the possibility that Eadwulf, and perhaps his sons, were able to exercise overlordship of the Northumbrian Danes in the 910s, and possibly at other times; see Woolf, *From Pictland to Alba*, 138–44.

69 *HSC*, c.22–c.24, 60–3.

tribute. King Rögnvald died in 921 and was succeeded by his brother Sigtrygg, who in turn was succeeded by Æthelstan of Wessex. After the accession of the last, northerners begin appearing in English royal charters, including several *duces* with Anglo-Saxon names, including at least two Eadwulfings. Among the others are Ælfred, Ælfstan and Æscbriht, figures who (as *Historia de Sancto Cuthberto* alleged) were forced to abandon Eadwulfing hegemony and recognise Rögnvald.[70] At this stage common West Saxon overlordship probably encouraged decentralisation, but after Æthelstan's death the Northern English and Norse of York would have been free to renew competition over the region and the allegiance of smaller regional 'big men' like Ælfred, Ælfstan and Æscbriht.

As we saw above, there is evidence that Æthelstan's nephew Edgar formally recognised or assigned Eadwulf *Yvelcild* jurisdiction of territory as far south as the Tees, but it is open to question whether or not a ruler based far to the north in Bamburgh would have be able to exercise much authority in the heavily Scandinavian-settled Teesside region. Norse landowners there, like Rögnvald's follower Scule lord of Castle Eden (County Durham, about halfway between modern Hartlepool and Sunderland), appear to have held other lands as far south as East Anglia, and would have naturally gravitated to the Uí Ímair or any other rulers of York and Lincoln.[71] One strategy, perhaps, would have been to use the Cuthbertine church and its charismatic cult. As early as the reign of Edward the Elder, Tilred abbot of Heversham and abbot of Norham (who appears in Anglo-Norman-era episcopal lists as bishop), is said to have purchased land at Castle Eden for the Cuthbertine church. Other Cuthbertine documents preserve what appear to be genuine notices of grants elsewhere in the settlement-zone, including Crayke in Yorkshire.[72] By the eleventh century the Cuthbertine church was claiming certain rights of sanctuary and powers of arbitration among the northern Anglo-Danes, *Consuetudines Sancti Cuthberti*, which the church claimed had been granted to Cuthbert by their first king,

---

70 *Sawyer*, nos 379, 393, 403, 405, 407, 410, 412–13, 416–18, 422–3, 425, 428, 450; S. Keynes, *An Atlas of Attestations in Anglo-Saxon Charters, c. 670–1066*. I, Tables, ASNC Guides, Texts, and Studies 5 draft edn (Cambridge, 2002), table 38; and McGuigan, 'Neither Scotland nor England', 49–50.
71 *HSC*, c.23–c.24, 60–3; *Liber Eliensis*, ii.36–7, ed. E. O. Blake (London, 1962), 111.
72 *Northern Chrs*, nos 18–20.

Guthred, and by Alfred of Wessex.[73] Then, of course, there was the church of Chester-le-Street on the river Wear, located at about seven miles south of the Tyne. Writers at Durham in the later eleventh century came to believe that Chester-le-Street had hosted the shrine and bishops of St Cuthbert for most of the Viking Age.[74] On the other hand, the ability of the Eadwulfings to benefit from Cuthbertine authority is up for question, and we cannot assume that the Eadwulfings were always able to exercise much control over their ecclesiastical colleagues. In the Norman poem *Moriuht*, written around 1000, a nunnery at Corbridge on the Tyne seems to have been regarded as part of a Norse rather than English zone.[75] This would not mean that Corbridge was beyond Bamburgh's power, but might be read to suggest that its relationship with Bamburgh was quite loose at best in the later tenth century.

Several Norman-era texts carry accounts of how 'Lothian' fell under the rule of Scottish kings involving implausible single-act transfers from either the Northern English ruler (Eadwulf *Cudel*) or from the King of England himself (either Edgar or Edward the Confessor). Unfortunately, all of these accounts appear to have been based on speculation or very late legend. Moreover, the term 'Lothian', with more than six different meanings after 1100, would be too vague to be of much historical use for understanding pre-1100 political geography *even if* we had cause to believe any single one of these accounts in some way reproduced some pre-Conquest tradition.[76] Better evidence suggests that the area east of the Esk and south of the Lammermuir remained in Northern English hands until the 1040s at least, perhaps until the reign of Máel Coluim III.[77] The *Chronicle of the Kings of Alba* tells us that Edinburgh was

---

73 *CMD*, 524; *HSC*, c.13, 52–3.
74 *HSC*, c.20, 58–9. The story about the move to Chester-le-Street is not in *Cronica Monasterii Dunelmensis*. The author of the latter believed that the Cuthbertine shrine had already arrived at Durham by the reign of King Edmund, i.e. 939–46, for which see *CMD*, 526. Craster believed *Cronica* to have been later than *Historia de Sancto Cuthberto*, but this was based on his belief that *Historia* had been completed in the tenth century, a position that has largely been abandoned by modern scholars in favour of South's mid-to-late eleventh-century date.
75 Warner of Rouen, *Moriuht*, ed. and trans. C. J. McDonough (Toronto, 1995), 76–81.
76 McGuigan, 'Neither Scotland nor England', c.5, and Appendix IV.a.
77 Woolf, *From Pictland to Alba*, 235–6; McGuigan, 'Neither Scotland nor England', c.5. For the account of how, *c.* 1030, relics were taken from Tyninghame, Coldingham, Melrose, Hexham and other places to Durham by Ælfred son of Westou, father and contemporary of some of Symeon's informants, see *LDE*. iii.7, 162–5.

'abandoned to the Scots' in the time of Ildulb mac Causantín (r. 954–62).[78] This passage appears to be an interpolation, but may reflect some real development that someone took from a reliable tradition.[79] On the other hand, a successor of Ildulb, Cinaed mac Maíl Choluim (r. *c.* 977–95), is said to have 'walled the fords of Frew' after an invasion of *Saxonia*, suggesting that the south bank of the Forth was still foreign territory to the Scots later in the century.[80]

There is credible evidence that the 'Northern English' realm saw fluctuation of power in the west too. The Ayrshire and Galloway regions appear to have been given the name *Airer Saxan*, 'coastland of the English', by their Gaelic neighbours in the early tenth century; but it is very likely that Northern English power in the Firth of Clyde and northern Solway Firth regions had ceased to exist by the tenth century.[81] A tenth-century abbot of Heversham in Westmorland, Tilred, was able to became abbot of Norham and, possibly, bishop of St Cuthbert.[82] The implication might be that Westmorland and the Tweed basin shared membership of one political system as late as the time of Edward the Elder, although it is possible that Tilred was simply a refugee. Oswulf of Bamburgh's responsibility for the 'treachery of Stainmore', at the boundary of the future counties of York and Westmorland, may be read to suggest that he and the Northern English were responsible for the Westmorland side.[83] According to the *Chronicle of the Kings of Alba* Cináed mac Maíl Choluim in the later tenth century (probably the 970s or 980s) carried out a raid that 'plundered *Saxonia* as far as Stainmore', implying that the region to the north of Stainmore was 'English'.[84] The natural reading is that all the territory was in the Northern English polity. On the other hand, the Scottish author may not have been knowledgeable enough or interested enough to distinguish different political communities in northern England. An enigmatic entry in manuscripts D and E of the *Anglo-Saxon Chronicle* makes reference to a people called the *Westmoringas*. It is said that, in 966 (recte

---

78 *CKA*, 151, 159.
79 Woolf, *From Pictland to Alba*, 193–5; see also P. Dunshea, 'Edinburgh's Renown in the Early Middle Ages', this volume, 50–78, at 61–2.
80 *CKA*, 151, 161.
81 *AU* 913.5; for discussion of this region, see T. O. Clancy, 'The Gall-Ghàidheil and Galloway', *JSNS* 2 (2008), 19–50, particularly 43.
82 *HSC*, c.21, 58–61.
83 *RW*, s.a. 950, ed. Coxe, i, 402–3.
84 *CKA*, 151, 161.

962/3?), 'Thored, Gunner's son, ravaged *Westmoringa land*' (*Ðoreð, Gunneres sunu, forhergode Westmoringaland*).[85] The fact that the *Westmoringas* are attacked by a Yorkshire *dux* suggests that the region was detached from the West Saxon dominated Anglo-Danish region. Unfortunately, however, this says nothing directly about the relationship between the *Westmoringas* and the rulers of Bamburgh.

The issue of Strathclyde expansion, of course, affects how we should understand the Northumbrian 'west country' of the tenth century. A writer based in France around 1000 believed that the 'Northmen' and Cumbrians had shared a border in the 940s. We cannot know the extent to which the author's understanding of detail had become abstracted as a result of chronological and geographic distance, but taken at face value the information means that either the Norse rulers of York or the Cumbrians of Strathclyde had, at least in the 940s, subdued, or gained overlordship over, Bamburgh territory.[86] At some point in the mid eleventh century, a certain Gospatric issued a writ in relation to the lands in Allerdale (i.e. the western part of what would become the county of Cumberland); the writ shows the region under Northumbrian dominion, but the address clause refers to the people who 'dwell in all the lands that were Cumbrian' (*þeo þoonan on eallun þam landann þeo þeoron Cōmbres*).[87] Indeed, the area around Carlisle later took the name 'Cumberland'. It would be reasonable to conclude that, in the mid eleventh century, the territory had recently been under Strathclyde control. Originally borrowings from the British endonym (*Cymry* in modern Welsh), *Cumere, Cumbraland*, etc, likely represent the northern Old English terms for regions dominated by British speakers and, consequently, the people and territory of Strathclyde.[88] Although there is no direct evidence that the kings of Strathclyde conquered Allerdale or the area around Carlisle, some process or event like that is indirectly suggested by the application of 'Cumbrian' terminology. Strathclyde expansion is a strong possibility in the later tenth century, particularly when one of its

---

85 *ASC*, MS D 966, ed. Cubbin, 46, trans. Whitelock, 76.
86 Reimann of Metz, *De S. Cadroe Abbate*, in J. Bolland and G. Henschenius (eds), *Acta Sanctorum*, Martius, i (Antwerp, 1668), 469–81, at 476; W. F. Skene, *Chronicles of the Picts, Chronicles of the Scots* (Edinburgh, 1867), 116; trans. *ES*, i, 441.
87 *Northern Chrs*, no. 21.
88 A. Woolf, 'Reporting Scotland in the Anglo-Saxon Chronicle', in A. Jorgensen (ed.) *Reading the Anglo-Saxon Chronicle: Language, Literature, History* (Turnhout, 2010), 221–39, at 230–2.

rulers, King Máel Coluim, appears to have enjoyed significant power.[89] There is also a possibility that the area south of the Forth, but west of the Esk, lay in the Strathclyde sphere in the tenth or eleventh centuries.[90] One way or the other, it is difficult to deny some kind of revival of Cumbrian Britishness in the western parts of Northumbria. Together with the emergence of the *Westmoringas* by the 960s, it is tempting to conclude that Bamburgh power, at best, became very weak west of the Cheviots and Pennines for a significant period after *c.* 960. It is also worth noting that men from 'Northern England' were said to have made up a section of the army of Dublin that fought at Clontarf in 1014, suggesting perhaps that much of the Northumbrian 'west country' (and elsewhere) may have developed strong ties with Dublin by the early eleventh century.[91]

The picture overall suggests that the Northern English polity consisted of a core set of territories between the Forth and Tyne, perhaps running from roughly Eldbottle or Dunbar to somewhere like Warkworth on the River Coquet. It is also possible that for much of the tenth century the rulers of Bamburgh enjoyed some sort of extensive authority over a larger area, probably stretching as far south as the Tees, and perhaps for some time as far west as the Irish Sea in the south and West Lothian in the north. It is, moreover, likely that they competed for these regions, perhaps not always successfully, with the rulers of Scotland, Strathclyde and the Danelaw. In the period between 867 and 954, the 'Northern English' may have borne occasional subjection to the Anglo-Danes. This is what the early twelfth-century annalist who wrote about the kings after Ælla believed.[92] We have several instances of recorded conflict between the Northern English and Scandinavian Northumbrians, including the battle of Corbridge (918),[93] the burning of Tyninghame and enslavement of Lindisfarne (941),[94] a Norse victory in 952,[95] and the treachery of Stainmore in (traditionally) 954.[96]

---

89 For a recent discussion of Strathclyde expansion, see Edmonds, 'The Expansion of the Kingdom of Strathclyde', 43–66.
90 McGuigan, 'Neither Scotland nor England', 148, n. 448.
91 *Cogadh*, c.87, 150–2.
92 *RW*, s.a. 867, ed. Coxe, i, 298–9.
93 *AU* 918.4, fought at 'the Tyne in Northern England' (*Tine la Saxanu Tuaiscirt*); *HSC*, cc. 22, 24, pp. 60–1, 62–3.
94 *Chronicle of 957*, s.a. 941, ed. Arnold, ii, 94; cf. *RW*, s.a. 941, ed. Coxe, i, 396.
95 *AU* 952.2.
96 *RW*, s.a. 950, ed. Coxe, i, 402–3.

However, by the early eleventh century the status and territories of the rulers of Bamburgh were becoming increasingly tenuous, not because of the threat posed by their immediate neighbours, but because of the emerging superpower in the island: the West Saxon kingdom of England. The rulers of Bamburgh generally seem to have benefited from pursuing a friendly and co-operative relationship with them in the tenth century. A subordinate but loose relationship with the rulers of Wessex, fellow Englishmen, may have been an important strategy for Oswulf of Bamburgh and other Eadwulfings seeking power and independence in that era. During the time of Uhtred, the ruler of Bamburgh said to have fought at Carham, that relationship provided the Eadwulfings with an opportunity to reunite much of Northumbria. The following section attempts to understand how this opportunity emerged.

West Saxon government in Northumbria

One of the problems faced by the scholar of late tenth- and early eleventh-century Northumbria was the undue and misleading influence of Anglo-Norman-era texts. In the twelfth century, there were many attempts to get to grips with Viking Age Northumbria, but all of them tackled their subject from a twelfth-century perspective and with limited knowledge. The kingship of Northumbria, so famously documented by Bede's *Historia ecclesiastica*, was known to these scholars and regarded as very important. Reliance on Bede forced all English historians to see the early years of their (often adopted) country from the point of view of a Northumbrian. They were also aware that 'Northumbria' was the name of an earldom that, between 1100 and 1135, was in the hands of King Henry I. There were several attempts to reconstruct the successions of earls who had come before King Henry, and even to link them to the ancient kingship. One influential tradition (though not the only one)[97] sought to recount King Henry's predecessors as far back as the death of the King Erik in 954, which they believed marked the end of the independent Northumbrian kingship. The authors incorporated a story about the creation of the new earldom, the tradition we can call the 'Northumbrian Earldom Foundation Legend'. It survives in two variants.

---

97   Cf. *DNPB*, 32–4.

The first version, Version A, is attested in *De Primo Saxonum Adventu*. According to this, after the death of King Erik, Oswulf administered Northumbria for King Eadred; subsequently, Eadred's successor Edgar divided Northumbria, handing York to one Oslac and the land *a Teisa usque Myreforth* ('from the Tees to *Myreforth*') to a certain *Eadulf cognomento Yvelcild*.[98] An extended variant of this occurs in the thirteenth-century St Albans compilation known under the name John of Wallingford.[99] Version B, probably based on Version A as found in *De Primo Saxonum Adventu*, occurs in a tract inserted into *Historia Regum*, s.a. 1072, and into Roger of Howden's *Chronica*, s.a. 952. According to B, Eadred appointed Oswulf as earl over the territory taken from Erik, but then during the reign of King Edgar he was joined in office by Oslac. To Oswulf was assigned the land north of the Tyne (*ad Aquilonalem plagam Tinae*) and to Oslac York (*super Eboracum*).[100]

Neither variant was written before the 1100s, but the names employed in the 'Foundation Account', particularly Version A, suggest the influence of a lost source, one that reproduced some near-contemporary information. Oslac and Oswulf, it is true, could have been found in surviving annalistic material; but Eadwulf *Yvelcild* appears only as an obscure charter witness (and without any nickname).[101] It is unclear why there is disagreement about the mutual border of the two earldoms, the Tyne or the Tees alternatively. If *De Primo Saxonum Adventu* can be taken as the more authoritative version, as appears obligatory, it seems like the author of Version B has altered 'Tees' to 'Tyne' (perhaps, as Woolf has suggested, and as Woodman suggests elsewhere in this volume, because the Tyne emerged, by the 1120s, as the boundary between the new county of Northumberland and the franchise of Durham).[102] The term *Myreforth*, used in Version A, does not occur in any other text (so far as this author is presently aware, at least), and *Myreforth* is not the twelfth-century term for the Firth of Forth usually

---

98 *DPSA*, 382.
99 *Chron. Wallingford*, 54.
100 *HR*, s.a. 1072, ed. Arnold, ii, 197; *RHC*, s.a. 952, ed. Stubbs, i, 57.
101 *Sawyer*, nos 766, 771, 779, 806; Keynes, *Atlas*, table 56. Note his appearance as the escort of the Scottish king Cináed mac Maíl Choluim on his way to receive Lothian, which occurs in *De Primo Saxonum Adventu*, is also inserted into Roger of Wendover's obit of King Edgar's, s.a. 975, ed. Coxe, i, 416.
102 Woolf, *From Pictland to Alba*, 76; and Woodman, 'Annals 848 to 1118', 216–17.

used by Anglo-French writers of Latin, who in that century normally style the estuary something like 'Water of the Scots'.

The creation of an 'earldom' in the reign of Edgar may be a real event, and if so probably one of the most important in Northumbrian history. An entry in the *Anglo-Saxon Chronicle* tradition common to manuscripts 'D', 'E' and 'F', made in the eleventh century from a set of pre-existing northern annals, notifies us of a certain Oslac's accession to the ealdordom (*feng to ealdordome*), *sub anno* 966.[103] In the heartlands of his own kingdom, the West Saxon English rulers relied heavily on a subordinate known as an 'ealdorman', in Latin usually called *dux*; from the tenth century the similarly ambiguous term *eorl*, 'earl', is increasingly used to describe the status of this office holder. By the later tenth century ealdormen were drawn from high status lineages able to supplement royal power with their own resources, in turn boosting their own capabilities by acting as the delegate and ally of an irresistible monarch. The ealdorman had already become a province-based official in the late ninth-century *Laws of Ælfred*.[104] By the later tenth century the official ealdorman and bishop of a province (*scire*) seem to have been required to attend a biannual provincial assembly, the *sciregemot*.[105] The office brought a specific honour-price to its holder's kindred, as well as a range of judicial privileges.[106] If Northumbrian territories were to be integrated into the West Saxon kingdom of the English, the creation of an ealdordom was a necessity. Oslac's appearance as ealdorman in the *Anglo-Saxon Chronicle* is therefore an important contemporary notice.

Oslac's charter attestations as *dux* appear to begin as early as 963.[107] As a date for Oslac's accession then, 966 appears problematic. This calls for a brief digression. Dorothy Whitelock suggested the possibility that the charters were at fault.[108] However, one very simple transcription mistake would explain the error in the annal, which is a much more

---

103 *ASC* MSS DEF 966, ed. Cubbin, 46, trans. Whitelock, 76.
104 *Laws of Alfred*, c.37, ed. and trans. F. L. Attenborough, *The Laws of the Earliest English Kings* (Cambridge, 1922), 62– 93, at 80– 1.
105 *III Edgar*, c.5, ed. and trans. A. J. Robertson, *The Laws of the Kings of England from Edmund to Henry I* (Cambridge, 1925), 24–9, at 26–7.
106 E.g. *Laws of Ine*, c.45, ed. and trans. Attenborough, *Laws*, 50–1; *III Æthelred*, c.1, ed. and trans. Robertson, *Laws*, 64–5.
107 *Sawyer*, nos 766, 771, 779, 806; Keynes, *Atlas*, table 56.
108 Whitelock, 'Dealings of the Kings of England with Northumbria', 78; for charter attestations of 965, see *Sawyer*, nos 732, 733, 734; for 963, see no. 716.

economical way of resolving the problem than attributing very specific problems to documents from two separate religious archives, especially as Oslac's 965 charter attestations are not obviously problematic.[109] There is further reason to doubt 966. King Edgar issued a set of ordinances in response to a plague afflicting his realm, which survives in a document known as the 'Wihtbordesstan Code' (*IV Edgar*). In the surviving form, the king orders that his decrees be followed by the king's English and Danish subjects, but as it closes it is stated that 'Further, Earl Oslac (*Oslác eorl*) and all the population dwelling in his ealdordom (*on his ealdordom*) shall promote the observance of this', adding that copies should be made for the ealdormen Ælfhere [of Mercia] and Æthelwine [of East Anglia].[110] Ælfhere attests as senior ealdorman 956–83, and Æthelwine 962–92, both having corresponding obits in *Anglo-Saxon Chronicle* tradition.[111] The plague we know elsewhere is mentioned s.a. 962 in manuscript A of the *Anglo-Saxon Chronicle*.[112] If this is the same plague, the ordinance is likely to have been issued around 962 or 963. Other complications about how this document can be interpreted are possible; but, on balance, while a later date in Edgar's reign is a possibility it seems more likely that Oslac obtained his position around 963.[113]

---

109 These are Abingdon (*Sawyer*, nos 732–4) and York (*Sawyer*, no. 716=*Northern Chrs*, no. 4); this point is addressed by Whitelock, who says 'the Newbald charter is preserved only in a late cartulary, while the three charters of 965 are all in an Abingdon cartulary and couched in identical form, so may share an error in date' (Whitelock, 'Dealings of the Kings of England with Northumbria', 78). An Oslac is also named in two other charters of 963, *Sawyer* nos 712 (=*Northern Chrs*, no. 4) and 712a, but is not titled *dux*. Whitelock pointed out ('Dealings') that an Oslac subscribed as more junior *minister* in 966 (i.e. *Sawyer* no. 738), which she read as supporting 966; however, it is surely at least as likely to be the Oslac who also attests in 970 (*Sawyer* no. 779) rather than the northern ealdorman. There is a useful recent discussion of early Oslac in Woodman, *Northern Chrs*, 123–4.
110 *IV Edgar*, c.15, ed. and trans. Robertson, 28–39, at 38–9.
111 *ASC* MS CDE 983 and 992, trans. Whitelock, 81, 82; Keynes, *Atlas*, tables 56, 62; D. Henson, *A Guide to Late Anglo-Saxon England from Ælfred to Eadgar: 871 to 1074 AD* (Hockwold cum Wilton, 1998), 127, 128.
112 *ASC* MS A 962, ed. Bately, 75, trans. Whitelock, 76; S. Keynes, 'Edgar, *Rex Admirabilis*', in D. Scragg (ed.), *Edgar King of the English, 959–975: New Interpretations* (Woodbridge, 2008), 3–59, at 11.
113 It is also worth noting the reservations about the *IV Edgar* and the 962 plague in P. Wormald, *The Making of English Law: King Alfred to the Twelfth Century: Vol. 1, Legislation and its Limits* (Oxford, 1999), 441–2, although these rely heavily (but not entirely) on accepting the northern recension of the *Anglo-Saxon Chronicle*'s date of 966.

The 'Northumbrian Earldom Foundation Legend' would suggest that Oslac's accession, which the charters put in 963 and the annal in 966, marked the beginning of the West Saxon ealdordom in Northumbria. Various Northumbrian and Danelaw *duces* were appearing long before even 963, but these *duces* were not ealdormen; almost certainly, they were local rulers or strongmen who, due to their high status and political role in northern society, were regarded by West Saxon bureaucrats as analogous to West Saxon ealdormen; whenever we know more about them, we know they have very high status and bear titles like 'hold', 'earl', or even 'king'; a few preside over regions similar in size to the pre-Viking-Age kingdoms of England.[114] As David Woodman has pointed out, the drafters of royal charters in the tenth century did not always know how to classify northern strongmen, and might be confused about how to represent their status.[115] Oslac, however, was a familiar figure. In the 'Wihtbordesstan Code', Oslac's position is not just that of a strongman benefiting from particular inherited status. He was responsible, to the English monarch, for an ealdordom. His political responsibilities are explicitly paralleled by Ælfhere ealdorman of Mercia and Æthelwine ealdorman of East Anglia.

Some recent discussions of ealdormen have come to the conclusion that Wessex itself had six of them until the first decade of the tenth century, but two (one for the shires west of Selwood, one for the shires to its east) from then until the reign of Cnut.[116] During the reign of Edward the Elder and the early reign of Æthelstan, the realm generally has four to seven *duces* attesting charters at any one time; however, during Æthelstan's time as overlord of Northumbria and the Danelaw, at least from 929 until 935, the appearances of miscellaneous northern *duces* raise this number as high as fifteen.[117] A large number of northern *duces* can still be counted in the early part of Edgar's reign. Among the names in charters issued in 958 and in 963, mostly at York it should be said, are *Anfred*, Leod, *Myrdach*, *Ascured*, *Ayered*, Cytelbearn, Oscytel, with

---

114 E.g. McGuigan, 'Neither Scotland nor England', 95–101.
115 Woodman, *Northern Chrs*, 123–4.
116 B. Yorke, *Wessex in the Early Middle Ages* (London, 1995), 98–101, following L. N. Banton, 'Ealdormen and Earls in England from the Reign of King Alfred to the Reign of King Æthelred II', DPhil dissertation (University of Oxford, 1981), which I have not been able to consult.
117 Keynes, *Atlas*, tables 35 and 38.

Urum, Gunner, Halfdan, Morcar and Uhtred representing continuity from earlier reigns. *Anfred, Ascured, Ayered*, Oscytel and Cytelbearn make only solitary attestations in Yorkshire-related charters, *Anfred* in 956, *Ascured* and *Ayered* in 958, Cytelbearn in 963, and Oscytel in 963.[118] Leod appears in three charters in three different years, 956, 958 and 959.[119] *Myrdach* (also spelled *Mirdach*) occurs in two charters, one of 958 and one of 963.[120] If the northern ealdordom existed before 963, the appearances of these *duces* make its ealdormen invisible; but the chances are better that King Eadred and King Edgar until *c.* 963 continued Æthelstan's strategy and attempted to rule and promote royal power through multiple direct relationships with various secular figures powerful enough to be thought of as *duces*, alongside, of course, the archbishops of York.

The 'Foundation Legend' and the picture of the 'Northumbrian earldom' in the Viking Age presented by Anglo-Norman sources seem be marred by an attempt to present false, anachronistic parallelism between the ealdordom created for Oslac and the older polity over which Oswulf presided. The Bamburgh-run polity in the north-east of Northumbria was certainly not a *creation* of either Eadred or Edgar, although as we saw above it is likely that Oswulf formally accepted some subordinate relationship with the Southumbrian monarchs. However, it is possible that part of Oswulf's deal with Eadred was some sort of junior overlordship that effectively made him the *de facto* ealdorman of the area around York. With the death of Oswulf, the potentate directly responsible for the removal of the last Norse king, the obligations owed to the Bamburgh family by the West Saxon

---

[118] Sawyer, nos 659, 679, 681, 716; *Prosopography of Anglo-Saxon England* [hereafter *PASE*] (online at http://www.pase.ac.uk/), s.v. 'Anfred 1', 'Ascured 1', 'Ayered 1', and 'Cytelbearn 1'. It is tempting to connect these *duces* to the emergence of new administrative units, which in this area would be the three Ridings of Yorkshire and, perhaps, adjacent groupings like the *Westmoringas*.

[119] *PASE*, s.v. 'Leod 1' and 'Leot 1'.

[120] Sawyer, nos 679, 712a. The name is the Gaelic Muiredach, which might lead one to suppose he was a ruler from (what is now) south-western Scotland or even an Irish king. It is also worth noting that the name was used in eastern Northumbria, as is shown by an inscription on a stone cross at Alnmouth, 'Myrdah made me' (*MYREDaH*MEH*wO*), though the latter Myrdah's origin is unknown and the rarity of his skills make it very likely that he did not originate locally; R. I. Page, 'How Long Did the Scandinavian Language Survive in England?', in P. Clemoes and K. Hughes (eds), *England Before the Conquest* (London, 1971), 165–81, at 176.

English kings were gone, freeing them to integrate their holdings in southern Northumbria. On that basis, it is tempting to date Oswulf's death to sometime around 962.

From about 963, around the time Oslac probably took power, the northern *duces* all but vanish, the general exception being the single northern *dux* regarded as the region's ealdorman (below). The other occasional exceptions to this in Edgar's reign are one appearance by a 'Malcolm' in 970 and four appearances 968–70 of one Eadwulf (almost certainly Eadwulf *Yvelcild*), clearly the rulers from Strathclyde and Bamburgh, whose territories lay beyond the dominion taken from the Uí Ímair in the 950s.[121] In 994, during Æthelred's reign, Oswulf's grandson Waltheof of Bamburgh makes a one-off appearance alongside a mysterious figure named Northman; both appear at the royal court, probably only very briefly, in the aftermath of a Scandinavian attack on Bamburgh.[122] In these cases, there is no good reason to think that either of them based their power inside regions subject to direct West Saxon English governance. Most likely they came from beyond the area gained from the Uí Ímair, and therefore outside the York ealdordom (and, also, presumably, outside the diocese of York).

The false parallelism is even more evident in the lists of earls that follow the 'Foundation Account' in two surviving versions. Both in the list of *De Primo Saxonum Adventu* and in the list following Version B, it is claimed that the two-fold 'earldom' was brought back together by Waltheof father of Uhtred. According to the account, Waltheof passed the reunited 'earldom' to his son Uhtred, and Uhtred to his brother Eadwulf *Cudel*, and Eadwulf to his nephews the sons of Uhtred until, in the time of the Mercian earl Morcar, Northumbria was again redivided.[123] This presentation, a reconstruction made in the early 1100s, falls apart when compared with contemporary sources. The relevant *Anglo-Saxon Chronicle* annals (written in the 1020s) tell us that the land over the Humber was governed by the Uhtred as earl until Cnut removed him from the position. Cnut appointed one Erik to Uhtred's office (*eorl*

---

121 Keynes, *Atlas*, table 56; Malcolm's appearance is *Sawyer*, no. 779 or *Liber Eliensis*, ii.5, ed. E. O. Blake (London, 1962), 76–8. The charter has him ranked before Eadwulf, which would suggest he was the reigning king or heir to Strathclyde rather than say, a successor to Muiredach's *ducatus*.
122 *Sawyer*, no. 992.
123 *HR*, s.a. 1072, ed. Arnold, ii, 197–9; *RHC*, s.a. 952, ed. Stubbs, i, 57–9.

eall swa Uhtred wæs).[124] According to the lists, Uhtred's successor was not Erik but his own brother Eadwulf *Cudel*. The twelfth-century earl lists have the earldom as a hereditary possession of the Bamburgh family from Waltheof onwards, but Erik was not even a member of the Bamburgh family, and indeed he is described in *Encomium Emmae Reginae*, written in the early 1040s, as 'earl and prince of the province that is called Norway' (*dux et princeps prouintiae quae Norduuega dicitur*).[125]

The lists make sense if the historian views them as built from genealogical material relating to the Bamburgh family supplemented by annalistic and historical references to the Northumbria-based ealdormen. Very few Bamburgh 'earls' are mentioned in surviving English chronicle material, but several of the ealdormen do appear. In the lists affiliated with the 'Northumbrian Earldom Foundation Account', Uhtred was succeeded by his brother Eadwulf *Cudel*; he, in turn, came to be succeeded by Uhtred's son Ealdred and then by another of Uhtred's sons, Eadwulf. Most likely, this depiction of the Bamburgh succession is roughly accurate, as Eadwulf son of Uhtred's existence seems to be confirmed by *ASC*, s.a. 1041.[126] What has happened is that the Anglo-Norman researchers have tried to patch together an account of the Northumbrian earldom centred on the Bamburgh family, but have confused the Bamburgh 'earldom' with the one that the West Saxon kings created for the area around York. During Henry I's reign, 1100–35, there was one earldom in Northumbria, held by the king in practice but with active historical claims centred on Matilda of Northampton, descended from both rulers of Bamburgh and from Siward, the Danish Northumbrian ealdorman. The men responsible for the above earl lists were back-projecting that earldom into the past.

We are well informed about the men who succeeded Erik of Hlaðir, and none of them was from the Bamburgh family – i.e. Siward (a Dane), Tostig (a West Saxon) and Morcar (a Mercian), followed by a series of

---

124 *ASC* MS C 1016, ed. O'Brien O'Keeffe, 101; trans. Whitelock, 94.
125 Text in *Encomium Emmae Reginae*, ii.7, ed. and trans. A. Campbell with S. Keynes (Cambridge, 1998), 22; see S. Keynes, 'Cnut's Earls', in A. Rumble (ed.), *Reign of Cnut* (London, 1994), 43–88, at 57–8, 70. The entry s.a. 1016, as we have seen elsewhere in this volume (p. 12), may have been a reflective comment rather than a direct description of the year. *ASC* MSS CDE 1017 suggests that Cnut as king may not have appointed Erik officially until 1017.
126 *ASC* MSS CD 1041, trans. Whitelock, 106.

Normans.[127] We are also able to trace a clear and probably exhaustive succession to the ealdordom prior to Erik. Oslac's successor was a magnate named Thored, who was followed in turn by Ælfhelm.[128] There is no period of charter overlap between these men, and other evidence we have seems to demonstrate that the three all held the same office. According to the northern recension of the *Anglo-Saxon Chronicle*, Oslac was expelled from England in 975, seemingly as part of the political turmoil produced by the death of King Edgar the same year. Oslac is never heard of again, but Thored witnesses charters after the succession of Edgar's son, Æthelred. Archbishop Oswald of York seems to have claimed that he lost lands to Earl Thored, which would indeed link him to the region.[129] Ælfhelm is specifically titled in two charters *dux transhumbranae gentis* and *Norðanhumbrensium provinciarum dux*.[130] Ælfhelm was killed in 1006, possibly at the instigation of his fellow ealdorman and fellow Mercian, Eadric Streona.[131]

Conclusion: aborted unification of Northumbria

The next ealdorman on record is Uhtred son of Waltheof,[132] the lord of Bamburgh named by *Historia Regum* as the opponent of Máel Coluim mac Cinaeda at Carham in 1018. It is possible that King Edgar had intended some sort of overlordship over the Bamburgh-governed Northern English as one of the powers of the new ealdormen in Northumbria. Even if this were the case, however, such overlordship is unlikely to have gone much beyond diplomatic formalities. With the

---

127 For the origins of Siward, see T. Bolton, 'Was the Family of Earl Siward and Earl Waltheof a Lost Line of the Ancestors of the Danish Royal Family', *Nottingham Medieval Studies* 55 (2007), 41–71.

128 Whitelock, 'Dealings of the Kings of England with Northumbria', 79–80; A. Williams, A. P. Smyth and D. P. Kirby (eds), *A Biographical Dictionary of Dark Age Britain: England, Scotland and Wales, c.500–c.1050* (London, 1991), s.v. 'Ælfhelm ealdorman 993–1006', 9, and s.v. 'Thored ealdorman 979–92', 223; Kapelle, *The Norman Conquest of the North*, 14; Fletcher, *Bloodfeud*, 70, 73; Henson, *Guide to Late Anglo-Saxon England*, 129.

129 *Sawyer*, no. 1453, trans. Whitelock, *EHD*, i, 565.

130 *Sawyer*, nos 891, 1380; the witness list in which this phrase is contained can be found in J. Caley, H. Ellis and B. Bandinel (eds), *Monasticon Anglicanum* (1823–1849), VI.3, 1446.

131 *ASC* MSS CDE 1006, trans. Whitelock, 87.

132 *ASC* MSS CDE 1013, trans. Whitelock, 92.

disappearance of independent Scandinavian rulers in England after the 950s neither the West Saxons nor the Northern English had the same incentive to continue their alliance. Or, at least, the alliance no longer merited any significant political price. After the 950s, indeed, the Northern English ruler's relationship with the West Saxon English kings seems to have been more like that of the kings of Gwynedd or Strathclyde than that of the northern ealdorman's. An *Eadulf Dux*, almost certainly Eadwulf *Yvelcild*, appears around 970, a period when an equally elusive bishop of Lindisfarne also shows up, Ælfsige;[133] but it is not until 994 that anyone from the region re-appears in Southumbria. Again, the context of Earl Waltheof's lone attestation is also very specific, falling a year after Bamburgh had been sacked by an army of non-Insular Scandinavians.[134] The next bishop thought to be associated with the Northern English realm is Ealdhun, whose first definitive appearance does not come until 1009 – a significant fact, given that the body of surviving charters is substantial at this stage and that most English bishops, including York, attest such charters regularly.[135] The appearance in 1009 is almost certainly due to the appointment of Waltheof's son Uhtred to the ealdordom, which may have taken place in 1006.[136] The appointment represents a revival of the Bamburgh–Winchester alliance.

In 1006, the Irish sources (alone) record a battle between the Scots and Northumbrians (*Bellum eter fhiru Alban & Saxanu*), in which the English side was victorious.[137] An Anglo-Norman-era text, *De Obsessione Dunelmi* ('On the Siege of Durham'), reproduced a tradition that Æthelred had promoted Uhtred to the earldom of York as a result of this victory over the Scots, a tradition that fits strangely well with contemporary information.[138] The victory may have impressed Æthelred, and certainly would have made Uhtred a more appealing ally, a figure with proven martial success whose charisma and skills might help him contain and control the northern Danelaw and boost English resistance

---

133 *Sawyer*, no. 779; Keynes, *Atlas*, table 56, for Eadwulf's last appearance; *Sawyer* no. 781, Keynes, *Atlas*, table LIV, for Ælfsige's.
134 *ASC* CDE 993.
135 *Sawyer*, no. 992.
136 *Sawyer*, nos 921, 921; Keynes, *Atlas*, table 62.
137 *AU* 1006.5.
138 *DOD*, 215–16, trans. C. J. Morris, *Marriage and Murder in Eleventh-Century Northumbria: A Study of 'De Obsessione Dunelmi'*, Borthwick Papers 82 (York, 1992), 1–2.

to the armies of Denmark. Resurrecting the old alliance of Eadred's era allowed the West Saxons to utilise the Bamburgh family's resources, at least on a temporary basis. Æthelred cemented the alliance by giving one of his daughters to Uhtred in marriage. For Uhtred, the marriage boosted his profile and tied his family's future to that of the West Saxon dynasty. The ealdordom was also licence to expand his family's power further and deeper into the Danish settlement-zone of Yorkshire and Country Durham, a goal that Uhtred may have pursued with his earlier marriages.[139] The authority that Æthelred gave him in 'England proper' may have extended into Lindsey and, in 1013 at least, included command of the king's army north of Watling Street.[140]

The alliance with Uhtred was probably a sign of Æthelred's weakness, and it was this weakness that prevented the Eadwulfings from realising the full potential of the alliance. Æthelred's fight with the Danes was, famously, a losing one. Although Uhtred may have survived the king's immediate downfall, his marriage-link with the fallen regime probably excluded the possibility of any permanent accommodation with Cnut. Hostility from the invading Danes, the Scots and the aristocracy of Yorkshire could have proved too much for Uhtred. According to the *Anglo-Saxon Chronicle*, Cnut not only removed him from the ealdordom but was also, at some unclear date, responsible for his death.[141] The act itself, according to the tradition presented by *De Obsessione Dunelmi*, was the work of a Danish hold named Thurbrand, possibly lord of Holderness in Yorkshire.[142] The *Anglo-Saxon Chronicle* appears to tell us that Erik, Uhtred's successor as royal ealdorman, was put in place in 1017. Uhtred, presumably, was still able to preside over Bamburgh. If the date of Erik's appointment is correct, 1018 would have been an opportune year for the Scots and Clydefolk to attack the homeland of Uhtred.

The polity that the Scots fought in 1018 was a shadow of the former kingdom of Northumbria. Still, a thousand years after the battle of Carham few historians would hesitate about calling the *Angli* who

---

139 For some astute analysis of this dynamic, see W. M. Aird, *St Cuthbert and the Normans: The Church of Durham, 1071–1153* (Woodbridge, 1998), 47–8.
140 *ASC* MSS CDE 1013. Gaimar described him as 'Earl Uhtred *de* Lindsey' (*Li quens Uctreid de Lindeseie*), for which see Geffrei Gaimar, *Estoire des Engleis/History of the English*, line 4145, ed. and trans. I. Short (Oxford, 2009), 226–7.
141 *ASC* MS C 1016, ed. O'Brien O'Keefe, 101, trans. Whitelock, 95.
142 *DOD*, 217–18, trans. Morris, *Marriage and Murder*, 3. For an engaging account of this, and the subsequent acts of revenge, see Fletcher, *Bloodfeud*.

fought at Carham in 1018 'Northumbrians'. In the early eleventh century, the idea of Northumbria was still alive in various forms. One of the most important reasons for this is the career of Uhtred of Bamburgh. His success restored some form of unity to the old realm, and so between *c.* 1006 and *c.* 1017 the *Angli* across their southern border presented a threat to the Alpinid Scottish kings not thitherto experienced. From *c.* 900 to *c.* 1016 England's kings formed alliances with Bamburgh when it helped them contend with the Danes; after 1016, England's rulers were themselves Danes. By the 1040s, Uhtred's power in the north of England had come to be replicated by one of his successors as ealdorman, another Dane named Siward. Indeed, none of Uhtred's successors as ealdormen was Northumbrian, but were Danes, West Saxons, Mercians and Continentals. Uhtred of Bamburgh was Northumbria's last chance, it seems, to re-establish a native-run Northumbrian kingdom. If the battle of Carham marked the end of Uhtred's prospects then, in that sense at least, it can be seen as a legitimate part of how we understand the end of Northumbria and the rise of a direct Anglo-Scottish border.

APPENDIX

Rulers of the Northern English, 867–1041 (certain and possible)

The following is an attempt to provide a preliminary list of Northern English rulers – certain and possible – between 867 and 1041, based on the evidence modern historians have to hand at the present time.

Osberht (fl. 866–867) *Libellus de Exordio* dated Osberht's accession to 849/850,[143] and the St Albans annals associated with Roger of Wendover to 848.[144] Both dates may be the result of misguided guesswork and deduction by twelfth-century scholars; analysis of the numismatic evidence has tended to suggest a date for Osberht's accession that is much later, possibly in the 860s.[145] It is likely, on similar numismatic evidence, that his reign overlapped with the episcopate of Wulfhere, archbishop of York; however,

---

143 *LDE*, ii.5, 94–5.
144 *RW*, s.a. 848, ed. Coxe, i, 282–3; it is worth noting that the annal includes notice of a solar eclipse.
145 H. E. Pagan, 'Northumbrian Numismatic Chronology in the Ninth Century', *British Numismatic Journal* 38 (1969), 1–15, esp. at 9; C. S. S. Lyon, 'Ninth-Century Northumbrian Chronology', in D. M. Metcalf (ed.), *Coinage in Ninth-Century*

our ability to date Wulfhere (fl. c. 872) is not much more exact.[146] Osberht's only firm date is provided by the *Anglo-Saxon Chronicle*, which says there was an attempt to depose him in 866. The *Anglo-Saxon Chronicle* appears to say that Osberht died at the battle of York, fought between Northumbrians and the Norse 'Great Army' in March 867.[147] The annal is usually read to suggest that Osberht fought against the Great Army. Another possibility is that Osberht was on the Norse side, perhaps relying on the Great Army's support for his bid to retain the throne against his rival, Ælla. Two of the three Northumbrian kings after Ælla bear a name that shares a dithematic suffix with Osberht, a possible indication that Osberht's dynasty benefited from Ælla's death.[148] Osberht was one of the last Northumbrian kings known to Anglo-Norman-era scholars, and so his name featured in various pseudo-historical episodes. According to one twelfth-century tradition, reproduced by the Anglo-French metrical chronicler Geoffrey Gaimar, Osberht raped the wife of a vassal, *Buern Bucecarle*. The story goes on to tell us that *Buern* obtained his revenge by summoning the Great Army, having sought refuge among the Danes and solicited their aid.[149] The eleventh-century *Historia de Sancto Cuthberto* presents a claim that Osberht confiscated Tillmouth and Warkworth from St Cuthbert.[150] On current evidence Osberht is the last native Northumbrian ruler to issue his own coins.

    Northumbria: The Tenth Oxford Symposium on Coinage and Monetary History, BAR British Series 180 (Oxford, 1987), 27–41; D. N. Dumville, 'Textual Archaeology and Northumbrian History Subsequent to Bede', in Metcalf (ed.), *Coinage in Ninth-Century Northumbria*, 43–55.

146 C. S. S. Lyon, 'A Reappraisal of the Sceatta and Styca Coinage of Northumbria', *British Numismatic Journal* 28 (1955), 227–43, at 31; Pagan, 'Northumbrian Numismatic Chronology', 3. The *Chronicle of 957*, ed. Arnold, ii, 92, says Wulfhere died in 892; Roger of Wendover says 895 (*RW*, s.a. 895, ed. Coxe, i, 61); both put Wulfhere's accession at 854 (for survey of dates, see Pagan, 'Northumbrian Numismatic Chronology', 5), surely not reliable but the claim that Wulfhere was expelled from his see in 872 occurs as part of a group of detailed notices fossilising seemingly secure personal synchronisms and, possibly, reliable chronology; if so, we could assign Wulfhere a *floruit* of 872.

147 *ASC* MS A 867, ed. Bately, 47, trans. Whitelock, 45; the phrase 'both kings were slain', *þa cyningas begen ofslægene*, seems surely to refer to Osberht alongside Ælla; unless the text is seriously defective, the only other possibility is that the phrase also refers to a separate, unnamed leader of the Norse.

148 McGuigan, 'Ælla and the Descendants of Ivar', 21–2, n. 10.

149 Geffrei Gaimar, *Estoire des Engleis*, lines 2587–2722, ed. and trans. Short, 142–9.

150 *HSC*, c.10, 50–1.

Ælla (d. 867) As previously stated, Ælla appears in the *Anglo-Saxon Chronicle* as part of the chronicle's account of Northumbrian affairs, 866–7. According to this source, the Great Army captured York in 866 during a Northumbrian civil war where some part of Northumbria had risen against Osberht and placed Ælla in the kingship. It was not until early 867 that the Northumbrians attacked the occupiers of the city. Ælla, and probably Osberht too, died during the battle.[151] The battle of York is documented in Irish annals, where alone Ælla is the 'king of the Northern English' killed by the 'Dark *Gaill*' (*Dubgaill*) (*Bellum for Saxanu Tuaisceirt i Cair Ebhroc re n-Dubghallaib, in quo cecidit Alli, rex Saxan Aquilonalium*).[152] In contrast to Osberht, the *Anglo-Saxon Chronicle* describes Ælla as 'unnatural king' (*ungecyndne cyning*), probably meaning he was not of royal descent.[153] The chronicle's description may mirror pro-Osberht propaganda better than reality, but it does indicate that Osberht and Ælla were probably not brothers (as claimed two centuries later in *Historia de Sancto Cuthberto*).[154] Ælla's name may be a hypocoristic form of Ælfwine.[155] His death at the hand of pagans does not appear to have produced a saint's cult (unlike his contemporary King Edmund of East Anglia).[156] Despite his short reign, he had an extraordinary literary afterlife, much greater than Osberht's. It is Ælla and not any East Anglian or Mercian or West Saxon who comes to be remembered as the principal English foe of the Great Army in later Norse sagas, particularly in the cycle associated with Ragnar Loðbrók and his son Ivar 'the Boneless'. The explanation for this, most likely, is that this cycle originated in Norse-speaking lands in Britain and Ireland, where the descendants of Ivar, the *Uí Ímair*, ruled over various territories, including southern and western Northumbria.[157] Ælla is also significant in Anglo-Norman England. In the twelfth-century 'Tale of

---

151 See above for detail regarding *ASC* MS A 867.
152 *AU* 867.7.
153 See above, p. 133, n. 147.
154 *HSC*, c.12, 50–1.
155 See in particular the interchangeability of the names for Ælfwine bishop of Lichfield (acceded in 928 according to a very doubtful annal: *RW*, s.a. 928, ed. Coxe, i, 287); F. Colman, *Grammar of Names in Anglo-Saxon England: The Linguistics and Culture of the Old English Onomasticon* (Oxford, 2014), 139; S. Wilson, *Means of Naming: A Social History* (London, 1998), 74.
156 But see Orderic Vitalis, *Ecclesiastical History*, iv.201, ed. and trans. M. Chibnall, 6 vols (Oxford, 1969–80), ii, 240–1.
157 McGuigan, 'Ælla and the Descendants of Ivar', 22–4.

the Wife of Arnulf', Ælla is given the role of royal rapist that Gaimar had given to Osberht.[158] *Historia de Sancto Cuthberto* accused Ælla of confiscating some of St Cuthbert's estates, including Crayke and Billingham; like the claim about his predecessor Osberht, this is almost certainly a fiction.[159] An Anglo-Norman-era pedigree claims that Ælla had a daughter named Æthelthryth from whom the later rulers of Bamburgh were descended.[160] Other female relatives, probably fictional but perhaps ultimately inspired by some real figure, are mentioned in Scandinavian and Anglo-French sagas, with one tradition making Ælla an ancestor of the kings of Denmark.[161]

Ecgberht I (d. 873) He is one of three immediate successors of Ælla presented to us by certain Anglo-Norman-era sources. The latter consist of king-lists and annals that appear, because of unusual specificity and detail, to have been influenced by some early source. These name Ecgberht as Ælla's replacement on the Northumbrian throne after the battle of York. However, according to *Historia Regum*, Ecgberht I reigned only 'beyond the Tyne'.[162] In Roger of Wendover, Ecgberht only 'obtained the kingship under the power of the Danes' (*sub Danorum potestate regnum adeptus*).[163] It was, indeed, the belief of Symeon of Durham that Ecgberht had been placed over the Northumbrians by the Great Army.[164] *Historia Regum*'s judgement about the Tyne, however, appears to conflict with incidental detail in an annal for 872, where we

---

158 *Narratio de uxore Aernulfi ab Ella Rege Deirorum violata*, in T. D. Hardy and C. T. Martin (eds), *Lestorie des Engles solum la translacion Maistre Geffrei Gaimar*, 2 vols, Rolls Series 91 (London, 1888–9), 328–38.
159 *HSC*, c.10, 50–1.
160 *DNPB*, 33.
161 *Ragnarssona þáttr* mentions a daughter of King Ælla, named Blaeja. She is said to have been married to Sigurd Snake-in-the-Eye, a union that produced Harthacnut, father of Gorm the Old, King of Denmark (and great grandfather of Cnut the Great). In Gaimar his sister's son (*le fiz ta sour*) Orrum is given a comical but important role at the battle of York. For Gaimar and *Orrum*, see Gaimar, *Estoire des Engleis*, lines 2729–2834, ed. and trans. Short, 150–5; for *Ragnarssona þáttr*, see Waggoner, *The Sagas of Ragnar Lodbrok* (New Haven, 2009), 70.
162 *HR*, s.a. 867, ed. Arnold, ii, 106; *RHC*, s.a 867, ed. Stubbs, i, 38.
163 *RW*, s.a. 867, ed. Coxe, i, 299.
164 Symeon of Durham, *Epistola ad Hugonem de archiepiscopis Eboraci*, ed. Arnold, *Sym. Op.*, i, 222–8, at 225. Symeon of Durham, *Epistola*, 225, had a piece of information that told him the archbishop had taken refuge from the Danes at Addingham in Wharfedale.

are told that the Northumbrians expelled King Ecgberht and Archbishop Wulfhere of York.[165] The archbishop of York could hardly be expelled from a kingdom limited to territory north of the Tyne! The reviser here, working in the 1120s, is probably telescoping the battle of York and the post-875 settlement arranged by Halfdan.[166] According to Roger of Wendover, Ecgberht and the archbishop fled to King Burhred of Mercia.[167] According to our annals, Ecgberht died in 873 and was succeeded by Ricsige.[168]

Ricsige (d. 876) The *Anglo-Saxon Chronicle* tells us that in 875 the Great Army wintered on the river Tyne and proceeded to subjugate surrounding lands; three of the Great Army's leaders departed south leaving behind a section of the army for the settlement of Northumbria, which was carried out in 876 under the leadership of a certain Halfdan.[169] Our Anglo-Latin annalists tie this event to the death of Ricsige and the succession of Ecgberht II – Roger of Wendover even claimed that the settlement caused Ricsige to die of grief![170] A certain Eadred of Gainford, named 'son of Ricsige', appears to have lived during the time of Edward the Elder (r. 899–924), and to have had sons of his own, named *Esbrid* and *comes* Ælfstan. There is a possibility that Eadred was Ricsige's son, an idea that is particularly appealing because Ricsige is a very rare name.[171]

Ecgberht II (fl. 876×883) The text that, apparently, supplied the names of the three kings after Ælla appears to have ceased its usefulness at the

---

165 *HR*, s.a. 872, ed. Arnold, ii, 110; *RHC*, s.a 872, ed. Stubbs, i, 41; *RW*, s.a. 872, ed. Coxe, i, 323–4.
166 Perhaps it is worth noting some other potential explanations. For instance, separate expulsions carried out by two different groups of Northumbrians may have occurred. Another marginal possibility is that the problematic *HR* annal originated in a region that, from a Durham perspective, lay 'beyond the Tyne'; if so, 'beyond the Tyne' would mean south of the Tyne, thus resolving the 'contradiction'. These appear overly-convoluted and unnecessary rationalisations, hardly justified given the commonplace nature of such telescoping (e.g. Wendover, s.a. 867, which relates that the Danes reduced and enslaved Northumbria as far as the Tyne, a case of related telescoping).
167 *RW*, s.a. 872, ed. Coxe, i, 324.
168 *HR*, s.a. 873, ed. Arnold, ii, 110; *RHC*, s.a. 873, ed. Stubbs, i, 41–2; *RW*, s.a. 873, ed. Coxe, i, 325.
169 *ASC* MS A 875, 876, ed. Bately, 49–50, trans. Whitelock 48.
170 *HR*, s.a. 876, ed. Arnold, ii, 111; *RHC*, s.a. 876, ed. Stubbs, i, 42. *RW*, s.a. 876, ed. Coxe, i, 327.
171 For this Eadred, see *HSC*, c.24, 62–3.

accession of Ecgberht II. *Historia Regum* claims that Ecgberht was still reigning in 883; the comment forms part of a long extract, of dubious contemporary worth, relating to the accession and munificence of a Danish king called Guthred.[172] It is, nonetheless, very likely that this era is key to the emergence of a polity beyond the Tyne (or at least the Tees) distinct from the Norse settlement-zone. Traditions about Guthred, who appears to be a genuine ruler in the Danelaw (below),[173] relate that he spent his early years in captivity to the 'widow of Whitting(e)ham(e)', a mysterious woman whose location (probably Northumberland, possibly East Lothian) suggests she was based in the Northern English polity.[174]

Guthred (d. 895) Some Anglo-Norman-era lists of Northumbrian rulers make Guthred, son of Harthacnut, successor rather than just, as *Historia Regum* claimed, the colleague of Ecgberht II.[175] The eleventh-century 'Donation of Guthred' presents a tradition that Guthred was inaugurated on a mound called *Oswigesdune* on the south bank of the river Tyne near a fording place called *Wircesforda*, both unidentified.[176] We are told that here Guthred granted St Cuthbert a series of privileges and lands.[177] Ritual proclamation on an inauguration mound is known from other parts of northern Britain to have been part of what made 'law' a 'reality', meaning that the detail had to be accurate in the minds of the audience or else it would not have been useful to anyone claiming validity for the law.[178] Although the 'Donation' likely reflects a

---

172 *HR*, s.a. 883, ed. Arnold, ii, 114. The key phrase *Egbert vero super Northimbros* is absent from the Howden version.
173 See below; for a recent discussion of Guthred (or Guðrøðr), see Downham, *Viking Kings of Britain and Ireland*, 75–8.
174 *CMD*, 524; *HR*, s.a. 883, ed. Arnold, ii, 114; *RHC*, s.a. 882, ed. Stubbs, i, 44; and *RW*, s.a. 882, ed. Coxe, i, 335; see also *HSC*, c.13, 52–3.
175 *DPSA*, 377; *Series Regum Northymbrensium*, ed. Arnold, ii, 391; *RW*, ed. Coxe, 248; versus *HR*, s.a. 883, ed. Arnold, ii, 114 ([Guthred] *regnauitque super Eboracum*; *Egbert vero super Northimbros*); see also D. P. Kirby, *The Earliest English Kings* (London, 2000), 175.
176 With no more information or insight, the best guess is, perhaps, that a mound was close to the Tyne's first fords or tidal limit, so probably on the south side of the river between Blaydon and Prudhoe; Scone, Kingston-upon-Thames and Govan, all probable inauguration sites in the Viking Age, were at such locations on major rivers. See M. Adams, *Ælfred's Britain: War and Peace in the Viking Age* (London, 2017), 169, for the suggestion of a mound at Ryton near Newburn.
177 The 'Donation of Guthred' is at *HSC*, c.13, 52–3; *CMD*, 524. See also McGuigan, 'Ælla and the Descendants of Ivar', 30.
178 Scottish kings were, according to a chronicle material of likely thirteenth-century origin,

real eleventh-century historical belief about the location of Northumbria's inauguration mound, the event itself is almost certainly a fiction. There is also no contemporary evidence that Guthred's kingship applied outside the Danish settlement-zone. *Historia de Sancto Cuthberto* reproduces a tradition that Guthred led an army into battle, against the Scots, in the vicinity of Norham.[179] This is probably the best evidence that Guthred exercised leadership, if not kingship, beyond the Tyne. However, the story is probably recycled folklore taken from the Danelaw, resembling another legendary battle between the Scottish king Causantín mac Cinaeda and the Hiberno-Norse that was reproduced in the *Cogadh*.[180] Adam of Bremen appears to make him the father of Rögnvald (d. 921) and Sigtrygg Cáech (d. 927), rulers of the *Dubgaill/ Anglo-Danes* in the 920s.[181] Æthelweard, who styles him *rex Northhymbriorum*, places his death in 895.[182]

Osberht II (fl. 901) The *Chronicle of 957*, annals that form an appendage to *Historia Regum* 'Part 1', contain a notice *sub anno* 901 telling us that 'Osberht was expelled from the *regnum*' (*Osbrith regno pulsus est*).[183] *Regnum* here almost certainly means 'kingdom' in the sense of

---

'accustomed to proclaim judgments, laws and statutes to their subjects' on the mound of Scone (*Scone monticulum quo reges . . . iudicia, leges et statuta subditis soleant propalare*). Máel Coluim II was said to have given away all of Scotland in title to his followers, but retained the mound at Scone to preserve his privileges. In the 1500s, the second son of James III gave up the earldom and dukedom of Ross, but similarly retained the mound at Dingwall to preserve his legal privileges. See Walter Bower, *Scotichronicon*, iv.48, ed. and trans. J. MacQueen and W. MacQueen, *Scotichronicon by Walter Bower in Latin and English: Volume 2, Books III and IV* (Aberdeen, 1989), 414–17; and W. J. Watson, *Place-Names of Ross and Cromarty* (Inverness, 1904), 93. For the potential thirteenth-century date of this Scottish chronicle, see D. Broun, *Scottish Independence and the Idea of Britain: From the Picts to Alexander III* (Edinburgh, 2007), c.9.

179 The text is printed and translated *HSC*, c. 33, 68–71. Note that this episode, 'Guthred's Dream', occurs outside *HSC*, in an independent manuscript of the twelfth century that focused on Anglo-Saxon material (Paris, Bibliotheque Nationale, Fonds Latin 5362). For discussion of this extract, see South, *HSC*, 116–17, M. Lapidge, *The Cult of Swithun* (Oxford, 2003), 555, n. 26, and B. Colgrave, *Two Lives of Saint Cuthbert* (Cambridge, 1950), 35.

180 *Cogadh*, c.25, 26–7. The common feature is that the earth opens up against the Scottish army.

181 Adam of Bremen, *Gesta Hammaburgensis Ecclesiae Pontificum*, ii.22, ed. B. Schmeidler, 4th edn, *Monumenta Germaniae Historica, Scriptores rerum Germanicarum* 2 (Hannover, 1917), 84; translation in F. J. Tschan (New York, 2002), 70–1.

182 Æthelweard, *Chronicon*, iv.3, ed. and trans. A. Campbell (London, 1962), 51.

183 Cambridge, Corpus Christi College, MS 139, fol. 75r; and *Chronicle of 957*, s.a. 901, ed. Arnold, ii, 92.

'kingship'. The annal may open up a very small window on the kingdom at the beginning of the tenth century, but owing to the fragmented nature of surviving Northumbrian evidence the event remains disembodied in obscurity. Based on our understanding of the relationship between names and kinship in Anglo-Saxon England, Osberht is likely to have been related to other rulers using the *-berht* element in their name, but we can say no more. It is possible that this entry is chronologically misplaced, which could mean that he is the same character as the predecessor of Ælla who was also said to have been forced out of his kingship.

Eardwulf (fl. 899×924) *Historia de Sancto Cuthberto* presents information about one 'prince' Eardwulf (*Eardulfum principem*) who lived, according to its synchronisation, in the time of Edward the Elder. In the Middle Ages *princeps*, 'prince', is a style generally applied to an independent or semi-independent ruler (it does not, like today, mean 'son of a king'). However, it may also signify some other leadership position, like head of a monastery. Eardwulf may have been based in Westmorland when he met his death. The text tells us that Eadred son of Ricsige, discussed above, 'rode westwards over the mountains' (*equitauit uersus occidentem ultra montes*), killed 'Prince' Eardwulf, and captured the deceased's wife.[184]

Eadwulf (d. 913) He is *Etulbb ri Saxan Tuaiscirt*, 'Eadwulf King of the Northern English', in the *Annals of Ulster*, s.a. 913;[185] a year matched by Æthelweard's obit of *Aðulf*, who 'as *actor* presided over the fortress of Bamburgh' (*præerat actori oppidi Bebbanburgh condicti*).[186] The tract 'On Northumbria after the Britons' names his mother as Æthelthryth daughter of King Ælla, which if true opens the possibility that Eadwulf was not a Northumbrian by agnatic lineage, but perhaps a West Saxon or Mercian. *Historia de Sancto Cuthberto* describes him as a *dilectus*, 'esteemed one', of Alfred the Great.[187] The genealogical tract makes him the first 'earl' of Northumbria, but there is no contemporary evidence suggesting he used that title and the belief is adequately explained by Eadwulf's

---

184 *HSC*, c.24, 62–3.
185 *AU* 913.1; see also *FA* 456, s.a. 912 [913] *Etalbh, rí Saxan tuaisgirt*.
186 Æthelweard, *Chronicon*, iv.4, ed. and trans. Campbell, 53.
187 *HSC*, c. 22, 60–1.

apical position in the genealogy of the later Bamburgh family.[188] The *Anglo-Saxon Chronicle* gives an account of a meeting between King Edward the Elder and the northern rulers of Britain in 920 at Bakewell, on the Northumbria–Mercia border in the Peak District. The rulers mentioned are the king of the Scots (presumably Causantín mac Áeda), Rögnvald (king of the Anglo-Danes), 'the sons of Eadwulf' and the king of Strathclyde.[189] This wording suggests that Eadwulf's sons had some sort of power-sharing arrangement in 920. None is named on this occasion, but several are known elsewhere and at least one of them, possibly more, were rulers of Bamburgh and given the title of king.[190]

Ealdred Eadwulfing (fl. 927–933) In the *Anglo-Saxon Chronicle* MS D's account of the meeting *æt Eamotum* in 927, 'Ealdred son of Eadwulf from Bamburgh' is named among 'all the kings who were in this island' (*ealle þa cyngas þe on þyssum iglande wæron*) taken under the lordship of Æthelstan; he appears alongside Causantín of Scotland and rulers from Wales.[191] The equivalent annal in *Chronicon ex Chronicis*, in part an early-twelfth-century translation of some lost version of the *Anglo-Saxon Chronicle*, says something a little different: Ealdred was expelled (*exturbauit*) from Bamburgh in 927.[192] Another surviving annal, *Anglo-Saxon Chronicle* MS E 927, tells us about Æthelstan's ejection of Guthfrith son of Sigtrygg Cáech that year.[193] It seems quite possible that the annal in *Chronicon ex Chronicis* represents a partially botched attempt to merge these two *Anglo-Saxon Chronicle* traditions, i.e. the entries represented best in surviving form by the annals in MS D and MS E. The Latin verb *exturbauit* may have been added to understand the English *from Bebbanbyrig*, thus erroneously giving the impression that Ealdred was expelled from Bamburgh.[194] For what it is worth, the claim in *Chronicon*

---

188 *DNPB*, 33.
189 *ASC* MS A 920, ed. Bately, 69, trans. Whitelock, 67.
190 I have omitted one of the sons, Uhtred (named at *HSC*, c.22), because he is never named explicitly as a ruler.
191 *ASC* MS D [927], ed. Cubbin, 41, trans. Whitelock, 68–9.
192 *Chronicon ex Chronicis*, ii, 386–7.
193 *ASC* MS E 927, ed. S. Irvine (Cambridge, 2004), 55, trans. Whitelock, 69.
194 It is worth noting that an annal in the St Albans collection similar to *Chronicon ex Chronicis* names the son of Eadwulf as Ælfred (*Alfredum . . . filium Eadulfi*), but this is most likely a scribal error; see *RW*, s.a. 926 [recte 927], ed. Coxe, i, 386; but compare Matthew Paris, *Chronica Majora*, s.a. 926 [927], ed. H. R. Luard, 7 vols, Rolls Series 57 (1872–84), i, 447.

ex Chronicis does not sit very well with other information. *Historia de Sancto Cuthberto* describes Ealdred as Edward the Elder's 'esteemed one' (*dilectus*); the same source says that King Rögnvald expelled Ealdred from his territory, whereupon he fled to Scotland and sought the aid of King Causantín; it relates that he and his brother Uhtred survived the ensuing battle of Corbridge, in 918.[195] They may have fled to Southumbria after the battle. According to two 926 charters, men named Ealdred and Uhtred had purchased land in the Danelaw under the authority of Edward the Elder and 'Ealdorman' Æthelred of Mercia (d. 911).[196] The documents survive from two different archives, but were probably issued at the same time.[197] Although their paternity is not specified, historians have sometimes identified them as the above Eadwulfings.[198] Ealdred and his brother Uhtred may be the men, generally found together, who appear in English royal charters until 933.[199]

Adulf mcEtulfe (d. 934) *Adulf mcEtulf* of the *Annals of Clonmacnoise* is the last named ruler of the Northern English specifically named and, also, styled king. *Adulf mcEtulf* in Irish orthography represents Æthulf son of Eadwulf, where Æthulf is a (at this time common) contraction of the name Æthelwulf.[200] Adaptation to Irish orthography has made the name orthographically almost identical to the name Eadwulf (e.g. in Æthelweard),[201] but fortunately Anglo-Saxons of this time almost never bore their father's name and in this instance the *Annals of Clonmacnoise* specifically distinguished *Adulf* from Eadwulf, *Adulf* and *Etulf*.[202] The name *Adulf* is Æthelwulf as it stands, but there remains a small

---

195 *HSC*, c.22, 60–1.
196 For Uhtred's charter, see *Sawyer*, no. 397, and *Charters of Burton Abbey*, ed. P. H. Sawyer (Oxford, 1979), no. 3; for Ealdred's charter, see *Sawyer*, no. 396, and *Charters of Abingdon*, ed. S. E. Kelly (Oxford, 2000–1), no. 21.
197 F. M. Stenton, *Types of Manorial Structure in the Northern Danelaw* (Oxford, 1910), 74–5; S. Keynes, *The Diplomas of King Æthelred 'The Unready'* (Cambridge, 1980), 42–3.
198 *The Crawford Collection*, ed. A. S. Napier and W. H. Stevenson (Oxford, 1895), 74–5; P. H. Sawyer, 'The Charters of Burton Abbey and the Unification of England', *NH* 10 (1973), 28–39, at 33–4; Williams, Smyth and Kirby (eds), *A Biographical Dictionary of Dark Age Britain*, s.v. 'Ealdred of Bamburgh 913–c.930', 116–17.
199 Charters they appear in together are *Sawyer*, nos 403, 412–13, 416–17, 418–19; no. 413 is the exception.
200 *AClon* 928 [934], ed. Murphy, 149.
201 Æthelweard, *Chronicon*, iv.4, ed. and trans. Campbell, 53.
202 McGuigan, 'Ælla and the Descendants of Ivar', 25, n. 25.

possibility that the translator himself 'corrected' some other, similar name to *Adulf* or has otherwise misled us.[203] *Adulf mcEtulfe* died the same year that King Æthelstan launched a major expedition against the Scottish king Causantín mac Áeda.[204] It is tempting to link the two events. However, the same year also witnessed the death of Guthfrith son of Sigtrygg Cáech. He was the father of Olaf Guthfrithson who in 937 fought alongside the Scots at Brunanburh.[205] According to lost historical material used by William of Malmesbury in the twelfth century, Guthfrith had fled to Scotland after his expulsion from England by Æthelstan in 927.[206]

Ealdwulf (fl. 927) William of Malmesbury tells us that when Æthelstan obtained the Northumbrian lands ruled by his former brother-in-law Sigtrygg Cáech, he drove out 'a certain Ealdwulf who was in revolt'(*expulso quodam Aldulfo qui rebellabat*).[207] This is not likely to be a mistake for Ealdred; more likely is Alex Woolf's suggestion that he is *Adulf mcEtulfe*, but it is also possible that Ealdwulf is another Eadwulfing or, indeed, someone from a different group of Northumbrian magnates.[208]

Oswulf Eadwulfing (fl. 934–954) A *dux* named Oswulf subscribes in charters of Æthelstan in 934 and 935.[209] It is not certain that this Oswulf is the ruler of Bamburgh, but Oswulf of Bamburgh certainly does appear in the charters of Æthelstan's brother, King Eadred. He seems to have been present at Eadred's inauguration at Kingston-upon-Thames in 946, and makes a series of appearances 949–50 where he is usually listed over all the *duces*, above the West Saxon ealdormen as well as regional rulers from the Danelaw. The figure in Eadred's reign is described as 'high

---

203 It is theoretically possible that he encountered it in the Irish obit for Æthelwulf King of Wessex who died in 858, which is *Adulf rex Saxan* in the *Annals of Ulster* (*AU* 858.2). Note also that in *AClon*'s obit for *Adulf mcEtulf*'s father the form is *Edulfe King of the North Saxons*, for which see *AClon* 904 [913], ed. Murphy, 145.
204 *Chronicle of 957*, s.a. 934, ed. Arnold, ii, 124; *AClon* 928 [934], ed. Murphy, 149; *ASC* MS C 934, ed. O'Brien O'Keeffe, 77, trans. Whitelock, 69.
205 For references to Guthfrith in Irish annals, see Downham, *Viking Kings of Britain and Ireland*, 254–5.
206 *GRA*, ii.134, ed. and trans. Mynors *et al.*, 212–15; on William's sources, see Foot, *Æthelstan*, 251–8.
207 *GRA*, ii.131.3, ed. and trans. Mynors *et al.*, 206–7.
208 Woolf, *From Pictland to Alba*, 164–5.
209 Sawyer, nos 407, 425, 434. Keynes, *Atlas*, table 38.

reeve', a title not used for any other ruler of Bamburgh.[210] Oswulf had cause to seek closer alliance with the West Saxon kings. In 941, Olaf Guthfrithson and the 'men of York' burned Tyninghame and enslaved the population of Lindisfarne.[211] It is not certain that Oswulf was ruler of Bamburgh in 941, but he was presumably the English leader who, as part of a coalition also containing Britons and Scots, suffered defeat to Scandinavians in 952.[212] Oswulf is best known for the 'treachery at Stainmore', where Erik king of the Northumbrian Danes was killed on the moor that separates the North Riding of Yorkshire from Westmorland. The deed itself was carried out by forces led by a certain Macon or Maccus, but Oswulf was held to have had ultimate responsibility.[213] Although Roger of Wendover's annals place the event in 950, version D (and E) of the *Anglo-Saxon Chronicle* has Erik in power until 954.[214] According to the twelfth-century 'Northumbrian Earldom Foundation Legend', King Eadred left Northumbria to Oswulf's supervision, an arrangement that came to an end under Eadred's successor King Edgar. In the latter's reign, an ealdorman named Oslac was assigned responsibility for Wessex's Northumbrian territories, leaving the area beyond the Tees (or Tyne) to Oswulf's successor in Bamburgh.[215] This had probably happened by 963, but certainly by 966, perhaps suggesting that Oswulf died in the early or mid 960s.[216] According to our only source of information about his genealogy, he was the son of Eadwulf grandson of Ælla, and thus the brother of Ealdred, Uhtred and *Adulf*.[217]

Eadwulf *Yvelcild* (fl. c. 963–970) He is almost certainly the *dux* who appears in charters of King Edgar in a brief period between 968 and 970.[218] During this period he was joined in the south by his ecclesiastical colleague, the Cuthbertine bishop Ælfsige.[219] As we saw above, King

---

210 *Sawyer*, nos 520, 544, 546, 550, 552a. Keynes, *Atlas*, table 45.
211 *Chronicle of 957*, s.a. 941, ed. Arnold, ii, 94; cf. *RW*, s.a. 941, ed. Coxe, i, 396.
212 *AU* 952.2 (*Cath for Firu Alban & Bretnu & Saxonu ria Gallaibh*).
213 *RW*, s.a. 950, ed. Coxe, 402–3; and in the 'Northumbrian Earldom Foundation Legend', i.e. *HR*, s.a. 1072, ed. Arnold, 197, and *RHC*, s.a. 952, ed. Stubbs, i, 57.
214 *ASC* MS D 954, ed. Cubbin, 45, trans. Whitelock, 73.
215 *DPSA*, 382; *Chron. Wallingford*, 54. *HR*, s.a. 1072, ed. Arnold, ii, 197; *RHC*, s.a. 952, ed. Stubbs, i, 57.
216 See above, 123–7.
217 *DNPB*, 33.
218 *Sawyer*, nos 766, 771, 779, 806. Keynes, *Atlas*, table 56.
219 *Sawyer*, no. 781 (dated 970). We also know from his own hand that the Cuthbertine

Edgar was said to have delegated to Eadwulf the land between the Firth of Forth (*Myreforth*) and the Tees (*Teisa*), or at least the Tyne, by the 'Northumbrian Earldom Foundation Legend'. The same legend gives him the nickname *Yvelcild*, 'evil child', possibly meant to be understood in apposition to his forename, viz. 'happy wolf, evil child'.[220] In Version A of the legend, it is stated that Eadwulf and Ealdorman Oslac escorted the Scottish king Cinaed mac Maíl Choluim to the court of King Edgar, where Cinaed was granted Lothian in return for perpetual Scottish homage to the kings of England. The latter seems to be a twelfth-century fiction, and although it is possible that Eadwulf escorted Cinaed southwards to Edgar, the inclusion of Cinaed as king of Scotland in any event dating to the reign of Edgar is chronologically difficult.[221] The story about the grant of Lothian is borrowed and reused in the St Albans annals, in their obit of King Edgar, s.a. 975.[222] No descendants of Eadwulf are known.

Ealdred (fl. mid tenth century) The Anglo-Norman-era genealogy of Earl Waltheof of Northampton tells us that Oswulf Eadwulfing's son, and the link to all the later earls, was named Ealdred; and it describes him as 'earl', *comes*.[223] There is no reason to take that title too seriously, however. A Cuthbertine bishop with the name Ealdred, the predecessor of Ælfsige, appears in some early charters of King Edgar, 958–9.[224] Given the close association of the Cuthbertine bishops and the rulers of Bamburgh, it is hardly out of the question that they are the same figures. Ealdred may have been placed on the Cuthbertine seat when Oswulf had expected another son, perhaps Eadwulf *Yvelcild*, to succeed in Bamburgh.

---

prepositus, Ealdred, was present at Oakley in Wessex (*Áclee on Westsæxum*) around this time, 10 August 970; for which, see Jolly, *Community of Cuthbert*, 66–8, 325–6.
220 For legend references, see above 122–3. For comment on *Yvelcild*, see G. Fellows-Jenson, 'By-Names', in M. Lapidge *et al.*, *The Blackwell Encyclopaedia of Anglo-Saxon England* (Oxford, 1999), s.v., at 77.
221 Woolf, *From Pictland to Alba*, 207–12.
222 *RW*, s.a. 975, ed. Coxe, 415–17; Matthew Paris, *Chronica Majora*, s.a. 975, ed. Luard, 467–8; cf. *Chron. Wallingford*, 54–5, which shows that it came to St Albans as part of the 'Northumbrian Earldom Foundation Legend'.
223 *DNPB*, 33.
224 *Sawyer*, nos 675, 679, 681.

Waltheof (fl. 994) The single contemporary documentation of Waltheof is a charter of King Æthelred 'the Unready' in 994, where he appears as number seven and last among the witnessing *duces*.[225] His appearance is almost certainly connected with the sack of Bamburgh by Norse forces the previous year, an event recorded in the *Anglo-Saxon Chronicle*.[226] According to the Anglo-Norman-era text *De Obsessione Dunelmi*, the Northern English land was invaded by the Scots during Waltheof's period in office. The text claims that Waltheof's son Uhtred defeated the attackers while the elderly Waltheof shut himself up in Bamburgh.[227] A variant of the Northumbrian earl list traditions gives Waltheof the nickname *Cudel*, 'Cuttlefish'.[228] The cuttlefish in classical and medieval church literature was one of the animals known to 'protect themselves by hiding', in this case by using ink.[229]

Northman (fl. 994) *Historia de Sancto Cuthberto* lists a Northman alongside three separate earls granting estates to St Cuthbert during the time of Bishop Ealdhun, whom the author probably believed to have been bishop between 990 and 1018.[230] Ealdhun appears in a English royal charter of 1009.[231] Preserved in the Durham *Liber Vitae*, in Old English, is a purported gift by *Norðman eorle* of the estate of Escomb (Durham) and 'a quarter of the territory of Ferryhill (Durham)'.[232] He appears in the same 994 charter as Waltheof but, curiously, is placed immediately above him, number six, in the list of 'ducal' witnesses allegedly present.[233] It is possible that Northman and Waltheof were brothers; both appear to have Norse or Norse-influenced names,[234] which may

---

225 *Sawyer*, no. 881.
226 *ASC* MS C, ed. O'Brien O'Keefe, 86–7, trans. Whitelock, 83.
227 *DOD*, 215, trans. Morris, *Marriage and Murder*, 1–2.
228 Alfred of Beverley, *Annales*, ed. Hearne, 133.
229 C. B. Schmitt, 'Aristotle as a Cuttlefish', *Studies in the Renaissance* 12 (1965), 60–72, at 63–6.
230 *HSC*, c.31, 64–7.
231 *Sawyer*, no. 922.
232 *Liber Vitae Ecclesiae Dunelmensis*, ed. J. Stevenson (London, 1841), 57, who speculates on the erasure of earlier lines; printed with translation *Anglo-Saxon Charters*, ed. A. J. Robertson (Cambridge, 1959), no. 67; and recently Rollason and Rollason (eds), *Durham Liber Vitae*, i, 140 (text runs Her syleð Norðman eorl into S(an)c(t)e Cuðberhte Ediscum (and) eall þ(aet) ðær into hyreð. (and) ðone feorðan æcer æt Feregenne).
233 *Sawyer*, no. 881.
234 Rollason and Rollason (eds), *Durham Liber Vitae*, ii, 181, 242.

either suggest a Scandinavian or Anglo-Scandinavian mother; or, at least, increasing interest in the Danelaw (indeed the estates granted to Cuthbert are located in the Scandinavian settlement-zone). As we saw in 920, the Northern English polity may have been split among brother rulers, a custom not widespread in England but well-established in the Norse-speaking world.[235] If Northman was Waltheof's brother, lack of successful descendants probably explains his comparatively low profile in surviving sources.

Eadred (fl. c. 1000) Alongside Earl Northman and Earl Uhtred, an earl named *Ethred* appears in *Historia de Sancto Cuthberto* as a patron of St Cuthbert during the episcopate of Bishop Ealdhun.[236] There is a possibility that Eadred is named in the famous *Gospatric's Writ*, where the grantor Gospatric refers to a predecessor of himself as Eadred (*on Eadread dagan*).[237]

Uhtred (fl. 1009–1018) We have more information about Uhtred than any other ruler of Bamburgh. A son of Waltheof (fl. 994), from 1009 until 1015 he witnesses English royal charters as *dux*, usually alongside Ealdorman Eadric Streona (Mercia), Ealdorman Ælfric (eastern Wessex) and Ealdorman Leofwine (Hwicce).[238] Since rulers of Bamburgh hardly ever appear in English royal charters, it is almost certain that Uhtred had obtained the viceregal ealdordom of York/Northumbria by 1009. He was given control of York by King Æthelred, according to the Anglo-Norman-era *De Obsessione Dunelmi*, after defeating the Scots in battle. King Æthelred allowed Uhtred to marry one of his daughters, Ælfgifu. The text says that Uhtred's father Waltheof still ruled Bamburgh during the Scottish invasion; that perhaps seems unlikely, but it is not impossible.[239]

---

235 K. L. Maund, "'A Turmoil of Warring Princes'", *The Haskins Society Journal* 6 (1994), 29–47, at 33.
236 *HSC*, c.31, 64–7.
237 Writ printed and discussed in F. W. Ragg, 'A Charter of Gospatrik', *The Ancestor* 7 (1903), 244–7; H. W. C. Davis, 'Cumberland before the Norman Conquest', *EHR* 20 (1905), 61–5; F. E. Harmer (ed.), *Anglo-Saxon Writs*, 2nd edn (Stamford, 1989), no. 121, with discussion by Harmer, 419–24; Phythian-Adams, *Land of the Cumbrians*, 174–81; and most recently *Northern Chrs*, no. 21, with discussion by Woodman at 371–8.
238 *Sawyer*, nos 921, 922, 926, 931, 931b, 933, 934; Keynes, *Atlas*, table 62.
239 *DOD*, 215–16, trans. Morris, *Marriage and Murder*, 1–2.

We know from Irish sources that the Scots were defeated by the English, almost certainly the Bamburgh-ruled English, in 1006.[240] Thus, the relative chronology offered by *De Obsessione Dunelmi* seems to be in harmony with the indirect testimony of contemporary sources. Uhtred's duties as an ealdorman brought him to the attention of the *Anglo-Saxon Chronicle* at several points. In 1013, Uhtred was at Gainsborough, where he and the Northumbrians, as well as the people of Lindsey and the Five Boroughs (Lincoln, Stamford, Nottingham, Derby and Leicester), submitted to the Danish king Sweyn Forkbeard.[241] Sweyn died the following year and left his army to his son Cnut. It is in relation to Cnut that Uhtred appears again, in 1016. Uhtred, in support of the ætheling Edmund Ironside, son of King Æthelred, is found ravaging Mercia, an action that targeted allies of Cnut. The last, the account continues, outmanoeuvred Uhtred by invading Northumbria, and Uhtred was forced to retreat and come to terms with the Danish leader. Uhtred offered hostages in exchange for peace but, the annalist adds, 'nevertheless he was killed by the advice of Ealdorman Eadric, and with him Thurcetel, Nafena's son' (*7 hine mon ðeah hwæþere ofsloh ðuruh Eadrices ræd ealdormannes, 7 Þurcytel Nafenan sunu mid him*).[242] This statement is the basis for the belief that Uhtred died in 1016; the entry was written in the 1020s, and since 1976 many historians have come to see it as a 'parenthetical' comment reflecting on a subsequent injustice rather than an event of 1016 itself.[243] As we have seen elsewhere in this volume, Uhtred is named in 1018 as leader of the losing English side at the battle of Carham, though only by *Historia Regum*.[244] The *Anglo-Saxon Chronicle* tells us that Cnut was responsible for Uhtred's death, but *De Obsessione Dunelmi* offers more detail. It relates that Uhtred was invited to a place called *Wiheal* (unidentified), where the followers of a Yorkshire hold named Thurbrand emerged from hiding in the hall and killed Uhtred.[245] Prior to his marriage with Ælfgifu, daughter of King Æthelred, *De Obsessione Dunelmi* tells us that he had been married to a

---

240 *AU* 1006.5.
241 *ASC* MS C 1013.
242 *ASC* MS C 1016, ed. O'Brien O'Keefe, 101, trans. Whitelock, 95.
243 Based upon the arguments of A. A. M. Duncan, 'The Battle of Carham, 1018', *SHR* 55 (1976), 20–8; for further details of this problem, see introduction to this volume, 10–16.
244 *HR*, s.a. 1018, ed. Arnold, 155–6.
245 *DOD*, 217–18, trans. Morris, *Marriage and Murder*, 3.

certain Ecgfrida, daughter of Bishop Ealdhun, whom he had discarded for a certain Sige, daughter of Styr son of Ulf, a wealthy Anglo-Dane who was a landowner in southern County Durham and, most likely, a citizen of York.[246] By the twelfth century, Uhtred was credited with supervising the establishment of an episcopal seat, and a new residence for St Cuthbert, at Durham, an event that Durham scholars of the early 1100s dated to 995, a date that contradicts *De Obsessione*'s chronology.[247] There is contemporary evidence, however, that the body of St Cuthbert remained at Norham on the Tweed until *at least* 1013; if reliable this would mean that, if the move to Durham happened at all during Uhtred's time, it was after 1013.[248] Despite Uhtred's temporary success bringing eastern Northumbria back together, no Bamburgh-based ruler would repeat his achievement.

Eadwulf *Cudel* (fl. *c.* 1020) There are no contemporary sources for Eadwulf, and we rely entirely on Anglo-Norman-era tracts. These tell us that he was another son of Waltheof, and thus brother of Uhtred.[249] He is given the nickname *Cudel*, 'cuttlefish', a nickname that, as we have seen, may also have been borne by his father. *De Obsessione Dunelmi* tells us that he was 'very lazy and timid' (*ignavus valde et timidus*), and that, hoping to avoid conflict, he handed Lothian over to the Scots in compensation for the deaths inflicted by Uhtred in his earlier victory.[250]

Ealdred (fl. *c.* 1030) According to the twelfth-century lists, Eadwulf *Cudel* was succeeded by his nephew Ealdred, the son of Uhtred by Ecgfrida, daughter of Bishop Ealdhun.[251] There are no contemporary sources for Ealdred's tenure either, but we are told by *De Obsessione Dunelmi* that he sought and obtained revenge for his father's death, killing Thurbrand the Hold. After this, the story goes, Ealdred tried to reconcile with Thurbrand's son Carl, and they even set out together for Rome on pilgrimage. Severe weather compelled them to abort their

---

246 *DOD*, 215–16, trans. Morris, *Marriage and Murder*, 2. For more on Styr, see *HSC*, c.29, 66–7, and pp. 111–12 for commentary by South.
247 *LDE*, iii.2, 148–9; *ALD*, 486.
248 See above, note 64.
249 E.g. *DPSA*, 383.
250 *DOD*, 218, trans. Morris, *Marriage and Murder*, 3.
251 *DPSA*, 383.

journey, however, and return to one of Carl's residences. After entertaining his guest, Carl slew Ealdred in a forest known as 'Risewood'.[252] We have no specific year for Ealdred's death.

Eadwulf (d. 1041) The quality of our information improves for Ealdred's brother and alleged successor, Eadwulf son of Uhtred.[253] The year of his death is supplied by the *Anglo-Saxon Chronicle*, which tells us that in 1041 he was betrayed by King Harthacnut (in violation of a safe-conduct).[254] The Anglo-Norman-era material attributes his death to Siward, ealdorman, who, it says, subsequently ruled the whole of Northumbria (including the land subject to Bamburgh).[255] We are told by *Historia Regum* (and Howden) that Eadwulf 'brutally devastated the British' (*Brittones satis atrociter deuastauit*).[256] This particular comment is not in *De Primo Saxonum Adventu*, and has been added by one of *Historia Regum*'s contributors in the 1120s or later. The event is dated three years prior to Eadwulf's death. This may suggest that he was using a northern version of the *Anglo-Saxon Chronicle* that included notice of Eadwulf's demise in 1041 and, uniquely, a campaign against the Cumbrians/Strathclyders in 1038. It is worth noting that this particular part of *De Primo Saxonum Adventu* is subject to other alteration.[257] In either 1039 or 1040 a Scottish army, led by Donnchad son of Crínán of Dunkeld, unsuccessfully attacked Durham. It was presumably Eadwulf who held Bamburgh at that point, but we are not told which side he supported or anything about his role.[258] Eadwulf's mother was not

---

252 *DOD*, 218, trans. Morris, *Marriage and Murder*, 3.
253 Genealogy given at *HR*, s.a. 1072, ed. Arnold, ii, 197, 198; *RHC*, s.a. 952, ed. Stubbs, i, 57, 58; *DPSA*, 383.
254 *ASC* MS C 1041, ed. O'Brien O'Keeffe, 107; *ASC* MS D 1041, ed. Cubbin, 66, trans. Whitelock, 106.
255 *DPSA*, 388; *HR*, s.a. 1072, ed. Arnold, ii, 198; *RHC*, s.a. 952, ed. Stubbs, i, 58.
256 *HR*, s.a. 1072, ed. Arnold, ii, 198; *RHC*, s.a. 952, ed. Stubbs, i, 58. Interestingly, where *HR* simply has *Brittones*, Howden's adds *id est Walas*, which might be evidence that the latter version has incorporated a gloss.
257 *De Primo Saxonum Adventu* places Eadwulf's death in Edward's reign, demonstrating that its author had not been able to figure out the chronology accurately (and, thus, cannot have been directly influenced by the northern version of the *Anglo-Saxon Chronicle*); however, in the other version of the Northumbrian earl tract the error is explicitly corrected by dropping the reference to Edward the Confessor and replacing it with Harthacnut; see *DPSA*, 383 and compare *HR*, s.a. 1072, ed. Arnold, ii, 198.
258 *LDE*, iii.9, 168–9.

Ealdred's mother, i.e. Ecgfrida, daughter of Bishop Ealdhun; nor was she Ælfgifu, daughter of the king Æthelred; and so he (and his brother Gospatric, never earl) was probably the son of Sige (*Sigen*) daughter of Styr; or son of (some other) wife or concubine.[259]

Acknowledgements

I would like to thank all those whose comments or assistance have, at various stages, contributed to the development of this article, in particular Alex Woolf, David Broun, John Hudson and Keri McGuigan.

---

259 *Sigen* is named in *DOD*, 216, trans. Morris, *Marriage and Murder*, 2.

CHAPTER SIX

Early Medieval Carham in its Landscape Context

DAVID PETTS

Introduction

Unlike many early medieval battles recorded in documentary sources, we at least can locate the battle of Carham on a map, because unlike for example Brunanburh, Carham still exists as a clearly identifiable location in the modern landscape. It is unlikely it will ever be possible to identify the precise point in the terrain of North Northumberland where the two sides came to blows, but we can home in on a stretch of river valley and upland edge, around ten kilometres by six kilometres in extent that comprises the later parish of Carham. Whilst there is a small group of dwellings at Carham village, this is largely a landscape of dispersed settlement and the use of the name 'Carham' in the sources should best be understood as not referring to a specific settlement, but rather its associated territory. Work on the territorial boundaries in Northumbria, particularly township boundaries, suggests that these units remained stable entities and earlier territories, for instance the *vills* mentioned in the various documentary sources, such as the *Historia Sancto Cuthberto* and the works of Symeon of Durham, can probably be mapped with reasonably certainty onto the later townships with the same names.[1]

Given the impossibility of identifying the precise location of the battle, any attempt to write a tactical account of the conflict in relationship to specific landscape features is doomed to failure. Nonetheless, it is possible to explore the wider landscape within which the clash took place. Recent scholarship on early medieval warfare in Britain and beyond has emphasised that when considering battlefields it is important to be cautious of understanding military conflict in this period

---

1   *HSC*, 48–9, 125–6.

from an ahistorical perspective that ignores the cultural specificity around the conduct of conflict and the symbolism and significance of battlefields.[2] Whilst ultimately one purpose of warfare was to resolve tensions and conflict between two opposed groups, the framework of the resolution of such conflict was embedded within culturally prescribed norms and expectations as to how and where battles should take place. This means that the choice of battlefield by commanders was not just framed by ahistorical notions of "inherent military probability" but influenced by a range of other more culturally specific factors that interact with strategic and tactical concerns.[3] Thus any consideration of the landscape of an early medieval battle must do more than consider the tactical affordances offered by the terrain and address the wider symbolic framework and rules of conduct within which the leaders of the opposing forces were operating.

Focusing on a slightly earlier period than Carham, several locational analyses of battles named in English sources between AD 600 and 850 (excluding civil wars and Viking attacks) have indicated that they were regularly associated with ancient monuments or river crossings;[4] whilst many of these records are written after the event, the association of battles with such locations seems to have been embedded within the early medieval mindset. The known battle sites recorded in Northumbria all seem to bear this out. The battle of Heavenfield (AD 633/4) took place adjacent to Hadrian's Wall close to where it crossed the North Tyne and close to Dere Street.[5] The battle of Corbridge (AD 918) was also located adjacent to a river crossing near the remains of an important

---

2   K. Cathers, '"Markings on the Land" and Early Medieval Warfare in the British Isles', in P. Doyle and M. R. Bennett (eds), *Fields of Battle: Terrain in Military History* (London, 2002), 9–17; G. Halsall, *Warfare and Society in the Barbarian West* (London, 2003); B. Raffield, '"Plundering the Territories in the Manner of the Heathens": Identifying Viking Age Battlefields in Britain', *Rosetta* 7 (2009), 22–43; T. J. Williams, 'Landscape and Warfare in Anglo-Saxon England and the Viking cCampaign in 1006', *Early Medieval Europe* 23.3 (2015), 329–59; T. J. Williams, 'The Place of Slaughter: Exploring the West Saxon Battlescape', in R. Lavelle and S. Roffey (eds), *Danes in Wessex: The Scandinavian Impact on Southern England, c.800–c.1100* (Oxford. 2015), 35–55.
3   T. J. Williams, 'Landscape and Warfare', 329–39.
4   G. Halsall, 'Anthropology and the Study of Pre-Conquest Warfare and Society', in S. C. Hawkes (ed.), *Weapons and Warfare in Anglo-Saxon England* (Oxford, 1988), 155–78; S. Semple, *Perceptions of the Prehistoric in Anglo-Saxon England* (Oxford, 2013), 84–9.
5   Bede, *Historia Ecclesiastica Gentis Anglorum*, ed. B. Colgrave and R. A. B. Mynors (Oxford, 1969), 216–7.

Roman fort and *vicus*, and again, close to Dere Street.[6] Whether the site of the battle of Degsastan (AD 603) is located at Dawston in the Scottish Borders or not, its very name seems to attest to its proximity to a notable stone or boulder (Degsas-stone).[7] There seems to have been a consistent attempt to intentionally select sites with propitious ideological symbolism, whether key border points or associated with locations imbued with connections to the past, as a location for battle.[8]

The consistency in the location of early medieval battles may partly be interpreted from a strategic perspective; early medieval warfare was not in essence about manoeuvre. One of the key challenges would have been for relatively small armies operating in landscapes with low population densities in modern terms to locate each other and bring their opponents to battle. Having a repertoire of cultural acceptable locations at which conflict might take place would have helped.

Understanding the environment

The drift geology of the area is not complex. Close to the course of the Tweed are alluvial sands and silts forming a relatively flat area of land of the type known locally as haughs. To the south of these (roughly south of the B6350) these are replaced by the gentle rolling landscape of Devensian Till. This is also found to the north of the Tweed where it forms the characteristic landscape of the area known as the Merse. To the east of the parish around Cornhill and Learmouth is a larger area of the sands and gravels with a flatter topography. In the south of the parish relief increases where the Till meets the andesite of the Cheviot Volcanic Formations, which is cut by a series of small river valleys including the courses of the Bowmont and the Kale Water that drain into the Tweed.

Not surprisingly there are a complex series of routeways that transect the Tweed and its hinterland.[9] At a wider regional level there were a

---

[6] *HSC*, 61.
[7] Bede, *Historia Ecclesiastica*, ed. Colgrave and Mynors, 116–17.
[8] Semple, *Perceptions of the Prehistoric*, 87–9.
[9] S. Semple, B. Buchanan, C. Harrington, D. Oliver and D. Petts, 'Power at the Edge, Yeavering, Northumberland, England', in S. Semple, C. Orsini and S. Mui (eds), *Life on the Edge: Social, Religious and Political Frontiers in Early Medieval Europe* (Wendenburg, 2017), 102–8.

number of key Roman routeways beyond Hadrian's Wall running through North Northumberland and into southern Scotland. The path of Dere Street runs up Coquetdale, where it drops down from the complex of camps at Chew Green, high in the Cheviots, down to the camp at Pennymuir from where it then heads towards Trimontium. To the east of the sandstone uplands which overlook the coastal plain runs the road known as the Devil's Causeway, which crosses the Tweed in the vicinity of Tweedmouth. Whilst no Roman route crosses the Tweed in the vicinity of Carham there is a small cluster of Roman camps of probable Flavian (AD 69–96) About 500m south of Carham village (at NT7985 3770) traces of a probable Roman camp survive as cropmarks, whilst at the east end of the parish at East Learmouth traces of another camp survive.[10] Another is known at Wooden Home Farm just to the west of Sprouston.[11] It is possible that these camps, probably of Flavian date, may have been intended to prevent lateral movement along the southern side of the Tweed. They may also have been sited to exercise control over key crossing points along this stretch of the river. The Wooden House Farm camp lies close to the modern bridge over the river to Kelso, originally the site of a ford.

At present, a number of other fording points are known; with fords known between Cornhill and Coldstream, one at Wark and another near Redden. There is, though, no longer a surviving ford at Carham itself, although a road from Birgham, north of the river, does run straight south towards Carham before terminating at the river edge. There is a need for some caution in identifying probable crossing points. The precise course of the Tweed itself has obviously changed over time; the presence of palaeochannels to the north of Carham village are testament to this.[12] The construction of weirs, including one just to the north of Carham, may also have changed the hydraulic character of the river, making previously crossable points unfordable. Indeed, it is clear from earlier sources that there were more crossing points along this section of the Tweed. In 1541 the Border Commissioners recorded a total

---

10   H. Welfare, *Roman Camps in England: The Field Archaeology* (London, 1995), 82, 95–6.
11   R. Jones, *Roman Camps in Scotland* (Edinburgh, 2011), 319.
12   D. Passmore and C. Waddington, 'Geoarchaeology of the Milfield Basin, Northern England: Towards an Integrated Archaeological Prospection, Research and Management Framework', *Archaeological Prospection* 9 (2002), 71–81.

of thirty-one fords between Berwick and Carham, with two (Houleford of Carham; Crabbestreams) adjacent to Carham village.[13]

At a local level there are a number of routeways which give access to the lower lying haughlands and areas of glacial till in the vicinity of Carham. Lateral movement along both sides of the Tweed is easy. From the point where Dere Street crosses the Teviot at its confluence with the Jed it is relatively simple to follow the course of the Teviot and then Tweed towards Carham. To the east from the Tweedsmouth, where the Devil's Causeway presumably crossed the Tweed, it is equally easy to head upstream along the Tweed through Norham and Cornhill to reach Carham.

To the south-east, the massif of the Cheviots superficially appears to impede movement. However, there are some corridors that do allow access through this area of upland; most significantly, by following the course of the Glen westwards to the point where it is formed by the joining of the Bowmont Water and the College Burn. Following the valley of the Bowmont Water westward leads to Kirk Yetholm where it is easy to strike straight westwards to Kelso or, by crossing the short watershed between the Bowmont and the Kale Water via Morebattle, easily reach Roxburgh and the Teviot. Alternatively, it is possible to take a shorter, higher altitude path, known as the Staw Road, heading south from Kilham towards Stawford and Yetholm.

Going back eastwards along the Bowmont Water it is simple to strike north from Mindrum towards Learmouth. The presence of Roman camps at both Mindrum and East Learmouth may testify to the recognition by the Romans of the importance of this route.[14] Much later the presence of a reiver trysting point just over a mile west of Mindrum at Stawford near Yetholm Mains may reflect the importance of this Glen–Bowmont Water route until the post-medieval period, although it is now very much an isolated backroute.[15] Incidentally, it makes more sense of the location of the siting of the royal centre of Yeavering if

---

13 R. Carlton, 'Further Research on the Routeways Taken by the Army of James IV', in J. Miller, L. Bankier and A. Bowden (eds), *Flodden: Legends and Legacy* (Berwick, 2016), 87–96; J. Hodgson, *History of Northumberland* (Newcastle, 1828), 194–202.
14 Welfare, *Roman Camps*, 181.
15 J. Bain (ed.), *The Border Papers: Calendar of Letters and Papers Relating to the Affairs of the Borders of England and Scotland Preserved in Her Majesty's Public Record Office, London* (Edinburgh 1894–8), i, 357, 374, 531, 660, 661, 663; ii, 101.

Glendale is seen not as a cul-de-sac off the more fertile Milfield Basin, but controlling access along the easiest way from the Milfield Basin to important locations along the middle Tweed, and in particular, Dere Street.[16]

There were also upland routeways across the Cheviots of some antiquity. Dere Street itself, known as Gamelspeth along its Cheviot section, runs across high ground between the Roman forts at High Rochester and Chew Green. The droving route known as Clennell Street (earlier known as Hernespeth or Yearnspeth) heads high over uplands from Alwinton via Windy Gyle, a known later cross-border trysting point, before dropping down towards the headwaters of the Bowmont Water at Cocklawfoot, from where Kirk Yetholm is a short journey.[17] This was later a key route linking the Cistercian foundation at Newminster with their vaccaries in this area. Another known upland route across this northern corner of the Cheviots is the droveway known as The Street, which runs from Upper Coquetdale, above Alwinton, to Hownam and the upper reaches of the Kale Water. There are many other small routes making use of the minor cleughs and sikes of the uplands. The survival of the name Harpath Sike (NT9095118784) may be a rare northern example of a *herepath* ('army path') placename.[18] Although seemingly very remote now, Harpath Sike is close to a trackway (Salters Road) that ran westwards from the top end of the Breamish valley joining the route known as Butts Road, which ran down to Cocklaw Foot where it joined Clennel Street.[19]

Ancestral landscapes of Carham

As earlier analysis of battlefields highlighted, early medieval fields of conflict in Britain were regularly associated with ancient monuments, of both Roman and prehistoric date.[20] Given this, it is worthwhile

---

16 Semple *et al.*, 'Power at the Edge'.
17 D. Jones with the Coquetdale Community Archaeology, *The Old Tracks through the Cheviots: Discovering the Archaeology of the Border Roads* (Newcastle upon Tyne, 2017).
18 A. Mawer, *The Placenames of Northumberland and Durham* (Cambridge, 1920), 102.
19 RCAHMS, *An Inventory of the Ancient and Historical Monuments of Roxburghshire*, vol. 2 (Edinburgh, 1956), 363–5, no. 758.
20 Halsall, 'Anthropology'; Semple, *Perceptions of the Prehistoric*; Williams, 'The Place of Slaughter'.

considering to what extent earlier monuments and settlements may have been preserved within the early medieval landscape.

While most of the Tweed valley is likely to have been occupied in prehistory, there is relatively little direct evidence for a Neolithic or Bronze Age presence in the immediate vicinity of Carham, although Bronze Age vessels found at Lamb Knowe, near Wark, and at Howburn are probably all that remains of ploughed-out round barrows.[21] A Bronze Age dagger was found in Carham in 1853, and a Bronze Age axe was found near Cornhill, although a lack of further context makes their interpretation difficult.[22] Cropmark evidence from Wark does show a probable Neolithic mortuary enclosure just to the east of the village.[23] This suggests that there may be other prehistoric structures surviving subsurface within the parish, although detailed plotting of cropmarks in the west of the parish has not been carried out. There are hints that known crossing points on the Tweed may be associated with prehistoric ritual landscapes, for example, at Norham (Ubbanford) a number of prehistoric ring ditches and later Iron Age enclosures survive as cropmarks.[24]

Towards the east of the parish, crop marks of probable Iron Age and Roman Iron Age enclosures survive, and the more substantial remains of similar sites survive in the Cheviot fringe, including a multi-vallate fort at Camp Hill, Downham,[25] and at Mindrum Mill.[26] Over the border into Scotland, other Iron Age forts such as Hownam remain as upstanding monuments at higher altitudes. The discovery of the tip of a late Iron Age sword and chape from the Tweed itself, opposite Carham, is perhaps a tentative hint that, as is known elsewhere (e.g. the Thames, the Witham), the river itself may have been used for votive deposition and perhaps marks the symbolic importance of the crossing at Carham.

21 A. Gibson, *Bronze Age Pottery in North-East England* (Oxford, 1978), 13; M. H. Dodds, *A History of Northumberland*, vol. 14 (Newcastle upon Tyne, 1935), 56.
22 C. B. Burgess and S. Gerlof, *The Dirks and Rapiers of Great Britain and Ireland* (Munich, 1981), 52, no. 369; Anon. 'Donations to and Purchases for the Museum', *PSAS* 80 (1945), 151; Anon. 'Notes on a Bronze Age Battle-Axe Found near Cornhill', *History of the Berwickshire Naturalists Club* 30 (1938–46), 229.
23 D. Passmore and C. Waddington, *Managing Archaeological Landscapes in Northumberland*, Till-Tweed Studies, vol. 1 (Oxford, 2009), 102.
24 *Ibid.*, 107–8; Semple *et al.*, 'Power at the Edge'.
25 G. Jobey, 'Hill Forts and Settlements in Northumberland', *Arch. Ael.*, 4th Ser. 43 (1965), 43, 62.
26 Dodds, *History of Northumberland*, 62.

Similar associations of votive weapon deposition and battle location are known elsewhere in Britain.[27]

The early medieval tenurial landscape

It is not easy to reconstruct the landscape of North Northumberland in terms of landholdings and tenurial responsibility. Unlike other parts of the country, particularly Wessex, this region lacks an extensive corpus of early medieval charters.[28] However, some useful sources for landholding survive in the eleventh and early twelfth century, primarily *Historia Sancto Cuthberto* and *Libellus de Exordio* by Symeon of Durham.[29] Conveniently, these works are all closely associated with the community of St Cuthbert, which had its origins in the monastic foundation at Lindisfarne and held significant holdings of land in North Northumberland and the Scottish borders, including Carham itself.

The first reference to Carham comes from the *Historia Sancto Cuthberto* when following Ecgfrith's defeat of the Mercian Wulfhere in AD 674 he donates Carham 'and whatever pertains to it' (*et quicquid ad eam pertinent*) to Cuthbert.[30] This phrase and similar ones are commonly used to imply that Carham was the centre of a network of associated *vills* and formed the core of what was probably a small shire.[31] It seems that this putative 'Carhamshire' was part of a larger block of land in the possession of the community of St Cuthbert running along the southern side of the Tweed; Carham was given to the Augustinian Priory at Kirkham alongside the contiguous parishes of Kirknewton and Ilderton, potentially helping to further define the extents of 'Carhamshire'.[32] To the east lay the territory that became

---

27   M. Macgregor, *Early Celtic Art in North Britain*, vol. 2 (Leicester, 1976), no. 136; Semple, *Perceptions of the Prehistoric*, 77–84.
28   D. Rollason, *Northumbria, 500–1100: Creation and Destruction of a Kingdom* (London, 2003), 10.
29   Symeon of Durham, *Libellus de Exordio atque procursu istius hoc est Dunhelmensis Ecclesiie*, ed. and trans. D. Rollason (Oxford, 2000) [*LDE*]; *Historia Sancto Cuthberto: A History of Saint Cuthbert and a Record of his Patrimony*, ed. and trans. T. Johnson South (Woodbridge, 2002) [*HSC*].
30   *HSC*, c.7, 49.
31   B. Roberts, *Landscapes, Documents and Maps: Villages in Northern England and Beyond AD 900–1250* (Oxford, 2008), 151–87; *HSC*, 124–9; G. W. S. Barrow, *The Kingdom of the Scots* (London, 1973), 24.
32   *RRAN*, ii, no. 1459.

known as Norhamshire, comprising an area running from Cornhill-on-Tweed to Horncliffe with its centre at Norham. To the east of Horncliffe lay the northern extent of Islandshire, centred on Lindisfarne but reaching as far north as Tweedmouth. To the south-east of Carham lay another piece of land associated with Cuthbert, a set of estates probably gifted by Oswiu running along the course of the Bowmont Water and perhaps centred on Kirk Yetholm.[33] This area was later dissected by the Anglo-Scottish border, with some land ending up in Scotland and Mindrum becoming a township belonging to Carham.[34] Carham is probably recorded later as *Carnham* s.a. 854 in the *Historia Regum* along with a number of other estates between the Teviot and the Tweed.[35]

It is clear that by the early eleventh century, almost all the land in the vicinity of Carham, particularly to the south of the Tweed, was part of the patrimony of Saint Cuthbert. As Alex Woolf has noted, the location of the battle on the Tweed makes it likely that the site was not a border between England and Scotland in this period, as early medieval battles rarely occur on such borders.[36] Yet, while not taking place on a national border, there are strong arguments that a site such as this, close to the Tweed, was on an internal administrative boundary, with the Tweed forming the boundary between two blocks of land under the control of the Community of Saint Cuthbert.

Early medieval settlement

We can be clear then that most of this Middle Tweed region was land held by the community of St Cuthbert and was well connected by routeways with the surrounding region; but what can we say about the way in which this land was actually occupied? It is possible to get a more general sense of the use of the landscape in the Carham area over the latter half of the first millennium AD. We know of a series of extensive, early

---

33   The estates in question are Sourhope?, Staerough, Old Graden, Pawston, Clifton, Shereburgh?, Colewell, Halterburn, Thornington(?), Shotton, Kirk Yetholm and Mindrum; see *HSC*, 43.
34   C. O'Brien, 'The Early Medieval Shires of Yeavering, Bamburgh and Breamish', *Arch. Ael.*, 5th Ser., 30 (2002), 53–73.
35   *HR*, s.a, 854, ed. Arnold, ii, 101.
36   A. Woolf, *From Pictland to Alba 789–1070* (Edinburgh, 2007), 237.

medieval settlement sites in North Northumberland. The most intensive area of known Anglo-Saxon settlement lies just across the northern tip of the Cheviots in the Milfield Basin, where the presence of two major royal centres are known. Yeavering, standing on the river Glen, is certainly the royal vill of *Ad Gefrin* associated with Edwin, whilst a major complex of cropmarks nearby at Milfield is probably the site known as *Maelmin*, which according to Bede replaced Yeavering as a royal estate centre.[37] Only Yeavering has seen archaeological excavation and Hope-Taylor's landmark work produced a series of excellent sequences of relative stratigraphy, although the overall chronology of the site remains frustratingly untethered at either end.[38] Ultimately the assumption that the site fell out of use by the early eighth century remains purely based on textual sources. Although Bede states, 'This town, under the following kings, was abandoned, and another was built instead of it, at the place called Maelmin', it is not clear whether this means the site was entirely abandoned or simply reduced in status.[39] Equally, whilst Bede implies that *Maelmin* was a royal vill whilst he was writing in the 720s–30s, since there has been no excavation the dates of the beginning and cessation of occupation at this site remain unknown. A site with strong parallels with Milfield and Yeavering survives at Whitemuirhaugh, Sprouston, only a few miles south-west of Carham.[40] This is an extensive multiphase site lacking any excavation. There may be early, perhaps Roman Iron Age phases, but the presence of large timber halls implies an early medieval date for its floruit. The presence of what appears to be a small church and associated cemetery recognisable on the cropmarks imply that it probably continued to be used into at least the seventh century AD, but once again, the date that it fell out of use remains unclear. Although a small silver ingot, possibly Viking Age, was found by a metal detectorist close to the Sprouston cropmarks, the association is not close

---

37 B. Hope-Taylor, *Yeavering: An Anglo-British Centre of Early Northumbria* (London, 1977); T. Gates and C. O'Brien, 'Cropmarks at Milfield and New Bewick and the Recognition of Grübenhauser in Northumberland', *Arch. Ael.*, 5th Ser. 16 (1988), 1–9; Bede, *Historia Ecclesiastica*, ed. Colgrave and Mynors, 188–9.
38 C. Scull, 'Post-Roman Phase 1 at Yeavering: A Reconsideration', *Medieval Archaeology* 35 (1991), 51–63; C. O'Brien, 'The Great Enclosure', in P. Frodsham and C. O'Brien (eds), *Yeavering: People, Power, Place* (Stroud, 2005), 145–52.
39 Bede, *Historia Ecclesiastica*, ed. Colgrave and Mynors, 188–9.
40 I. Smith, 'Sprouston, Roxburghshire: An Early Anglian Centre of the Eastern Tweed Basin', *PSAS* 125 (1991), 197–236.

enough for it to date continued occupation into the ninth/tenth century.[41] Combined, the evidence from Sprouston, Milfield and Yeavering suggests a well-developed landscape in the Tweed-Till region, with a series of substantial settlement foci implying considerable wealth and the ability to exploit the surrounding landscape effectively.[42] The importance of this area is underlined by the fact that two of the handful of gold tremisses known from Bernicia are found in this area, one a contemporary gold-plated forgery excavated at Yeavering and one from a metal-detector find near Coldstream.[43]

In addition to these large sites, a number of smaller Anglo-Saxon settlements have been identified in the Milfield Basin, including sites at Thirlings, Lanton Quarry and Cheviot Quarry. Unlike the major sites, these have produced a series of radiocarbon dates.[44] Together these suggest that the settlements were occupied, broadly speaking, between AD 400 and AD 700, with little evidence for later occupation. This means that there may have been some kind of shift in the settlement pattern, perhaps in the seventh or eighth century. But there seems to have been a further shift in settlement between the tenth and twelfth centuries. This can be detected by the presence of new churches being established with associated settlement cores and the lack of any obviously later medieval activity on the cropmark sites. At Yeavering, the nearby settlement of Kirk Newton develops; its name being a clear testament to the fact that it was a new development associated with a church, although in a charter of Henry I it is simply called 'Newton in Glendale'.[45] Although the current church has its origin in the thirteenth century, a sculpture within it depicting the Adoration of the Magi is probably twelfth century in date, or even earlier.[46] At Sprouston, whilst the current church is

---

41 A. Heald, 'Whitmuirhaugh, Scottish Borders (Sprouston Parish), *Ingot*', *Discovery Excav. Scot.*, 6 (2005), 125.
42 Semple *et al.*, 'Power at the Edge'.
43 Hope-Taylor, *Yeavering*, 182–3; Smith, pers. comm.
44 B. Johnson, 'Prehistoric and Dark Age Settlement Remains from Cheviot Quarry, Milfield Basin, Northumberland', *Archaeological Journal* 165/1 (2008), 107–26; C. O'Brien and R. Miket, 'The Early Medieval Settlement Site at Thirlings, Northumberland', *Durham Archaeological Journal* 7 (1991), 57–91; C. Waddington, 'A Note on Neolithic, Bronze Age and Anglo-Saxon Remains at Lanton Quarry near Milfield, Northumberland', *Arch. Ael.*, 5th Ser. 38 (2009), 23–30.
45 *RRAN*, ii, no. 1459.
46 R. Cramp, *Corpus of Anglo-Saxon Sculpture: County Durham and Northumberland* (Oxford, 1977), 251.

post-medieval in date, it is on the site of a medieval structure. It is recorded that the monks of Kelso dedicated the church of 'Spruwestun' (Sprouston) to St Michael in 1140, and the presence of a stone cross-base from the site may indicate a late Anglo-Saxon date for the church.[47] The excavation of a small church at the Hirsel, close to Coldstream, has suggested that the earliest phase of the structure, a simple, unicameral building, dates broadly to the tenth/eleventh century AD, perhaps also indicating a new phase of settlement activity at the site around the turn of the millennium.[48]

Tentatively then, we may suggest that there were two realignments in the settlement pattern in this region; one in the late sixth or seventh century AD when the small sites such as those at Lanton and Cheviot Quarry cease to be active and another in the tenth–twelfth century when we see the emergence of small stone churches, seemingly in new locations and perhaps associated with new settlement cores. How the chronology of Yeavering, Sprouston and *Maelmin* fits into this pattern is unclear and serves to emphasise the need for more work to better understand these important sites.

As well as considering settlement evidence, we can also think about the actual landscape between occupation centres. Although limited in scale, the environmental evidence from the Hirsel can help us get some sense of the range of crops being grown. An examination of the plant macrofossils suggests that oats were the most commonly grown species, with smaller quantities of wheat, rye and barley, as well as peas and beans.[49] There is very little comparative material from the Border regions, although the asssemblages from the Anglo-Saxon monastery at Hoddom (Dumfriesshire) also indicate a predominance of oats as the main cereal crop.[50] Pollen evidence from Broad Moss, near Harthope, show the cultivation of oats and wheat in the Cheviots and its vicinity.[51]

---

47   RCAHMS, *An Inventory*, 433, no. 970, figs 266, 466.
48   R. Cramp, *The Hirsel Excavations* (London, 2014).
49   J. Huntley 'Analysis of Carbonised Plant Remains', in Cramp, *The Hirsel*, 137–50.
50   T. Holden. 'The Botanical Evidence', in C. Lowe, *Excavations at Hoddom, Dumfriesshire: An Early Ecclesiastical Site in South-West Scotland* (Edinburgh, 2006), 150–5.
51   R. Young, 'Peat, Pollen and People: Palaeoenvironmental Reconstruction in Northumberland National Park', in P. Frodsham, *Archaeology in Northumberland National Park* (York, 2004), 156–90; G. Davies and J. Turne, 'Pollen Diagrams from Northumberland', *New Phytologist* 82 (1979), 783–804.

As far as animal husbandry is concerned, there were only low numbers of animal bones from the Hirsel; nonetheless, they seem to indicate that in the tenth/eleventh century AD, cattle and sheep were being consumed in roughly equal numbers, with lower numbers of pig.[52] Large areas of ridge and furrow survive in North Northumberland, and in the Carham area patches survive as earthworks (sometimes only visible on Lidar) and cropmarks. There are several clearly discernible lobes of such ridge and furrow centring on the village of Carham itself, between the church and the hall. Dating the emergence of such field systems is fraught with difficulty, but the reorganisation of the settlement system postulated as occurring around the turn of the millennium might be a persuasive context for their establishment.

All the sites discussed so far have been located in low-lying valley bottoms. However, much of the landscape south of Carham is dominated by the northern Cheviots. These upland areas also seem to have been occupied in this period, although direct evidence is slim. The seventh-century grant by Oswiu of the Bowmont Water estates to Lindisfarne implies that they were seen to have some economic value – though some of these vills were on the floodplain and river terraces of the Bowmont, others were clearly located in areas of greater relief. Evidence from elsewhere in the Cheviots does suggest early agricultural exploitation of the Cheviot uplands. Radiocarbon dates from a cross-ridged dyke near Brough Law, a low walled boundary at Little Haystack and beneath a stone revetment at Ritto Hill, all in the Breamish Valley, suggest that arable agricultural activity was taking place here in the mid first millennium AD.[53]

We have only a poor understanding of the nature of upland settlement in this period. Enclosed settlements and small univallate and multivallate hillforts clearly continued to be used in the Cheviots throughout the Roman period.[54] However, the point at which this tradition was replaced by the emergence of unenclosed settlements with rectangular buildings is not clear, partly due to the difficulty in dating early medieval activtiy in the absence of any distinctive diagnostic

---

52 L. Gidney, 'The Animal Bones', in Cramp, *The Hirsel*, 150–61.
53 P. Frodsham and C. Waddington, 'The Breamish Valley Archaeological Project 1994–2002', in Frodsham, *Archaeology*, 171–89.
54 P. Frodsham, A. Oswald, S. Ainsworth and T. Pearson, *Hillforts: Prehistoric Strongholds of Northumberland National Park* (London, 2007).

material culture. There have been arguments for continuity of activity into the early medieval period at Yeavering Bell, and post-Roman actvity has been conjectured at the Dunion, a substantial hillfort near Jedburgh.[55] One site that has produced early medieval material culture is Crock Cleugh (Roxburghshire) in the upper Bowmont Valley, where excavation of an enclosure of Iron Age origin recovered a Leeds type F Anglo-Saxon annular brooch of sixth-century date.[56] However, it is not clear whether this indicates continued occupation or whether it is merely a chance loss. An Anglo-Saxon loom weight was discovered at Sourhope during building work near the farm, but little is understood about its context.[57]

There are no securely dated early medieval upland settlements with rectangular structures known from the North Cheviots, but there are others from the wider region. Nineteen miles to the north at Kersons Cleugh in the Lammermuirs excavation in advance of a windfarm development has revealed a small building of broadly seventh–ninth century AD date.[58] Even further afield excavation at sites such as Simy Folds (County Durham), Gauber High Pasture (Cumbria), Bryant's Gill (Cumbria) and Upper Pasture, Horton-in-Ribblesdale (North Yorkshire), all show that these upland areas were well used, certainly by the Middle Anglo-Saxon period.[59] It is possible that these are early examples of small upland shielings, indicative of the pastoral

---

55 R. Miket, 'Understanding British/Anglo-Saxon Continuity at Gefrin: Brian Hope-Taylor's Excavations on Yeavering Bell', *Arch. Ael.*, 5th Ser. 42 (2013), 133–60; RCAHMS, *An Inventory*, 62–4, no. 33, fig. 96; J. Rideout, 'Dunion Hill (Bedrule p). Fort, Houses, Walls', *Discovery Excav. Scot.* 2 (1984); J. Rideout, 'Excavation of an Iron-Age Fort at The Dunion, Roxburghshire', *PSAS* 117 (1987), 361.
56 K. Steer and G. Keeney, 'Excavations in Two Homesteads at Crock Cleugh, Roxburghshire', *PSAS* 81 (1946–7), 138–57; Alice Blackwell pers. comm.
57 Anon., 'Donations to and Purchases for the Museum and Library', *PSAS* 104 (1971–2), 316, no. 21.
58 I. Suddaby, *Excavation at the Confluence of Dye Water/Kersons Cleugh, Fallago Rig Windfarm, Longformacus*, Unpublished Report (Edinburgh, 2011).
59 D. Coggins, K. J. Fairless, C. E. Batey, K. Brown, A. Donaldson, D. Wright and R. Young, 'Simy Folds: An Early Medieval Settlement Site in Upper Teesdale, Co. Durham', *Medieval Archaeology* 27/1 (1983), 1–26; A. King, 'Gauber High Pasture, Ribblehead: An Interim Report', in R. A. Hall (ed.), *Viking Age York & the North* (York, 1978), 21–5; D. S. Johnson, 'Excavation of a Late Seventh Century Structure in Upper Ribblesdale', *Yorkshire Archaeological Journal* 86 (2014), 80–105; S. Dickinson, 'Bryant's Gill, Kentmere: Another "Viking-Period" Ribblehead', in J. R. Baldwin and I. D. Whyte (eds), *The Scandinavians in Cumbria* (Edinburgh, 1985), 83–8.

transhumance practices that are known to have taken place in many parts of upland northern England until the early post-medieval period.[60]

Amidst this landscape of secular settlement and agricultural activity there was also the ever-present evidence of the church. We have already seen that there were probably eleventh- or twelfth-century churches at Sprouston and the Hirsel with potentially slightly earlier origins. Not surprisingly, given that most of the land in the area was under the control of the powerful community of St Cuthbert and acquired when they were still based at Lindisfare, there is good evidence for a number of other churches in the vicinity. At Carham itself the church is of eighteenth-century date, but replacing a medieval predecessor. The presence of three fragments of sculpture with a late first millennium AD date indicates a likely Anglo-Saxon date.[61] The dedication of the church to Cuthbert reminds us of the Lindisfarne connections. Given Carham's position at the centre of a group of vills it is not surprising to find a church here; a similar situation can be found at Norham, the centre of Norhamshire, which was clearly the site of an important church, and the first site to which the community of St Cuthbert moved following their departure from Holy Island.[62] At Carham it is possible that there are still traces of an early enclosure associated with an ecclesiastical foundation at the village. A large sub-oval banked enclosure lies to the north side of the road, with the church and its graveyard occupying the south-western quarter. The north-east of the enclosure is clearly overlain by medieval ridge and furrow, which runs over the enclosure bank; this stratigraphic relationship implies a relatively early date for the enclosure and confirms that it is not a headland or selion related to the ridge and furrow in the immediate area.

Tillmouth, between Cornhill and Norham, was listed in the *Historia Regum* as belonging to the community of St Cuthbert, alongside a number of other sites including Auldham, Coldingham, Norham, Pefferham (probably Aberlady) and Tyninghame. These other places can all be

---

60 A. L. Winchester, *The Harvest of the Hill: Rural Life in Northern England and the Scottish Borders, 1400–1700* (Edinburgh, 2001).
61 R. Cramp, *Corpus of Anglo-Saxon Stone Sculpture: Volume 1, County Durham and Northumberland* (London, 1984), 169–70, plates 161–3; see also Thompson in this volume.
62 *HR*, s.a. 854.

identified as early ecclesiastical sites, which suggests Tillmouth may also have been a church or monastic site. Today, a heavily restored medieval chapel, dedicated to Saint Cuthbert, still stands on land at the confluence of the Tweed and the Till, adjacent to a fording point recorded as 'chapel ford' by the sixteenth-century Border Commissioners.[63] The site has not had any modern archaeological investigation, but the cropmarks of a possible large circular enclosure are visible surrounding the chapel.[64] Tillmouth is thus a strong candidate for the site of a previously unrecognised early medieval monastic site. In the case of Norham, Carham and Tillmouth, the position of the church in low-lying land close to a river (particularly those with crossings) is widely paralleled in other early medieval ecclesiastical sites in Northumbia, including Old Melrose, Sockburn, Gainford, Alnmouth, Jarrow and Wearmouth. The enclosures at both Tillmouth and Carham are strong candidates for small-scale targeted fieldwork, including geophysical survey and excavation to identify and evaluate any surviving sub-surface remains.

Just two and a half miles north of Carham is Eccles, a village with a placename clearly derived from the Latin *ecclesia* meaning 'church', a placename element that can also be found in Berwickshire at Bunkle.[65] Simon Taylor has argued that these southern Scottish simplex *eccles* names may well be relatively early, probably predating *c.* AD 650.[66] This may imply the presence of an early ecclesiastical site. However, little survives of any such putative early church site. A possible long cist was excavated at Eccles House to the south of the church in the nineteenth century, although this may well be related to a later Cistercian convent known to have existed here.[67] The church was dedicated to Cuthbert by 1248, perhaps implying that at some point before this it had come under the control of the community of St Cuthbert.[68]

---

63 J. Hodgson, *History of Northumberland* (Newcastle upon Tyne), 194–202.
64 Passmore and Waddington, *Managing Archaeological Landcapes*, 104, fig. 3.19.
65 C. Hough, 'Eccles in English and Scottish Place-Names', in E. Quinton (ed.), *The Church in English Place-Names* (Nottingham, 2009); S. Taylor, 'Place-Names and the Early Church in Eastern Scotland', in B. Crawford (ed.), *Scotland in Dark Age Britain* (Aberdeen, 1996), 93–110; S. Taylor, 'Place-Names and the Early Church in Scotland', *Records of the Scottish Church History Society* 28 (1998), 1–22.
66 Taylor, 'Place-Names and the Early Church in Scotland'.
67 *The New Statistical Account of Scotland by the ministers of the respective parishes under the superintendence of a committee of the society for the benefit of the sons and daughters of the clergy, 15v.* (Edinburgh, 1834–45), 58.
68 H. Scott *et al.* (eds), *Fasti ecclesiae scoticanae*, new edn, vol. 11 (Edinburgh, 1917), 12.

The parish of Eccles was divided into four quarters, each with its own chapel; Birgham, one of these quarters, lies between Eccles and Carham. The site of the chapel just to the south of the village is known, but again, there is nothing to suggest a particularly early foundation. The sites of similar non-parochial churches or chapels are also known at Mindrum (Carham),[69] Pressen (Carham)[70], Stawford (St Aetheldreda, Yetholm),[71] Wark (Carham),[72] Hoselaw (Linton parish)[73] and, of course, the Hirsel.[74] Cramp's excavations at the Hirsel have shown that it may date as early as the tenth century. If the other chapels have a similar date, this provision of subordinate townships or vills with places of worship may be of the same period as the postulated settlement shift occurring around the turn of the first millennium AD and be broadly contemporary with the battle.

A landscape of assembly

A final dimension of the early medieval landscape to consider is what might be termed the 'administrative' landscape. It is clear from extensive research both further south in Anglo-Saxon England and more recently in Scotland that many judicial, administrative and military activities were carried out at open-air assembly sites.[75] These might be marked by

---

69 K. H. Vickers, *A History of Northumberland, Vol. XI* (Newcastle upon Tyne, 1922), 15–16; M. Culley, 'Old Epitaphs in Mindrum Graveyard in the Chapelry of Carham and the Parish of Kirknewton', *History of the Berwickshire Naturalists Club* 22 (1914), 191–6.

70 R. N. Hadcock, 'A Map of Mediaeval Northumberland and Durham', *Arch. Ael.*, 4th Ser. 16 (1939), 144–220, at 164.

71 R. Carlton and P. Ryder, 'Ecclesiastical Establishments in the Scottish Borders Potentially Associated with the Battle of Flodden', in Miller *et al.*, *Flodden*, 96–104, at 102–3.

72 Vickers, *History of Northumberland*, 16; Anon., 'Erskine Monument and Wark Castle', *History of Berwickshire Naturalists Club* 29 (1935), 11–12; J. Wallis, *The Natural History and Antiquities of Northumberland and so much of the County of Durham as lies between the rivers Tyne and Tweed (Vol. 2)* (London, 1769), 467; J. Hardy, *History of the Berwickshire Naturalists Club* 13 (1890–1), 80.

73 RCAHMS, *An Inventory*, 259.

74 Cramp, *The Hirsel*.

75 A. T. Skinner and S. Semple, 'Assembly Mounds in the Danelaw: Place-Name and Archaeological Evidence in the Historic Landscape', *Journal of the North Atlantic* 8 (2015), 115–33; S. Semple and A. Sanmark, 'Assembly in North West Europe: Collective Concerns for Early Societies?', *Journal of European Archaeology* 16.3 (2013), 518–42; A. Pantos, '"On the edge of things": The Boundary Location of

distinctive natural features such as stones or trees or be associated with prehistoric monuments. It is also clear that most were located on or near borders between administrative units. There was also a hierarchy of assembly sites, ranging from the local to the regional.

However, Northumberland comprises a lacuna in the research into such assembly sites and there has been no systematic review of the evidence for such locations in this region. Nonetheless, it is possible to identify a number of candidate sites, primarily by identifying later locales which were recorded as fulfilling similar roles. The presence of the border between England and Scotland, and the long-lived conflict between the two polities, as well as endemic unrest during the sixteenth century between local 'reivers' in this debated territory means that the later documentary record is well furnished with references to trysting locations and mustering sites.

At Carham itself, the best-known trysting place was Hadden Stank (also known as Redden Burn), a small stream that formed the border between England and Scotland at the point that it left the course of the Tweed and turned southwards. It became the site of a series of major border meetings between the English and Scots throughout the medieval period and into the sixteenth century, and was also the site of a battle between the two sides in 1540.[76] In 1245, English knights attempted to commence a perambulation of the border from Redden Burn to White Law before being forced to withdraw after facing violent opposition.[77] This incident gives a nice indication of how key locations on political boundaries could become the locus of conflict through acting as the point of origin for perambulation and other modes of asserting claims to land. Of course, the key issue here is whether the fallout of the battle at Carham led to this location becoming a significant node on an international border and thus emerging as a trysting site or whether the presence of a pre-existing assembly site resulted in the battle taking place here. The latter is more likely, but

---

Anglo-Saxon Assembly Sites', *Anglo-Saxon Studies in Archaeology and History* 12 (2003), 38–49; O'Grady, 'Judicial Assembly Sites in Scotland: Archaeological and Place-Name Evidence of the Scottish Court Hill', *Medieval Archaeology* 48 (2014), 104–35.

76 Joseph Bain (ed.), *Calendar of Letters and Papers Relating to the Affairs of the Borders of England and Scotland*, 2 vols (1894–6), vol. 1, 347, 352, 353, 355, 358; vol. 2, 566–7.

77 R. Oram, *Alexander II 1214–1249 King of the Scots* (Edinburgh, 2012), 175.

ultimately unprovable. Within Carham, the only other probable administrative location is Gallows Knoll at the eastern end of the parish, midway between Carham and Wark. Antiquarian references record a 'circular mount' from which at least one skeleton had been recovered.[78] It has been suggested that the field known as Battle Place overlooked by the hill was the site of a skirmish between the English and the Scots in 1370.[79]

Just over one kilometre beyond the eastern boundary of Carham, in the parish of Crookham, stands the King's Stone, also known as the 'Stone of Crookham More' [sic].[80] Probably originally a prehistoric standing stone, it was regularly listed as a muster point in the sixteenth century, and in 1533 troops were mustered here following the destruction of Cornhill and Wark. In 1545, the Earl of Hertford ordered that 'all his army had a day appointed to mytte at the Stannyngston on Crocke-a-More [Crookham Moor]'. Its name came from the belief that James IV was killed here at the Battle of Flodden. Further afield, Stawford on Bowmont Water lies on the border and is also recorded as being the site of several cross-border meetings and warden courts during the sixteenth century.[81] As noted above, it is also at the point where the Staw Road reaches the lower-lying valley bottom and is close to a probable chapel site. Another known assembly point was Cocklaw (Windy Gyle) on the watershed of the Bowmont Water, close to the route of Clennel Street, again recorded as an important meeting place on the March in the sixteenth century.[82] A key feature of this site is the presence of a large cairn of potential Bronze Age date; now known as Russell's Cairn it allegedly marks the spot where Lord Russell met his death on the day of a truce in 1565.[83] To the north of Carham on the Scottish side of the Tweed, the hillfort at Hirsel Law seems to have been used as a site for settling legal disputes and executions as late as the

---

78 E. Mackenzie, *An Historical, Topographical, and Descriptive View of the County of Northumberland: And of those Parts of the County of Durham Situated North of the River Tyne, with Berwick Upon Tweed, and Brief Notices of Celebrated Places on the Scottish Border, Volume I* (Berwick upon Tweed, 1825), 356.
79 M. Rayner, *English Battlefields: An Illustrated Encyclopaedia* (Stroud, 2004), 87.
80 *History of the Berwickshire Naturalists' Club* 10 (1908); Anon., *Proceedings of the Society of Antiquaries of Newcastle*, 3rd Ser. 4 (1910), 213–220, at 220.
81 Bain, *Border Papers*, vol. 1, 357, 374, 531, 660, 661, 663; vol. 2, 101.
82 *Ibid.*, vol. 2, 179, 180, 184.
83 RCAHMS, *Inventory*, 361–2, no. 720, fig. 5.

seventeenth century.[84] Further afield, sites such as Ellemford, north of Duns, were also historically attested muster sites for Scottish armies.[85]

In many cases, these various assembly sites are only first recorded as such in the sixteenth century; it is unlikely though that their importance was only a recent development and, given that other assembly sites such as Hadden Stank are of greater antiquity, it is highly likely that these sites too are older. It is true that the high level of border conflict in this region may have both catalysed and distorted the development of such sites in the landscape and thus some of the sites mentioned may in a sense be a result of, rather than a context for, the 1018 battle. In practice, the parish of Carham was bounded on all sides by assembly sites associated with prehistoric monuments, boundaries and routeways, and it would have been virtually impossible to enter the parish from any direction without passing hard by a site attested as being an assembly place at some point. This dense distribution of assembly sites of various forms and scales in Carham and its hinterland helps towards an understanding of the reason why it became the site of a key battle such as that of 1018. Indeed, the wider area along the Tweed between the confluences with the Kale water downstream to the Tillmouth has a remarkable density of medieval battles. In addition to the battle of Carham itself, there were the conflicts at Haddon Stank and the 1370s battle as well as the battle of Piperdean (1435), all in the parish of Carham itself; surely making Carham one of the most fought over parishes in Britain. Further east were the battles of Homildon Hill (1402), Yeavering (1415), Hedgeley Moor (1464), Grindon (1558) and of course Flodden (1513). Supplementing these major confrontations, there were numerous incidents of lower level violence throughout the medieval and early post-medieval period. Indeed, in the mid-sixteenth century several parts of the parish around Carham and Wark were categorised as 'bateable lands', patches of land that although south of the Tweed and east of the Redden Burn still claimed by both Scotland and England.[86] The importance of assembly sites in the bringing together of armies and other groupings, and as sites for negotiation of peace and opening hostilities is clear. The intersection of routeways, the river, settlements and

---

84 Cramp, *The Hirsel*, 18–19, 26.
85 D. Caldwell, 'Scottish Ways to War 1513: The Mobilisation for the Flodden Campaign', in Miller *et al.*, *Flodden*, 81–5.
86 Bain, *Border Papers*, vol. 1, 31–2.

pre-existing landscape features, not to mention the importance of the junction between lowland arable farming and upland pastoral transhumance, condensed within a relatively small areas with associated patterns of assembling and dispersing landscape, mean that the area of Carham was a complex one. Fording points and passes are likely to have been particularly sensitive points; constraining and channelling movement, a process which would have inevitably provoked a sense of anxiety and tension. The bringing together of people was not just an activity that took place within settlements, but at other key positions in the landscape such as these.

In essence, battles might be seen as just one particular aspect of the wider range of assembly practices that took place in early medieval (and later) contexts. These might include assembling people and resources for purposes of economic and social exchange, judicial decisions, and other forms of dispute resolution. Indeed, from a *longue durée* perspective, the records of the sixteenth-century Wardens of the Marches make it clear how easily administrative meetings at tryst sites with formal truces in place could spill over to small- and large-scale violence.[87] Equally, armies might be assembled and then demobbed without actually fighting, the classic Northumbrian example being Oswine's assembling of an army at *Wilfaresdun* and then disbanding it when he realised Oswiu's army was stronger.[88]

Conclusions

While we can never know in which field or at which Ordnance Survey gridpoint the meeting of the Scottish and Northumbrian armies took place, this paper has shown it is possible to get some sense of the physical and to an extent, social landscape within which the forces came together. This was an inhabited tract of land, and perhaps one undergoing change. It is broadly around this time that new villages appear to have been coalescing; they would go on to form the armature for the later medieval countryside of the middle Tweed Valley. Centred on small stone churches and their graveyards, and probably surrounded by lobes of heavily farmed fields, these settlements are likely to have been

---

87 Bain, *Border Papers*, vol. 1, vol. 2.
88 Bede, *Historia Ecclesiastica*, ed. Colgrave and Mynors, 3.14.

enveloped in larger areas of less intensively farmed outfields, probably used seasonally for grazing, particularly on the low-lying haughs close to the river. Depending on the time of year that the armies marched they may have either passed fields green with ripening oats, intermingled with a wide range of weeds and wildflowers, or the stubble of harvested crops. Crossing these fields and meadows would have been the roads and tracks that served to link the local inhabitants with areas of upland grazing where sheep or cattle were sent during the summer, probably along with the young unmarried men and women who would have tended them. Although the roads themselves would have soon disappeared from the immediate line of sight as they crossed the river or headed south into the more rolling countryside, they would have served to remind the population of how their small patch of the Middle Tweed was connected to their immediate neigbours, small towns such as Kelso, Coldstream and Kirk Yetholm, but also, a little further, important monastic sites, such as Norham and Jedburgh. But side-by-side with this landscape of farming and movement were also places and spaces where people came together. At times of peace they would convene to make decisions, hear disputes and exchange goods, as well as to meet neighbours from adjacent villages; but at times of war, they would have assembled to hear news of advancing armies, take orders from leaders and arm themselves for defence or to go on the offensive. These assembly places would have acted as valves where tensions within and between communities may have been eased but also stoked.

There is still much to do to unpick the nature of the landscape of Carham at the turn of the first millenium AD. A better understanding of the chronology at sites such as Sprouston is key to refining the tempo of settlement change in this area, whilst the large enclosure visible on Lidar around the church at Carham needs to be better understood; did it bound a monastic site or did it have some other function? Finally, there is a strong case to be made for a better understanding of the landscape of assembly in this region. At least some of the sites that have been identified are likely to be where men who took part in the battle of 1018 came together in the days and hours before fighting started. These are likely to have been places long-known to them and burnished by generations of gatherings. Work on such sites elsewhere has demonstrated the material correlates of such convocations, yet the assembly sites of Bernicia are probably the least understood of any in Britain.

Acknowledgements

I would like to thank all those who commented on this work or provided useful information to help me better understand the landscape of Carham; in particular thanks are due to Alice Blackwell, Sarah Semple, Victoria Thompson and Andrew Tibbs. Thanks also to the editors for suggestions, corrections and support.

CHAPTER SEVEN

A New Reading of Late Anglo-Saxon Sculpture in and around the Tweed Valley: Carham, Lindisfarne, Norham and Jedburgh

VICTORIA THOMPSON

Introduction

Three fragmentary stone crosses, now in the Great North Museum in Newcastle, plausibly come from late Anglo-Saxon Carham.[1] Broken and deracinated as they now are, with notably austere ornament, little can be said about them directly. However, this article will seek to reanimate the sculptural landscape of the Tweed and its hinterland in the generations around the battle of Carham, first by appraising the story of a stone cross written by Symeon of Durham, then by re-evaluating the role of carved stones at Lindisfarne, Norham and Jedburgh, the three sites in the vicinity with large collections of ninth- to eleventh-century sculpture. The sculpture from this area has been discussed in detail by Rosemary Cramp in a range of publications; the aim here, therefore, is not to list exhaustively or to describe, but rather to suggest new angles and interpretations.[2]

---

1 R. Cramp, *Corpus of Anglo-Saxon Stone Sculpture: Volume 1, County Durham and Northumberland* (Oxford, 1984), 169–70, plates 161–3. Images of all stone sculpture in England referred to in this study can be accessed via the Corpus of Anglo-Saxon Stone Sculpture website: <http://www.ascorpus.ac.uk/>

2 R. Cramp, 'The Anglian Tradition in the Ninth Century', in J. T. Lang (ed.), *Anglo-Saxon and Viking Sculpture* BAR BS 49 (Oxford, 1978), 1–32; 'The Anglian Sculptures from Jedburgh', in A. O'Connor and D. V. Clarke (eds), *From the Stone Age to the Forty-Five: Studies Presented to R. B. K. Stevenson, Former Keeper, National Museum of Antiquities of Scotland* (Edinburgh, 1983), 269–84; *County Durham and Northumberland*, 31–2, 161–2, 194–214; 'The Artistic Influence of Lindisfarne within Northumbria', in G. Bonner, C. Stancliffe and D. Rollason (eds), *St Cuthbert, His Cult and His Community to AD 1200* (Woodbridge, 1989), 213–28; 'Heads You Lose', in E. Cambridge and J. Hawkes (eds), *Crossing Boundaries: Interdisciplinary Approaches to the Art, Material Culture, Language and Literature of the Early Medieval World* (Oxford and Philadelphia, 2017), 15–22.

No pre-Conquest account tells us in detail what carved stones, whether in the form of free-standing stone crosses, or shrines, or grave-markers, meant to their Anglo-Saxon patrons, makers or audiences. However, in his history of the St Cuthbert community, the *Libellus de Exordio atque procursu istius hoc est Dunhelmensis ecclesie*, Symeon gives an enchanting account of an inscribed stone cross:

> *Fecerat iste de lapide crucem artifici opere expoliri, et in sui memoriam suum in eo nomen exarari. Cujus summitatem multo post tempore, dum ipsam ecclesiam Lindisfarnensem pagani devastarent, fregerunt, sed post artificis ingenio reliquae parti infuso plumbo, ipsa fractura est adjuncta; semperque deinceps cum corpore sancti Cuthberti crux ipsa circumferri solebat, et a populo Northanhymbrorum propter utrumque sanctum in honore haberi, que etiam usque hodie in huius (id est Dunelmensis) ecclesie cimiterio stans sullimus utrorumque pontificum intuentibus exhibit monimentum.*

He [Æthelwald] had had embellished by the work of craftsmen a stone cross, and in memory of the saint he had his name inscribed on it. Much later the heathens broke the top of this cross when they sacked the church of Lindisfarne, but afterwards with the ingenuity of a craftsman the broken part was joined again to the remainder by means of pouring in lead. Always afterwards it was the custom to carry this cross round with the body of St Cuthbert, and for it to be held in honour by the people of Northumbria on account of both saints. Down to the present day it stands loftily in the cemetery of this church (that is the church of Durham), and it exhibits to onlookers a monument to both bishops.[3]

There can be little doubt that Symeon is describing a monument that he knows intimately. We may, however, justifiably doubt details of the back-story he provides for it, while at the same time interrogating his account as a way of understanding the numinous power and personality of these monuments. Symeon was writing in the early twelfth century, approximately a hundred years after the battle of Carham; and although he was probably of Norman extraction, he identifies

---

3   *LDE*, i.12, 60–1.

himself with the traditions of the pre-Conquest St Cuthbert community.[4]

These three major sites with sculpture in Carham's hinterland, Lindisfarne, Norham and Jedburgh, are also intimately connected with the cult of St Cuthbert, as well as those of associated seventh-to-eighth-century holy men such as St Aidan, founder of the monastery on Lindisfarne, and St Ceolwulf, the king of Northumbria who abdicated to become a brother of the Lindisfarne community. Both Norham and Jedburgh are recorded in much later sources as being linked to Lindisfarne from the first half of the ninth century, and Norham was also a monastery, though the precise nature of the relationship between these different monastic houses is not clear.[5] In the ninth century, the community of St Cuthbert left Lindisfarne, taking its relics; and according to historiography based on Anglo-Norman accounts they embarked on a journey that took them first to Norham, then presumably back to Lindisfarne before leaving again in 875 for an eight-year odyssey before settling far to the south in Chester-le-Street in 883 and relocating finally to Durham in 995. However, Neil McGuigan has recently made a powerful case for privileging accounts contemporary to the ninth, tenth and eleventh centuries over later retrospectives, even if those later narratives are more detailed; and he unpicks the narratives of the 'Symeonic school' to show their mythopoeic character. This methodology leads to the conclusion that St Cuthbert's body probably rested at Norham into the early eleventh century.[6]

This is not the place to reproduce McGuigan's complex and technical argument in detail. However, any attempt to write the story of the sculpture of the Tweed Valley is, inevitably, intimately bound up with our understanding of the narrative of the St Cuthbert community. Efforts to contextualise the sculpture have largely been contained within the framework deduced from the writing of the Anglo-Norman historians.

---

4   J. Crook, *English Medieval Shrines* (Woodbridge, 2011), 149.
5   D. Rollason, *Northumbria, 500–1100: Creation and Destruction of a Kingdom* (Cambridge, 2003), 133.
6   McGuigan is far from being the only scholar to raise anxieties about this narrative. N. McGuigan, 'Neither Scotland nor England: Middle Britain, c.850–1150', PhD thesis (University of St Andrews, 2015), 74ff; *HSC*, 32–3, 84–5. 100–1; J. Barrow, 'Danish Ferocity and Abandoned Monasteries: The Twelfth Century View', in M. Brett and D. A. Woodman (eds), *The Long Twelfth-Century View of the Anglo-Saxon Past* (London, 2016), 77–94, 86.

The sophistication of the Norham sculpture – and the comparative crudity of that from Chester-le-Street – has long been a puzzle, as has the situation on Lindisfarne, where an interest in monumental sculpture appears largely, possibly wholly, to post-date the community's supposed departure from the region. Another long-standing conundrum is the context for the sophisticated shrine fragment from Jedburgh. This article will therefore use McGuigan's 'Norham hypothesis' as a lens through which to re-examine the sculpture from Lindisfarne, Norham, Jedburgh and Carham. If nothing else, McGuigan's reassessment, which suggests more continuity and agency for the St Cuthbert community, albeit diffused across several sites, indicates the fragility of the existing explanatory framework.

What was Anglo-Saxon sculpture for?

Before looking at the sites in detail, we will first consider the nature and purpose of the sculptural record, and then interrogate Symeon of Durham's narrative of the stone cross. The sculpture of northern Northumbria appears in two main forms: large crosses and smaller funerary stones.[7] Carham only has crosses, but Norham also has a cross-marked slab, and Lindisfarne a range of grave-markers. In addition to its crosses, Jedburgh has a fragment of elaborate late-eighth to early-ninth-century shrine, unrivalled in the region. Crosses and grave-stones in northern Northumbria exhibit a wide variety of shapes and decorative motifs; and their functions could overlap: a large cross might have marked a grave, or provided a devotional focus in a cemetery, whereas a cross-marked grave-slab might easily prompt compunction, penance and prayer. Both categories of monument need

---

[7] Two sites in Carham's vicinity, Edrom and Old Cambus, have hogbacked gravestones which Lang suggested were eleventh-century, and the initial intent here was to reassess their dating and speculate on their place within the devotional and monumental landscape of Carham's hinterland. However, Edrom was lost a long time ago, and the ruined church of St Helen at Old Cambus is so thoroughly overgrown with couch grass that tracing the two recumbents is impossible without a major campaign of clearance. Unfortunately, the photographic record is poor, and so the decision was taken to omit these stones from the present study. A. Reid, 'The Churches and Churchyard Memorials of St Helens on the Lea and Cockburnspath', *PSAS* 48 (1914), 210–22; J. T. Lang, 'Hogback Monuments in Scotland', *PSAS* 105 (1972–4) 206–35, 224 and 231. I am grateful to Anna Ritchie and Jamie Barnes for discussing Old Cambus with me.

to be read eschatologically, as well as their providing clues to the social and cultural environments in which they were made, preserved and reused or destroyed. Almost all the sculpture under discussion here is damaged, often severely; none is in its original place, or serving its original function. What we see now is the equivalent of a skeleton – often no more than a few scattered bones: we need to reclothe these fragments in flesh, and dress them, and breathe life back into them.

Listing and describing surviving sculpture is a reasonably straightforward process; interpreting it presents more of a challenge. Sculpture frequently survives at sites for which there is no other early evidence for Christian ritual activity. Usually there is little basis for ascribing a date other than style and, to a lesser extent, technique. Both methods – as scholars are well aware – are riddled with subjectivity.[8] The temptation is always to fall back on a historical narrative established through other data, although this always risks circularity. While sculpture is often dated by reference to art in other media, such as metalwork and manuscripts, the dating of these, too, is seldom solid.[9] In the absence of secure contexts, datable inscriptions and complete monuments, it is hard to do more than spot likenesses, suggest typologies, and hypothesise influence based on very unstable chronology.[10] Those few comparatively complete monuments with human figures and/or inscriptions, are more susceptible to interpretation which does not depend on a wider historical narrative, or their place in a typology. This is exemplified by the scholarly attention paid to the Ruthwell, Bewcastle and Sandbach crosses; and here to the fragmentary but figural Lindisfarne 3 and 8, analysed in detail below.[11] The present

---

[8] Cramp, 'The Anglian Tradition' gives a helpful overview both of this anxiety and its historiography.

[9] The Lindisfarne Gospels is a good example, usually dated to the early eighth century and ascribed to Lindisfarne on the basis of Aldred's Colophon, but for the concerns around this text see n. 16 below.

[10] F. Orton, 'Rethinking the Ruthwell and Bewcastle Monuments: Some Deprecation of Style; some Consideration of Form and Ideology', in C. E. Karkov and G. Hardin Brown, *Anglo-Saxon Styles* (Albany, 2003), 31–68; J. Hawkes, 'Reading Stone', in C. E. Karkov and F. Orton, *Theorizing Anglo-Saxon Stone Sculpture* (Morgantown, 2003), 5–30.

[11] F. Orton, I. Wood and C. Lees, *Fragments of History: Rethinking the Ruthwell and Bewcastle Monuments* (Manchester, 2007); E. Ó Carragáin, *Ritual and the Rood: Liturgical Images and the Old English Poems of the* Dream of the Rood *Tradition* (Toronto, 2005); J. Hawkes, *The Sandbach Crosses: Sign and Significance in*

discussion seeks not to impose a new hegemonic interpretation but to open up debate.

The cross of St Æthelwald

The historiography of the sculpture associated with the St Cuthbert community is preoccupied by a vanished monument: the cross commissioned by Æthelwald of Lindisfarne, an object known only from those two sentences in Symeon's *Libellus de Exordio*. On the basis of this testimony, Clare Stancliffe has recently suggested that Æthelwald is a good candidate for the commissioner of the Ruthwell cross; Eric Cambridge looks in vain for the influence of Æthelwald's cross at Chester-le-Street and wonders whether therefore it might instead have been taken directly from Lindisfarne to Durham in the eleventh century; and Rosemary Cramp argues in several places that sculpture at Durham and related sites may owe its conservatism to Æthelwald's cross having been a revered model, 'a pattern book in itself'.[12] Other scholars repeat Symeon's claim that it was taken from Lindisfarne after pagan attacks and accompanied the body of St Cuthbert.[13] But what do we know really know about this haunting object?

Anglo-Saxon Sculpture (Dublin, 2002); Karkov and Orton, *Theorizing Anglo-Saxon Stone Sculpture*, in which five of the six contributions focus mainly or wholly on the Ruthwell and Bewcastle crosses.

12 C. Stancliffe, 'The Riddle of the Ruthwell Cross: Audience, Intention and Originator Reconsidered', in E. Cambridge and J. Hawkes (eds), *Crossing Boundaries: Interdisciplinary Approaches to the Art, Material Culture, Language and Literature of the Early Medieval World* (Oxford and Philadelphia, 2017), 3–14, at 11; E. Cambridge, 'Why did the Community of St Cuthbert Settle at Chester-le-Street?', in G. Bonner, C. Stancliffe and D. Rollason (eds), *St Cuthbert, His Cult and His Community to AD 1200* (Woodbridge, 1989), 367–86, at 378, n. 43; R. Cramp, 'The Pre-Conquest Sculptural Tradition in Durham', in N. Coldstream and P. Draper (eds). *Medieval Art and Architecture at Durham Cathedral* (Leeds, 1980), 1–10; R. Cramp, 'The Artistic Influence of Lindisfarne within Northumbria', in Bonner, Stancliffe and Rollason (eds), *St Cuthbert, His Cult and Community*, 213–28, at 224, 227–8; Cramp, Durham 1 in *County Durham and Northumberland*, 32 and 66–7.

13 D. Petts, '"A Place More Venerable Than All in Britain": The Archaeology of Anglo-Saxon Lindisfarne', in R. Gameson (ed.), *The Lindisfarne Gospels: New Perspectives* (Leiden, 2017), 1–18, at 7; M. P. Brown, '"A Good Woman's Son": Aspects of Aldred's Agenda in Glossing the Lindisfarne Gospels', in J. Fernández Cuesta and S. M. Pons-Sanz, *The Old English Gloss to the Lindisfarne Gospels: Language, Author and Context* (Berlin, 2016), 13–36, at 20–1.

From the opening paragraph of his *Libellus*, Symeon stresses the links between his home, the newly-rebuilt Durham cathedral, and its deep past, going back to the community's seventh-century origins. As Petts notes, Æthelwald's cross embodies the abstract concept of continuity.[14] This account is one of the first pieces of information for which Symeon does not rely on Bede, and we may wonder what his sources were for his exciting story. He tells us that the stone cross was first raised on Lindisfarne in honour of St Cuthbert and inscribed with the saint's name (*Fecerat iste de lapide crucem artifice opera expoliri, et in sui memoriam suum in eo nomen exarari*). Later, its top was broken (*summitatem . . . fregerunt*) by pagans when Lindisfarne was attacked, but repaired with lead; it was carried in company with the body of St Cuthbert, and venerated as a relic associated with both Cuthbert and Æthelwald; and it was standing tall in the Durham cemetery at the time of writing (*usque hodie . . . stans sullimis*).[15] In the light of McGuigan's demonstration of the myth-making capacities of Symeon's master-narrative, it is also appropriate to call into question the smaller stories of which it is composed, and ask if this anecdote can be taken at face value.

A close analysis of this brief but rich text shows us how Symeon constructed a cross's biography and used it to create meaning. His narrative starts with the intimate relationship between the living Æthelwald and his dead predecessor Cuthbert, and Æthelwald's commissioning of the cross as a materialisation of the spiritual connection between the two men. Æthelwald summons the cross into being but he does not make it: that is the job of the skilled craftsmen, the *artifices*, who smooth or decorate it (*expoliri*) it. The late-tenth-century colophon to the Lindisfarne Gospels, a text which Symeon seems to have known as he quotes it or something very similar, also depicts Æthelwald in connection with the arts. In the colophon Aldred, a priest of the St Cuthbert community, writes that Æthelwald, bishop of Lindisfarne, 'bound and covered [the book] on the outside, as he well knew how', whereas Symeon's rendition has Æthelwald commissioning a treasure binding (*auro gemmisque perornari iusserat*).[16] Symeon's successive references to Æthelwald as patron

---

14 Petts, 'A Place More Venerable Than All in Britain', 7.
15 *LDE*, i.12, 60–1.
16 *LDE*, i.12, 120–1. Aldred's colophon is a much-debated text, and need not be taken at face value, although the gospel of St John found in St Cuthbert's coffin attests to the existence of at least one beautifully-bound book whose covers employ a range of motifs

prompt us to visualise the bishop both composing the inscription on his cross and designing any decorative programme, even if the work of quarrying and carving was delegated.

Symeon has nothing to say about where the cross stood when first erected on Lindisfarne, or at the interim locations his narrative implies; but at Durham he describes it in the open air, among the graves of the monastic community. The dimensions of the cross are indicated by the reference to it 'standing sublime', *sullimis*, an adjective which is used consistently in the Vulgate to describe great height (e.g. the heights of heaven, tall trees, mountain tops, fortifications). In Symeon's day the cross thus probably stood at least high enough that a person of average stature had to look up to view the cross-head. The size of the cross, as well as its fragility, adds to the wonder of the account of it being customarily carried around (*crux ipsa circumferri solebat*).

In its circumambulations, the body of St Cuthbert is always (*semper*) accompanied by the cross, a visual metaphor both for the body of Christ and that of St Æthelwald, reminding the faithful to venerate both bishops together (*utrorumque pontificum ... monumentum*). There is no narrative of Æthelwald's own death and burial in the *Libellus*, although much later in his account, when describing Bishop Eardwulf's decision to leave Lindisfarne in 875, Symeon depicts the community amassing their relics and placing Æthelwald's bones in Cuthbert's coffin.[17] The cross bears Cuthbert's name but not, it seems, Æthelwald's own: it is therefore presented as embodying both written and oral tradition, the name of its original commissioner being passed down through the community over the 350 years between Æthelwald's day and Symeon's.

Æthelwald, Cuthbert and the cross are the main characters in this narrative, but there are a host of others. The wealth and skill of the

---

with analogies in sculpture. K. Jolly, *The Community of St Cuthbert in the Late Tenth Century* (Columbus, 2012), 53; F. L. Newton, F. L. Newton, Jr and C. R. J. Scheirer, 'Domiciling the Evangelists in Anglo-Saxon England: A Fresh Reading of Aldred's Colophon in the "Lindisfarne Gospels"', *ASE* 41 (2012), 101–44; J. Roberts, 'Aldred: Glossator and Book Historian', in J. Fernández Cuesta and S. M. Pons-Sanz (eds), *The Old English Gloss to the Lindisfarne Gospels: Language, Author and Context* (Berlin, 2016), 37–60; J. Roberts, 'Aldred Signs off from Glossing the Lindisfarne Gospels', in A. Rumble (ed.), *Writing and Texts in Anglo-Saxon England* (Woodbridge, 2006), 28–43; L. Webster, 'The Decoration of the Binding', in C. Breay and B. Meehan (eds), *The St Cuthbert Gospel: Studies on the Insular Manuscript of the Gospel of St John* (London, 2015), 65–82.

17 *LDE*, ii.6, 100–3.

community are implied by the two references to talented craftsmen, makers and menders. The community remain present implicitly, as readers of the cross, as victims of the pagans, as resilient survivors, as devoted and hard-working curators of their saints, come at last to haven in Durham. The violence and ignorance of the pagans is encapsulated by the vignette of the smashing of the cross. Finally, we meet the whole *populus Northanhymbrorum* who venerated the cross when it was being ferried about, and their successors, the *intuentes* (by inference the male monastic community) contemplating it in Symeon's present, in their cemetery at Durham. The cross has meaning because it is embedded in a nexus of human activity, emotion and understanding: it has become a member of the Cuthbert community, and an exemplary one.

Symeon's dream of Æthelwald's stone rood, with its complex materiality and object biography, embodies the continuity and rootedness of the St Cuthbert community, despite a fractured and mobile history. Its stone emerges from the very landscape of Lindisfarne to take on form and voice, its cross-shape brackets Christian history, referring back to the historical moment of the Crucifixion and ahead to 'the sign of the Son of Man in heaven' as a herald of the Last Judgement (Matthew 24: 30). It testifies in its brokenness to the resilience of the community; and it stands tall, in Symeon's now, uniting the living and the dead, heaven and earth, past, present and future. Symeon's brief account helps us to see the pieces of stone that survive from Carham and other nearby sites, including Norham, as more than mere shattered and unhappy fragments. It is a tribute to Symeon's story-telling power that scholars have read this account as literal truth.

Nonetheless, we should be wary of taking his tale at face value. There is no reason to doubt that there was a venerable cross in the monastic cemetery at Durham in the early twelfth century, plausibly inscribed and repaired, which may well have had legends attached to it. The cross from St Oswald's (Durham 1) indicates that by Symeon's time there were old monuments on the Durham peninsula.[18] If, however, the cross he describes had been imported from elsewhere, by Symeon's own

---

18 Cramp argues that this 'one of the most difficult chronological problems of all the Durham pieces' is late tenth–early eleventh century, and conservative in style, perhaps inspired by 'Aethelwold's cross, which surely when it was set up as the first monument in the churchyard on the peninsula, must have been very influential': Cramp, *County Durham and Northumberland*, 32 and 66–7, ills 37–8.

testimony this must have been generations before he himself came to Durham, and well before the 1083 displacing of the old community by the new monastic one to which he belonged.[19] For the cross to embody the community's fractured history, he needs it to have travelled; but he never saw it move. Symeon avoids mentioning the cross when he is detailing the vicissitudes and wanderings of the St Cuthbert community in the late ninth century; nor does he list any of the interim destinations of the community in his tale of the cross: it is likely that he was aware of the implausibility (even the unintended comedy) of the image of a small, harried group of men toting a large and fragile stone object around with them (it is not easy to establish the weight of early medieval crosses, but the granite Downpatrick town cross weighs over a thousand kilograms).[20] He seems to have had no anecdotal information about Æthelwald other than that provided by the Lindisfarne Gospels colophon. Faced with a name in a list, a cross in a churchyard, and an allusion to artistic patronage, it seems likely that he combined them into an inspired micro-narrative, twining the tale of the cross into his over-arching story, possibly prompted by in-house legend.[21] This reading exorcises the ghost of Æthelwald's cross as a genuine eighth-century artefact, the goal towards which study of Cuthbertine sculpture strives; it allows us instead to use Symeon's story as a myth that enriches our understanding of the *numen* the extant crosses embodied as late as the eleventh and twelfth centuries.

Lindisfarne, Norham and Jedburgh

Lindisfarne
'Demolishing' Æthelwald's cross goes some way to solving one of the problems presented by the Lindisfarne sculptural assemblage: that there is no convincing evidence for interest in monumental sculpture on the

---

[19] W. M. Aird, *St Cuthbert and the Normans, 1071–1153* (Woodbridge, 1998), 138–9.
[20] *LDE*, i.12, 60–1 *contra* 101–5 and 111–21. Thanks to Mike King of the Down County Museum for the information about the Downpatrick cross, which was weighed recently when moved into the museum.
[21] Symeon claims elsewhere to have had local informants, e.g. for the miracle story in *LDE*, iii.3, which he heard from 'certain devout and entirely trustworthy priests who saw it and who are now advanced in age'. See *LDE*, iii.3, 150–1.

island before the late eighth century at the very earliest, and even the ninth century evidence is minimal. Putting Norham back at the heart of the St Cuthbert community's activities also helps to reframe Lindisfarne, only thirty kilometres distant. Can we see the two sites as complementary in some way, each the focus of investment at different periods by an interlinked, multi-focal community?

Certainly, Lindisfarne has a very different monumental environment from Norham's ninth-century extravaganza (discussed below): busy in the later period but very sparse before *c.* 900. Might early large-scale sculpture still be awaiting discovery? Various campaigns of excavation at Lindisfarne have turned up over forty pieces of sculpture (more than twice as many as at virtually unexcavated Norham), so the difference is likely to be real.[22] For two centuries Lindisfarne was the seat of the bishop, the home of a great cult, a supremely wealthy house, capable of producing the Lindisfarne Gospels; but one would guess little of this from the seventh-to-ninth-century sculpture.[23] Petts comments that 'as much sculpture appears to post-date the departure of the community for Norham as precedes it' but (once Æthelwald's cross is removed from the equation) the bulk of the 'preceding' material is composed of the only stones from the island with text, the simple and diminutive name-stones, which may have been designed to go into, rather than over, a burial.[24]

The name-stones indicate that, well before 800, Lindisfarne's culture embraced masons who could identify high-quality stone, competent carvers, literacy in two alphabets, and a commemorative or funerary environment that admitted women as well as men, but apparently very little interest in free-standing crosses.[25] Where more prominent monuments are concerned, one lost fragment with incised interlace may have come from a late eighth-century cross (Lindisfarne 10). A new interest in monumentality is evinced by a finely-carved cross (1 and possibly

---

22 Petts, 'A Place More Venerable Than All in Britain', 2, 7.
23 Lindisfarne 1 is the only cross which looks as though it has anything in common with Insular manuscript art. Cramp, *County Durham and Northumberland*, 194.
24 Petts, 'A Place More Venerable', 16. The Lindisfarne name-stones were found *ex situ* but the evidence from Hartlepool suggests they may have been grave-goods: C. Maddern, *Raising the Dead: Early Medieval Name Stones in Northumbria* (Turnhout, 2013), 2–11.
25 Lindisfarne 24, which is exceptionally high quality, has the female name Osgyth.

fragment 18) from the late eighth to mid ninth century.[26] However, the majority of the better-preserved material – at least ten crosses and two grave markers (2, 3, 4, 5, 6, 7, 8, 9, 11, 14, 37, 38) – sits most happily in the later period; and the same ratio holds when fragments and the lost and poorly-recorded stones are factored in.[27] This later material emerges from the same contexts as the early, a powerful indicator of continuity of use.[28] Although Lindisfarne is largely absent from the written sources after the late ninth century, other than its sack by Olaf Guthfrithson in 940, the sculpture from the island together with a closely-related cross from Alnmouth suggests at least one major campaign of investment. A tenth-century revival of sculptural activity on Lindisfarne would align it with other sites to which it had historic connections, such as Iona and Whithorn.[29] Furthermore, two of these late crosses, Lindisfarne 3 and 8, indicate an ambitious, well-furnished and well-connected environment.

Lindisfarne 3

One broad face of the cross-shaft Lindisfarne 3 has an oblong panel divided into quarters, with a central roundel; the other surviving carving consists of interlace interspersed with plain panels.[30] The roundel contains a haloed front-facing figure whom Cramp interpreted as 'squatting' but it is in fact shown foreshortened and seated, with a semi-circular

26 Cramp ascribes the three cross-bases to this period (Lindisfarne 19, 775×850, Lindisfarne 20 and 21, 775×900) but, as she readily admits, the evidence for any precise date is extremely weak. Cramp, *County Durham and Northumberland*, 201–2.

27 In her overview of material Cramp ascribes Lindisfarne 2, 3, 4, 6, and Alnmouth to the 'early ninth century', but in the catalogue proper they are given the dates of 'ninth century', 'last quarter of ninth to end of tenth century', 'ninth century', 'last quarter of ninth to first half of tenth century', and 'late ninth to early tenth century' respectively. 'Early ninth' seems significantly too early for this material; they have a lot of features in common and are surely broadly contemporary; and here the catalogue dates will be followed. Okasha calls the Alnmouth inscription 'probably tenth century'. Cramp, *County Durham and Northumberland*, 27, *contra* 162, 195–7.

28 Petts, 'A Place More Venerable Than All in Britain', 17.

29 Iona, pers. comm. K. Forsyth and A. Maldonado; I. Fisher, *Early Medieval Sculpture in the West Highlands and Islands* (Edinburgh, 2001), 126–35; Whithorn: P. Hill, *Whithorn and St Ninian: The Excavations of a Monastic Town, 1984–9* (Stroud, 1997), 52–4.

30 The division of the scene on Lindisfarne 3 is identical to that on an eleventh-century ivory plaque from southern Italy, in which the central roundel contains the Agnus Dei and the four quarters the evangelist symbols. Metropolitan Museum of Art, New York, Accession no. 17.190.38.

feature below its feet.³¹ Each of the four quarters contains a figure shown in three-quarter view, facing inwards. The upper two are dressed in short tunics, standing and proffering books, with what appear to be trumpets coming from their mouths. The lower pair sit on chairs; they have no apparent clothing, and they hold scrolls.³² The figure in the roundel is surely Christ. The seated figure of Christ, combined with the layout, and the likelihood that the four men with books or scrolls are the evangelists, suggests that a *Majestas Domini* scene is intended. Christ enthroned is a common theme in Anglo-Saxon art, but no close parallel for Lindisfarne 3 suggests itself. This is not the same layout as is found on the lid of St Cuthbert's coffin, where the standing Christ is surrounded by evangelist symbols; and it bears only a little more resemblance to the *Majestas* in the Codex Amiatinus, where the seated Christ has his feet on a footstool which represents the earth (e.g. Matthew 5: 35: *terram, quia scabellum est pedum eius*), is flanked by angels and enclosed in a circular mandorla, with the standing human evangelists and their symbols in the corners of the frame (f.796v). The very existence of these two scenes suggests that a range of models was available from an early date in northern Northumbria, and the evangelists and their symbols in the Lindisfarne Gospels suggest even more complexity: Matthew's book-holding, trumpet-blowing angel on f.25v has some similarities with the two standing figures on Lindisfarne 3. Mark's lion in the Lindisfarne Gospels also has a trumpet or perhaps a speech-scroll; a mould from Hartlepool (a site associated with Lindisfarne) shows Luke's calf with a trumpet or scroll. (The very familiarity of the Lindisfarne Gospels images may hinder us from seeing how unusual these trumpets are: other than the examples listed here the only parallel is in the Luke and Matthew portraits in the much later Copenhagen Gospels, which appear to depend directly on Lindisfarne as a model.)³³

The overall composition of the seated Christ with a long torso and small, fore-shortened legs, elbows bent and hands placed in front of his torso, is closely paralleled on the eighth-century altar from Cividale, and

---

31 Unweathered, it may have looked more like Billingham 12: Billingham was another holding of Lindisfarne. Rollason, *Northumbria*, 245.
32 The evangelists in the Lindisfarne Gospels hold a mixture of books (John and Luke) and scrolls (Matthew and Mark).
33 C. Farr, 'Style in Late Anglo-Saxon England: Questions of Learning and Intention', in C. Karkov and G. Hardin Brown (eds), *Anglo-Saxon Styles* (Albany, 2003), 115–30, at 117–20; M. Brown, *The Lindisfarne Gospels: Society, Spirituality and the Scribe* (Toronto, 2003), 354–5.

in the Godescalc Evangelistary (f.3r).³⁴ The curving suppedaneum at Christ's feet on Lindisfarne 3 is an allusion to the globe as footstool, as in the Weingarten Gospels (f.1v) or sits, as in the Vivian Bible/First Bible of Charles the Bald (f.329v). On Lindisfarne 3 the lower, seated, figures are on carefully depicted chairs, which have parallels in numerous images of the evangelists, such as those on Ottonian *Majestas Domini* ivory plaques, and such a plaque is a feasible model.³⁵ A rectangle divided into four quadrants is a common lay-out for depicting the evangelist symbols in various media, though much less so for their human forms.³⁶ Lindisfarne 3 has a close parallel in concept if not in layout with the Boulogne Gospels (f.7r) where Christ is seated on a cloud-swathed rainbow, flanked by standing, symbol-free evangelists, the inner pair of whom carry scrolls, the outer, books, in an image which both emphasises the gospels' harmonious witness to Christ's life and the heavenly inspiration of their testimony.³⁷

A major objection to this reading is that the four smaller figures on Lindisfarne 3 are, apparently, in contemporary lay male dress, inappropriate for evangelists.³⁸ However, Cramp sees this movement from 'sub-classical [dress] to what seems to be contemporary native' as a trend in Northumbrian sculpture from the ninth century onwards.³⁹ The angel in the cross-head Durham 5 (which may be the symbol of

---

34 L. Chinellato, *Arte longobarda in Friuli: l'Ara di Ratchis a Cividale. La ricerca e la riscoperta delle policromie* (Udine, 2016), 102ff.

35 There are two *Majestas* ivories in the Bode Museum in Berlin which clearly derive from a model such as the Vivian Bible, in one Christ is framed in a quatrefoil mandorla, in the other in a lenticular mandorla which overlaps the circular globe: either could easily be interpreted as depicting a semi-circular footstool below Christ. Bode Museum, Berlin, accession nos DSC03616 and DSC03627.

36 See for example the Book of Durrow, the Trier Gospels and the MacDurnan Gospels: J. J. G. Alexander, *Insular Manuscripts 6th to 9th century* (London, 1978), cat. 6, pl. 13; cat. 26, pl. 114; cat. 70, pl. 325.

37 Boulogne BM MS 11, f.7r: T. H. Ohlgren, *Anglo-Saxon Textual Illustration* (Kalamazoo, 1992), 313, fig. 5.11; R. Gameson, *The Role of Art in the Late Anglo-Saxon Church* (Oxford, 1995), 133. Compare the symbol-free evangelists in two gospel manuscripts from Canterbury associated with the scribe-artist Eadwig Basan: T. A. Heslop, 'Art and the Man: Archbishop Wulfstan and the York Gospelbook', in M. Townend (ed.), *Wulfstan, Archbishop of York* (Turnhout, 2004), 278–308, at 298 ff.; C. Karkov, 'Writing and Having Written: Word and Image in the Eadwig Gospels', in A. Rumble, *Writing and Texts in Anglo-Saxon England* (Woodbridge, 2006), 44–61.

38 N. Netzer, *Cultural Interplay in the Eighth Century: The Trier Gospels and the Making of a Scriptorium at Echternach* (Cambridge, 1994), c.8 generally.

39 Cramp, 'Anglian Tradition', 10.

St Matthew) is similarly dressed in a short, flared tunic; and very few of the holy figures on the Durham cross-heads have haloes.[40] On the contemporary cross-shaft from Alnmouth, the figures of Stephaton and Longinus, the Roman soldiers present at Calvary who are shown flanking the crucified Christ, are in dress identical to that of the upper pair of postulated evangelists on Lindisfarne 3, and overall the figural carving is handled in a very similar way on both monuments: chunky bodies and legs, stiff beards and tunics, shown in three-quarter view with a degree of depth of field and muscular tension. These carvings on Alnmouth and Lindisfarne 3 are by far the most dynamic depictions of the human form to be found at this period between the Tyne and the Forth.[41]

Alnmouth, also known as the 'Myredah' cross, has other features in common with Lindisfarne 2, 3 and 4.[42] All four carvings are distinguished by solid, competent interlace in small panels; in an unusual detail Alnmouth and Lindisfarne 3 have plain panels interspersed with the decorated ones. Alnmouth gets its name from the inscription, *myredah meh wor[hte]* (Myredah made me) on Face C, thus transforming it into a 'speaking object'.[43] Could the blank panels have had further, painted, inscriptions? Stephaton and Longinus on Alnmouth are so like the upper figures on Lindisfarne 3 that it is tempting to think Myredah was at work on both.[44] Alnmouth is also striking because the shaft of the cross on which Christ is shown crucified is carved with two tiny panels of finely-rendered interlace, thus assimilating the True Cross of

---

[40] Durham 5-7: Cramp, 'Pre-Conquest Sculptural Tradition', in Coldstream and Draper, 8; *County Durham and Northumberland*, 68-71. Other evidence for holy figures wearing short tunics is suggestive, though slight. The Tidfirth stone (Monkwearmouth 3) shows two figures flanking a cross and a rectangle, on which latter they rest their hands. It is plausibly an altar, and the men priests, but they are in short tunics. Additionally, the central standing figure on Barwick-in-Elmet 1 (W. Yorks) is almost certainly Christ, but shown in a short tunic. The broken figure of Christ on the cross from Monifieth (Angus) wears a flared skirt but this may be a loincloth.

[41] Compare figural sculpture from *c*. 850×*c*. 1050 at Bedlington, Bothal, Jedburgh, Ovingham, Tynemouth and Warkworth.

[42] Cramp, *County Durham and Northumberland*, 27.

[43] C. Karkov, *The Art of Anglo-Saxon England* (Woodbridge, 2011), 134ff..

[44] Cramp dates Alnmouth to late ninth century/early tenth century, and Lindisfarne 3 to late ninth century to *c*. 1000, but the basis for dating both is subjective and highly inferential. On both Lindisfarne 3 and Alnmouth Christ is assertively haloed while the attendant figures lack haloes and are in contemporary lay dress.

Calvary directly to its many Northumbrian instantiations.[45] The suggestion that Alnmouth and Lindisfarne 3 can both be ascribed to Myredah cannot be proven, but his Irish or Scottish Gaelic name (Muiredach) is especially intriguing considering the first reading of Lindisfarne 8 proposed below.[46]

Lindisfarne 8
Lindisfarne 8 is the lowest part of a large, damaged and weathered cross-shaft. Faces C and D have fragments of interlace, while A depicts two profile male figures, unhaloed and in contemporary dress, facing each other with a long thin vertical element dividing them: Cramp sees this as a pillar, placing the two figures under separate arches. However, the top of the stone is damaged, making this reading speculative; and the central vertical object appears to be shorter than the men. Moreover, the men are grasping the central element with both their hands, interacting with it and each other in a way that would be very odd for an architectural frame. It is more likely that they inhabit the same space and the vertical element is a significant object: if so, they are a very close match for the scene on the identical location on the Cross of the Scriptures at Clonmacnoise.[47] This image, showing a warrior and a cleric facing each other and grasping a carved pole with both hands, is usually seen as a reference to the monastery's foundation legend in the vernacular *Life of St Ciarán*, in which St Ciarán and King Diarmait jointly plant the first post of the building.[48] The Cross of the Scriptures is

---

45   There are two smaller figures flanking this cross, above Stephaton and Longinus, very damaged but also both in contemporary male dress. Their identity is a mystery: they do not appear to be the thieves crucified with Christ, as no crosses are evident. Their short tunics preclude them being the Virgin and St John, who appear above and behind Stephaton and Longinus on the Romsey Abbey rood, and on a ninth-century ivory crucifixion from Reims (Victoria & Albert Museum, accession no. 303–1867); or abstract personifications such as Ecclesia and Synagogue, who appear on another from Metz (Victoria & Albert Museum, accession no. 250–1867); and they do not look like angels.

46   K. Hughes, 'Evidence for Contacts between the Churches of the Irish and the English from the Synod of Whitby to the Viking Age', in P. Clemoes and K. Hughes (eds), *England before the Conquest: Studies in Primary Sources Presented to Dorothy Whitelock* (Cambridge, 1971), 49–68, 66.

47   P. Harbison, *The High Crosses of Ireland*, i, 49, 202–3; A. Kehnel, *Clonmacnois – the Church and Lands of St Ciar'an: Change and Continuity in an Irish Monastic Foundation (6th to 16th Century)* (Munster, 1997), 106–7.

48   The Irish and Latin *Lives* of St Ciarán only survive in high-to-late medieval redactions,

broadly contemporary with Lindisfarne 8, and has often been associated with Abbot Colmán and King Flann Sinna on the grounds of a debatable inscription, although recent re-evaluation suggests that the crosses of this group may be mid-ninth century not c. 900.[49] The Clonmacnoise image may therefore either represent the founding of the monastery, or the refounding, or conceivably both. Where the Cuthbert community is concerned, Symeon's description of Earl Uhtred and Bishop Ealdhun supervising the clearing of the site at Durham suggests that analogous narratives of Church and State cooperating to found or refound churches were also in circulation in Northumbria.[50] A reading of Lindisfarne 8 as an image of an event in the community's deep past is also possible, and here the obvious candidates would be King Oswald and St Aidan. Oswald's raising of the wooden cross at Heavenfield might underlie such an image; it might also conceivably allude to the miraculous fire-proof buttress against which Aidan was leaning when he died, which by the early eighth century had itself become a source of healing.[51]

Since the object between the two men on Lindisfarne 8 could be a cross, the image also has points in common with images of donation in a variety of media.[52] Parallels in Northumbrian stone sculpture include the unhaloed men flanking but not holding a cross at Great Urswick (Cumbria), which commemorates a named individual, and the man and woman in contemporary dress and holding a cross at Kirkby Wharfe (W. Yorks), which is probably a donor image.[53] The Clonmacnoise

---

but may contain significantly earlier material. Kehnel suggests a ninth–eleventh-century context for the Irish *Life*: Kehnel, *Clonmacnois*, 18.

49 P. Harbison, *High Crosses of Ireland*, i, 49; R. Stalley, 'Artistic Identity and the Irish Scripture Crosses', in R. Moss (ed.), *Making and Meaning in Insular Art* (Dublin, 2007), 153–66.

50 *LDE*, iii.2, 148–9.

51 Bede, *Historia Ecclesiastica Gentis Anglorum*, ed. Colgrave and Mynors, 218–19 and 264–5.

52 Manuscript: the New Minster Liber Vitae drawing of Cnut and Emma offering a cross to the altar (where however only Cnut touches the cross) BL Stowe MS 944; metalwork: Abbess Matilda and Otto of Swabia both grasping and flanking a cross, shown on an enamel plaque below the feet of Christ on a late tenth-century gold processional crucifix from Essen. K. G. Beuckers, 'Das Otto-Mathilden-Kreuz im Essener Münsterschatz. Überlegungen zu Charakter und Funktion des Stifterbildes', in K. Bodarwé and T. Schilp (eds), *Herrschaft, Liturgie und Raum. Studien zur mittelalterlichen Geschichte des Frauenstifts Essen* (Essen, 2002), 51–80.

53 R. Bailey and R. Cramp, *Corpus of Anglo-Saxon Stone Sculpture, Volume 2: Cumberland, Westmorland and Lancashire North-of-the-Sands* (London, 1988),

parallels are strongest, however, with both male figures facing towards the centre and grasping the post or cross with both hands, and the scene located at the base of the cross-shaft; but in the absence of any other evidence we cannot know whether Lindisfarne 8 illustrates refoundation, commemoration or donation. The height of these two crosses is unknown but they are large pieces of stone: Lindisfarne 3 is 35 centimetres wide, the same as the early ninth-century Rothbury cross; Lindisfarne 8 is 41 centimetres wide, and they represent serious and confident investment. A continuing link with Irish churches later than the late ninth century is an interesting possibility.[54]

It is not enough simply to spot visual parallels: we also need to think of the role these crosses may have played in the life of the community. Lindisfarne 3 provides a devotional focus: the Christ in Majesty was probably at around eye-level, governing the way that viewers of the cross would have physically interacted with the image. The back of the cross is lost: it may have been decorated with panels of interlace; it could have been inscribed or have had more figural imagery, such as a Crucifixion (all are found at Alnmouth). The cumulative testimony of all these Lindisfarne crosses, those with surviving figural imagery and those without, is that there was a great deal going on, on the island, of which we know nothing. Lindisfarne 3 could well be inspired by an ivory *Majestas*, perhaps incorporated into a treasure binding. Whatever ceremony is commemorated by Lindisfarne 8, it demonstrates both ritual and investment. We do not know how and when these crosses were destroyed but the majority have been found in excavation, unstratified. From around 900 the church community at Lindisfarne evidently felt a powerful need for large stone crosses, an urge which had only sporadically been experienced in the past. It is likely that these crosses divided areas within the monastery, suggesting a new or revitalised interest in the articulation of sacred space. Myredah's cross at Alnmouth includes a damaged inscription which may refer to the 'soul of Eadwulf', suggesting a

---

148–50 and ills 564–6, 568–9; E. Coatsworth, *Corpus of Anglo-Saxon Stone Sculpture, Volume 8: Western Yorkshire* (London, 2008), 185–7 and ills 440–3 where, however, the image is interpreted as Ss Mary and John flanking an empty cross. For the donation argument see V. Thompson in prep.

54 F. Edmonds, 'St Cuthbert, St Columba and Ireland: Movements of Relics in the 870s', in N. R. McGuire and C. Ó Baoill (eds), *Rannsachadh na Gàidhlig 6* (Aberdeen, 2013), 1–29.

commemorative or funerary function (like the lost *pro anima* inscription on Norham 9b, discussed below).[55] In terms of the number of monuments, their size and their sophistication of design and reference, late Anglo-Saxon Lindisfarne looks like a confident and assertive church.

Norham

Norham has long been understood as a significant place in the story the St Cuthbert community told itself: one of the resting places of St Cuthbert, as well as St Ceolwulf, the former king (and Bede's patron) who had retired to become a monk of Lindisfarne; the site where St Aidan's wooden church was rebuilt when the focus of the community first shifted from Lindisfarne.[56] However, previous discussion of Norham's sculpture has been predicated on the idea that the church was only briefly important, in the earlier ninth century; what might it look like if we accept for the sake of argument that Norham was the seat of the bishop and the home of the cult for the best part of two centuries, playing Kells or Dunkeld to Lindisfarne's Iona?[57]

All but one of the Norham fragments were found in 1833, in the churchyard, immediately to the east of the present mid-twelfth-century church in association with an undated but probably earlier building.[58] Unfortunately, Canon Gilly, writing thirteen years later, does not clarify whether they were reused in the walls or found loose in the soil, although Ryder argues that they were reused in later fabric.[59] Norham is surely a

---

55   E. Okasha, *Hand-List of Anglo-Saxon Non-Runic Inscriptions* (Cambridge, 1971), 47–8, plates 2a–c.

56   The dating of the earliest Cuthbertine activity at Norham relies on the dates of 830–45 for the bishopric of Ecgred in the *Historia Regum* cross-referred with the *HSC*, c.9. J. Hodgson-Hinde (ed.), *Symeonis Dunelmensis Opera et collectanea, Volume 1* (Durham, 1868), 42 and see n. 81 below.

57   Cramp, 'The Anglian Tradition', in Lang (1978), 11–13; *County Durham and Northumberland*, 208–14.

58   Eighteen of these, including the lost fragments, are illustrated in Cramp, *County Durham and Northumberland*, as above; the nineteenth was found in 1983 in a garden approx. 200 metres south of Norham church. R. Bailey and R. Cramp, *Corpus of Anglo-Saxon Stone Sculpture, Volume 2: Cumberland, Westmorland and Lancashire North-of-the-Sands* (London, 1988), 85–6 and ill. 675, stressing parallels to Carlisle 2; R. Cramp, 'Heads You Lose', in E. Cambridge and J. Hawkes (eds), *Crossing Boundaries: Interdisciplinary Approaches to the Art, Material Culture, Language and Literature of the Early Medieval World* (Oxford and Philadelphia, 2017), 15–22, 16 and fig. 2.2a–c.

59   W. S. Gilly, 'Our Churches and Churchyards: 1. Norham', *History of the Berwickshire Naturalists' Club 1842–1849* (1846), 177–90; P. Ryder, 'The Parish Church of St

prime candidate for a campaign of research-oriented archaeological investigation.[60] These fragments were subsequently cemented together to make a pillar (now in the north nave aisle of the church), in what Gilly describes as a conscious evocation of the Bewcastle cross.[61] It is possible that carved faces are concealed, and impossible to be sure whether any of the fragments come from the same original monument. The extant shafts certainly all come from different crosses, as they are not only very various in style and motif, but the carving techniques and border mouldings are also distinct, suggesting a range of craftsmen and models. In a couple of cases, similarity of style renders it possible that a fragment of shaft and one of cross-head or -arm belong together, although they are in slightly different types of local stone. If the crosses were plastered and painted, however, the natural colour of the stone would be immaterial.[62]

We thus have at least eight crosses and probably more, some of which (e.g. Norham 1) were on an impressive scale. The fragments date from the early ninth to the late eleventh century, but the period of great investment is the ninth century. Norham's sculpture is an anthology of

---

    Cuthbert, Norham: Analysis of the Fabric and Archaeological Assessment' carried out for the Diocese of Newcastle March 2005, <http://www.newcastle.anglican.org/userfiles/file/Newcastle%20Website/Diocesan%20Office/Diocesan%20Advisory%20Committee/Norham%2C%20St%20Cuthbert%20-%20March%202005.pdf>. Accessed 18 January 2018.

60 R. Finlayson *et al.*, *Norham: Northumberland Extensive Urban Survey* (Morpeth, 1995–7, revd 2009), 8–9.

61 Gilly, 'Our Churches and Churchyards: 1. Norham', 181.

62 Norham is on carboniferous red sandstone, which outcrops locally by the castle site, just to the east of the village. In 1978 Cramp suggested that the shaft Norham 2 and the arm Norham 14 may form part of one monument, as they share a similar plant-scroll motif, but she has since retreated from this hypothesis as the two fragments are of different types of sandstone. However, given that the upper and lower sections of the Ruthwell cross, in Dumfries and Galloway, are also of different stone types; and that the yellow sandstone of Norham 2 and red sandstone of Norham 14 are both available locally, Cramp's original argument carries considerable force. Norham 4 (shaft) and 10 (head) also share very similar plant scroll, though again the sandstone of the two fragments is different in colour. T. Pearson, *Norham Castle, Northumberland* (English Heritage Survey Report, 2002), 3; R. Cramp, 'The Anglian Tradition in the Ninth Century', in J. T. Lang (ed.), *Anglo-Saxon and Viking Age Sculpture and its Context* ([British Archaeological Reports] BAR BS XLIX, 1978), 1–32, 12; Cramp, *Northumberland and County Durham*, 209; F. Orton and I. Wood with C. Lees, *Fragments of History: Rethinking the Ruthwell and Bewcastle Monuments* (Manchester, 2007), 43; Cramp, *County Durham and Northumberland*, 212–13.

contemporary ornament, covering almost the full range of interlace, fret pattern, inhabited and uninhabited plant scroll, as well as human figures and inscription – everything but spiral scroll patterns (which are vanishingly rare in Anglo-Saxon stone sculpture). The ninth-century Norham crosses are also consistent in their technical excellence, and regular, confident designs: Cramp remarks of Norham 5 that its fret patterns 'make everything at Lindisfarne look so tentative that the Lindisfarne crosses may well be copies'.[63] Norham's aesthetic is also profoundly embedded in that of Northumbria as a whole.[64]

Sadly, four of the fragments are now lost and only recorded in eighteenth- or nineteenth-century illustrations. Two of the lost pieces (9a and 9b) bore inscriptions: the one on 9b was an intercessory prayer in Latin, beginning *pro anima*, while 9a's was badly damaged, but apparently incorporated the christogram IHS and *Nazaraios*, the Greek form of Nazarene and therefore a title of Christ, hinting at a degree of literacy in Greek (if the reading *Nazaraios* is correct) as well as Latin.[65] One of the extant figural fragments has an angel, plausibly from an Annunciation; another has a haloed saint. The crosses from which they came bear comparison with Rothbury and the crosses of the Yorkshire Dales at sites like Masham, Easby and Dewsbury. This is an impressive campaign of investment at a major church.

In the tenth century, however, this interest in sculpture at Norham appears, for whatever reason, to dwindle.[66] In the early tenth century

---

63 R. Cramp, 'The Artistic Influence of Lindisfarne within Northumbria', in Bonner, Stancliffe and Rollason, *St Cuthbert, His Cult, and His Community to AD 1200*, 213–28, at 227.

64 Cramp, 'The Anglian Tradition', in Lang (1978), 12–13.

65 Okasha, *Hand-List of Anglo-Saxon Non-Runic Inscriptions*, 103–4, plates 95 and 96. If this is an accurate transcription, the cross may have had the Greek form of the inscription which is recorded in John 19: 20 as being posted above the crucified Christ in Greek, Latin and Hebrew: *Iesous Ho Nazaraios Ho Basileus Ton Ioudaion*, recalling the use of *hagios* rather than *sanctus* in the Lindisfarne Gospels evangelist portraits, and the Lord's Prayer in Greek but using Roman letters in Durham A II 10.

66 This is based on the CASSS dating, which is broadly accepted here. However, there is nothing about the fret and interlace on Norham 5 which absolutely precludes it being tenth–eleventh century; and the fragments Norham 6 and 12 have enough in common with material from Durham that they too could be later than the ninth-century dates ascribed to them. Cramp, *County Durham and Northumberland*, 208 ff.; R. Trench-Jellicoe, 'A Richly Decorated Cross-Slab from Kilduncan House, Fife: Description and Analysis', *PSAS* 135 (2005), 505–59, at 524–5 and n. 21.

Tilred, formerly abbot of Heversham, became abbot of Norham.[67] Heversham has its own handsome cross from *c.* 800, but if Tilred was responsible for sponsoring new sculpture in early tenth-century Norham there is no evidence that he was inspired by the surviving art of his previous incumbency. The encircled pattern of Norham 7a/b and the crouched beast of Norham 3 (the best candidates for tenth-century creations) are quite unlike the slender, organic plant-forms of the eighth-century cross at Heversham.[68] It should be emphasised that these plausibly later sculptures at Norham are all highly competent in design and execution: there was still time and money. Norham's cross-marked grave-slab may be roughly contemporary with Tilred, but it is closely paralleled at Lindisfarne (Norham 16 and Lindisfarne 38). A late eleventh-century cross-marked stone which could have been a dedication cross, or indicated a liturgical station, suggests that by this late date there may have been a stone church, but no earlier architectural fragments have been securely identified.[69]

Given that almost all the material at Norham was found in a single excavation, it is plausible that the destruction of the sculpture post-dates the late eleventh century. Norham castle, built by Ranulph Flambard in 1121, saw battle in 1136 and was devastated in the siege of Norham in 1138: there is clearly scope here for such an episode of destruction.[70] The present church dates from the mid twelfth century. At the time of the battle of Carham in 1018, therefore, it is probable that these magnificent and ambitious crosses were all still *in situ* and serving their original function. Why so many crosses? By analogy with Irish high crosses,

---

67 McGuigan, 'Neither Scotland or England', 247–8.
68 Aird, *St Cuthbert and the Normans*, 24; *HSC*, 48–9; Bailey and Cramp, *Cumberland, Westmorland and Lancashire North-of-the-Sands*, 183–4 and 351–4; McGuigan, 'Neither Scotland not England', 248.
69 Cramp, *County Durham and Northumberland*, 245–6. Eric Cambridge argues that Norham 7a/b may be architectural (and that they are eighth- or early-ninth-century), but their fragmentary condition and the similarity of their encircled patterns to those on crosses at Jedburgh and Morham (East Lothian) leaves this hypothesis, at best, unproven. E. Cambridge, 'Why did the Community of St Cuthbert settle at Chester-le-Street?', in Bonner, Stancliffe and Rollason (eds), *St Cuthbert, His Cult and His Community to AD 1200*, 367–86, 371 and n. 11.
70 W. M. Aird, *St Cuthbert and the Normans: The Church of Durham, 1071–1153* (Woodbridge, 1998), 258; M. Strickland, 'Securing the North: Invasion and the Strategy of Defence in Twelfth-Century Anglo-Scottish Warfare', in M. Chibnall (ed.), *Anglo-Norman Studies XII: Proceedings of the Battle Conference 1989* (Woodbridge, 1990), 177–98, at 186.

some may have marked entrances to the monastic enclosure, bounding and controlling access to the sacred space; others may have been votive and/or commemorative, or prompts for devotional or penitential activity.[71] It is quite possible that one cross performed numerous functions. Perhaps the comparative lack of tenth-century material merely indicates that by around 900 Norham's sculptural landscape was already crowded.

Jedburgh

Jedburgh may have been given to Lindisfarne in the early ninth century, though the evidence for this comes in a passage of the *Historia de Sancto Cuthberto* with notoriously confused chronology.[72] Towards the end of the eleventh century Eadwulf *Rus* was buried there, and later exhumed in retaliation for his murder of Bishop Walcher: this is the earliest – and purely inferential – hint at a church on the site.[73] Jedburgh lies twenty-six kilometres south-west of Carham, reached by following the valleys of the Tweed, Teviot and Jed upstream. Jedburgh's carved stone has been described in detail by Cramp.[74] Whereas both Lindisfarne and Norham have a degree of house style, the main impression left by the sculpture from Jedburgh is its sheer variety. The earliest and certainly the most elaborate monument is the shrine with inhabited vine-scroll, two pieces of which survive. While there is no record of a major early shrine at Jedburgh, it is possible that there was an important cult of which we now know nothing; and the other sculpture suggests considerable investment in the site in the ninth to eleventh centuries. It includes a fragment with encircled interlace (a close match for Norham 7a/b); a fragment of a cross with variations on plant-scrolls on all four faces; a cross-shaft whose confronted animals have parallels in Pictland at Meigle as well as at Lindisfarne; a cross-head which patently alludes to metalwork designs (again paralleled at Norham); three fragments of an ambitious cross depicting several profile human figures who could

---

71 M. Herbert, *Iona, Kells and Derry: The History and Hagiography of the Monastic Familia of Columba* (Dublin, 1996), 106; A. Hamlin, 'Crosses from Early Ireland: The Evidence from Written Sources', in M. Ryan (ed.), *Ireland and Insular Art AD 500–1200* (Dublin, 1985), 138–40.
72 *HSC*, 48–50; McGuigan, 'Neither Scotland nor England', 11–12.
73 Aird, *St Cuthbert and the Normans*, 153.
74 R. Cramp, 'The Anglian Sculptures from Jedburgh' in A. O'Connor and D. V. Clarke, *From the Stone Age to the Forty-Five: Studies Presented to R. B. K. Stevenson, Former Keeper, National Museum of Antiquities of Scotland* (Edinburgh, 1983), 269–84, at 269.

easily be secular; and a cross-shaft which appears to show Christ in Glory above and chaotic, naked figures below: presumably a Last Judgement, full of expressionist vigour. This last has the intriguing detail that all the figures, including Christ, have their ribs or abdominal muscles indicated with incised lines.[75] One is left with the impression that fashions changed radically at Jedburgh in every generation between *c.* 800 and *c.* 1100; and no patron or sculptor saw any need to fit in with existing monuments. Alternatively, some of the sculpture may have been imported as building rubble from other sites, as Ralegh Radford suggested for the shrine.[76]

This idea, that the shrine was originally from a different site, was taken seriously enough by Cramp that she discusses it in an appendix to her Jedburgh article, rather than the main chapter; and it is also repeated (and rightly described as speculative) by Crook.[77] Ralegh Radford expressed anxiety about associating such elaborate shrine fragments too closely with an unrecorded early church and cult, suggesting instead that they originally belonged sixteen kilometres north, at Old Melrose, and were associated with the shrine of St Boisil, Cuthbert's mentor; that by the eleventh century, when Alfred Westou 'collected' the relics of Boisil to enshrine them at Durham, Old Melrose was already derelict; and that building stone, including the shrine fragments, was subsequently brought to Jedburgh after the foundation of the priory in 1138.[78] None of this is susceptible of proof. There is no surviving early sculpture at the site of the original monastery at Old Melrose, though several fragments from various periods have been found reused locally, including a plausibly tenth-century cross fragment in a wall at nearby Gattonside, now in the National Museum of Scotland.[79]

---

75 This piece is not discussed by Cramp. Historic Environment Scotland claim this for the ninth or tenth century (site museum label) but figural detail and the compass-drawn circles used as a decorative motif suggest this date is surely too early. Its closest analogy is with the Newent (Gloucs.) stone book, and the later eleventh century is a more plausible context. V. Thompson, *Dying and Death in Later Anglo-Saxon England* (Woodbridge, 2004), 88–90; R. Bryant, *Corpus of Anglo-Saxon Stone Sculpture, Volume X: The Western Midlands* (Oxford, 2012), 236–9, ills 401–12, figs 31F, 32G.

76 C. A. Ralegh Radford, 'Two Scottish Shrines; Jedburgh and St Andrews', *Archaeological Journal* 112 (1955), 43–60, 46.

77 J. Crook, *English Medieval Shrines*, 102–3.

78 C. A. Ralegh Radford, 'Two Scottish Shrines; Jedburgh and St Andrews', *Archaeological Journal* 112 (1955), 43–60, 46; Boisil's relics: *LDE*, iii.7, 164–5.

79 *Old Melrose, Near Melrose, Scottish Borders: Archaeological Desk-Based Assessment,*

However, the Jedburgh assemblage has some extremely close parallels with Norham. The fragment with circular interlace is virtually identical in design to Norham 7a/b; and the elaborate cross-head with its complex concentric boss and knotwork in the arms is very like the head found near Norham church in 1983.[80] Ralegh Radford suggested Boisil as the original inhabitant of the Jedburgh shrine because of the proximity of Melrose to Jedburgh, and because he had no reason to think of Norham as the long-term home of a major saint; but Norham, like Melrose, is on the Tweed, and not much further away. There was a major episode of destruction at Norham at the time of the foundation of the priory at Jedburgh. If – and it is a big if – the shrine fragments were brought from elsewhere, then Norham, with its glorious assemblage of plant-scroll, seems as reasonable a possibility as Melrose. The quality of the Jedburgh fragment, both the plant-scroll with its vivacious parrot- and bushbaby-like inhabitants, and the adjacent run of interlace, is exceptional. Ralegh Radford justifies the claim that this shrine may have been Boisil's by comparing it with Bede's description of Cuthbert's original shrine on Lindisfarne, but it is not beyond the bounds of possibility that the shrine fragment now at Jedburgh was originally that of a saint culted at Norham, perhaps Ceolwulf, or even Cuthbert himself.[81] Given the uncertainty over the sources for Ecgred's episcopal dates, and the uncertainty over the dating of the shrine fragment, this may be unlikely but it is not impossible.[82]

Oxford Archaeology North December 2007, The Trimontium Trust Issue No: 622, 30. https://library.thehumanjourney.net/2204/1/Old%20Melrose%20DBA.pdf

[80] Cramp, 'Jedburgh', 276.

[81] The idea that St Cuthbert's stone shrine might have moved is given tantalising substance by the tradition recorded by Hutchinson, and later given poetic form by Walter Scott in *Marmion*, that his stone coffin floated from Melrose to Tillmouth. W. Hutchinson, *The History and Antiquities of the County Palatine of Durham, Volume 3* (Carlisle, 1794), 413.

[82] Dates ascribed to the shrine fragment vary wildly, with Cramp putting it later than Ruthwell and Bewcastle, but before Rothbury, which allows for a date range of c. 740×c. 850. Cramp, 'Jedburgh', 281; McGuigan, 'Neither Scotland nor England', 65–6. The dates of Ecgred's episcopacy are based on episcopal lists incorporated into the *Historia Regum* associated with Symeon, but the only contemporary evidence is Ecgred's undated letter to Wulfsige, archbishop of York (whose own dates are approximate). *EHD*, i, no. 214, at 875–6; Rollason, *LDE*, xlviii–l.

Carham, and conclusions

What then of Carham? There are three surviving fragments of late Anglo-Saxon carved stone associated with the battle location: two cross-shafts and a piece of a shaft or more probably cross-head, from what were clearly three separate monuments. All are in a yellow sandstone which is locally common, although no quarry site has been suggested.[83] None has a clear provenance: they are now in the Great North Museum in Newcastle, and have been linked with Carham since being presented by a local land-owner in 1902.[84] The presumption here is that they come from the site of St Cuthbert's church, Carham.[85]

Although they differ in execution, the three fragments have a strong family resemblance. All but one of the surviving faces are decorated exclusively with plain interlace and/or moulding: there are no human figures, no animals, birds or plants; and no other forms of abstract ornament. The exception (Carham 2C) carries an incised depiction of a cusp-armed cross (CASSS type D9).[86] None of these three can be dated other than on stylistic grounds. Only one carved face survives on Carham 1; Carham 2 has been luckier, with all four faces showing some carving. Carham 3 has carving on two adjacent faces, and dowel holes indicating how the larger monument was fitted together. Cramp ascribes Carham 1 to the tenth century based on its large field of pattern D interlace, which associates it locally with sculpture which clusters late (although it is found on one of the finest fragments of cross-head from Norham).[87] However its width-depth ratio is comparatively square (identical to the Bewcastle cross), which could shunt it earlier as later cross-shafts tend to be more slab-like; and its carving is assured, with the plump, sinuous interlace giving a convincing impression of three-dimensional cord.[88] Carham 2's interlace is conceived

---

83 J. M. Ragg, *The Soils of the Country Round Kelso and Lauder* (HMSO, Edinburgh, 1960), 18.
84 Cramp, *County Durham and Northumberland*, 169–70, plates 161–3.
85 See Petts, this volume.
86 R. Cramp, *Grammar of Anglo-Saxon Ornament* (1991), xvi, fig. 2.
87 Norham 14; compare Durham 1 (St Oswald's), and cross-heads 5, 6, Billingham 6 (lost) and 12, Lindisfarne 2, 6, 11, 15; Jarrow 4.
88 Although pattern D is more common in later sculpture Bewcastle has a register of pattern D on face B. Cramp suggests that the cross-base Lindisfarne 20 may date from 775x900 on the basis of its 'squarish' socket. Bailey and Cramp, *Cumberland,*

much more two-dimensionally, ribbon rather than cord, on all three faces. Their complexity emphasises the austerity of the fourth face, with its incised double-cusped cross: this, as Cramp observes, looks like an image of an object. If the frame around the cross is integral to this object, it looks like 'a grave-marker or a headstone', and there are parallels with the grave-slabs Norham 16 and Lindisfarne 38.[89] It could also depict a free-standing cross, with a double-cusped head like Rothbury, Norham 10, 11, 12 and 14, Monkwearmouth 1, Tyninghame and possibly Lindisfarne 15 and 16. Whether a grave-slab or a cross is alluded to, it is intriguing that one monument should reference another in this way, and Myredah's cross at Alnmouth provides a possible parallel, with its depiction of Christ's cross at Calvary decorated with interlace. These stones conflate sacred space and time on many levels. Carham 3 is another competent fragment, crisply carved with well-modelled cords and a free, roomy use of space, very different from the close-packed 1 and 2. Where this sense of spaciousness is concerned, the closest parallel locally is Norham 5D, and there is no pressing case for putting this stone into the late-tenth- to early-eleventh-century slot.

In some ways, these crosses tell us little or nothing about Carham in 1018. We do not know what they looked like when complete, or where they stood; we cannot even be absolutely sure they come from Carham. However, we can use them and the other sculptural survivals around the Tweed to poke at established orthodoxies. What does this landscape look like, if we hypothesise Norham as a spiritual and political superpower into the early eleventh century, with the community and their treasures only leaving for Durham around the time of the battle of Carham? Was Carham itself an important church? How might we think differently about Lindisfarne, with its new investment and reshaping of its identity in the tenth century? What new possibilities are opened up around the Jedburgh shrine fragment? Who was buried under Norham 16 and Lindisfarne 38, those elaborate slabs with their double-cusped crosses, both plausibly ninth century, a time when a vanishingly small number of people were interred under an elaborately-carved stone?

Westmorland and Lancashire North-of-the-Sands, 64; Cramp, *County Durham and Northumberland*, 202.
89   Cramp, *County Durham and Northumberland*, 169.

These and other questions may help us to look at the region of the modern Anglo-Scottish border with new eyes.

Acknowledgements

I am very grateful to Neil McGuigan, David Petts, and Niamh Whitfield for their comments on drafts of this paper.

CHAPTER EIGHT

Annals 848 to 1118 in the Historia Regum

DAVID A. WOODMAN

There has been significant scholarly discussion about the battle of Carham.[1] One point of difficulty is that surviving sources give different fundamental details about the battle, including its date and the identities of those involved. An important account can be found in annal 1018 in the *Historia Regum* (hereafter *HR*), as it is preserved in C[ambridge], C[orpus] C[hristi] C[ollege] 139.[2] This is the only source to provide the name of Uhtred, son of Earl Waltheof, on the side of the *Angli*,[3] a detail which has shaped arguments about the battle's date. *HR* survives in its fullest form in CCCC 139; there are abbreviated versions of the text found in other manuscripts.[4]

---

1   B. Meehan, 'The Siege of Durham, the Battle of Carham and the Cession of Lothian', *SHR* 55 (1976), 1–19; A. A. M. Duncan, 'The Battle of Carham, 1018', *SHR* 55 (1976), 20–8; and A. Woolf, *From Pictland to Alba, 789–1070*, The New Edinburgh History of Scotland 2 (Edinburgh, 2007), 236–7; and introduction to this volume, 1–32.
2   *HR* 8, *s.a.* 1018, ed. Arnold, ii, 155–6; the *HR* is cited from *Sym. Op.*, ii, 3–283. In this contribution, references to *Historia Regum* follow Hunter Blair's schema, outlined below (e.g. *HR* 8 for *Historia Regum*, section 8).
3   Meehan, 'Siege', 13.
4   CCCC 139's copy of *HR* is the principal focus of this chapter. Related material/versions include Paris, Bibliothèque nationale, nouv. acq. Lat. 692, which is a copy of the late twelfth or early thirteenth century (on which see H. S. Offler, 'A Medieval Chronicle from Scotland', *SHR* 47 (1968), 151–9, reprinted in, and cited from, A. J. Piper and A. I. Doyle (eds), *North of the Tees: Studies in Medieval British History* (Aldershot, 1996), essay XI). The *Historia post Bedam*, extant in three manuscripts (Oxford, St John's College 97, British Library, Royal 13 A. vi and London, Inner Temple, Petyt 511.2), was originally compiled in the mid twelfth century at Durham. It has entries to 1148, and was itself borrowing from the *HR* and therefore forms another important witness to the *HR*'s text. It survives today embedded in the work of Roger of Howden (see *RHC*, i). Finally, both Liège, Bibliothèque Universitaire, 369C (for the view that this manuscript was written at Durham, see B. Meehan, 'Geoffrey of Monmouth, *Prophecies of Merlin*: New Manuscript Evidence', *Bulletin of the Board of Celtic Studies* 28 (1978), 37–46) and BL, Cotton Caligula A. viii, contain annals from 1066 to 1119 which are derived from the *HR*. For recent comments about all of these copies, see D. Rollason, 'Symeon of

The *HR* is highly complex. Although known by one title, the *HR* as preserved in CCCC 139 is actually a compilation of a range of quite different items. Hunter Blair showed that it was composed of the following:

1) The Kentish Legends.
2) The Early Northumbrian Kings.
3) Material derived mainly from Bede.
4) A Chronicle from 732 to 802.
5) A Chronicle from 849 to 887, derived mainly from Asser.
6) A Chronicle from 888 to 957.
7) Extracts from William of Malmesbury.
8) A Chronicle from 848 to 1118, derived mainly from Florence of Worcester.
9) A Chronicle from 1119 to 1129.[5]

Hunter Blair observed that sections 1–5 of the above list were marked by their use of a very mannered kind of Latin prose that involved devices like 'bombastic circumlocutions', the use of three verbs in consecutive fashion and a fondness for elaborate superlatives.[6] Michael Lapidge later showed that this style of Latin was so distinctive that it could be attributed to Byrhtferth of Ramsey, a monk whose *floruit* belongs to the period *c*. 970 to *c*. 1020.[7] The entry about the battle of Carham occurs in section 8, that part of the *HR* that relies heavily on a copy of the Worcester *Chronicon ex Chronicis* (hereafter *Chronicon*)

Durham's *Historia de Regibus Anglorum et Dacorum* as a Product of Twelfth-Century Historical Workshops', in M. Brett and D. A. Woodman (eds), *The Long Twelfth-Century View of the Anglo-Saxon Past* (Farnham, 2015), 95–111. For related material in the *Chronicle of Melrose*, see D. Broun and J. Harrison, *The Chronicle of Melrose Abbey: A Stratigraphic Edition. Volume I: Introduction and Facsimile Edition*, Scottish History Society 6th Ser. (Edinburgh, 2007), 48–53.

5 P. Hunter Blair, 'Some Observations on the '*Historia Regum*' attributed to Symeon of Durham', in N. K. Chadwick (ed.), *Celt and Saxon: Studies in the Early British Border* (Cambridge, 1964), 63–118, where this list appears at 76–7. Hunter Blair also showed (at 117) that these nine sections of the *HR* could be grouped further into three main divisions, the first comprising items 1–5 in the list, the second comprising item 6 and the third in the chronicle comprised of items 8 and 9.

6 *Ibid*., 96–8 (at 97).

7 M. Lapidge, 'Byrhtferth of Ramsey and the Early Sections of the *Historia Regum* Attributed to Symeon of Durham', *ASE* 10 (1981), 97–122, reprinted in his *Anglo-Latin Literature, 900–1066* (London and Rio Grande, 1993), 317–42; and M. Lapidge (ed.), *Byrhtferth of Ramsey: The Lives of St Oswald and St Ecgwine* (Oxford, 2009), xxxix–xlii.

attributed to John of Worcester.[8] CCCC 139, which contains an array of texts in addition to the *HR*, was itself judged by Hunter Blair to have been written *c.* 1170 in Sawley, Yorkshire,[9] although the manuscript's origin has proved contentious and, while some have proposed Hexham and Fountains as other possibilities, others have suggested a Durham origin as more likely.[10] Hunter Blair thought that the copying of the *HR* into CCCC 139 had been completed by 1164.[11] He also thought that sections 8 and 9, which together form a chronicle covering the years 848 to 1129, were very likely originally composed at Durham (even if he judged the whole manuscript to have been produced at Sawley). In CCCC 139, a rubricator attributed the *HR* to Symeon of Durham himself, and Hunter Blair concluded, 'There seems to be a fair case for regarding the additional northern material inserted into Florence's work and the writing of the entries for 1119–29 as being the contribution of Symeon himself. It is possible, though not certainly known, that the interruption of the work after the end of the entry for 1129 was due to Symeon's death in or soon after 1130.'[12]

---

8   R. R. Darlington and P. McGurk (eds), J. Bray and P. McGurk (trans.), *The Chronicle of John of Worcester, Volume II* (Oxford, 1995); and P. McGurk (ed. and trans.), *The Chronicle of John of Worcester, Volume III* (Oxford, 1998).

9   Hunter Blair, 'Observations', 70, 72–6. See also D. N. Dumville, 'The Corpus Christi "Nennius"', *The Bulletin of the Board of Celtic Studies* 25 (1974), 369–80.

10 See, for example, B. Meehan, 'Durham Twelfth-Century Manuscripts in Cistercian Houses', in D. Rollason, M. Harvey and M. Prestwich (eds), *Anglo-Norman Durham, 1093–1193* (Woodbridge, 1994), 439–49 (at 440–2); C. Norton, 'History, Wisdom and Illumination', in D. Rollason (ed.), *Symeon of Durham: Historian of Durham and the North* (Stamford, 1998), 61–105 (at 72, 87 and 101–4); J. Story, 'Symeon as Annalist', in Rollason (ed.), *Symeon*, 202–13, at 210–13; and D. Rollason, 'Symeon's Contribution to Historical Writing in Northern England', in Rollason (ed.), *Symeon*, 1–13, at 10. See the works cited in these examples for references to either Hexham or Fountains as other possible origins of CCCC 139. The date of production of the manuscript as a whole has likewise been debated and B. Meehan, 'A Reconsideration of the Historical Works Associated with Symeon of Durham: Manuscripts, Texts and Influences', unpublished PhD dissertation (University of Edinburgh, 1979), 109, after considering a range of evidence and the composite nature of CCCC 139, suggests a date of *c.* 1180 as perhaps more plausible.

11 This opinion has not received universal acceptance. See, for example, H. S. Offler, 'Hexham and the *Historia Regum*', *Transactions of the Architectural and Archaeological Society of Durham and Northumberland*, new series ii (1970), 51–62, reprinted in H. S. Offler, *North of the Tees: Studies in Medieval British History*, ed. A. J. Piper and A. I. Doyle (Aldershot, 1996), no. X.

12 For all of this, see Hunter Blair, 'Observations', 107–12 (at 112 for the quotation). The attribution to Symeon is discussed further below.

This chapter offers reflections primarily on annals 848 to 1118, section 8 in Hunter Blair's list above. The majority of this part of the *HR* is so heavily dependent on the Worcester *Chronicon* that Hunter Blair considered it 'of only slight value as a primary source'.[13] This dependence on the Worcester text means that any deviation from its source becomes particularly interesting, and questions need to be asked about the cause of such differences. Are they the result of authorial intervention on the part of the *HR* author, or do they actually reflect on the Worcester text used as an exemplar?[14] As will be seen, there are several occasions when the nature of the divergence – containing details about Northumbrian history or items of local interest – is such that authorial intervention seems the most reasonable explanation. It would be difficult to suggest that these additions reveal some kind of overriding and uniform purpose on the part of the *HR* author of these annals, for the complexity and composite nature of the *HR* text as a whole makes this unlikely.[15] But they certainly help in revealing some of the prevailing concerns of the author(s) in making use of, and embellishing, the Worcester annals and thus provide important contextual information when reading entries like that for the battle of Carham. One further complexity is that we no longer possess the autograph copy of the *HR*: that preserved in CCCC 139 was judged by Hunter Blair to have been made *c.* 1164, that is, some thirty-five years after this part of the *HR* was originally composed. This means that we have to contend with the possibility that any divergence between this part of the *HR* and the Worcester *Chronicon* could actually be the result of an addition

---

13 Hunter Blair, 'Observations', 107.
14 Surviving copies of the Worcester *Chronicon ex Chronicis* reveal three stages in the composition of that text (for which, see Darlington and McGurk, *The Chronicle, Vol. II*, lxvii–lxxiii). A comparison of annals 848 to 1118/1119 in the *HR* with those in the *Chronicon* reveals that the *HR* author had access to an 'early state' of the Worcester text (M. Brett, 'John of Worcester and his Contemporaries', in R. H. C. Davis and J. M. Wallace-Hadrill (eds), *The Writing of History in the Middle Ages: Essays Presented to R. W. Southern* (Oxford, 1981), 101–26). There are also indications that the *HR* author may have had an exemplar of the *Chronicon* which was slightly different from those surviving today.
15 On the difficulties in detecting authorial purpose in chronicles, see P. Hayward, *The Winchcombe and Coventry Chronicles: Hitherto Unnoticed Witnesses to the Work of John of Worcester*, 2 vols (Tempe, 2010), i, 11–61. For an alternative view, see E. A. Winkler, *Royal Responsibility in Anglo-Norman Historical Writing* (Oxford, 2017), 16–18.

made at some point between the original composition of the *HR c.* 1129 and its copying *c.* 1164. Scattered throughout CCCC 139's annals are various near-contemporary annotating hands, which demonstrate that this kind of annalistic history was not static: in fact, scribes continued to engage with the text after *c.* 1164, changing and correcting passages here and there. The second part of this chapter analyses some of these changes, to demonstrate the concerns and interests of those involved in the annotating process.

Authorial additions to annals 848–1118

There are certain differences between the Worcester *Chronicon* and the corresponding annals of the *HR* where it is clear that the differences are the result of authorial insertions by those working on the *HR*. One way in which this can be seen is by the use of earlier sections of the *HR* itself. For example, *HR*'s 866 annal begins with a verbatim borrowing from annal 866 in the *Chronicon*, but then inserts a quite long passage about Alfred which is virtually identical to the corresponding element of annal 866 from earlier in *HR* (section 5).[16] This happens numerous times in *HR* section 8 where its annals overlap with those of previous sections.[17]

Other elements in *HR* are so overtly northern in terms of their interest and contents that the most logical explanation for their insertion is that the responsibility lies with the author(s)/compiler(s) of *HR*. One striking result of this can be seen in *HR*'s annal for 854. This begins with details of Wulfhere being made archbishop of York and Eardwulf receiving the 'bishopric of Lindisfarne' (*episcopatum Lindisfarnensem*), but then continues with a relatively long interpolation about the possessions of the Lindisfarne see, before concluding its annal with details of a viking victory at Thanet, and a marriage between Burgred, king of the Mercians, and the daughter of Æthelwulf, king of the West Saxons, which are taken once more from the Worcester *Chronicon*. This list of possessions of the Lindisfarne see is very interesting. Some (but not all)

---

16 See *HR* 8, *s.a.* 866, ed. Arnold, ii, 104–5 and *HR* 5, *s.a.* 866, ed. Arnold, ii, 73–4. Ultimately, this text about Alfred comes from Asser's *Vita* of that king, but the nature of these borrowings in *HR* 8 makes it clear that the compiler is taking them directly from the earlier *HR* section rather than independently from Asser. For discussion, see Hunter Blair, 'Observations', 107–9.

17 See, for example, annals 848, 851, 852, 853, 854, 855 and so on in section 8 of *HR*.

of the places mentioned can be found described in Durham's *Historia de Sancto Cuthberto* (hereafter *HSC*),[18] a mid- to late-eleventh-century text which combines hagiographical elements with detail about property ownership.[19] And, while there are important differences between this part of the *HR* and corresponding parts of the *HSC*,[20] some of its elements share verbal parallels with different chapters of the *HSC*. This makes it possible that the author of this element in the *HR* was borrowing/adapting text from the *HSC*, or a source common to both, and inserting it here in partially similar form (and structural order) into the *HR*.[21] The inclusion of this list of estates is one feature which links the *HR* to Durham very particularly.[22] It demonstrates the author's concern to document the landed possessions of his church, and its insertion at this point may have been triggered by the mention of Bishop Eardwulf at the beginning of the annal.[23]

Another example occurs in annal 1072. Having begun its entry by detailing William the Conqueror's expedition to Scotland against Máel Coluim III (r. 1058–93) which borrows from the *Chronicon*,[24] and then also describing how William deprived Gospatric of the Northumbrian earldom, the *HR* interrupts its usual narrative and inserts a long passage giving a history of the earls of Northumbria.[25] It is likely that it was the mention of Gospatric that prompted CCCC 139's copy of the *HR* to insert this interpolation at this point in its text, under annal 1072. But various

---

18 For the places not mentioned, and for discussion of this part of *HR* in general, see W. Aird, *St Cuthbert and the Normans* (Woodbridge, 1998), 13–15.
19 For the difficulties involved in dating the *HSC*, see the discussion in the most recent edition, T. Johnson South (ed. and trans.), *Historia de Sancto Cuthberto* (Woodbridge, 2002), 25–36 (and references therein to previous scholarship).
20 See the contributions of McGuigan and Woolf in this volume.
21 Verbal borrowings from, and structural similarities to, *HSC*, cc.8, 9, and 11 (ed. and trans. Johnson South, 49–51) can be seen in this part of the *HR*. And see also *HSC*, c.4, 46–7.
22 Hunter Blair, 'Observations', 110. For the suggestion that this element of the *HR*'s 854 annal had originally been part of one copy of Symeon's *Libellus de Exordio* (hereafter *LDE*), only to be erased, see D. Rollason, 'The Making of the *Libellus de Exordio*: The Evidence of Erasures and Alterations in the Two Earliest Manuscripts', in Rollason (ed.), *Symeon*, 140–56, at 149–50.
23 For the records of land transactions likely available at this stage in Durham, and for texts like the *Cronica monasterii Dunelmensis* that are related to the *HSC*, see D. A. Woodman (ed.), *Charters of Northern Houses* (Oxford, 2012), 323–8.
24 *HR* 8, s.a. 1072, ed. Arnold, ii, 195–6.
25 *HR* 8, s.a. 1072, ed. Arnold, ii, 196–200.

phrases which serve to cross-reference other parts of the *HR* indicate that this may not have been its original position. In fact, as Arnold noted, it may be that this history of the earls of Northumbria had at one time been placed in annal 952 rather than annal 1072.[26] And, because the *Historia post Bedam* (hereafter *HpB*) includes this interpolation about the earls of Northumbria in its entry for 952, at exactly the moment that that source describes Northumbria as no longer being subject to the rule of kings,[27] it may be confirmation that it belongs properly to this earlier position in *HR*.[28] The different position of this interpolation (either in annal 952 or in 1072) raises the question of whether we can regard it as part of the original core of the *HR* as it was first composed *c.* 1129 at Durham, or whether it was added (or moved) at a subsequent stage, at some point between *c.* 1129 and *c.* 1164 when CCCC 139 was copied. Arnold noted that the *HR*'s history of Northumbrian earls accorded very well with that in another Durham text written in the late eleventh century or early twelfth century, and known as the *De Obsessione Dunelmi* (*DOD*).[29] A perhaps even closer resemblance, however, is borne to a further Durham text, known as the *De Primo Saxonum Adventu* (*DPSA*).[30] The two share many similarities, not least in the order of the earls presented and in the starting-point of Earl Oswulf and then also of the ending-point of King Henry keeping the earldom in royal hands. It seems that the *modus operandi* for the author/compiler (or reviser if this interpolation was added at some point between *c.* 1129 and *c.* 1164) of this part of the *HR* was, at points considered appropriate in his copy of the Worcester *Chronicon*, to insert passages of prose inspired by, or taken from, near-contemporary Durham texts, thus lending a northern bias to certain parts. Once the interpolation about the Northumbrian earldom has finished in 1072, annal 1073 resumes by once more borrowing from the corresponding annal of the Worcester *Chronicon*, and then ending with detail about

---

26 Arnold, *Sym. Op.*, ii, 196, n. a. This was also the view of Hunter Blair, 'Observations', 111.
27 *HpB*, in *RHC*, s.a. 952, ed. Stubbs, i, 57, where the passage about the earls is introduced by the following sentence: *Iam deficientibus (ut supra diximus) Northimbrensium regibus, qualiter uel quibus comitibus ipsa prouincia subiacuerit, hic placet inserere.*
28 See also Arnold, *Sym. Op.*, ii, 196, n. a.
29 Arnold, *Sym. Op.*, ii, 197, n. a; and see C. J. Morris, *Marriage and Murder in Eleventh-Century Northumbria: A Study of the 'De Obsessione Dunelmi'*, Borthwick Paper no. 82, University of York (York, 1992).
30 *DPSA*, 365–84 (at 382–4 for the section on the Northumbrian earls).

the actions of Earl Waltheof which seem to be inspired by a corresponding part of the *DOD*, or by a source common to both.[31]

From its annal for 1069, the *HR* has a tendency to show greater divergence from its source, adding material and, in some ways, changing details received via the Worcester *Chronicon*. The *HR*'s annal for 1088, for example, is strikingly different from that in the *Chronicon*. Both record details of the rebellion early in William Rufus's reign, during which leading Norman figures turned against their new king and looked instead to his brother, Robert Curthose, duke of Normandy, for leadership.[32] One prominent leader of the rebellion was Odo, bishop of Bayeux, and the *Chronicon* lists others involved at high levels, concluding by saying 'what is worst of all, William, bishop of Durham. At this time the king (who knew him well) relied on Bishop William's wisdom as a true counsellor, and the affairs of all England were managed by his advice'.[33] Thus the *Chronicon* declares William of St Calais, bishop of Durham, to have been among the leaders of the rebellion and also someone that, although trusted by the king and involved in the running of the country, had nevertheless failed to support him.[34] It is not hard to see why a northern author, upon receiving a version of the *Chronicon*

---

[31] Compare this sentence in *HR* 8, s.a. 1073, ed. Arnold, ii, 200: *Comes Waltheouus, missa manu ualida Northymbrensium, necem aui sui Aldredi comitis crudeliter ulciscitur; siquidem filios Carl, qui eum occidi fecerat, apud Seteringetun simul conuiuantes gladius insidiantium consumpsit*, with these sentences in *De Obsessione*: *comes Waltheof, erat enim filius filiae illius, missa multa iuuenum manu aui sui interfectionem grauissima clade uindicauit. Erant namque filii Carl conuiuantes simul in domo fratris sui maioris in Seteringetun, non longe ab Eboraco; quos inopinate qui missi fuerant preoccupantes seva clade simul peremerunt, preter Cnutonem, cui pro insita illi bonitate uitam permiserunt*. See *DOD*, 219.

[32] For comments about the rebellion, see S. Harvey, *Domesday: Book of Judgement* (Oxford, 2014), 268–70.

[33] *Chronicon ex Chronicis*, s.a. 1088, ed. and trans. McGurk, iii, 48–9: *quod etiam erat peius, Willelmus episcopus Dunholmensis, ea quoque tempestate rex predictus illius, ut ueri consiliarii, fruebatur prudentia, bene enim sapiebat, eiusque consiliis totius Anglie tractabatur respublica*.

[34] For the power and influence of William of St Calais, see W. M. Aird, 'An Absent Friend: The Career of Bishop William of St Calais', in Rollason *et al.*, *Anglo-Norman Durham*, 283–97; for the famous trial of William, see H. S. Offler, 'The Tractate *De iniusta uexacione Willelmi episcopi primi*', *EHR* 66 (1951), 321–41 and M. Philpott, 'The *De iniusta uexacione Willelmi episcopi primi* and Canon Law in Anglo-Norman Durham', in Rollason *et al.*, *Anglo-Norman Durham*, 125–37. For text and translation of the extant account, see R. C. van Caenegem, *English Lawsuits from William I to Richard I*, 2 vols (London, 1990–1), i, no. 134, at 90–106; there is another translation in *EHD*, ii, no. 84, at 652–69.

that so explicitly criticised a recent bishop of Durham, desired to alter its own telling of this annal. The annal begins by borrowing from the corresponding annal in the *Chronicon*. But, on reaching the part that names the leaders of the revolt, it removes William of St Calais' name from the record and instead inserts a more general statement, that the 'more senior nobles of all England, except Archbishop Lanfranc' (*excellentiores principes totius Anglie, excepto Lanfranco archiepiscopo*) were involved.[35] The *HR* annalist nevertheless felt that some mention of William of St Calais had to be made and so his departure from England is recorded factually at the end of the annal. This comes after a passage that describes further treacherous behaviour from Bishop Odo, which ultimately resulted in his departure from England and arrival in Normandy. In following this description of Odo's behaviour with the detail that William of St Calais also left the country, the *HR* annalist betrays his implicit understanding that this exile was likewise necessitated by William of St Calais's treachery. But the annalist tries to downplay this in two ways: by beginning the sentence with the particle *etiam*, thus distancing this entry from what had gone before about Odo; and by referring plainly to the 'bishop of Durham' without naming him (the hand of a later reader of CCCC 139 annotates the annal at this point by inserting the name 'Willelmus' in an interlinear position).[36]

This annal in the *HR* raises other issues. As noted above, it begins by using the *Chronicon* for its opening sentences. But it soon afterwards shares some of its text with the abbreviated version of the *Chronicon*, known as the *Chronicula*,[37] and also with a Worcester compilation

---

35 *HR* 8, s.a. 1088, ed. Arnold, ii, 214–15.
36 *HR* 8, s.a. 1088, ed. Arnold, ii, 217. Arnold's rendering of the relevant sentence does not accurately follow what is in the manuscript, which reads *Etiam Dunholmensis episcopus 'Willelmus' viii anni sui episcopatus et multi alii Anglia exierunt*. Arnold does not indicate that the word 'Willelmus' is a later addition. This sentence is not found in the *HpB* at the relevant point (see *RHC*, s.a. 1088, ed. Stubbs, i, 142). The Paris manuscript has no record for this year and the Liège manuscript, on f.96v, has a related, but abbreviated entry: *Willelmus episcopus Dunelmensis de Anglia exiuit*, virtually identical to that found in Cotton Caligula A. viii on f.39r: *Guillelmus episcopus Dunelmensis de Anglia exiuit*.
37 The *Chronicula* (Dublin, Trinity College 503) is a small manuscript written mainly in the hand of John of Worcester, but, from 1124 to 1141, it was continued by someone working at Gloucester in the mid twelfth century. The relationship between the *Chronicula* and the *Chronicon* is not straightforward; see Darlington and McGurk, *The Chronicle, Vol. II*, lix-lxiv.

which brings together extracts from the *Chronicon* and also William of Malmesbury.[38] The remainder of the annal, apart from the last two sentences, appears then to be derived from the corresponding entry in the *Anglo-Saxon Chronicle*.[39] The proximity of this part of the *HR* both to the *Chronicula* and to the Worcester compilation raises questions about what Worcester text lies behind the *HR* at this stage.[40] Was it simply an earlier version of the *Chronicon* which has not survived in that extant form, or did the *HR* for some reason have access at this moment to another Worcester tradition/source that was different from the *Chronicon* in its received form?[41]

Other annals in the *HR* exhibit authorial changes of a kind that help to reveal some of its priorities. The date of 1093 is important in Durham history, for it was the year in which the building of Durham cathedral began. The *HR* begins its entry for 1093 with the usual borrowing from the *Chronicon*; then, at an appropriate point, it moves away from the *Chronicon* by recording the construction of the new Durham church and using a dating-clause which has similar (if not identical) elements to that found in Symeon's *LDE*.[42] The *HR* then returns to using the *Chronicon* as its source in providing detail about relations between King William Rufus and King Máel Coluim III of Scotland, and then also about the deaths of various prominent figures, including Paul, the abbot of the monastery of St Albans. At the introduction of Paul's name, the *HR* author once more breaks off from the *Chronicon* source and inserts an addition which states that Paul, having illegally deprived the Durham monks of possession of the church of Tynemouth, was taken by illness there and subsequently died at Settrington, near York.[43] This recalls a similar episode in chapter 13 of the Durham community's *Liber de miraculis et translationibus sancti*

---

38   This was noted by Brett, 'John of Worcester', 122, n. 1 (with reference to F. Liebermann, *Engedruckte Anglo-Normannische Geschichtsquellen* [Strasbourg, 1879], 15–24 [with relevant overlapping material at 22]).
39   See also McGurk, *John of Worcester, vol. III*, 48, n. 1.
40   Brett, 'John of Worcester', 122, n. 1.
41   I have an article forthcoming which examines in greater detail the links between Worcester and Durham texts in this period.
42   Compare the similar elements in the dating-clause in *HR* 8, *s.a.* 1093, ed. Arnold, ii, 220 and in *LDE*, iv.8, 244–5. On Symeon's use of dating-clauses, see K.-U. Jäschke, 'Remarks on Datings in the *Libellus de Exordio atque procursu istius hoc est Dunhelmensis ecclesie*', in Rollason (ed.), *Symeon*, 46–60.
43   *HR* 8, *s.a.* 1093, ed. Arnold, ii, 221.

Cuthberti.⁴⁴ The aim of including it here, in an annal of the *HR* commemorating the beginning of the Durham church, was clearly to ward off would-be defrauders of Durham property or possessions.⁴⁵ The message is made even clearer only two sentences later in the same annal when, having detailed the death of King Máel Coluim III of Scotland – a man who had raided Northumbria on various occasions – at the hands of Earl Robert, the *HR* states that he had been justly killed thanks to the judgement of an avenging God.⁴⁶

Three other annals in the *HR* – those for 1107, 1114 and 1116 – reveal, both in their manipulation of the Worcester *Chronicon* and in their addition of material, their concern for the status of the York church as an archbishopric in relation to Canterbury. In its account of events in 1107, the *Chronicon* describes how Archbishop Anselm was assisted in his consecration of various bishops by 'the suffragans of his see, Gerard, archbishop of York, Robert of Lincoln, John of Bath, Herbert of Norwich, Robert of Chester, Ralph of Chichester, Ranulf of Durham'.⁴⁷ The *HR*, although relying on the *Chronicon* for a large part of its 1107 annal, deliberately changes this list of those who aided Anselm, to read more generally, 'the suffragans of his see aided him in this service. And Gerard, archbishop of York, was present at their consecration, at Anselm's request'.⁴⁸ Although the *HR*'s annal had previously defined Gerard's relationship to Canterbury, this rewriting of the *Chronicon*'s

---

44 This is noted in Arnold's edition, *Sym. Op.*, ii, 221. For this Durham text, see B. Colgrave, 'The Post-Bedan Miracles and Translations of St Cuthbert', in C. Fox and B. Dickins (eds), *The Early Cultures of North-West Europe* (Cambridge, 1950), 305–32; W. M. Aird, 'The Making of a Medieval Miracle Collection: The *Liber de translationibus et miraculis sancti Cuthberti*', *NH* 28 (1992), 1–24; and Rollason, *LDE*, lxxv–lxxvi.

45 In this way it is reminiscent of the tone of parts of the *HSC*: T. Johnson South, 'Changing Images of Sainthood: St Cuthbert in the *Historia de Sancto Cuthberto*', in S. Sticca (ed.), *Saints: Studies in Hagiography*, Medieval and Renaissance Texts and Studies, vol. 141 (New York, 1996), 81–94. The possession of Tynemouth continued to be an issue for the Durham community into the late twelfth century, as evidenced by a group of forgeries: D. Bates, 'The Forged Charters of William the Conqueror and Bishop William of St Calais', in Rollason *et al.*, *Anglo-Norman Durham*, 111–24 (at 115–16).

46 *HR* 8, s.a. 1093, ed. Arnold, ii, 221: *In cuius morte iustitia iudicantis Dei aperte consideratur* ...

47 *Chronicon ex Chronicis*, s.a. 1107, ed. and trans. McGurk, iii, 112.

48 *HR* 8, s.a. 1107, ed. Arnold, ii, 239: *ministrantibus sibi in hoc officio suffraganeis ipsius sedis. Gerardus etiam Eboracensis archiepiscopus eorum consecrationi, rogatu Anselmi interfuit*. And cf. the *HpB*'s entry at the same point: *RHC*, s.a. 1107, ed. Stubbs, i, 164.

annal was effected in such a way that it did not have to name York (and Durham) as suffragans of the southern archbishopric.[49] A similar stance can be seen in *HR*'s 1114 entry, where, as part of an addition to an annal that is otherwise wholly taken from the *Chronicon*, a sentence is found about the excellence of character and way of life of the deceased archbishop of York, Thomas II.[50] The *HR*'s handling of annal 1116 offers the most obvious example of the modification of the *Chronicon*'s text in order to maintain York's status in the face of Canterbury claims. Both the Worcester and *HR* annals describe the dispute that was taking place between Ralph, archbishop of Canterbury, and Thurstan, archbishop-elect, about Canterbury's insistence that York make a profession of obedience. But the *HR* adds a relatively long and unique insertion which cites historical precedents for why York should not be required to profess obedience.[51] The *HR* annal then returns to verbatim borrowing from the corresponding annal in the *Chronicon* but, in its phrase about King Henry's recognition of Thurstan's position, the *HR* crucially changes the sense of the *Chronicon*'s *Rex autem Heinricus, ubi aduertit Turstanus in sua peruicacia stare*, by emending *peruicacia* ('obstinacy') to *sententia* ('opinion'/'decision').[52] This alteration removed any negative judgement about Thurstan's actions and lays clear one aspect of the *HR*'s agenda.[53]

---

49 For more about the primacy debate, see F. Barlow, *The English Church 1066–1154: A History of the Anglo-Norman Church* (New York, 1979); M. Brett, *The English Church under Henry I* (Oxford, 1975); and R. Bartlett, *England under the Norman and Angevin Kings, 1075–1225* (Oxford, 2000). As Martin Brett points out to me, not even Canterbury claimed that Gerard was Anselm's suffragan.

50 Those words added in this annal read: *uir eximie religionis... qui cum ceteris sanctarum uirtutum operibus, etiam in uirginitatis puritate perrexit ad Dominum. Quanta uero morum probitate et uite innocentis puritate ante episcopatum et in episcopatu enituerit, nullis humanis uerbis digne explicari posse arbitror* (*HR* 8, s.a. 1114, ed. Arnold, ii, 248). And cf., for example, the entry in Cotton Caligula A. viii, f.42r, which has the detail about the death of Thomas, but without this description of his character.

51 *HR* 8, s.a. 1116, ed. Arnold, ii, 249–50. This passage does not appear in the *HpB* (*RHC*, s.a. 1116, ed. Stubbs, i, 171), nor in the Liège manuscript (which is highly abbreviated at this point, on f.99r), nor in Cotton Caligula A. viii (on f.42v), nor in the Paris manuscript (on f. 39v).

52 *Chronicon ex Chronicis*, s.a. 1116, ed. and trans. McGurk, iii, 138 and *HR* 8, s.a. 1116, ed. Arnold, ii, 250.

53 The omission of the long addition citing historical precedent for York's status from the *HpB* (see above, n. 51), and the *HpB*'s retention of *peruicacia* rather than *sententia*, raises the possibility that the addition and rewriting happened after the original *HR* was compiled. Such a conclusion depends on a detailed comparison of all extant versions of the *HR*, which is beyond the scope of this chapter. For the *HR*'s views about

As will be seen in the next section, it is possible that various additions by annotating hands in CCCC 139 were made on the basis of a reading of Symeon's *LDE*.[54] The relationship of section 8 of the *HR* (attributed to Symeon) and the earlier *LDE* raises interesting questions. The two are, in certain parts, closely connected, to the extent that some passages of the *HR* adopt similar structures in their Latin formulation and similar vocabulary when describing the same events. But, in the vast majority of cases, such similarities do not represent verbatim copying by the author of *HR* from *LDE*, and in fact relevant phrases have been modified and recast somehow. Given that the *HR*, when relying on the Worcester *Chronicon* for passages, most often copies its text verbatim and without modification, it is important to question why this is not the approach in the case of its handling of the *LDE*. Some of *HR*'s annals demonstrate a relatively minor, but nonetheless intriguing, level of engagement with the *LDE*. For example, in its annal for 867, which describes the victory of viking forces at York, the *HR* borrows mostly verbatim from the Worcester *Chronicon*. But, on three occasions, it has phrases or sentences which cannot be found in the Worcester text and are instead related to the *LDE*. The first phrase is *omniaque uastauerunt usque Tinemutham*, which may represent a summary of the relevant part of *LDE*;[55] the second is the addition of a dating-clause which bears relation to the same part of the *LDE*;[56] and the third is the addition of two sentences which read: *Quibus predicti pagani sub suo dominio regem Egbertum prefecerunt. Egbertus uero regnauit post hec super Northumbros ultra Tine vi. annis.*[57] These are clearly related to a similarly structured, but not identical, sentence in the same chapter of *LDE*: *Quibus (ut dictum est) interfectis, regem Northumbris qui supererant Ecgbertum Dani constituerunt, qui eis tantum qui ad septentrionalem plagam fluminis Tini habitabant sub eorum dominio imperaret.*[58] Because the *HR* author is

---

the primacy debate, see also A. Gransden, *Historical Writing in England c. 550–1307* (New York, 1974), 151.

54   Below, 220–8.
55   See *LDE*, ii.6, 94–105.
56   The dating-clause in this annal in *HR* is more detailed than that found in *LDE*, which does, however, share its date of 21 March (*duodecimas Kalendas Aprilis*): *LDE*, ii.6, 96.
57   These two sentences are further discussed below, 223.
58   *LDE*, ii.6, 98. The *HR* adds the detail that King Ecgberht ruled for six years.

here adding material about Northumbrian history, it is possible that he was so well acquainted with the details, and with the *LDE* itself, that similar vocabulary and turns of phrase automatically slip through into the *HR*'s text, without being copied verbatim. If we can accept that the author of this part of the *HR* was indeed Symeon himself,[59] it would readily explain this kind of relationship between the two texts.[60]

Some of *HR*'s annals exhibit an evolving and complex relationship with the *LDE*. That for 883 is one such example. This annal begins with a sentence about the seizing of Condé which is drawn from the Worcester *Chronicon*'s 883 annal, but it quickly moves to a long entry which is not in the Worcester source and which relies on northern sources. The remainder describes how St Cuthbert appeared in a dream to Abbot Eadred and how the latter was then instrumental in the election of a king (Guthred) for the viking army;[61] how after this election St Cuthbert's see was moved from Lindisfarne to Chester-le-Street; the rights of sanctuary that were bestowed on St Cuthbert's church; that the land between the Tyne and the Tees also be given to St Cuthbert's church, and so on.[62] Much of this detail can be found in the *HSC*, principally in chapter 13 of that text.[63] And there is also overlapping material in the *Cronica Monasterii Dunelmensis* (*CMD*), which itself

---

59 Below, 217–20.
60 Other verbal echoes of the *LDE* can be seen in, for example, *HR*'s annals 870 (with *LDE*, ii.6); 872 (with *LDE*, ii.6 – and note in CCCC 139's copy of this annal the interesting confusion of names with *Werefrithum* being miscopied for a second time in the same annal, and on the basis of the mention of the bishop by the same name earlier in the annal. This was later corrected and *Werefrithum* was expuncted and *Wlfere* inserted); 1043 (with *LDE*, iii.9); 1069 (with *LDE*, iii.15); and 1087 (with *LDE*, iv.7). For further comments about Symeon's authorship, at least of annals 1119–29 in the *HR*, see M. Gullick, 'The Hand of Symeon of Durham: Further Observations on the Durham Martyrology Scribe', in Rollason (ed.), *Symeon*, 14–31, at 21–2. Story, 'Symeon as Annalist', 208, argues that Symeon was in addition the compiler of the annals known by the title *Annales Lindisfarnenses et Dunelmenses*, which also show 'information in common' with Symeon's *LDE*; and, at 212–13, Story makes a case on the basis of the contents and arrangement of CCCC 139 for Symeon's involvement in the compilation of the *HR*.
61 On Guthred, see C. Downham, *Viking Kings of Britain and Ireland, the Dynasty of Ívarr to AD 1014* (Edinburgh, 2007), 75–9.
62 *HR* 8, *s.a.* 883, ed. Arnold, ii, 114–15.
63 *HSC*, c.13, 52–3; that chapter of the *HSC* does not, however, mention the establishment of the Lindisfarne see at Chester-le-Street, which can be found later in *HSC*, c.20, 58–9.

relied in parts on the *HSC* and which then formed another source for the *LDE*.[64] But there are elements in this part of *HR* which seem to rely ultimately on the *LDE* rather than the *HSC* or the *CMD*. Firstly, the detail about Eadred's surname being *Lulisc* can be found in almost identical terms in the *LDE*;[65] secondly, the causal link between the movement of St Cuthbert's see to Chester-le-Street and Guthred's election seems unique to *LDE*;[66] thirdly, the detail that anyone contravening the terms of sanctuary be fined ninety-six pounds as if the king's peace had been broken;[67] and fourthly the formulation of a sanction-like clause which threatens anyone contravening the terms just outlined, which likewise finds parallel in the same chapter of the *LDE*.[68] The second similarity listed above makes it particularly apparent that the author of the *HR* 883 annal had the *LDE* in mind when creating his entry. And it is interesting that it was thought important to include detail about the fine due for contravention of the sanctuary terms and likewise of the wording of the otherworldly sanction. These additions are of the same nature as the list of possessions of the Lindisfarne see that was added to annal 854 in the *HR*.[69] While they demonstrate the kind of sources available to the *HR*,[70] they also show that one concern of the *HR* in creating this annalistic version of history was to insert exact information about the rights, possessions and privileges of St Cuthbert's church. It is therefore important to note that, by the time this part of the *HR* was compiled, its author was able to claim that the land granted to the community in 883 stretched from the Tyne to the Tees, a notable extension of the same clause found earlier in the corresponding part of the *LDE* (and of the *HSC*), where it was from the Tyne to the Wear.[71] It seems unlikely that this was a slip of the pen, and more likely that it was an up-to-date statement of what the Durham church

---

64 See H. H. E. Craster, 'The Red Book of Durham: I. Liber Ruber', *EHR* 40 (1925), 504–32 (at 524 for the relevant text, and at 530 for discussion of the relationship to Symeon's *LDE*).
65 *LDE*, ii.6, 100.
66 *LDE*, ii.13, 122; and n. 78.
67 *Ibid.*, 126.
68 *Ibid.* There are related items in the *CMD*, at 524.
69 Above, 206–7.
70 The *HSC* and the *CMD* preserve related details about property rights and possessions.
71 See *LDE*, ii.13, 124 and *HSC*, c.13, 52.

believed it owned,[72] placed within the context of a historical text which, by its nature as an annalistic record, lent credibility to its claims, and which may therefore have been designed for a readership beyond Durham itself.

Sometimes annals in the *HR* show a striking change in emphasis when compared to corresponding parts of the *LDE*. For example, annal 1070 in the *HR*, having begun by inserting a verbatim borrowing from the Worcester *Chronicon*,[73] then continues by giving details of Bishop Æthelwine of Durham's plans to leave his see.[74] One reason given for Æthelwine's plan to vacate the bishopric is that, following events of 1069 and William the Conqueror's 'harrying of the North', and likewise following William's despoiling of English monasteries in 1070, he was unwilling to bear the 'weighty rule' (*graue dominium*) of a foreign people.[75] But Symeon's *LDE*, in recounting Æthelwine's attempted departure, and providing reasons for it, makes for very different reading. For the *LDE* is heavily critical of Æthelwine, accusing him of theft from the Durham church and then recounting a story which demonstrates that Æthelwine was guilty of perjury.[76] One explanation for this difference in tone and character would be to suppose that Symeon is not the author of this part of the *HR*, and various scholars have upheld this view.[77] But others have suggested that discrepancies between the *LDE* and the *HR* may instead represent Symeon changing his mind.[78] If Symeon is thought to be behind this addition to the *HR*, there could be reasons why his tone towards Æthelwine has changed between the writing of the two texts. It may simply be that the passing of time in this

---

72 This was not the first time that St Cuthbert's community claimed to possess lands stretching to the Tees; see the map between pages 118 and 119 in *HSC*.
73 The beginning of annal 1070 in the *HR* (*HR* 8, s.a. 1070, ed. Arnold, ii, 189), about the ransacking of monasteries, is taken from the annal for the same year in the Worcester *Chronicon*.
74 *HR* 8, s.a. 1070, ed. Arnold, ii, 190.
75 Ibid.
76 *LDE*, iii.17, 192–5.
77 J. Hodgson Hinde (ed.), *Symeonis Dunelmensis opera et collectanea*, vol. 1, Surtees Society (Durham, 1867), xxvi–xxvii. Gransden, *Historical Writing*, 149, queries Symeon's authorship of the *HR* and, in discussing the *LDE* as well, she suggests 'it is unlikely that he wrote both since internal evidence suggests that they were by different authors'.
78 H. S. Offler, 'Medieval Historians of Durham', in Offler, *North of the Tees*, 9; and Rollason, *LDE*, xlix.

particular case led to the softening of Symeon's memory about Æthelwine, whose term as bishop of Durham ended *c.* 1071.[79] Or it may be that the two texts had different purposes and different intended audiences, thus shaping how events were construed.[80]

Two other annals in the *HR* are related to sections of Symeon's earlier *LDE*, but again show interesting differences. *HR*'s entry for 1074 begins with a section taken verbatim from the Worcester *Chronicon*,[81] before inserting extra detail about the revival of monasticism in the North.[82] The passage narrates how three monks, Aldwin, Elfwy and Reinfred, desired to restore Northumbria's holy places. In doing so, they were joined by many others, including a man named Turgot. The *HR* then provides further detail about Turgot's life, that he established a relationship with King Olaf of Norway, that he eventually came to Durham and succeeded Aldwin as prior there, that he then became bishop of St Andrews in Scotland, but that he encountered difficulties there, returned to Durham in infirmity and eventually died and was buried in the chapter-house there in 1115. In its entry about the revival of monasticism in Northumbria, this part of the *HR* is clearly related to corresponding chapters in Symeon's *LDE*.[83] But the *LDE*

---

79 It is also interesting that *HR*'s 995 annal about the translation of St Cuthbert's church from Chester-le-Street to Durham is so brief, not only because it is such an important event in the community's history, but also when compared to the detailed account given in *LDE*, iii.1, 144–9.

80 For the suggestion that the *LDE* was written as part of an attempt to protect the Durham community against the predations of Ranulf Flambard, see W. M. Aird, 'The Political Context of the *Libellus de Exordio*', in Rollason (ed.), *Symeon*, 32–45. Given that Ranulf Flambard died in 1128, and that the *HR* may have originally been written *c.* 1129, there may well have been different concerns for Symeon by the time he turned his attention to these parts of the *HR*. Symeon himself had noted Ranulf Flambard's death in the Durham Martyrology: Gullick, 'Hand of Symeon', 22. On Ranulf Flambard, see further, H. S. Offler, 'Ranulf Flambard as Bishop of Durham (1099–1128)', *Durham University Journal* 64 (1971), 14–25, reprinted in Offler, *North of the Tees*, no. VII.

81 *HR* 8, *s.a.* 1074, ed. Arnold, ii, 200–1, where the detail about the election of Hildebrand as pope and his holding of a synod are taken from *Chronicon ex Chronicis*, *s.a.* 1074, ed. and trans. McGurk, iii, 22.

82 *HR* 8, *s.a.* 1074, ed. Arnold, ii, 201–5. Once this account has finished, the *HR* annal returns to a verbatim borrowing from the corresponding annal in the Worcester *Chronicon*. The Paris copy of the *HR* does not include this text about the revival of monasticism in Northumbria, while the *HpB* does: *RHC*, ed. Stubbs, i, 128–31, and there is a much abbreviated version in Liège, Bibliothèque Universitaire, 369C, f. 95rv and also in Cotton Caligula A. viii, f.37rv.

83 *LDE*, iii.21–3, 200–17.

gives more detail about the revival itself and does not contain so much information about Turgot who, at the time of the *LDE*'s publication, is described with these words, that he 'still to this day holds in the church of Durham the office of prior'.[84] It may be that, by the time the *HR* was composed, and after the death of Turgot himself, a detailed account of that prior's career was felt appropriate for insertion in the history books of the Durham community, thus slightly changing the emphasis from how it appears in the corresponding part of the *LDE*. A similar shift may be seen in relation to accounts of the murder of Bishop Walcher of Durham in 1080. Symeon's *LDE* gives an account of Walcher's gruesome death, describing how his failure to stop his own men from offending and harming native Northumbrians led to his murder.[85] The *LDE* apportions little blame to Walcher himself and in fact distances him from having been involved in the actions which led to disagreement between his household and native Northumbrians.[86] By the time of the *HR*'s composition, things had clearly moved on. Relying almost verbatim on the Worcester *Chronicon*, and its account of the murder of Walcher, much more circumstantial detail is given about the reasons for Walcher's death.[87] We learn, for example, that this took place in revenge for the killing of Liulf, a powerful and well-connected Northumbrian, a man who was a 'brave and noble thegn' (*nobilis generosique ministri*).[88] We are also told that the killing of Liulf had occurred at the request of Walcher's chaplain, Leobwine, who in turn requested the help of a man called Gilbert. Although Walcher, in the *HR*'s account, goes on to send messengers throughout Northumbria denying his own involvement, it is clear that the actions of his own chaplain, Leobwine, and of Gilbert implicated Walcher in this murder of Liulf to an extent not seen in Symeon's *LDE*. It is perhaps the case that Symeon, writing the *LDE* at a time closer to these events, could not provide much detail about a situation that was clearly politically sensitive and resulted in

---

84   *LDE*, iii.22, 206–7.
85   *LDE*, iii.23 and particularly iii.24, 212–21.
86   Note this sentence at the beginning of *LDE*, iii.24: 'On the day which had been agreed for the bishop's knights who had done the injuries and those who had suffered them to be reconciled in peace and concord, the bishop and his men came to the place called Gateshead...', 216–17.
87   *HR* 8, *s.a.* 1080, ed. Arnold, ii, 208–10.
88   *HR* 8, *s.a.* 1080, ed. Arnold, ii, 208.

William the Conqueror sending Odo of Bayeux northwards in retaliation for the murder of Walcher.[89] The *HR*, composed later in time, was free of such constraints and able to provide a different picture, relying on the Worcester *Chronicon*.[90]

The fluidity of the annalistic genre: later changes to *HR* in CCCC 139

There are occasions when text that differs between the *Chronicon* and *HR* occurs in part of CCCC 139 that is written over erasure, or made as an addition (various different, near-contemporary annotating hands can be found throughout this part of CCCC 139),[91] or as text that has somehow been altered. There are two possible explanations of why these passages occur in parts of the manuscript that have been erased or added at a different time and possibly by a different hand. It may be that a scribe, or scribes, working through the copy of *HR* made into CCCC 139, and comparing it against an exemplar (perhaps a version of the *HR* that had been composed *c.* 1129), found parts that somehow needed correction, to bring it into line with the text in front of them. Or it may be that those working on CCCC 139 after its copying *c.* 1164,[92] added detail not to be found in the original version of *HR* that they felt was needed at relevant points in the text, either to clarify particular information, or to add detail for its own sake, or on the

---

89 *LDE*, iii.24, 218–21; *HR* 8, *s.a.* 1080, ed. Arnold, ii, 210–11.
90 See also the comments of Rollason, *LDE*, 213, n. 96 and 218, n. 102. One further borrowing in the *HR* from the *LDE* can be found in *HR*'s annal for 1093 and its description of the building of Durham cathedral: Ecclesia noua Dunelmi *est incepta iii. idus Augusti, feria v.*, episcopo *Willelm*o, et Malcolmo rege Scottorum, et *Turgot*o *prior*e *po*nentibus *primos in fundamento lapides* (*HR*, *s.a.* 1093, ed. Arnold, ii, 220), where the italicised words (and parts of words) depend on *LDE*, iv.8, 244.
91 Arnold only rarely identified text that had been added by later hands and so it is very important to recognise which parts of the *HR*'s text in CCCC 139 may have been added at a stage that post-dates its original composition. For further comment about the hands involved in writing CCCC 139, where some of the annotating hands are dated to the twelfth and also to the early thirteenth centuries, see Meehan, 'A Reconsideration', 104–5. For the appearance of annotating hands throughout CCCC 139, not just against the copy of the *HR*, see Dumville, 'Corpus Christi', 372, where the manuscript is described as 'very much a living document', as a result of these additions and corrections.
92 For the possible places of origin of CCCC 139, see above, 204.

basis of sources that had not so far been fully exploited.[93] If this is judged the more likely explanation, then this would represent later layers of text being added to the HR as it was originally composed c. 1129.[94] Sometimes these extra layers can be tentatively identified by comparison with other manuscripts which contain versions of at least parts of the HR.[95]

Some additions made to CCCC 139's version of the HR may simply demonstrate a reader comparing its text with that of the exemplar and making changes. For example, in annal 1010 (on f.90r of CCCC 139), above the place-name *Mirenheafed*, the words *id est eque caput* have been added directly above by a near-contemporary hand in an ink that is lighter than that of the main text. The same annotating hand can be found making other changes to this particular annal in the HR. For, two lines below *Mirenheafed*, the same scribe can be seen correcting *exstiterunt* to *restiterunt* and inserting *regis* interlineally between the words *gener* and *Ethelredi*.[96] These latter two changes/additions have the effect of bringing this part of HR's text closer into line with its ultimate source, the *Chronicon*. This may suggest that this annotating hand was running through this part of CCCC 139's copy of HR and comparing it afresh perhaps with an earlier version of the HR that was closer to that composed c. 1129.

In various sections of CCCC 139's copy of HR there are other minor portions of text that have been corrected or added. This can be seen, for example, with the words *eadem tempestate* in annal 855 (f.78r), which have been added in darker ink over erasure by a thicker pen,[97] or with the word *est* in annal 867 (f.78v).[98] With these kinds of minor changes – which are not in the Worcester *Chronicon* – it is difficult to know whether they were made by cross-reference to the exemplar of HR used by CCCC 139, or whether they were added authorially by scribes at

---

[93] For the extensive marginalia in CCCC 139, see Meehan, 'A Reconsideration', 183–221.
[94] We know that interpolations concerning Hexham have been added to the HR: Offler, 'Hexham and the *Historia Regum*'; and see also Offler, 'Medieval Historians of Durham', 8–9.
[95] For these manuscripts, see above, 202, n. 4.
[96] These changes are obscured by Arnold's edition: HR 8, s.a. 1010, ed. Arnold, ii, p. 142.
[97] HR 8, s.a. 855, ed. Arnold, ii, 103.
[98] HR 8, s.a. 867, ed. Arnold, ii, 105.

work on CCCC 139 after *HR* had been copied for the first time. This difficulty remains for additions like that found in the bottom margin of f.102r for annal 1066, where the words *pridie nonas Ianuarii* appear. A *signe de renvoi* indicates that these words are to be inserted to give greater detail for the date when King Edward the Confessor died.[99] It may be judged more likely that it was the original version of the *HR* which preserved this extra element, since it is the kind of detail that appears relatively frequently in the *Chronicon*, *HR*'s ultimate source. Nevertheless, the fact that the copy of *HR* in the Paris manuscript does not preserve this same phrase on its f.25r should perhaps make us pause for thought.[100] The Parisian manuscript contains an abbreviated version of the *HR*, so this type of omission may have been routine practice and may not necessarily reflect an earlier version of *HR*. But it is interesting that these are the only words from this sentence not found in the Paris manuscript, the rest being exactly the same as that found in CCCC 139. This raises the possibility that the words *pridie nonas Ianuarii* were an authorial change by a scribe working on CCCC 139 after it had first been copied.

Some changes or additions made to CCCC 139 are effected seemingly on the basis of reference to sources other than the Worcester *Chronicon*. At times annals from section 8 of the *HR*, which runs from 848 to 1118, clearly borrow turns of phrase or sentences from annals that can be found in earlier parts of the *HR* itself, namely section 5, which covers the years 849 to 887 and is based mainly on Asser, and section 6, which covers the years 888 to 957.[101] Sometimes these borrowings from earlier sections have been inserted after the initial copying of CCCC 139. At the beginning of annal 853, for example, on f.77v, after the initial dating clause, a scribe has added above the line the phrase, *natiuitatis Elfredi .v.*,[102] which matches the corresponding annal from section 5 of the *HR*.[103]

---

99   *HR* 8, *s.a.* 1066, ed. Arnold, ii, 179. Arnold's edition does not indicate that these words were added later to the work of the main text, and in the bottom margin of the page. See the comments of Meehan, 'A Reconsideration', 179–81.
100 The *HpB* annal likewise does not contain this element: *HpB*, in *RHC*, *s.a.* 1066, ed. Stubbs, i, 108.
101 See above, 206.
102 *HR* 8, *s.a.* 853, ed. Arnold, ii, 101, where this phrase is not identified as an interlinear addition.
103 *HR* 5, *s.a.* 853, ed. Arnold, ii, 70.

Annal 867 offers a particularly interesting example of a later addition being made to section 8 of the *HR*. This annal describes the moment that the Northumbrian kings Osberht and Ælla put aside their mutual hostilities in an attempt to repel the viking threat, only to be routed by Scandinavian forces at York. The greater part of this entry is taken wholesale from annal 867 in the *Chronicon*, except for a few additions, including these two sentences: *Quibus predicti pagani sub suo dominio regem Egbertum prefecerunt. Ecbertus uero regnauit post hec super Northumbros ultra Tine .vi. annis*. The first sentence, from *Quibus* to *prefecerunt*, is added in the lower margin of f.79r.[104] The second sentence occupies part of the main text on that same folio. Because the first sentence has been added in the lower margin of CCCC 139, it is important to question whether it did belong to the original version of *HR* or whether it was added at some point after the copying of CCCC 139 as a unique insertion by a near-contemporary scribe. The fact that this sentence appears in virtually identical form in the *HpB* may suggest that it should be thought of as an original part of the *HR* (or, at least, the archetype of *HR*, made before the transcription of *HR* in *HpB*) rather than a later addition.[105] If so, its writing in the lower margin of CCCC 139 may show a scribe once more checking the version of *HR* in front of him with the exemplar and making corrections as he went. The source of the first sentence is very likely Symeon's *LDE*,[106] while the detail of Ecgberht's reign being for six years may come from a source like the regnal list attached to a late twelfth-century copy of Symeon's *LDE* in Cambridge, University Library, Ff. i. 27.[107]

---

104 *HR* 8, *s.a.* 867, ed. Arnold, ii, 106.
105 *HpB*, in *RHC*, *s.a.* 867, ed. Stubbs, i, 38.
106 *LDE*, ii.6, 98–9, where a very similar sentence can be found: *Quibus (ut dictum est) interfectis, regem Northumbris qui supererant Ecgbertum Dani constituerunt, qui eis tantum qui ad septentrionalem plagam fluminis Tini habitabant sub eorum dominio imperaret*.
107 This detail about the length of Ecgberht's reign can be found on f.129v of Cambridge, UL, Ff. i. 27: *Postea regnauit Ecgbert .vi. annis*. Like CCCC 139, this Cambridge manuscript is thought to be a Durham production which belonged at one time to Sawley Abbey. See discussion in Rollason, *LDE*, xxiv-xxvii and, for the length of reign attributed to Ecgberht by different northern sources, see Rollason, *LDE*, 99, n. 43. Meehan, 'Durham Manuscripts', 442, raises the possibility that the annotators at work on the *HR* in CCCC 139 may have had the very copy of the *LDE* in Ff. i. 27 in front of them: 'The annotator's source may have been a copy of that work, perhaps even the copy in CUL Ff.1.27, since connections between the two manuscripts have long been noted.'

An entry which records the death of Wigred, bishop of St Cuthbert's church, and the succession of Uhtred to the same role, has been inserted as an addition at the end of annal 941 in *HR* (where it is clear that CCCC 139's original annal for that year previously ended with the words *Normannorum dux*).[108] The details may be based once more on Symeon of Durham's *LDE*, or on a common Durham source that underlies both texts.[109] On this occasion the same entry cannot be found at the relevant points in either the abbreviated version of *HR* found in the Paris manuscript, or in the *HpB*. Does this suggest that the scribe responsible for this addition to CCCC 139's text, who was working after the main text of the *HR* had been copied, was comparing this part of the *HR* to other Durham sources, like Symeon's *LDE*, and inserting entries that were thought particularly important for the history of the Durham church? The possibility that this was a later accretion to the original core of the *HR*, made at some point after 1164, should be registered.

An addition of a similar kind, again about episcopal succession at St Cuthbert's church, provides further evidence of the comparing of CCCC 139's *HR* with Symeon's *LDE*.[110] The addition can be found in the lower margin of f.85r in CCCC 139, where the following sentence occurs: *Anno .dccccxlviii. Aldredus qui post Uchtredum fuit episcopus, obiit, et Ailsi ei successit*.[111] Here it is striking that this addition actually results in internally conflicting repetition, since the *HR*'s own annal for 968 then records this death of Aldred and succession of Ælfsige once more.[112] Fortunately, it is not difficult to explain why this mistaken addition was made at this point in CCCC 139. Symeon's *LDE* is once more the likely source of this information – and thereby also of this error. In book 2, chapter 20 of that text, Symeon begins his entry by recording the death of King Edmund and accession of his brother, Eadred. In

---

108 *HR* 8, s.a. 941, ed. Arnold, ii, 125: *Wigredus episcopus obiit, et Getredus successit*. Arnold's transcription of the word *Getredus* could equally well be read as *Uctredus* or as *Uetredus*.
109 *LDE*, ii. 18, 138–9.
110 See also the comments of Meehan, 'A Reconsideration', 251.
111 *HR* 8, s.a. 948, ed. Arnold, ii, 126. The hand making this addition in the lower margin is similar in form to that discussed above as responsible for an addition in the lower margin to annal 867 on f.79r. This entry cannot be found in either the Paris copy of the *HR* or in the *HpB*.
112 *HR* 8, s.a. 968, ed. Arnold, ii, 130.

doing so, Symeon is explicit in saying that this took place in the year 948. Having given this date of 948, only two sentences later, and without any further detail about chronology, Symeon states: 'After Bishop Aldred's death, Ælfsige took over the government of the church in Chester-le-Street in his place...'[113] A careless reader mining Symeon's text for details of episcopal succession at Chester-le-Street could easily assume that this suggests Aldred's death and Ælfsige's succession also took place in 948. But if one continues reading this same chapter of Symeon, we are later told that, 'After he had spent twenty-two years as bishop, Ælfsige died and in his place was elected and consecrated as bishop Ealdhun, a man distinguished by his religion. This was in the year of Our Lord's Incarnation 990...'[114] This clearly dates Aldred's death and the succession of Ælfsige to 968, not 948. It also demonstrates that this later addition to CCCC 139 was probably made on the basis of a reading of Symeon's *LDE*, and that the two texts were being compared with one another.[115]

There are various other sentences which have been added subsequent to the main text of CCCC 139 being copied and which are not found in other copies of *HR* (i.e. in the Parisian manuscript, the *HpB* or in the Liège and Cotton Caligula manuscripts). For example, *HR*'s annal for 1069, on f.104r, begins with a sentence which has been added in the lower margin and reads, *Cenobium sancti Germani de Selebi sumpsit exordium*;[116] a similar kind of addition has been made at the beginning of annal 1098, with the sentence, *Cisterciense cenobium sumpsit exordium*.[117] The content of both annals (about the foundation of *coenobia*,

---

113 *LDE*, ii.20, 140–1.
114 *Ibid.*, 142–3.
115 An addition in the lower margin of f.96v of CCCC 139 (to be included in annal 1042), demonstrates a similar interest in episcopal succession at Durham: *Eadmundus episcopus obiit. Cui Edredus per pecuniam in episcopatum successit, et decimo mense moritur*. This is probably based on *LDE*, iii.9, 168–9. A not-dissimilar entry can be found added in the lower margin of f.100v: *Kinsi Eboracensis archiepiscopus, et Egelwinus Dunelmensis episcopus, et Tosti comes Eboraci deduxerunt regem Malcolmum ad regem Eadwardum* (*HR* 8, s.a. 1059, ed. Arnold, ii, 174). For similar comments about these additions concerning episcopal succession, see Meehan, 'Durham Manuscripts', 217–19 and 442.
116 *HR* 8, *s.a.* 1069, ed. Arnold, ii, 186.
117 Although Arnold has noted that this sentence is an interpolation, he has misplaced where the interpolation occurs, adding it to the end of annal 1097, instead of the beginning of 1098, which is where the *signe de renvoi* indicates it belongs: *HR* 8, *s.a.* 1097, ed. Arnold, ii, 228.

one at Selby and one at Cîteaux) and the similar verbal construction suggest they have been added by someone interested in locating the beginnings of religious communities within the chronological framework provided by *HR*.[118] Because these entries are not found in other copies of *HR*, it is possible – although not certain – that they were added to CCCC 139 at some point after c. 1164, and that they do not belong to the original/earlier version of that text.[119] In *HR*'s 1014 annal in CCCC 139, we are told, in words borrowed verbatim from the *Chronicon*, of King Swein's vision of St Edmund and of the King's eventual death. But, just after the death of Swein is recorded, CCCC 139's version preserves an addition in its lower margin of f.91v of the words, *et apud Eboracum sepultus fuit*. What is the source for this detail that Swein was buried at York? It may be that it was inserted into the margins of CCCC 139 on the basis of some local tradition or knowledge. But it should also be noted that Gaimar's *Estoire des Engleis* which is, in many parts, an Anglo-Norman verse adaptation of the *Anglo-Saxon Chronicle* written – as its most recent editor argues – c. 1137 in Lincolnshire, preserves the same detail about Swein's burial at York.[120] It would be hazardous to place too much weight on the testimony of Gaimar's verse text but, since it is based on earlier chronicle materials, its correspondence with this marginal addition in CCCC 139 is noteworthy.

---

118 Annal 1078 in CCCC 139's *HR* (on f.109v) reads: *fundata est abbatia sancte Marie Eboraci*. Its layout, with the words *Marie Eboraci* written in the lower margin of that folio, suggests that it was added at some point after the writing of the main text. It is not found in other copies of the *HR* (the Liège manuscript notes rather despondently that, for this annal on f.95v, *Nichil dignum*, as does Cotton Caligula A. viii, on f.37v), and so may be another example of a later addition being made to CCCC 139's text of *HR* about the foundation of a new religious house. An addition made in the lower margin of f.121r, to be inserted at the beginning of annal 1113, and again unique to this copy of *HR*, records the arrival of a group of monks in England.

119 As noted earlier (above, 221–2), the abbreviated nature of the other copies of *HR* means that they cannot be used definitively as guides to the contents of the original text of that chronicle.

120 Gaimar, *Estoire des Engleis*, in I. Short (ed. and trans.), *Geffrei Gaimar, Estoire des Engleis, 'History of the English'* (Oxford, 2009), ll. 4157–4162 (226–7; and 413 for a note highlighting a previous suggestion that this information, which is not found in the *Anglo-Saxon Chronicle*, may have come from Kirkstead Abbey). For the dating of Gaimar's text, and its place of origin, see Short, *Geffrei Gaimar*, xii.

The end of annal 1083 in CCCC 139's *HR* provides another interesting later addition. The vast majority of this annal is, as usual, taken verbatim from the *Chronicon*. But in its addition of a sentence at the very end of the annal which reads, *Hoc anno monachi primum in Dunelmum conuenerunt*, a later scribe has added the words *in Dunelmum* after the main text has been copied. This addition may be revealing. The record itself is of the famous introduction of monks into Durham in 1083, a subject that is of great importance to St Cuthbert's community, and is described by Symeon in his *LDE*.[121] It is here, in the *HR*, added to the end of an annal that is mostly otherwise about events at Glastonbury. Because the words *in Dunelmum* were inserted only at a later stage, it suggests that, either in the mind of the author/copyist of CCCC 139's exemplar, or of the main copyist of CCCC 139 itself, the event was so well known that its happening at Durham hardly needed explaining. A similar, although not identical, sentence in the *HpB* may suggest that the words *in Dunelmum* were omitted by the principal copyist of CCCC 139, rather than by whatever exemplar lies behind CCCC 139.[122] A later reader, going through this part of CCCC 139, then felt that this sentence required further clarification.[123]

These later changes and additions made into CCCC 139's text are interesting for showing the ways in which the *HR* continued to be studied and augmented after its first copying *c.* 1164. They demonstrate, for example, a desire to insert further information about northern events not already in *HR* and, in completing such additions, later scribes at work in CCCC 139 were cross-referencing earlier sections of the *HR* itself and also looking more widely at related sources like Symeon's *LDE*. The motivations for scribes at work in a northern religious house (whether that was Durham, Fountains or Sawley) in inserting extra

---

[121] *LDE*, iv.3, 228–35.
[122] *HpB*, in *RHC*, s.a. 1083, ed. Stubbs, i, 137: *Monachi in Dunelmum conuenerunt*; and the same sentence is preserved in Cotton Caligula A. viii on f.38r.
[123] If the omission of the words *in Dunelmum* belonged to the original version of *HR*, it could perhaps demonstrate that text's compilation at Durham, since a Durham author would naturally not feel the need for this kind of clarification about such a famous event in the community's history. But if the omission of these words occurred not in the original version of *HR* but rather at the moment that CCCC 139 was copied, could it confirm that the copyist of CCCC 139's own affiliations were at Durham rather than Sawley, and that the manuscript only later travelled to Sawley?

northern material are fairly clear. But their interests were not confined to northern history, as additions made into CCCC 139 in annals 1100 and 1101 demonstrate.[124]

Conclusion

The writing of history was alive and well in the early to mid-twelfth century and the use of the *Chronicon* in compiling the *HR* shows the scholarly interchanges that were taking place between Worcester and Durham. When making a copy of the *Chronicon*, the author of *HR* took care to insert passages and detail that suited his purpose: examination of these additions reveals – unsurprisingly – that the author had a pro-Durham agenda, seeking to hide any difficult information about illustrious Durham figures and to promote the possessions and rights of the Durham church. The *HR* author also inserted material with specifically northern interest, including, for example, amplification of the *Chronicon*'s 1018 annal with the addition of the record about the battle of Carham and the fact that Uhtred had acted on the side of the *Angli*. There are interesting echoes of Symeon's earlier work, the *LDE*, and, if Symeon can be considered the author of some of these additions to the *HR*, we can gain a fascinating insight into the way that this Durham historian's mind worked, and how his ideas and opinions changed depending on exactly when he was writing.[125] We know from the evidence of his handwriting that Symeon had a firm interest in annals, as he can be found at work on at least three other manuscripts with annalistic entries.[126] The *HR*

---

124 The addition to annal 1100 reads: *Constituuntur in Ierusalem canonici .xxx. tres in monasterio in quo sepulchrum Domini continetur, a Godefrido rege eiusdem urbis et patriarcha Wiberto* (ed. Arnold, ii, 230) and that to annal 1101 reads: *Henricus rex tenuit curiam suam Londoniae in natiuitate Domini, ubi interfuit Lodowicus electus rex Francorum* (ed. Arnold, ii, 232). Note that a variation of this second addition can be found in Cotton Caligula, A. viii, f.41r: *Rex Anglorum Henricus tenuit curiam suam in natale Domini apud Westmonasterium, huic curie interfuit Lothowicus electus rex Francorum, et ad mensam sedebat ad dexteram regis, inter regem scilicet Henricum et Anselmum archiepiscopum.*

125 Above, 217–20.

126 Rollason, *LDE*, xlvi; M. Gullick, 'The Scribes of the Durham Cantor's Book (Durham, Dean and Chapter Library, MS B.IV.24) and the Durham Martyrology Scribe', in Rollason *et al.*, *Anglo-Norman Durham*, 79–109; Gullick, 'Hand of Symeon', 14–31; and Story, 'Symeon as Annalist'. See also C. C. Rozier, 'Symeon of Durham as Cantor and Historian at Durham Cathedral', in K. A.-M. Bugyis, A. B. Kraebel and M. E. Fassler (eds), *Medieval Cantors and their Craft* (York, 2017), 190–206.

may provide further evidence of this interest. The last section of the *HR*, covering annals 1119 to 1129, abandons the Worcester *Chronicon* as its chief source,[127] and offers a quite full and vivid account of events in these years. Attention is given to canon law, major political events (like the White Ship disaster of 1120 that caused the death of several members of the royal family, including Henry I's heir William Adelin), and to some matters of interest to the Durham church. But the most prominent theme recurring throughout these entries is that of the status of the York archiepiscopal see and Thurstan's attempts to guarantee his, and his church's, position in the face of Canterbury assertions. In that way the concluding part of the *HR* continues a theme seen in the previous section when the *Chronicon* had been used as the principal source. The text breaks off after 1129 and it is thought that Symeon may have died at about this time.[128] In its last annal, the *HR* records how Henry I, having secured his position on the Continent, and married his daughter, Matilda, former empress, to Geoffrey of Anjou, returned triumphantly to England. But this prosperity did not last and *HR* reports that Matilda was repudiated by her husband and had to return to Rouen, a sequence of events that 'grievously annoyed the king's mind'. In writing this annal, and describing the oscillating fortunes both of Matilda and the king of England, the author of this part of the *HR* – perhaps Symeon – could not have known that things were to become even more difficult only six years later on the accession of Stephen.[129]

---

127 Nevertheless, Brett, 'John of Worcester', 119–20, draws attention to continuing traces of the *Chronicon*'s style into annal 1120 in the *HR*.
128 Rollason, *LDE*, xlix–l and Rollason, 'Symeon's Contribution', 10–11.
129 On Stephen's reign, see, for example, H. A. Cronne, *The Reign of Stephen, 1135–54: Anarchy in England* (London, 1970) and E. King, 'The Anarchy of Stephen's Reign', *TRHS*, 5th Ser. 34 (1984), 133–53. For the situation in Durham, see A. Young, 'The Bishopric of Durham in Stephen's Reign', in Rollason *et al.*, *Anglo-Norman Durham*, 353–68.

Acknowledgements

The writing of this chapter would not have been possible were it not for various generous research positions awarded to me by Trinity College, Dublin, and facilitated also by Trinity's Long Room Hub. I am sincerely grateful to all of those scholars and friends who made my stays in Dublin so welcoming and productive, in particular Professor Anna Chahoud, Dr Laura Cleaver, Dr Ashley Clements and Dr Bernard Meehan. At the beginning of my work on the Worcester *Chronicon*, I profited from Dr Patrick McGurk's unrivalled understanding of that text, about which he was extremely patient and generous in answering numerous queries. I am likewise indebted to Dr M. Brett, Prof. D. N. Dumville and Dr B. Meehan for reading an early draft of this paper, and to Dr N. McGuigan for many useful comments. I am responsible for any errors that remain.

CHAPTER NINE

The Diocese of Lindisfarne: Organisation and Pastoral Care

ALEX WOOLF

Whether or not the Battle of Carham marked a decisive point in the expansion of *regnum Scottorum*, it remains for us, 1,000 years later, a signifier for that ill-defined process that saw the boundary between England and Scotland emerge along the line of the lower Tweed and the Cheviots. Three hundred years earlier, in Bede's time, the Firth of Forth was conceived of as the boundary between the Picts, and the English and Northumbrian institutions extended at least as far west, along its southern shore, as Abercorn, a mile or two beyond the road and rail bridges that now join Fife to Laudonside.[1] The earliest notice we have of the expansion of the Scots into Northumbria is the frustratingly vague reference in the composite twelfth-century text, based on a tenth-century king list, known as *The Chronicle of the Kings of Alba* (henceforth *CKA*), which notes that during the reign of Ildulb (r. *c.* 954–62) Edinburgh was 'vacated and left to the Scots, as it is to this day'.[2] The perspective of this notice appears to be English and the reference to 'until this day' suggests a non-contemporary intervention at the very least, if not a retrospective composition in its entirety.[3] Post-conquest English sources claim that Lothian was granted to Cinaed II (†995) by Edgar (r. 959–75) in the late tenth century,[4] while *De Obsessione Dunelmi*, from *c.* 1100, claimed that Lothian was surrendered to the Scots by Eadwulf of Bamburgh, Uhtred's brother and

---

1 *HE*, i.12, and for a discussion see James E. Fraser, 'Bede, the Firth of Forth, and the Location of *Urbs Iudeu*', *SHR* 87 (2008), 1–25.
2 *CKA*, 151, 159. For the complexity of the text and the current preferred name see D. N. Dumville, 'The Chronicle of the Kings of Alba', in S. Taylor (ed.), *Kings, Clerics and Chronicles in Scotland, 500–1297*, (Dublin, 2000), 73–86; and Alex Woolf, *From Pictland to Alba, 789–1070* (Edinburgh, 2007), 88–93.
3 Woolf, *From Pictland to Alba*, 193–5. See also P. Dunshea, 'Edinburgh's Renown in the Early Middle Ages', this volume, 60–2.
4 Neil McGuigan, 'Neither Scotland nor England', PhD thesis (University of St Andrews, 2015), 141; Woolf, *From Pictland to Alba*, 211.

successor, shortly after the battle of Carham.⁵ It is possible that *CKA*'s statement synchronising the abandonment of Edinburgh with Ildulb's reign arose from a conflation of this Eadwulf with an early *dux* of Bamburgh who attested West Saxon charters in the period 968–70 and who seems to have succeeded Oswulf, who is last noted as one of those involved in slaying King Eric in 954 and would have had a *floruit* which overlapped with those of Cinaed and Edgar.⁶ It seems as if our present understanding of the sources does not allow us to state with any confidence the point at which parts or all of the northern portion of Northumbria passed into the control of the Scottish kings, though a later rather than an earlier date is perhaps to be preferred.

In this chapter I shall be looking at the diocese of Lindisfarne during the period when its see, or at least its chief relics, were located at Norham-on-Tweed, some ten or eleven miles downstream of Carham. The Church at Norham had been constructed by the ninth-century Bishop Ecgred. *Historia de Sancto Cuthberto*, one of the earliest of the Durham attempts to reconcile evidence relating to the cult of Cuthbert with their own sense of history as a house, relates that:

> Ecgred transported a certain church, originally built by Aidan in the time of King Oswald, from the island of Lindisfarne to Norham and there rebuilt it and translated to that place the body of Saint Cuthbert and that of King Ceolwulf and gave the villa itself to the holy confessor.⁷

How long Cuthbert's relics remained at Norham is not entirely clear. *Historia de Sancto Cuthberto* and later Durham sources claim that the body was moved to various locations starting in the later ninth century but the early eleventh-century text, known as *Secgan*, listing the resting places of saints, identifies Norham as the home to Cuthbert's relics.⁸ In

---

5   McGuigan, 'Neither Scotland nor England', 123, n. 390 and 145–6; and McGuigan, 'The Battle of Carham: An Introduction', this volume, at 31–2.
6   For Eadwulf as a witness, see Simon Keynes, *An Atlas of Attestations in Anglo-Saxon Charters, c. 670–1066* (Cambridge, 1998), table LVI. For a discussion, see McGuigan, this volume. Oswulf's involvement in the death of Eric is recorded by the thirteenth-century chronicler Roger of Wendover; the passage is reproduced and discussed in McGuigan, 'Neither Scotland nor England', 89–90.
7   *HSC*, c.9, 48–9.
8   David Rollason, 'Lists of Saints' Resting-Places in Anglo-Saxon England', *ASE* 7 (1978), 61–93, at 87.

his edition of the text Rollason argued that the northern section of the text contained unrevised ninth-century material but McGuigan has recently argued convincingly that there is no evidence to support this claim.[9] The earliest MS copy of the *Secgan* was written in 1031 and the *terminus post quem* for its composition is 1013 when the relics of St Florence were interred at Peterborough.[10] This might be taken to imply that Cuthbert still lay at Norham after 1013 suggesting, perhaps, that his translation to Durham was part of Alfred son of Westhou's collection of the relics of saints originally interred at Jarrow, Tynemouth, Hexham, Lindisfarne, Melrose, Coldingham and Tyninghame; a geographical spread within which Norham lies fairly centrally.[11] McGuigan produces other evidence suggesting that Cuthbert remained at Norham until the eleventh century and also that the combination of the Bernician bishoprics into a single see may have been somewhat later than has usually been assumed. There is no need to rehearse these arguments in full here.[12]

Instead I want to start by turning to a list of properties pertaining to the diocese of Lindisfarne which is preserved in both *Historia Regum Anglorum* 2 and Roger of Howden's *Chronica*.[13] These texts go back to a common exemplar and are very close in form. In both the list of properties is inserted after an account of events of the later ninth century. The passage begins by mentioning Carlisle, *Lugubalia id est Luel*, to which the *Historia Regum* version adds the gloss *nunc dicitur Carliel*, which is not present in Howden's version. The 'caer' prefix to the place-name is otherwise first attested in the eleventh century and may be a coinage of that era suggesting perhaps that the *id est Luel* phrase predates this period. Carlisle is followed by Norham and then a rather vague claim to all the churches between the Tweed and the southern Tyne and beyond the western desert. This last claim must date to the period after the diocese of Hexham and Lindisfarne were merged, but the lack of detail suggests that it has a different, later, origin than the text as a whole and has been added to the list of specific locations after the merging of the two dioceses. There then follows a more interesting

9   *Ibid.*, 68; McGuigan, 'Neither Scotland nor England', 77–8.
10 McGuigan, 'Neither Scotland nor England', 77.
11 *LDE*, iii.7; discussed in Woolf, *From Pictland to Alba*, 235–6.
12 McGuigan, 'Neither Scotland nor England', 58–81 and 178–206.
13 *RHC*, ed. Stubbs, i, 45; and *HR*, 101.

list of places described as *mansiones* ending with Norham (again). The *Historia Regum*'s list comprises *Carnham, Culterham*, two *Geddewrd* (on the south side of the Teviot), *Mailros, Tigbrethingham, Eoriercorn* (to the west), *Edwinesburch, Pefferham, Aldham, Tinnigaham, Coldingaham, Tillmuthe, Norham*. Howden's list is largely the same, with minor spelling differences but adds *Bricgham* before *Tillemuthe*. Most of these places are readily identifiable on the map today. *Geddewrd* is Jedburgh (and Bonjedward?); *Mailros*, Melrose; *Edwinesburch*, Edinburgh; *Aldham*, Auldhame; *Tinnigaham*, Tyninghame; *Coldingaham*, Coldingham; *Bricgham*,[14] Birgham; *Tillmuthe*, the confluence of the Till and the Tweed, perhaps represented by the present day St Cuthbert's farm. Less certain are the identifications of *Carnham, Culterham, Tigbrethingham, Eoriercorn* and *Pefferham*, though the last two are almost certainly Abercorn, the last Northumbrian church site known before one reaches the Antonine Wall, and Aberlady which lies at the mouth of the Peffer Burn and from where part of the shaft of a Northumbrian cross has been recovered.[15] *Tigbrethingham* might well be Stow-in-Wedale since this had a reputation for being an important and ancient church later in the Middle Ages and the name 'Stow' literally just means '[holy] place' and may not have been the site's original designation. This leaves us with *Carnham* and *Culterham*. The latter is not currently identifiable[16] but it has been common to identify the former with Carham-on-Tweed, partially on the basis of the similarity

---

14   The early forms of this name suggest that the first element is the word for 'bridge'. In recent times there was certainly a ford between Birgham and Carham and the possibility that there was at some point a bridge over the Tweed here is interesting, though it is perhaps more likely that the bridge referred to was a smaller affair crossing a stream or bog on the north side of the Tweed. I would like to thank David Petts and Alan James for discussing this with me.

15   Now in the National Museum of Scotland, item IB298, details can be found at: https://canmore.org.uk/event/1008847. More recent excavations at Aberlady have also produced material relating to this period, including a coin of Eanred, a ninth-century Northumbrian king, but these await full publication.

16   In 2007, following Ekwall, I tentatively suggested Holmcultram in Cumberland (*From Pictland to Alba*, 82), but this was probably grasping at straws. Coulter in Clydesdale also preserves the first element but is almost certainly too far west. The place name is English *-ham* combined with a British term made up of *cul* plus *tir* menaing a narrow strip of land, and the geographical positioning of the name in the list might suggest a site lying on the right bank of the Tweed between Carham and Jedworth at somewhere such as Sprouston or Crailing. Eilert Ekwall, *The Concise Oxford Dictionary of English Place-Names*, 4th edn (Oxford, 1960), s.v. 'Holme Cultram', at 246.

of the name (though this is not without problems)[17] and partially on the basis of geographical groupings. The list from Abercorn to Coldingham represents a clear geographical progression, west to east, through Lothian; similarly, it would be argued, the first four *mansiones* would seem to be located between Norham and the Teviot on the right bank of the Tweed, Melrose (presumably Old Melrose) is located between Teviot and Tweed and *Tigbrethingham* somewhere *en route* between Melrose and Abercorn. The final two *mansiones* prove slightly more problematic for this analysis. Birgham is directly opposite Carham, barely a kilometre away across the Tweed, while *Tillmuthe* would seem most naturally to fall on the right bank of the Tweed between Norham and Carham. Neither of these last two sites seems to follow particularly easily on from Coldingham and the fact that the latter is the only site in what is now Berwickshire, presumably one of the more populous districts in the diocese, is at first sight somewhat surprising but can probably be explained.

Before we go further we should probably ask ourselves what these *mansiones* were imagined to be. In light of the fact that nine of them have names terminating in either *-ham* or *-ingham* we should maybe turn our attention to Alan James's essay on these Old English place-name elements in Scotland, published in 2010.[18] An exhaustive study suggested that many, perhaps most of the places with such names in south-eastern Scotland, were in fact ecclesiastical sites. On our list Norham, Jedburgh, Melrose, Abercorn, Auldhame, Tyninghame and Coldingham certainly were ecclesiastical sites and, as we have seen, remains of a Northumbrian cross shaft have been recovered at Pefferham/Aberlady. Perhaps this is enough to go on to suggest that all of our *mansiones* were in fact church settlements and not merely estates owned by the bishop. It is equally clear, however, that this cannot be an exhaustive list of churches located in the diocese of Lindisfarne. This said, the Latin word *mansio* is not used for churches or monastic buildings themselves (although it is ultimately the source of Scots 'manse') so we might best imagine that what we are being told is that these are places where the bishop has a house, in most, perhaps all, cases lying

---

17 The place name Carham derives from OE *Carrum*; possibly our manuscript form derives from an original *Carrum* plus *ham*.
18 Alan G. James, 'Scotland's *-ham* and *-ingham* Names: A Reconsideration', *JSNS* 4 (2010), 103–30.

alongside a church complex. The *mansiones*, then, are perhaps best understood as residences owned by the bishop where he and his household, or his agents, might stay during visitations and that what the list effectively gives us is a rough guide to the episcopal circuit of the diocese. It is further possible that the original distribution of the *mansiones* in the list may have reflected secular division within northern Bernicia. Certainly in Lothian, with the exception of Auldhame for which a special explanation may be possible,[19] the *mansiones* are evenly spread along the coast and may each have been located in a separate shire paired with some royal centre.

If this were the case then we might look for a parallel in the Welsh text known as 'The Seven Bishop-Houses of Dyfed' which has been edited by Thomas Charles-Edwards.[20] This short tract lists seven locations of what it calls, in Welsh, *esgobty*, 'bishop-houses'. This lists includes Mynyw (St Davids), which was or after became the see, but also names a church site in each of the six other *cantrefi* or 'shires' which made up the seven cantrefs of Dyfed during the ninth to eleventh centuries. In his 1971 edition of the text, Chares-Edwards argues that each house had its own bishop, but by 2016 he was more cautious on this point, putting more stress on the fact that the tract itself says that the head of each house should be an abbot. I would like to reiterate a suggestion I originally made in 2007 that the episcopal connection with these houses was related to the circuit made by the bishop for visitation and tribute collection.[21] As Charles-Edwards points out in his 2016 discussion, the list of houses is not one of all the significant churches in the region, and the even distribution across the *cantrefi* is almost certainly of administrative significance. Returning to our own list of *mansiones*, the instability of the list in the section along the Tweed makes a definitive examination more complex, but something similar to the Lothian section and the Dyfed document may lie behind our extant versions.

---

19 Alex Woolf, 'Auldhame and Tyninghame', in Anne Crone and Erlend Hindmarch (eds), *Living and Dying at Auldhame: The Excavation of an Anglian Monastic Settlement and Medieval Parish Church* (Edinburgh, 2016), 166–70.

20 Thomas Charles-Edwards, 'The Seven Bishop-Houses of Dyfed', *Bulletin of the Board of Celtic Studies* 24 (1970–2), 247–62. Discussed most recently in Charles-Edwards, *Wales and the Britons, 350–1064*, 596–8.

21 Alex Woolf, 'The Expulsion of the Déisi from Dyfed', in Karen Jankulak and Jonathan Wooding (eds), *Ireland and Wales in the Middle Ages* (Dublin, 2007), 102–15, at 112.

I commented earlier on the absence of any *mansiones* between Coldingham and Norham and this may be compared with the absence of any holdings below Norham on the right bank of the Tweed. The solution to this, at first glance, surprising situation may be that the bishop of Lindisfarne held all the land in these regions. Islandshire, south of the Tweed, has long been recognised as falling into this category, but I would like to suggest that the lands opposite it on the left bank, which appear as dependent territories of Berwick in King Edgar of Scotland's charter of *c.* 1095 and which Geoffrey Barrow identifies as the earlier 'Berwickshire' (though it comprises only the southern portion of the modern county) were also originally episcopal holdings analogous to Islandshire and Norhamshire.[22] Edgar of Scotland granted this land, together with the much less wealthy Coldinghamshire, to Durham in their entirety, and it seems likely that this grant was a confirmation or restoration of an earlier situation aimed to reassure the community of St Cuthbert that the establishment of Scottish royal power in the region did not threaten their rights there.[23] This embryonic Berwickshire may well have started life as the northern portion of Islandshire, the block endowment of Lindisfarne. An assertion that such an early block endowment had been made appears in *Historia de Sancto Cuthberto* c.4, which makes a claim over all the land south of the Tweed between the Till and the sea as far south as the Warren Beck (which has its estuary between Bamburgh and the ford across to Lindisfarne) together with all the land north of the Tweed between the confluences of that river with the Leader and the Whiteadder. To this is added the lands appended to Tyninghame between Lammermuir and the Inveresk. Rather curiously the claim does not extend to encompass Coldinghamshire and Berwickshire east of the Whiteadder. Ted Johnson-South rightly points out that such a large endowment cannot date back to Cuthbert's own time and a later passage in the *Historia* (c.9) describes King Ceolwulf (r. 729–37) as the donor of Norham itself (which falls within the area outlined in c.4)[24] and *Historia Regum* 2 makes the claim that it was thanks to Ceolwulf's endowments that the Lindisfarne monks were able to regularly drink

---

22 For a map of the settlements included in this early 'Berwickshire', see G. W. S. Barrow, *The Kingdom of the Scots* (Edinburgh, 1973), 30, with discussion 28–32.
23 *ESC*, no.15. Discussed in *ibid*.
24 South, *HSC*, 79–80.

beer and wine rather than the water and milk to which they had been formerly confined.[25] Whether the huge territory claimed by *HSC* had really been given by Ceolwulf must remain doubtful. Balthere (d. 756), the founder of Tyninghame, was still alive when Ceolwulf abdicated, so the section north of Lammermuir was almost certainly not in the hands of the church of Lindisfarne in the eighth century or indeed at the time when our list of *mansiones* was compiled.

As it stands the list of *mansiones* would seem to date to some point in the period when Cuthbert's body, and the effective see of the diocese, lay at Norham, between about AD 830 and 1030. In his letter to Bishop Ecgberht of York, Bede made it clear that it was expected that Northumbrian bishops would tour their dioceses on an annual basis in order to confirm baptisms and consecrate new churches, and also that they would take their share of ecclesiastical dues in return for doing so.[26] If the interpretation put forward here is correct, that the *mansiones* at the ecclesiastical sites mentioned in this list represent episcopal residences used by the bishop and his household whilst making a circuit of his diocese, then we may have some of the best evidence for how bishops exercised their authority in the pre-conquest English Church. Our surviving evidence is so heavily skewed towards monastic or quasi-monastic foundations that we get few descriptions of bishops exercising their pastoral role, and when such episodes appear, for example in the lives of Wilfrid or Cuthbert, they are usually devoid of any information about the logistics involved.[27] Our inability to date the prototype of this tract more closely than *c.* 830–1030 remains frustrating, but is very much of a piece with most material relating to Northumbria in the Viking Age. It can only be hoped that closer textual analyses and archaeological chance may gradually help us to move forward. With regard to Carham we might, for

---

25   *HR*, 101.
26   Bede, 'Epistola ad Ecgbertum Episcopum', ed. C. Plummer, *Venerabilis Baedae Opera Historica*, 2 vols (Oxford, 1896) i, 405–23. For a discussion of Bede's agenda and the context see John Blair, *The Church in Anglo-Saxon Society* (Oxford, 2005), 108–17. For a wider discussion of episcopal rights and duties, see Catherine Cubitt, 'Pastoral Care and Conciliar Canons: The Provisions of the 747 Council of *Clofesho*', in John Blair and Richard Sharpe (eds), *Pastoral Care before the Parish* (Leicester, 1992), 193–211.
27   Blair, *The Church in Anglo-Saxon Society*, 94–5 describes well the difficulty in identifying this aspect of episcopal activity in England.

the time being, view this snapshot of the diocese of Lindisfarne/ Norham as reflecting the period immediately preceding the battle, and Alfred son of Westhou's collection of saints' relics from the region as acts of retrenchment following the Northumbrian defeat there.

Index

1006, battle of 9, 17, 19, 21–2, 91, 130–2, 147

Abercorn (West Lothian) 113–14, 231, 234–5
Aberlady (East Lothian) 113, 165, 234–5
Adam of Bremen, Saxon historian (†c. 1081) 138
Adam of Dryburgh, Carthusian writer (†c. 1212) 38n
Addingham (Yorkshire) 135n
Adulf mcEtulfe, king of Northern English (†934) 98, 105–6, 141–2
Áed mac Cináeda, king of Picts (†878) 17, 19
Aidan, saint (†651) 176, 190, 192, 232
Ælfgifu, daughter of Uhtred (fl. c. 1010) 22, 131, 146–7, 150
Ælfhelm, ealdorman in Northumbria (†1006) 129
Ælfhere, ealdorman in Mercia (†983) 124–5
Ælfric of Eynsham, English writer (†) 86n
Ælfric, ealdorman in Wessex (fl. 992–1016) 146
Ælfsige, bishop of St Cuthbert (fl. 970) 130, 143–4, 224–5
Ælfstan son of Eadred, Northern English magnate 116, 136
Ælla, king of Northumbria (†867) 98, 106–7, 120, 133–6, 139, 143, 223
Aelred of Rievlaux, Cistercian writer and abbot (†1167) 19n, 102n
Æscbriht (or *Esbrid*), son of Eadred, Northern English magnate 116, 136
'Æthelstan A', scribe 37n
Æthelflæd, 'lady' of Mercia (†918) 99

Æthelred II, the Unready, king of England (r. 978–1016) 10, 22, 80, 90, 92–3, 103, 127, 129–31, 145–7, 150
Æthelred, king of East Anglia (fl. 869×) 97
Æthelred, king of Mercia (†911) 99–100, 141
Æthelstan, king of Wessex and England (r. 924–39) 37, 83, 99, 104, 106n, 116, 125–6, 140, 142
Æthelthryth, daughter of King Ælla 135, 139
Æthelwald, bishop of Lindisfarne (†c. 740) 175, 179–81, 183
  cross of 179–84
Æthelweard, ealdorman and historian (fl. c. 980) 87n, 100, 104, 138–9, 241
Æthelwine, bishop of Durham (†c. 1071) 217–18
Æthelwine, ealdorman of East Anglia (†992) 124–5
Æthelwulf Eadwulfing, king of the Northern English see *Adulf mcEtulfe*
Æthelwulf, king of Wessex (†858) 142, 206
Æthelwulf, name 141
Airer Saxan ('coastland of the English') 118
Alba, Gaelic word 17, 37, 60
  see also Scotland; *Scotia*
Alcuin, Northumbrian scholar (†804) 107
Aldred see Ealdred
Aldwin, prior of Durham (fl. 1083) 218
Alexander I, king of Scotland (r. 1107–24) 42, 45–6, 64, 77
Alexander III, king of Scotland (r. 1249–86) 41
Alfred, king of Wessex (r. 871–99) 99, 117, 139, 206
  Laws of Ælfred 123

INDEX

Alfred, Northern English magnate (fl. 920s) 116
Alfred, possible Eadwulfing (fl. 927) 140n
Alfred, son of West(h)ou (fl. *c.* 1030) 117n, 197, 233, 239
Alfred of Beverley, chronicler (fl. *c.* 1150) 3n, 145
Allerdale (Cumberland), province 92, 101, 119
Aln, river (Northumberland) 25, 112n
Alnmouth (Northumberland) 166, 185, 188–9, 191, 200
Alnwick (Northumberland) 24, 26
Alt Clut *see* Dumbarton
Alwinton (Northumberland) 156
Aneirin, legendary Welsh poet 53–5
Anfred, Danelaw magnate (fl. 956) 125–6
Angers (Maine-et-Loire) 105
Anglo-Saxon Chronicle (*ASC*), English annal tradition 3, 9, 12–16, 67, 80–1, 83, 86n, 100, 104, 118–19, 123–4, 127, 129, 131, 133–4, 136, 140, 143, 145, 147, 149, 211, 226
Angus, Scottish province 19, 24, 25
Anjou, French province 105, 229
Annales Cambriae, Welsh–Latin annals 14–16, 83–4
Annandale (Dumfriesshire), border province 20, 42–4, 46, 48, 90, 101n
Annals of Clonmacnoise, Irish annals 59, 60, 98, 141
Annals of Tigernach, Irish annals 59, 98n
Annals of Ulster, Irish annals 17, 18, 59, 80, 97, 139
Anselm, archbishop of Canterbury (†1109) 212, 213n
Antonine Wall 234
Arfon (Caernarfonshire) 55–6
Argyll, Scottish region 18–19, 93
Arthur, legendary Welsh king 56, 68–9
Ascured, Danelaw magnate (fl. 958) 125–6
Asser, Welsh bishop (†909) 203, 206n, 222
Atholl (Perthshire), Scottish province 25
Auldhame (East Lothian) 113, 234–6
Ayered, Danelaw magnate (fl. 958) 125–6
Ayrshire 72, 108, 118

Bakewell (Derbyshire), congress of (920) 140

Bamburgh 11, 21, 27–8, 31, 95–6, 100, 104–5, 109, 111, 116, 139–40, 149, 232, 237
  deanery of 29
  'high reeve' at 101
  House of *see* Eadwulfings (House of Bamburgh)
  rulers of 21–3, 30–2, 79–80, 95–121, 126–31, 135, 140–9
  sacking of (993) 127, 130, 145
Bannockburn, battle of (1314) 1, 36
Balthere, saint (†756) 112, 238
Beattock Summit (Lanarkshire) 88
Bede, English historian (†735) 7, 69, 121, 160, 180, 192, 198, 203, 231, 238
Bedlington (Northumberland) 188m
Bernicia, early medieval kingdom 28, 105, 111, 161, 172, 233, 236
Berwick, 'shire' of 237; *see also* Merse
Bewcastle Cross 178, 179n, 193, 198n, 199
Birgham (Berwickshire) 9n, 29, 154, 167, 234–5
Blackadder (Berwickshire), river 109
Blaydon (Durham) 137n
Boisil, saint (†*c.* 661) 197–8
Bonedd y Saint, Welsh genealogical tract 56, 63, 65, 67, 76–7
Border Commissioners (16th century) 154, 166
Bothal (Northumberland) 188n
Boulogne Gospels 187
Bower, Walter 8, 36, 75
Bowmont Water, border river 109, 153, 155–6, 159, 163–4, 169
Breamish, river (Northumberland) 112, 156, 159n, 163
Brian Bóruma (Brian Boru), Irish high-king (†1013) 93
Britons *see* Strathclyde/Cumbrians
  language (Welsh, Cornish, Cumbric) 15, 20, 37, 51–2, 58, 64, 87–9, 91, 94, 119, 236
Brough Law (Northumberland) 163
Brunanburh, battle of (937) 1, 24, 99, 142, 151
Brough (Westmorland) 8
Brix, Adam de 44n
Bruce (de Brus), Robert, Norman magnate (†1142) 43–5, 48
Buchan, Scottish province 61–2

INDEX

Buern Bucecarle, literary character 133
Bunkle (Berwickshire) 166
Burgh-by-Sands (Cumberland) 8, 9n
Burhred (or Burgred), king of Mercia (†874×) 136, 206
Burton-on-Trent (Staffordshire) 70–1, 74
Byrhtferth of Ramsey, English Benedictine writer (fl. 1000) 203
Caddonlee (Selkirkshire) 25
Cait, region north of Dornoch Firth 18
Caithness, Scottish province 18
Calvary, Roman soldiers at 188–9
Canterbury 187n, 212–13, 228–9
cantref 236
Cardrona (Peeblesshire) 89
Carham (Northumberland) 26–9, 113, 154–6, 158–60, 163, 168–71, 174, 176, 232, 234–5
    battle of (c. 1018) 1–32, 33–5, 47, 50, 79–82, 84–6, 88, 90, 92, 94, 95–6, 121, 129, 131–2, 147, 151–2, 168, 170, 175, 195, 202–3, 205, 228, 231–2
    church/minster at 27–9, 113, 158–9, 165–7, 170–1, 200, 234–5, 238–9
    etymology of 26–7, 235n
    fords at 154–5
    sculpture at 174, 177, 182, 199–200
    'shire' of 20, 158
    Ulfchil, *clericus* of 28–9
Carl, son of Thurbrand the Hold (fl. c. 1030) 148–9, 209n
Carlisle (Cumberland) 8, 26–7, 44, 113, 119, 233
Castellum Puellarum see under Edinburgh
Castle Eden (Durham) 116
Catraeth (possibly Catterick, Yorkshire) 51
Causantín mac Áeda (or Constantine II), king of Scotland (†952) 83–5, 99
Causantín mac Cinaeda (or Constantine I), king of Picts (†877) 17, 138
Causantín mac Cuilén (or Constantine III), king of Scotland (†997) 17
Causantín, mormaer of Fife (fl. c. 1128) 102n
Ceolwulf, king of Northumbria (†764) 176, 192, 198, 232, 237–8
Charles the Bald (emperor; †877), First Bible of 187
charters 40, 112, 161
    Anglo-Saxon 83, 101–3, 105, 116, 122–7, 129–30, 141–6, 158, 232

Scottish royal 40–5, 46n, 47–8, 74, 112, 237
Chester 10, 77
    congress of 973 86, 122n, 144
Chester-le-Street (Durham) 117, 176–7, 179, 215–16, 218, 225
Cheviot Quarry 161–2
Cheviots 120, 153–7, 160, 162–4, 213
Chew Green (Northumberland) 154, 156
Chilnecase 70, 72
Chronica of Roger of Howden see Howden, Roger of
Chronicle of 957, *Historia Regum* 'section 6' 97, 138, 203, 222
Chronicle of Melrose 2–4, 75–6, 80n, 82, 202–3n
Chronicle of the Kings of Alba (*CKA*), tenth-century Scoto-Latin chronicle 50, 60–1, 72n, 76, 85, 103–4, 117–18, 231
Chronicon ex Chronicis, Anglo-Latin annals attributed to John of Worcester 2–3, 7, 80, 113, 140, 203–15, 217–223, 226–9
Chronicum Scotorum, Irish annals 60
Ciarán, saint (6th century) 189
Cinaed mac Ailpín (or Kenneth Mac Alpin), king of the Picts (†858) 6, 17, 22, 60
Cinaed mac Duib (or Kenneth III Mac Duff), king of Scotland (†1005) 17
Cinaed mac Maíl Choluim (or Kenneth II), king of Scotland (†995) 21, 23, 61, 103, 118, 122n, 144, 231–2
Cîteaux Abbey (Côte-d'Or) 226
Cividale del Friuli (Udine) 187–8
Clann Ruaidrí (House of Moray) 18–19
Clare, Gilbert de [Gilbert fitz Richard], Norman baron (†1117) 77
Clennell Street (Northumberland) 156
Clonmacnoise (Offaly), Cross of the Scriptures 189–91
Clontarf, battle of vii, 2, 15n, 93, 120
Clyde 34, 79
    Firth of 87, 93–4, 118
    'Clyde-folk' see Strathclyde
Clydesdale (Lanarkshire), region of southern Scotland 20, 25, 68, 90
Clydno Eidyn 55–6, 76
Cnut, king of England (r. 1016–35) 5, 8, 10, 12, 14, 22–3, 30, 80–1, 92, 125, 127–8, 131, 137, 147, 149, 190n, 209n

INDEX

Cocklaw (Northumberland) 156, 169
Cogad Gáedel re Gallaib, Irish text (12th century) 93, 120, 138
coins 97, 99, 132–3, 233, 234n
Coldingham (Berwickshire) 113, 117n, 165, 233–5, 237
  'shire of' 237
Coldstream (Berwickshire) 154, 161–2, 172
Colmán mac Ailella, ab. of Clonmacnoise (†926) 190
comet 5–6, 13, 80
Conchubranus, Irish hagiographer (fl. *c.* 1100) 67, 70–1, 73–4
Condé-sur-l'Escaut (Nord) 215
Copenhagen Gospels 186
Coquet, river (Northumberland) 120
Coquetdale 154, 156
Corbet, Walter (fl. 1160×1203) 29n
Corbridge (Northumberland) 117
  battle of (918) 21, 98, 115, 120, 141, 152
Cornhill-on-Tweed (Northumberland) 153–5, 157, 159, 165, 169
Cornwall 71, 77, 108n,
Crailing (Roxburghshire) 234n
Crayke (Yorkshire) 116, 135,
Crínán, ab. of Dunkeld (†1045) 149
Crock Cleugh (Roxburghshire) 164
Cronica Monasterii Dunelmensis (*CMD*), Anglo-Latint tract (*c.* 1080s) 113, 207, 215
Crookham (Northumberland) 169
Cuilén mac Ilduilb, king of Scotland (†971) 72n, 85–6
Culhwch ac Olwen, Welsh tale 56–7
Culterham, unidentified place-name 113, 234
Cumberland, English county 20, 39, 42n, 44, 92, 104, 119
Cumberland (Old English word) 93, 108n, 119
Cumbria/Cumbrians *see* Strathclyde
Cuthbert, saint (†687)
  bishops/episcopate of 28, 115n, 117, 144, 148, 224
  church/corporation/monastery of 91, 112–13, 116, 133–5, 137, 145–6, 159
  community of 5, 27, 101–2, 158–9, 165–6, 175–7, 179, 182–4, 190, 192, 217n, 227, 237

Consuetudines Sancti Cuthberti 116, 215
gospel book of St John (from Cuthbert's tomb) 180n
person/shrine 5, 112, 113n, 117, 137, 148, 166, 175, 178–81, 186, 192, 197–8, 215, 218n, 232–3, 237–8
See also Historia de Sancto Cuthberto
cuttlefish 145, 148
Cynesige, archbishop of York (†1060) 225n
Cytelbearn, Danelaw magnate (fl. 963) 125–6
d'Avranches, Hugh, earl of Chester (†1101) 77
Dacre (Cumberland) 104–5
Dál Riata (Dalriada), early Scottish polity 6, 93
Danes
  Anglo-Danes / Anglo-Norse 13–14, 21–2, 95, 101, 107–10, 116, 120, 133, 135–6, 138–40, 143, 148
  of Denmark/Scandinavia 60–1, 127–8, 130–3
  of Northumbria 95, 101, 103, 106, 115–17, 120, 137–40, 143
Danelaw, or Scandinavian England 21, 96, 99, 115–17, 120, 125, 137–8, 141–2, 146
  northern Danelaw 95n, 98, 100, 116, 130
  southern Danelaw 14, 99, 109
David I, mac Maíl Choluim, king of Scotland (r. 1124–53) 19n, 26, 35, 42–6, 48, 71, 74–6, 90, 114
Dawston (Roxburghshire) 153
De Obsessione Dunelmi (*DOD*), Anglo-Latin tract (*c.* 1100) 11–12, 15–17, 22, 30–1, 80n, 81, 91, 130–1, 145–8, 208–9, 231
De Primo Saxonum Adventu (*DPSA*), Anglo-Latin tract (*c.* 1120) 104n, 108n, 110–11, 122, 127, 149, 208
De Situ Albanie, Latin tract (*c.* 1200) 55
Deer, Book of 25
Degsastan, battle of (*c.* 603) 153
Deheubarth, Welsh kingdom 77
Derby 147
Dere Street 91, 152–6
Devil's Causeway (Northumberland) 154–5
Dewsbury (Yorkshire) 194

INDEX

Diarmait mac Cerbaill, Irish king (†565) 189
Dingwall (Ross) 138n
Domnall Bán mac Donnchada (or Donald III), king of Scotland (r. 1093/4–7)' 41, 62, 75
Domnall mac Causantín (or Donald II), king of Scotland (†900) 18n, 61
Donnchad mac Crínáin (or Duncan I), king of Scotland (r. 1034–40) 6–8, 9, 17, 33, 149
Donnchad mac Maíl Choluim (or Duncan II), king of Scotland (†1094) 33, 39–42, 112
Donnchad I, mormaer/earl of Fife (†1154) 36n
Dornoch Firth 18
Downham (Northumberland) 157
Downpatrick 183
Drip Ford (river Forth, Stirlingshire) 36n
Drumelzier (Peeblesshire) 89
Dub mac Maíl Choluim, king of Scotland (†967) 18
Dubgaill, Gaelic term for the Great Army and Anglo-Danes 106, 134, 138
Dublin vii, 60, 93, 94n, 96, 98–9, 120
Dumbarton (Alt Clut), northern British power centre 56, 58, 68–70, 83, 86–8, 93
Dunbar (East Lothian) 28, 120
  earls of 38n, 48
Dundonald (Ayrshire) 70
Dunfermline (Fife) 75
Dunion Hill (Roxburghshire) 164
Dunkeld (Perthshire) 67, 192
Dunnottar (Kincardineshire) 61
Duns (Berwickshire) 170
Durham 28, 41, 117, 148, 176, 179–83, 187–8, 200, 202n, 218
  battle at (1039) 17, 22n, 91, 130, 149,
  cathedral 40, 75n, 176, 180, 190, 197, 217
  community of 4, 7, 13, 40–2, 48, 82n, 92, 112n, 179, 204, 207–12, 216–18, 224, 227–9, 232–3, 237
  county of 114, 122, 131, 148
  diocese of 29, 111, 115n, 213, 217, 225n, 233
  Liber Vitae 145
  St Oswald's Church 182, 199n
  see also Cuthbert, church of

Dyfed, Welsh kingdom 77, 236

Éadaoin (Etain, Edana), Irish saint 73–4
Eadred, earl in northern England (fl. c. 1000) 146
Eadred, king of England (r. 946–55) 99–103, 106, 122, 126, 131, 142–3, 224
Eadred *Lulisc*, ab. of Lindisfarne (9th century) 215–6
Eadred son of Ricsige, Northern English magnate (fl. 899×924) 136, 139
Eadric Streona, ealdorman in Mercia (†1017) 10–12, 129, 146–7
Eadwulf, king of Northern English (†913) 21, 97–8, 100, 104, 110, 115n, 139–40, 141, 143
Eadwulf *Cudel*, ruler of Bamburgh (fl. c. 1020) 11–12, 24, 30, 81, 92, 117, 127–8, 148, 231–2
Eadwulf *Rus*, Northern English leader (fl. 1080) 196
Eadwulf *Yvelcild*, ruler of Bamburgh (fl. 968–70) 104, 116, 122, 127, 130, 143–4, 232
Eadwulf son of Uhtred, ruler of Bamburgh (†1041) 104, 128, 149–50
Eadwulfings (House of Bamburgh) 21–3, 32, 88, 91–2, 95–8, 105–21, 126–31, 140–2
Ealdhun, bishop of St Cuthbert (fl. 1009) 5–6, 9, 13, 16, 31, 130, 145, 146, 148, 150, 190, 225
ealdorman / ealdordom, West Saxon institution 22, 101–4, 123–5, 142–3
Ealdred (or Aldred), bishop of St Cuthbert (fl. 960s) 224–5
Ealdred (or Aldred), priest of St Cuthbert (fl. 970)
  colophon of 178n, 180–1n
Ealdred Eadwulfing, ruler of Bamburgh (fl. 927) 83, 104–5, 111, 115, 140–3
Ealdred son of Oswulf, possible bishop of St Cuthbert (fl. 958–9?) 21, 144
Ealdred son of Uhtred (fl. c. 1030) 128, 148–9, 150
Ealdwulf, rebel (fl. 927) 142
Eamont, river 83, 105
  at Eamotum, congress of 927 82–3, 104–5, 140

Eanred, king of Northumbria (9th century) 234n
Eardwulf, legendary bishop (9th century) 181, 206–7
Eardwulf, *princeps* in Northumbria (fl. 899×924) 97, 139
Earlsferry (Fife) 36
Easby (Yorkshire) 194
East Anglia or East Anglians, kingdom/people 28, 96, 106, 109, 116, 124–5, 134
East Lothian (or Haddingtonshire) 31
Eccles (Berwickshire) 166–7
Ecgberht I, king of Northumbria (†c. 873) 135–6, 214, 223
Ecgberht II, king of Northumbria (†876×) 97, 115, 136–7
Ecgberht, bishop of York (†766) 238
Ecgfrida, daughter of Bishop Ealdhun (fl. c. 1000) 147–8, 150
Ecgfrith, king of Northumbria (†685) 27, 158
Ecgred, bishop of Lindisfarne (9th century) 192n, 198, 232
Eddleston or *Penteiacob* (Peeblesshire) 89
Edgar, king of England (r. 959–75) 22, 86, 104n, 110–11, 116–17, 122–7, 129, 143–4, 231–2
Edgar, king of Scotland (r. 1097–1107) 31, 35, 39–42, 47–8, 237
Edinburgh 25, 31, 50–78, 113–14, 234
  as *Castellum Puellarum* 68–9, 72, 74
  'vacating' of 61–2, 91, 117–18, 231–2
Edmund (II), bishop of Durham (†c. 1040) 31
Edmund, king of England (r. 939–46) 86, 117n, 224
Edmund Ironside, king of England (†1016) 10, 80, 147
Edmund the Martyr, king of East Anglia (†869) 97, 134, 226
Edrom (Berwickshire) 177n
Edward the Confessor, king of England (r. 1042–66) 31–2, 104n, 117, 149n, 122
Edward the Elder, king of Wessex (r. 899–924) 97, 99, 115–16, 118, 125, 136, 139–41
Edwin, king of Northumbria (†632/3) 160
Eldbottle (East Lothian) 120
Elidir Mwynfawr 55

Ellemford (Berwickshire) 170
Encomium Emmae Reginae, biographical text (c. 1040) 128
England/English, kingdom/people 22, 27, 29, 38n, 95, 105, 107–8, 168–9, 231
  church in 106–8, 130, 238
  kings / kingship of 39, 45, 48, 86, 96, 99–100, 106, 116, 121–9
  language (Old English) 3, 26, 70, 74, 87, 89, 108n, 109, 112, 119, 234n, 235
  see also East Anglia; Mercia; Northumbria; Wessex
Eochaid mac Ilduilb, Scottish royal son (†971) 85
episcopal houses (or *esgobty*) 113, 235–8
episcopal lists 116, 198n
Eric (Erik) son of Harald, king in Northumbria (†c. 954) 100–1, 121–2, 129, 143, 232
Eric (Erik) of Hlaðir (Eiríkr Hákonarson), ealdorman in Northumbria (fl. 1016–18) 10, 92, 127–8, 131
Escomb (Durham) 145
Eskdale, border province 88
Espec, Walter, Anglo-Norman magnate (†1153) 27–8
Esk, river (East Lothian) 109, 112, 114, 117, 120
Ettrick Forest (Selkirkshire) 90, 115
Ewen son of Erwegende/Ulien 63–5

Falaise, Treaty of (1174) 39
Falkirk (Stirlingshire) 25
Fantosme, Jordan, writer (fl. 1170s) 24
Fergus mac Eirc, legendary king of Scotland 6
Ferryhill (Durham) 145
Fife, Scottish province 19, 25, 36n, 42n, 66, 72, 102n, 231
Findláech mac Ruaidrí, ruler in Moray (†1020) 18
Five Boroughs 109, 147
Flann Sinna, Irish high-king (†916) 190
Flodden, battle of (1513) 169–70
Florence, saint (seventh century) 233
Fordun, John of viii, 8–9, 75, 85
Forres 18
Forth, river/firth 25, 36, 55, 64, 66–7, 76–7, 90, 95, 108–9, 110–11, 118, 144, 231
  Gweryd as name for 55, 111n

INDEX

Fortriu, Pictish kingdom 34n
Fothad II (†1093), bishop of St Andrews 112
Fountains Abbey (Yorkshire) 204
France 34, 105, 119
French, language 27, 74n, 133, 135, 226
Frew, fords of 25, 36n, 118,

Gaelic (Irish) language 15, 20, 31, 61, 64, 66, 72, 74, 89n, 93, 105–6, 110, 118, 126n, 189
  orthography 141–2
  (modern) Scottish Gaelic 52
Gaimar, Geoffrey, historian (fl. 1130s) 131n, 133, 135, 226
Gainford 136, 166
Gainsborough (Lincolnshire) 147
Gall-Goídil (Gall-Ghàidheil, Galwegians) 93–4
Galloway, region/kingdom 70–1, 74, 94, 118
Gamelspeth (Northumberland) 156
Gateshead (Durham) 219n
Gattonside (Roxburghshire) 197
geweorc, Old English word 26–7
Geoffrey Plantagenet, count of Anjou (†1151) 229
Geoffrey of Burton (fl. 1114), hagiographer 71
Geoffrey of Monmouth, bishop and writer (†c. 1155) 35, 63–9, 72, 89–90; see also Gaimar, Geoffrey
Gerard, archbishop of York (†1108) 212
Gilbert, kinsman of Walcher (fl. 1080) 219
Glasgow 38, 63
  church/diocese of 29, 64, 67, 77, 90, 113
  'Glasgow Inquest' 113–14
Glasserton (Wigtownshire) 74
Glastonbury Abbey (Somerset) 36, 227
Glen, river (Northumberland) 109, 155, 160
Glendale (Northumberland), district 156, 161
Godescalc Evangelistary 186–7
Gododdin (Votadini), people/kingdom 50, 53, 77
  Y Gododdin, medieval Welsh poem(s) 50–3, 55–6, 58, 60, 66, 76–8
Gospatric (Cospatrick), name 91
Gospatric, ruler of Bamburgh (fl. 1067–72) 92, 207

Gospatric, son of Uhtred (fl. c. 1020) 91, 150
Gospatric's Writ 92, 119, 146
Govan 87, 176n
Gowrie (Perthshire), Scottish province 25
Great Army 96, 98, 106, 109, 115, 133–6
  see also Danes; *Dubgaill*
Great Urswick Cross 190
Grið, legal tract (c. 1000) 107–8
Grim, fictional king of Scotland 9
Grindon, battle of (1558) 170
Gruffudd ap Cynan, king of Gwynedd (†1137) 77
Gunner (fl. c. 960) 126
Guthfrith, son of Sigtrygg Cáech, Hiberno-Norse leader (†951) 106n, 140, 142
Guthred, son of Harthacnut, king of Anglo-Danes (†895) 117, 137–8, 215–16
  'Donation of Guthred' 137, 216
Gwarchanau, Welsh poems 52–3
Gwent, Welsh kingdom 83, 105
Gwynedd, Welsh kingdom 21, 55, 77, 130
Gwŷr y Gogledd ('Men of the North') 55–6, 78

Hadden Stank (or Redden Burn), border stream 168, 170
Hadrian's Wall 154
Halfdan, Danelaw magnate (fl. c. 960) 126
Halfdan, Norse leader (†877) 106, 126, 136
Harald Maddadsson, earl of Orkney (†1206) 19
Harleian genealogies 56, 78, 82–3
Harrying of the North (1069–70) 217
Harthacnut, father of Guthred (9th century) 135n
Harthacnut, king of England (†1042) 104, 149
Harthope Burn 162
Hartlepool (Durham) 116, 184n, 186
Hastings, battle of (1066) 1
haughs 153, 155, 172
Heavenfield, battle of (633/4) 152, 190
Hebrides 18, 93
Hedgeley Moor, battle of (1464) 170
Henry I, king of England (r. 1100–35) 27–8, 42n, 44–5, 77, 113, 121, 128, 161, 208, 213, 229

Henry II, king of England (r. 1158–89) 24, 39
Henry 'the Young King', Plantagenet heir (†1183) 24
Herbert, bishop of Glasgow (†1162) 38n, 63
Herbert de Losinga, bishop of Norwich (†1119) 212
Hereford *Mappa Mundi* 38
Heversham (Westmorland) 116, 118, 194–5
Hexham (Northumberland) 117n, 204, 221n, 233
Hexham, Richard of, Augustinian writer (fl. *c.* 1140) 26–7
Hiberno-Norse 21, 24, 98, 101n, 138
high-reeve, Anglo-Saxon institution 101–3
High Rochester, Roman fort (Northumberland) 156
Hirlas Owain, Welsh poem (12th century) 58, 78
Hirsel, the (Berwickshire) 162–3, 165, 167
Hirsel Law (Berwickshire) 169
Historia Brittonum, Welsh–Latin compilation 54n, 55–6, 69, 108n
Historia de Regibus Anglorum et Dacorum see *Historia Regum*
Historia de Sancto Cuthberto (*HSC*), Anglo-Latin tract 27, 97, 107n, 112–17, 133–5, 138–9, 141, 145–6, 196, 207, 212n, 215–16, 232, 237
Historia post Bedam see Howden, Roger of
Historia Regum (*HR*), Anglo-Latin annals 2–4, 7, 11, 14–16, 19–20, 26, 79–82, 97, 104n, 113, 122, 129, 135, 137, 138, 147, 149, 159, 165–6, 192n, 198n, 202–29, 233–4, 237; see also *Chronicle of 957*
Hoddom (Dumfriesshire) 162
Holderness (Yorkshire) 131
Holmcultram (Cumberland) 234n
Holyrood Abbey (Edinburgh) 75n, 76
Homildon Hill, battle of (1402) 170
Horncliffe (Northumberland) 159
Hoselaw (Roxburghshire) 167
Howden, Roger of
Chronica of, Anglo-Latin annals 2–4, 7, 48, 80n, 82, 104n, 113, 122, 137n, 149, 202, 208, 210n, 212n, 213n, 218n, 222–5, 227, 233–4
Hownam (Roxburghshire) 156–7

Humber, river 21, 108
Hywel Dda, Welsh king (†*c.* 950) 83
Ilderton (Northumberland) 28–9, 158
Ildulb mac Causantín, king of Scotland (†962) 50, 60–3, 72n, 91, 118, 231–2
Inchcolm, island in Firth of Forth 36
Inglewood, forest 90
Inveresk (East Lothian) 112, 237
Iona 37, 59, 185, 192
Ivar 'the Boneless', Hiberno-Norse leader († *c.* 873) 107, 134
dynasty of Ivar see Uí Ímair
Ireland vii, 7, 37, 72n, 74, 107, 134

James IV, king of Scotland (r. 1488–1513) 169
Jarrow (Durham) 166, 199n, 233n
Jed, river (Roxburghshire) 155, 196
Jedburgh (Roxburghshire) 109, 164, 172, 174, 176–7, 188n, 195n, 196–8, 200, 234–5
Jocelin, bishop of Glasgow (†1199) 38
Jocelin of Furness (fl. *c.* 1200), Cistercian writer 38, 64, 67
John, bishop of Glasgow (†1147) 46n, 67
John of Tours, bishop of Bath (†1122) 212
John of Worcester see *Chronicon ex Chronicis*

Kale Water (Roxburghshire) 153, 155–6, 170
Kells (Meath) 192
Kelso, village and abbey (Roxburghshire) 29n, 154–55, 162, 172
Kentigern, saint 63–5, 67, 77
Life of Kentigern (Jocelin of Furness) 38, 64, 67
Fragmentary ('Herbertian') *Life of Kentigern* 63–4, 66, 72
Kepduf (East Lothian) 66–7
Kersons Cleugh 164
Kilham (Northumberland) 155
Kincardineshire see Mearns
king-lists
English and Northumbrian 135
Scottish 6–8, 18n, 62, 82n, 85
Kingston-upon-Thames (Surrey) 137n, 142
Kirkham Priory (Northumberland) 28–9, 158
Kirkmaiden (Wigtownshire) 74
Kirknewton (Northumberland) 28–9, 158, 161

Kirk Yetholm (Roxburghshire) 155–6, 159, 172
Kirkby Wharfe (Yorkshire), cross at 190
Kyle (Ayrshire), province 108

Lailoken 89
Lamb Knowe (Northumberland) 157
Lammermuir 46, 91, 112–13, 117, 164, 237–8
Lanton Quarry (Northumberland) 161–2
Leabhar Leacain ('Book of Lecan') 59–60
Leader, river (Berwickshire) 109, 237
Learmouth (Northumberland) 153–5
Leath, ward in Cumberland 104
Leicester 147
Lennox, province 93
Leod, magnate (fl. 950s) 125–6
Leofwine (or Leobwine; fl. 1080) 219
Leofwine, ealdorman in Hwicce (†c. 1023) 146
Letha (Brittany) 60
Liber de miraculis et translationibus sancti Cuthberti, text (early 12th century) 211–12
Lincoln 96, 99, 116, 147
Lincolnshire 10, 226 *see also* Lindsey
Lindsey (Lincolnshire) 131, 147
Lindisfarne or Holy Island (Northumberland) 111, 143, 159, 179, 181, 192, 198, 232
  bishops of 130, 237–8
  diocese of 21, 113–15, 206, 215–16, 231–9
  Gospels 102, 180–1, 183
  mansiones of the bishop of 113, 235–8
  monastery of 27, 109, 111–12, 120, 158, 163–5, 233
  sculpture at 174–8, 180–2, 183–92, 194–6, 199n, 200
  'shire of', Islandshire 159, 237
Linton (Roxburghshire) 29, 167
Liulf (fl. 1080) 219
Llyfr Aneirin ('Book of Aneirin') 50, 52–3
Loch Lomond 37
Loth/Leudonus (Lewdwn) 38n, 63–4, 67–8
Lothian (or Tweed–Forth region) 1, 11–12, 20, 25, 30–1, 33–5, 38–9, 41–2, 46, 48, 50, 58–61, 63, 65–8, 72, 74, 76, 80–1, 89, 91, 110–13, 117, 122, 137, 144, 148, 231, 235–6

Macbeth, king of Scotland (†1057×8) 7–8
Macon (Maccus), *consul* in northern England (fl. c. 954) 101, 143
Máel Coluim I (or Malcolm I), mac Domnaill, king of Scotland (†954) 86
Máel Coluim II (or Malcolm II), mac Cinaeda, king of Scotland (r. 1005–34) 1, 4, 6–9, 14–19, 21–23, 33, 79, 81–2, 84, 95, 129, 138
Máel Coluim III (or Malcolm III), mac Donnchada, king of Scotland (r. 1058–93) 24, 25, 31, 42, 63, 75, 77, 112, 117, 207, 211–12, 220, 225
Máel Coluim son of Dyfnwal (Domnall), king of Strathclyde (†997) 120, 127
Máel Coluim son of Máel Brigte, ruler in Moray (†1029) 18
Máel Sechnaill mac Maíl Ruanaid, Irish high-king (†862) 62
Majestas Domini 186–7, 191
Makerstoun (Roxburghshire) 29n
Man(n), isle of 92–3
mansio 235
manuscripts
  Boulogne-sur-Mer, Bibliothèque municipal 11 *see* Boulogne Gospels
  Cambridge, Corpus Christi College 139 (CCCC 139) 4, 15–16, 97, 138n, 202–8, 210, 214–15, 220–8
  Cardiff, National Library of Wales, Peniarth 1 53n
  Cardiff, National Library of Wales, Peniarth 4 & 5 53n
  Cardiff, National Library of Wales, Peniarth 16 53n
  Cardiff, National Library of Wales, Peniarth 45 56
  Dublin, Trinity College 503 210n
  Dublin, Royal Irish Academy 23 P 2 *see Leabhar Leacain*
  Durham, Cathedral Library A.IV.19 102
  Liège, Bibliothèque universitaire 369C 3n, 202n, 210n, 213n, 225, 226n
  London, British Library, Cotton Claudius D.ii 108n
  London, British Library, Cotton Caligula A.viii 3n, 202n, 210n, 213n, 218n, 225–8

London, British Library, Cotton Cleopatra A.ii 70–1
London, British Library, Cotton Domitian A.vii *see under* Durham *Liber Vitae*
London, British Library, Cotton Tiberius B.v 86–7n
London, British Library, Cotton Titus A.xix 64n, 65n
London, British Library, Stowe 944 190n
Oxford, Jesus College 29 108n
Oxford, Jesus College 111 53n
Paris, Bibliothèque nationale, fonds lat. 5362 138n
Paris, Bibliothèque nationale, nouv. acq. lat. 692 3–4, 202n, 210n, 218n, 222, 224–5
Paris, Bibliothèque nationale lat. 4126 6, 61
Mar (Aberdeenshire), Scottish province 15n, 25
Margaret, daughter of King William of Scotland 38
Margaret of Wessex, queen of Scotland (†1093) 32, 36n, 74–6
Masham (Yorkshire) 194
Matilda, empress (†1167) 229
Matilda of Northampton, queen of Scotland (†c. 1130) 128
Matilda of Scotland, queen of England (†1118) 28, 45n
May, island in Firth of Forth 66
Mearns (Kincardineshire), Scottish province 19, 25
Meigle (Perthshire) 196
Melrose (Roxburghshire) 89, 109, 113, 117n, 198, 223–4
    Old Melrose 166, 197, 235
    see also Chronicle of Melrose
Mercia, Mercians, kingdom/people 96–7, 99–100, 109, 128–9, 132, 134, 139–40, 147
Merse or Berwickshire 25, 31, 41, 48, 153, 166, 235
Michael, archangel 71, 72n, 162
Milfield / *Maelmin* (Northumberland) 156, 160–2
Mindrum (Northumberland) 155, 157, 159, 167
Monenna, saint 67, 69–74

Monkwearmouth (Durham) 166, 188n, 200
Mons Agned 68–9
Mons Dolorosus 68
Moray, Scottish province 18–19, 68
Morcar, Danelaw magnate (fl. c. 960) 126
Morcar, ealdorman in Northumbria (†1087×) 127–8
Morebattle (Roxburghshire) 29, 155
Morham (East Lothian) 195n
Moriuht, Norman–Latin poem (c. 1000) 117
Mounth (Grampian massif) 19
Mowbray, Robert de, earl of Northumbria (†1125) 111, 212
Mynydawc 58
Myrdah (or Muiredach), magnate (fl. c. 960) 110n, 125–6
Myredah's cross, Alnmouth 126n, 188–9, 191, 200
Myreforð 110–11

Narratio de uxore Aernulfi ab Ella rege Deirorum violate, Anglo-Latin saga (c. 1100) 135
Newburn (Northumberland) 137n
Newminster Abbey (Northumberland) 156
Newcastle upon Tyne 25, 39–40, 174, 199
Nottingham 147
Norðhymbra Cyricgrið, legal tract (c. 1000) 108
Norðleoda laga, legal tract (c. 1000) 92, 101–2
Norham on Tweed 41, 138, 157, 165, 234–5, 237–8
    castle at 26–7
    church/minster of 112n, 113, 115n, 116, 118, 155, 157, 166, 172, 232, 238–9
    'Norham hypothesis' 113n, 148, 198, 233
    sculpture at 174, 177, 182, 184, 192–6, 198–200
    'shire' of 158–9, 165, 176–7
Normans/Normandy 24, 27, 42, 44–5, 71, 111–12, 117, 128–9, 175, 209–10
Norse
    Old Norse language 18, 60, 94n, 109 –10, 134, 143–4
    see also Danes; *Dubgaill*; Great Army; Hiberno-Norse; Scandinavia

INDEX

Northman, earl (fl. 994) 127, 145–6
Northumbria, Northumbrians, kingdom/
 people 1, 5, 10, 12, 14, 19, 20n, 30, 32,
 59, 80–1, 90, 92, 94, 95, 108–10, 121,
 129–32, 151, 175, 177, 205, 212, 215,
 223
 breakup of 86–8, 96–7
 Church in 27–8, 101, 107–8, 113–14,
  189–90, 218, 231–9
 Danes in 21, 95, 98–100, 106, 109, 120
 ealdordom in Northumbria/earldom of
  York 21–2, 48, 88, 90–2, 121–9,
  127–30, 143–4, 146–7
 kingship in 97–8, 100, 103–4, 107, 115,
  132–44, 176
 law in 101, 107–8, 116–17, 215–16
 'Northern English' / Bamburgh polity in
  1, 21–5, 31–2, 82, 95–150; see also
  Eadwulfings; Bamburgh, rulers of
'Northumbrian Earldom Foundation
 Legend' 121, 125–6, 143, 144n,
 208–9
Norway 128

Oakley (Hampshire) 144n
Odo of Bayeux (†1097) 209–10, 220
Olaf *Cuarán* (or Olaf Sigtryggsson),
 Hiberno-Norse king (†980) 99–100
Olaf Guthfrithsson, Hiberno-Norse king
 (†941) 99, 142–3, 185,
Olaf *Kyrre* (or Olaf III Haraldsson), king of
 Norway (1067–93) 218
Old Cambus, St Helen's Kirk (Berwick-
 shire) 177n
Orkney 18, 60
Osberht, king in northern England
 (†901×) 138–9
Osberht, king of Northumbria
 (fl. 866) 132–5, 139, 223
Oscytel, archbishop of York (†971) 107
Oscytel, Anglo-Danish magnate
 (fl. c. 960) 125–6
Otto of Brunswick (or Otto IV), emperor
 (†1218) 38–9
Oslac, ealdorman in Northumbria
 (†975×) 122–7, 129, 143–4
Oswald, archbishop of York (†992) 129
Oswald, king of East Anglia (fl. 869×)
 97
Oswald, king of Northumbria
 († c. 642) 190, 232

Oswiu (or Oswig), king of Northumbria
 (†670) 159, 163, 171
Ovingham (Northumberland) 188n
Oswigesdune, inauguration mound 137
Oswulf Eadwulfing, ruler of Bamburgh
 (fl. c. 954) 21, 100–3, 105, 110, 118,
 121–2, 126–7, 142–4, 208, 232
Owain Cyfeiliog, Powys prince (†1197)
 78
Owain of Gwent/Strathclyde (fl. 927) 83,
 105
Owain the Bald (or *Eugenius Calvus*), king
 of Strathclyde/Cumbrians (fl. 1018) 4,
 14–15, 19–20, 79, 82, 84, 90, 94
Owain son of Dyfnwal (or *Owinus filius
 Dunawal*; †1014×16) 14–16, 83

Paris, Matthew 35–6, 140n
Patrick, saint (5th century) 91
Peak District (Derbyshire) 108, 140
Peffer Burn (East Lothian) 234
Pennines 120
Pennymuir (Roxburghshire) 154
Penrith (Cumberland) 83
Penteiacob see Eddleston
Peterborough 233
Picts 37, 196, 231
Piperdean, battle of (1435) 170
Poland 34
Pressen (Northumberland) 167
Prophecy of Berchán, Irish metrical
 chronicle (12th century) 62
Prudhoe (Northumberland) 137n
Ptolemy (or Claudius Ptolemaeus),
 Roman–Egyptian geographer 111n
Puiset, Hugh de, bishop of Durham
 (†1195) 29

Qaṣr al-Banāt (Syria) 69
Quair Water, river (Peeblesshire) 89
Queensferry (Midlothian) 36

Raeburnfoot (Dumfriesshire), fort 88
Ragnar Loðbrók, literary character 134
Ragnarssona þáttr, Norse saga (c.
 1300) 135n
Ralph d'Escures, archbishop of Canterbury
 (†1122) 213
Ralph de Luffa, bishop of Chicester
 (†1123) 212
Ranulf Flambard (†1128) 195, 212, 218n

Ranulf le Meschin, earl of Chester (†1129) 44
Ravenna Cosmography, geographical text (c. 700) 111n
Redden (Roxburghshire) 154
Rhinns or Na Renna (Wigtownshire) 74, 101n
Rhun ab Arthgal, king of Strathclyde (†872) 82
Ricsige, king of Northumbria (†876) 136
Richard I, king of England (r. 1189–99) 38–9
Risewood, unidentified forest 149
Ritto Hill (Northumberland) 163
Robert Bloet, bishop of Lincoln (†1123) 212
Robert Curthose, duke of Normandy (†1134) 25n, 209
Robert de Limesey, bishop of Chester (†1117) 212
Rögnvald, Hiberno-Norse king (†921) 98, 115–16, 138, 140–1
Rome 67
  pilgrimage to 7, 71, 148–9
Ross, Scottish province 18, 138n
Rothbury (Northumberland) 191, 194, 198n, 200
Roxburghshire *see* Teviotdale
Russell's Cairn (Northumberland) 169
Ruthwell Cross 178–9, 193n, 198n
Ryton (Durham) 137n

Saint Albans (Hertfordshire) 122, 132, 140n, 144, 211
Saint Andrews (Fife) 8, 70–2
  bishops/diocese of 38, 67, 112, 218
  foundation legend(s) of 110
  see also Fothad II
Saint Davids (or *Mynyw*; Pembrokeshire) 84, 236
Saint-Sauveur-le-Vicomte, abbey of (Manche, Normandy) 44n
sanctuary 107–8, 116, 215
Sandbach Crosses 178
Sawley Abbey (Yorkshire) 204, 223n, 227n
Scandinavia 18
sciregemot 123
Scone (Perthshire) 42, 137–8n
Scotia, Latin word 33–4, 39n, 42, 77
Scotland (or Alba), Scots, kingdom/people 1, 7, 17–19, 24–5, 29–32, 33–48, 50, 60, 63, 70–4, 95, 105, 109, 120, 141–2, 159, 168, 170, 207, 231
  army of (or *Fír Alban*) 19, 24–5, 77, 98, 138n, 149
  relations with Northumbria 21–3, 31, 212
  territory/borders of 17–19, 28–9, 33–6, 62–3
Scule, Danelaw magnate (fl. c. 920) 116
seals/seal matrices 40n, 41, 45
Secgan (or 'On the Resting-Places of the Saints'), text (early 11th century) 113n, 232–3
Selby Abbey (Yorkshire) 226
Selwood, forest in Wessex 125
Seven Bishop-Houses of Dyfed, tract 236–7
Seymour, Edward, earl of Hertford (†1552) 169
Shires and Hundreds of England, Þe Syren and Hundredes of engelonde, tract (c. 1100) 108n
shire
  as juridsictional sphere 30, 158–9, 236–7
  'small shire' 108n
  as West Saxon administrative unit 103, 108, 123, 125
Sige, daughter of Styr (fl. c. 1000) 148, 150
Sigtrygg *Cáech*, Hiberno-Norse king (†927) 98–9, 104, 106n, 116, 138, 140, 142
Siward, ealdorman in Northumbria (†1055) 128, 129n, 132, 149
slaves, slavery 23, 120, 136n, 143
Slethemur 110
Sockburn (Durham) 166
Solway, firth 88, 93, 118
Sourhope (Roxburghshire) 159n, 164
Sprouston (Roxburghshire) 28–9, 109, 154, 160–2, 165, 172, 234n
Stainmore (Westmorland) 8, 118
  'treachery of' (c. 954) 101, 103, 118, 120, 143
Stamford (Lincolnshire) 10, 147
Standard, battle of the (1138) 19n
Stawford (Roxburghshire) 155, 169
  St Aetheldreda's Chapel at 167
Stephen of Blois, king of England (r. 1135–54) 45, 229
Stirling 36, 70, 72

INDEX

Stow of Wedale (Midlothian) 25, 113, 234
Strathclyde/Cumbrians (or 'Clyde-folk'), kingdom/people viii, 1, 8–9, 14–16, 19–25, 30, 33–5, 38, 42, 44–6, 48, 64–5, 79–94, 95, 109, 113, 118–21, 127, 130–1, 140, 149
Styr, son of Ulf (fl *c.* 1000) 148, 150
Suffolk 109
Suibne mac Cinaeda, king of the Gall-Goídil (†1034) 93
Sutherland, Scottish province 18
Sweyn Forkbeard, king of Denmark (†1014) 147
Symeon, archdeacon of Teviotdale (fl. 1174–95) 64
Symeon of Durham 2, 16, 151, 174
   Annales Lindisfarnenses et Dunelmenses 5–6, 215n
   Epistola ad Hugonem de archiepiscopis Eboraci 135
   Libellus de Exordio (*LDE*) 4, 6, 9–11, 13, 26, 80–1, 83, 132, 158, 175, 179, 211, 214–20, 223–8
   potential contribution to Anglo-Latin annals 6, 204, 215–18, 227–9
   see also Historia de Sancto Cuthberto; *Historia Regum*

Tacitus, Roman writer (fl. *c.* 100) 111n
Tay, river and firth 36, 110
Tees, river 5, 32, 46, 110, 115–16, 120, 122, 137, 143–4, 215, 216, 217n
Teviot, river 109, 113, 155, 159, 196, 234–5
Teviotdale (or Roxburghshire), border province 25, 28–9, 31, 64, 67–8, 76, 88, 90, 114
Taneu (or Thaney), Cumbric saint 63, 66–7
Thanet (Kent) 206
Thetford (Norfolk/Suffolk) 28
Thietmar of Merseburg, Saxon chronicler (†1018) 13
Thirlings (Northumberland) 161
Thomas II, archbishop of York (†1114) 213
Thored, ealdorman in Northumbria (†992) 129
Thored son of Gunner (fl. 960s) 91, 119
Thurbrand the Hold, Danelaw magnate (fl. 1010s) 30, 80–1, 131, 147–8
Thurcetel, Nafena's son (fl. 1016) 10–12, 147
Thurstan, archbishop of York (†1140) 213, 229
Tigbrechingham/Tigbrethingham 113, 234–5
Till, river (Northumberland) 109, 112, 153, 161, 166, 234, 237
Tillmouth (Northumberland) 113, 133, 165–6, 170, 198n, 234–5
Tilred, ab. of Norham (fl. 899×924) 116, 118, 194–5
Titlington (Northumberland) 28
Tostig Godwinesson, ealdorman in Northumbria (†1066) 128, 225n
Traprain Law (East Lothian) 66, 71, 77
Traquair (Peeblesshire) 89
Trimontium / Newstead (Roxburghshire) 154
Turgot, prior of Durham (†1115) 75, 218–20
Tweed, river 5, 25, 41, 42, 88, 109, 153–7, 159, 166, 170, 174, 196, 198, 200, 233, 234n, 235–7
   basin of 14, 22, 27, 32, 109–12, 114, 118, 159–61, 171–2, 176
   as border 9n, 29, 33, 35, 38, 47, 159, 168–9, 231
Tweeddale (or Peeblesshire), province 20, 25n, 67, 88–90, 114
Tweedmouth (Northumberland) 154, 159
Tynemouth (Northumberland) 118n, 211, 212n, 214, 233
Tyninghame (East Lothian) 28, 112–13, 117n, 120, 143, 165–6, 200, 233–8

Ubbanford *see* Norham-on-Tweed
Uhtred, Danelaw magnate (fl. *c.* 960) 126
Uhtred, ealdorman in Northumbria (fl. 1009–16×18) 9–10, 32, 121, 146–8, 231–2
   battle of 1006 9, 17, 19, 21–2, 91, 130–2, 147
   children of 138, 148–9
   death of 10–17, 30, 147–8
   as ealdorman 22, 90–2, 104, 127, 129–32, 147
   family of 21–2

founder of Durham 111, 148, 190
leader at Carham 4, 8, 17, 25, 79–84, 146, 202, 228
Uhtred Eadwulfing (fl. c. 920) 141, 143
Uí Ímair (Dynasty of Ívar) 86, 98–9, 106–7, 115–6, 127, 134
Urum, Danelaw magnate (fl. c. 960) 126

Vairement, Richard, *Céle Dé* historian (fl. c. 1250) 85
Wales 15, 37, 51–8, 63, 65, 77, 82, 104, 140
Walcher, bishop of Durham (†1080) 112n, 196, 219–20
Wallingford, John of, chronicle attributed to (13th century) 122
Waltheof son of Siward, earl/saint (†1076) 144
Waltheof, ruler of Bamburgh (fl. 994) 21, 104, 127–8, 130, 145–6, 148, 209,
Wark (Northumberland) 26–7, 154, 157, 167, 169–70,
Warkworth (Northumberland) 113n, 120, 133, 188n
Watling Street 131
Wearmouth *see* Monkwearmouth
Weingarten Gospels 187
Welsh language *see under* Britons
Wendor, Roger, chronicler (†1236) 101, 122n, 132–3, 135–6, 143, 232n
Wessex, West Saxons, kingdom/people 125, 132, 134, 139, 144n, 158, 232
 expansion of 22, 95–6, 99–100, 103, 116, 119, 121–9, 142–3
 kings of 21, 99, 100–7, 121, 130–1
 law in 92, 123–5
West Lothian (or Linlithgowshire) 89, 120
Westmoringas, people 118–20, 126n
Westmorland 91, 101n, 118, 139, 143
Whiteadder (Berwickshire), river 109, 237
Whitemuirhaugh (Roxburghshire) 160

Whithorn (Wigtownshire) 72, 101n, 185
Whittingham (Northumberland) 115n
Wigred, bishop of St Cuthbert (fl. 928–35) 224
Wiheal, unidentified hall 147
Wihtbordesstan Code (or 'IV Edgar') 124–5
Wilfaresdun 171
William, king of Scotland (r. 1165–1214) 7, 24, 36n, 38–9, 43, 48
William I, the Conqueror, king of England (r. 1066–87) 207, 217, 219–20
William II, Rufus, king of England (r. 1087–1100) 40–1, 44–5, 209, 211
William Adelin (†1120) 229
William of St Calais, bishop of Durham (†1096) 112n, 209–10
William of Malmesbury, English historian (†c. 1142) 83, 104–5n, 142, 203, 211
Wulfhere, archbishop of York (fl. c. 872) 133, 136
Wulfhere, king of Mercia (†675) 158, 206
Wulfstan II, archbishop of York (†1023) 92, 101, 107–8, 187n

Yarrow Water, river (Selkirkshire) 109
Yeavering (Northumberland) 109, 155–6, 160–2, 164
 battle of (1415) 170
Yetholm (Roxburghshire) 29, 155, 167
York 10, 88, 96, 98–9, 106–8, 118, 133, 146, 226
 archbishops/diocese of 106–7, 126–7, 130, 212–13, 228–9, 238; *see also individual named archbishops*
 battle of (867) 98, 133–35, 214, 223
 kingship based in 116
 army/citizens of York 116, 119, 125, 143, 148
 See also Northumbria, ealdordom in
Yorkshire 92, 105, 108–9, 118–19, 126, 131, 143, 147, 194